Modern Catholic Social Documents and Political Economy

Albino Barrera, O.P.

Georgetown University Press
Washington, D.C.

Georgetown University Press, Washington, D.C. 20007

Printed in the United States of America

10 9 8 7 6 5 4 3 2 1

2001

This volume is printed on acid-free, offset book paper.

In memory of my parents

Library of Congress Cataloging-in-Publication Data

Barrera, Albino.
    Modern Catholic social documents and political economy / Albino Barrera.
        p. cm.
    Includes bibliographical references (p.) and index.
    ISBN 0-87840-856-8 (cloth : alk. paper)
        1. Economics–Religious aspects–Catholic Church–History of doctrines.
    2. Sociology, Christian (Catholic)–History of doctrines. 3. Catholic
    Church–Doctrines–History. I. Title.

BX1795.E27 B37 2001
261.8'5'08822–dc21   2001023265

CONTENTS

LIST OF FIGURES AND TABLES

PREFACE

T he modern Roman Catholic social documents offer a treasure trove of teachings on political economy. This should not come as a surprise since these papal, conciliar, and synodal documents are theological reflections on the socioeconomic crises or opportunities of their time. *Rerum Novarum* (1891) speaks out on the condition of laborers in a then-maturing Industrial Revolution. *Quadragesimo Anno* (1931) responds to the deepening economic malaise of the Great Depression. *Mater et Magistra* (1961), *Pacem in Terris* (1963), and *Gaudium et Spes* (1965) examine a vibrant economic environment of great optimism in which many believed that poverty could be finally eliminated. *Populorum Progressio* (1967), *Octogesima Adveniens* (1971), *Justice in the World* (1971), and *Sollicitudo Rei Socialis* (1987) challenge the conventional wisdom in international economic relations given the growing relative inequality and the worsening plight of the Third World. *Laborem Exercens* (1981) urges a rethinking of and a renewed appreciation for the role of labor in social life. Reviewing the outcome of the Cold War, *Centesimus Annus* (1991) cautions against overlooking the shortcomings of the seemingly vindicated, triumphant capitalistic model of economic life.

A family wage for the worker, profit sharing, co-management, co-ownership of the means of production, guaranteed full employment, the right to the satisfaction of basic needs regardless of one's productive contribution to societal output, the state as the provider of last resort, disinterested and massive aid to poor nations–these are but a sampling of the Roman Catholic Church's wide-ranging teachings on political economy. They have been accorded a mixed reception, even described as "Ecclesiastical Economics: Envy Legitimized" (Bauer 1984).

These social documents have been predominantly about socioeconomic life. In spite of this, not much work has been done to examine the nature and the structure of their economic ethics. There is little by way of integrating the similarities and dissimilarities across these documents beyond reiterating the caveat that this modern social tradition does not offer an alternative school of thought between classical laissez-faire capitalism and socialist centralized planning. This amorphous presentation of modern Catholic social thought probably accounts for why a broad spectrum of political philosophy, from liberation theology to classical liberalism, can confidently claim selected texts of this tradition as an affirmation of their own positions.

This book has been written for scholars and students of economics, theology, and political science interested in religious social thought. It examines the modern Catholic social teachings on political economy within their historical context (part I), which includes both a retrospective accounting of their evolution from scholastic thinking on the just price (part II) and a comparison with contemporary, normative mainstream economic thought and policies (part III). It then looks ahead and weighs postindustrial social questions using key principles from the social documents (part IV) and concludes with a conceptual synthesis of this modern tradition's norms (part V).

Part I examines the economic dimensions of the social questions addressed in the twentieth century. Chapter 1 describes the distinctive contributions of Leo XIII and Pius XI to the principles of universal access and subsidiarity as they grappled with the competing claims of labor and capital. As argued in chapter 2, John XXIII's exposition on agriculture is a theological response to the import-substitution strategy in early development planning. The postconciliar turn toward a more activist egalitarianism is examined at length in chapter 3.

Part II accounts for differences in the economic ethics of scholasticism and the modern Catholic social documents. The radically changed conditions between the medieval and industrial economies explain much in the development of these teachings. In transposing scholastic just price into the labor market, chapter 4 argues that the modern Catholic social documents' stress on the living wage reflects the broader shift from a distributive to an allocative role for price as we move from a feudal to a modern wage-labor economy. Chapter 5 expands on this phenomenon by examining in greater depth this tradition's switch from the scholastic preoccupation with personal moral behavior to the modern documents' intense and persistent scrutiny of the sinful structures of society. The conduct of economic life in accordance with traditional custom, law, and usage has given way to the institutional, impersonal ways of the market. The informal social conventions of the medieval era rooted in family and religious ties have been replaced by legal safeguards. Thus, systemic failures in the economic order merit closer scrutiny.

Part III contrasts the economic thought of these modern social documents with normative economics. To lay the groundwork for such a comparison, chapter 6 briefly summarizes the anthropological assumptions of mainstream economic thought as rooted in eighteenth- and nineteenth-century philosophies. The latter's legacy and influence on contemporary economics are evident in the *homo oeconomicus* model and in the discipline's characteristic utilitarian cast. Chapter 7 differentiates this theological tradition from mainstream economics in its understanding of economic life. These dissimilarities are summarized in chapter 8 by examining the pattern of twofold economic objectives advanced by the modern Catholic social documents.

Part IV anticipates significant postindustrial social questions. The economic "signs of the times" in a globalized, knowledge-based economic life are sketched in chapter 9. Their attendant market-generated redistribution of burdens and benefits requires a guided and creative evolution of the principles of universal access and participation. Chapter 10 maintains that the Archimedean point of this further development may be found in the form of a postindustrial participative egalitarianism. As part of this reformulation, chapter 11 proposes a refinement in our understanding of the superfluous income criterion by highlighting the varied functions of goods in the necessary economic dimension of human flourishing.

Since the social documents are concerned with addressing the pressing economic problems of their day, they do not form a systematic, homogeneous exposition on economic ethics. Part V is a conceptual synthesis of the modern social documents' norms. Chapters 12 and 13 examine the teleological warrants and the complementarity of the mainstay principles. The common good is defined with a little more precision in chapter 14 by examining two characteristics that can be reasonably expected of it: *due order* and *due proportion*. The value of these interpretive models may well lie in their diagnostic framework for weighing competing claims. They also alert contending parties to those aspects of the common good that may be easily overlooked, put at risk, or be in apparent conflict with each other as various solutions to intractable social issues are considered. Moreover, due order and due proportion furnish an analytical means of incorporating the Catholic social principles within the language of the common good.

Four of the following fourteen chapters have been published previously. Chapter 2 was "*Mater et Magistra* and the Import-Substitution Strategy to Development," *Journal for Peace and Justice Studies* 9: 2 (1998), 69–86. Chapter 4 appeared as "Exchange Value Determination: Scholastic Just Price, Economic Theory and Modern Catholic Social Thought," *History of Political Economy* 29: 1 (spring 1997), 83–116. Chapter 5 is a revision of "The Evolution of Social Ethics: Using Economic History to Understand Economic Ethics," *Journal of Religious Ethics* 27: 2 (summer 1999), 285–304, and "From Obligations to Rights: Economic Progress and the Language of Ethical Discourse,"

The Downside Review 117: 406 (January 1999), 41–58. Chapter 11 was published in the *Review of Social Economy* 55: 4 (winter 1997), 464–86, as "Degrees of Unmet Need in the Superfluous Income Criterion." My thanks to these journals for permission to use these materials. Many have been generous with their time in the course of this project. Phil Smith, Stephen Brett, John Davis, Daniel Rush Finn, David Hollenbach, Thomas Massaro, Michael Naughton, Anthony Waterman, Diane Yeager, and Andrew Yuengert offered valuable suggestions in improving specific chapters. I am deeply grateful for their assistance and encouragement. Ernest Bartell read through the entire manuscript and raised numerous questions that were instrumental in sharpening my arguments and in tightening the organization of the book. I owe him a great debt of gratitude. My thanks to the editors, staff, and referees of Georgetown University Press for their excellent advice and help. Needless to say, any errors that remain are solely mine.

A distinctive contribution of moral theology lies in its reflections on competing visions of justice in the social order. There is need, however, for an interdisciplinary examination of its claims. Closing this gap in the literature requires much preparatory, critical scholarship in the dual task of evaluating the economics of these theological reflections while articulating, at the same time, the conceptual bases of their proposed economic norms. I offer this book as a small step in that direction.

ABBREVIATIONS

CST   Catholic social thought (teaching)

CA   *Centesimus Annus* (On the Hundredth Anniversary of Rerum Novarum)

CFL   *Instruction on Christian Freedom and Liberation*

CM42   Christmas Message, 1942

EC   *The Ecological Crisis: A Common Responsibility*

GS   *Gaudium et Spes* (Pastoral Constitution on the Church in the Modern World)

JW   *Justice in the World*

LE   *Laborem Exercens* (On Human Work)

LT   Instruction on Certain Aspects of "Liberation Theology"

MM   *Mater et Magistra* (Christianity and Social Progress)

OA   *Octogesima Adveniens* (The Coming Eightieth)

PEN   Pentecost Message, 1941

PP   *Populorum Progressio* (On the Development of Peoples)

PT   *Pacem in Terris* (Peace on Earth)

QA   *Quadragesimo Anno* (On Social Reconstruction)

RN   *Rerum Novarum* (On the Condition of the Working Classes)

SRS   *Sollicitudo Rei Socialis* (On Social Concerns)

Numbers refer to the paragraph order. In cases where the original document does not have numbered paragraphs (such as *Quadragesimo Anno* and *Laborem Exercens*), the numeration adopted is that of Carlen, *Papal Encyclicals, 1790–1981* (New Hampshire: McGrath Publishing, 1981). In documents where multiple paragraphs are assigned to a single number (as in the case of *Gaudium et Spes, Sollicitudo Rei Socialis*, and *Centesimus Annus*), letters (corresponding to the paragraphs) are appended to the numbers. Hence, GS #34c refers to the third paragraph of entry number 34 of *Gaudium et Spes*.

Part I

THE ECONOMICS OF THE MODERN TRADITION

New social problems serve as the springboard for the further development of earlier teachings and for the articulation of fresh principles and norms for the ideal economic life. Thus, *Rerum Novarum* reconciles the conflicting claims of labor and capital by advancing what subsequent documents eventually call the principle of universal access. In response to inhumane working conditions, the encyclical also provides a rudimentary form of what John Paul II would later call the primacy of labor principle. Alarmed by the economic concentration that threatened social cohesion, *Quadragesimo Anno* formalizes the principle of subsidiarity on the protection of private initiative and individual economic freedoms. *Mater et Magistra* highlights what some now call the principle of socialization where higher bodies are obligated to assist lower entities. John XXIII underscores this feature of Pius XI's principle of subsidiarity at a time of increasing societal interdependence. Taking stock of the Roman Catholic Church's pastoral role in the modern world, the Second Vatican Council affirms human dignity as the fundamental guide for social life in *Gaudium et Spes* and thus lays the groundwork for the principle of solidarity. Paul VI addresses the widening gap between rich and poor countries in *Populorum Progressio* and explains genuine integral human development. Joining the worldwide clamor for justice and participation, *Octogesima Adveniens* and *Justice in the World* probe the essential requirements for fairness in market operations. In *Laborem Exercens*, John Paul II provides a systematic reflection on the principle of the primacy of labor in reaction to the continued needful plight of workers in the marketplace. *Sollicitudo Rei Socialis* presents solidarity as a guiding principle for international relations. Finally, *Centesimus Annus* brings the tradition full circle by restating the principle of universal access as a cautionary reminder of the free market's limitations despite the collapse of the socialist economies and the resultant implied superiority of liberal, capitalist models of economic life.

Following the lead of *Rerum Novarum*, these social documents address the injustices of their day and, in so doing, provide fresh insights into the ethics of political economy by closely examining the fairness of market outcomes and processes. They reaffirm and refine the Christian vision of integral human development by situating economic life within a larger moral order.

METHODOLOGY

As used in this book, "political economy" deals with the distribution of the benefits and burdens of the common productive effort and is much broader in scope than the common usage of the term "economics" because it encompasses history, theory, moral values, and policy (Groenewegen 1987). The increasing sophistication of contemporary production processes with their concomitant division of labor has pushed the exchange of goods and services to an even more central and prominent role in the modern market economy. Exchange, initially in kind and subsequently monetized, has become the principal avenue for interaction among atomistic economic agents in a setting that has expanded in scope and complexity. Thus, different schools of thought in political economy can be distinguished from each other by their conception of economic freedom. The degree of acceptable market regulation differentiates various political economies from each other and is therefore a logical starting point in any thoughtful inquiry.

In searching for intelligible patterns in the economic ethics of the modern Roman Catholic social tradition, the next three chapters pursue a twofold task of exploring these documents' economic teachings within their historical context and of identifying the warrants for their proposed principles or norms. Much can be learned from what these theological reflections implicitly say about the marketplace: when it should be overridden, under what circumstances and why, how not to intervene, and what essential conditions for equity in outcomes and processes are to be pursued.

Chapter 1

BALANCING COMPETING
LABOR-MANAGEMENT CLAIMS

RERUM NOVARUM: JUST USE AS DISTINCT
FROM JUST OWNERSHIP

Alarmed by the growing rift between labor and management during the maturation of the Industrial Revolution in nineteenth-century Europe, Leo XIII breaks out of the "state of siege" (Bokenkotter 1990) in 1891 and decries the plight of workers in his encyclical *Rerum Novarum* (Camp 1969; Schuck 1991).[1] He appeals for balance in the competing claims of capitalists and workers. Extreme socialism proposes to resolve the dispute by abolishing the right to private property ownership, thereby removing an entire class of claims altogether.[2] Laissez-faire capitalism, on the other hand, simply refuses to acknowledge any problems by appealing to the trickle-down mechanism of economic progress. Allowing capitalists a free hand to blossom in their entrepreneurship creates employment for many along the way. Leo XIII avoids the extremes of these competing schools of political thought by affirming the legitimacy of both the workers' and the capitalists' claims through his deft distinction between just use and just ownership.

The deleterious consequences of massive industrialization and urbanization compel *Rerum Novarum* to deal with the growing animosity in labor-management relations.[3] Taking socialism to task as his starting point, Leo XIII, in effect, provides a commentary on how not to intervene in the marketplace. *Rerum Novarum* (#7–23) dismisses the idea of abolishing private property ownership as a de facto imposition of an extreme equality in outcomes, an undue and exaggerated assignation of powers to the state far beyond its legitimate role, and an impoverishment of the very workers socialism professes to protect. Implicit in his critique of this radical solution are the following significant affirmations on the nature and function of the market:

1. In dismissing class struggle as the governing dynamic of labor-management relations, *Rerum Novarum* sees nothing in the nature of economic life that makes it inherently contentious. The market per se can serve as a constructive avenue for harmonious, mutually beneficial interactions in the socioeconomic order.
2. In asserting the right of the owners of capital to share in output, Leo XIII (i) ascribes a proper function and role to entrepreneurial capital, (ii) acknowledges the rightful existence of nonpublic wage labor markets, and, consequently, (iii) affirms a legitimate place for private contractual agreements both as a necessary condition for the existence of the market system and as a venue for nurturing private initiative.
3. In staunchly defending the right to property ownership, *Rerum Novarum* invites attention to the unique role of private property in a vibrant economic life (i) as a guarantee of and means for facilitating individual freedom of action, (ii) as a needed incentive and just reward for private initiative, and (iii) as a channel for saving wage earnings.

Rerum Novarum goes beyond merely reacting to socialism's radical prescriptions. Its originality lies in the critical balance it strikes in situating particular interests (the capitalists' private initiative and economic freedom) within the larger requirements of the community (the general welfare and livelihood of workers). Even while affirming labor (just like socialism), Leo XIII also acknowledges the importance of doing so within a functioning marketplace. The encyclical upholds and then counterbalances the claims of both labor and capital through its two distinctive contributions of differentiating just ownership from just use and of delineating the boundaries of market operations.

Universal Access Principle

In what subsequent documents call the universal access principle, *Rerum Novarum* argues that the gifts of the earth are meant for the use of all; gaining legitimate titles of private ownership to these does not take away their primary finality of benefiting the entire community.[4] While ownership has a personal aspect to it, the utilization of such property has an additional dimension–a social character where goods are meant for the welfare of both the owners and their neighbors. St. Thomas's notion of superfluous income is invoked where wealth and income not necessary for one's own social standing must be used for others (Aquinas 1947/48, II–II, q. 32, a. 6, reply). Consequently, lawful ownership does not automatically confer legitimacy to whatever purpose or however owners choose to use such properties. Just ownership is not a sufficient condition for just use; the exercise of just ownership is not identical to just use (RN #35–36). The former is a right, the latter an obligation flowing from that right. Thus, in the case of labor-management relations, the just-use requirement means that capital has to profit both its legitimate owners and the propertyless wage earners who depend on such assets for their livelihood (RN #28–32). The universal access principle is discussed in greater depth in chapter 10.

Justice in the Marketplace as More Than Mutual Consent

A second distinctive contribution of *Rerum Novarum* is succinctly expressed in paragraphs #61–63. The essence of the market is the private contractual exchange struck by mutually consenting economic agents. The latitude accorded to free market operations is measured by the degree to which these private contractual agreements are allowed to stand on their own without external interference or oversight. *Rerum Novarum* dismisses the laissez-faire contention that mutual consent alone lends validity to these contractual exchanges. If true, this classical liberal claim would mean that the legitimacy of a wage-labor agreement is contingent merely on the consensual nature of the arrangement struck between the worker and the employer regardless of the working conditions and compensation agreed upon. Leo XIII notes that the content of the contract also matters. In other words, it is natural justice that is the final arbiter of market operations. In the case of wage-labor agreements, such justice encompasses a wide variety of considerations such as the provision of a wage that allows the worker to become propertied (RN #63, #64–65) and the maintenance of a humane working environment. Not surprisingly, *Rerum Novarum* does not consider state oversight and unionization as undue infringements on the rightful place of a freely operating market in a just economic order.

The implications of *Rerum Novarum*'s contributions extend well beyond labor-management relations. It not only foreshadows what *Laborem Exercens* later calls the primacy of labor principle, but it also situates this principle within the setting of a wage-labor market. Consequently, Leo XIII affirms the legitimacy and importance of private property ownership and market operations as essential building blocks in a just, harmonious, and functional economic order. While staunchly affirming the essential role of individual economic initiative and freedoms, the social encyclical also defines minimum conditions and sets limits to societal outcomes and processes. Complementary extra-market mechanisms are required such as social security, labor legislation, and unionization. Whether in criticizing socialist prescriptions or in advancing its own position of limiting market operations and private property use, *Rerum Novarum* appeals to human dignity as the primary value to uphold and protect. In fact, because human dignity is owed to God and not owned by the person (RN #57), it cannot even be voluntarily surrendered, given away, or bartered whether in the marketplace or elsewhere.

QUADRAGESIMO ANNO: FULL EMPLOYMENT AT A LIVING WAGE AND WITH SUBSIDIARITY TO BOOT

Founded on a reappropriation of key features of the medieval guilds, *Quadragesimo Anno*'s (Pius XI 1931) vocational groupings constitute one of the more unusual proposals advanced on the amelioration of worker welfare in the modern era. It is a surprising policy recommendation because the suggestion is made at a time when industrialization has replaced economic customs, laws, and usages that harkened from a medieval organic hierarchical view of society (Polanyi 1944). Vocational groupings are never broached again after Pius XI, in part because of its association (rightly or wrongly) with the Italian fascism of that period (Cawson 1986; Halevi 1987). However, the encyclical's principle of subsidiarity has survived as a singular contribution in gaining coinage in political discourse beyond theological circles (see, for example, Peterson 1994; and Kinsley 1995). The *Oxford English Dictionary* (1986) credits initial use of the term to Pius XI.

Why does *Quadragesimo Anno* suggest a retrieval of salient features of the medieval guilds in the 1930s? In what ways are these proposed vocational groupings different from the various strands of corporatism? Answers to these questions may be found in the microeconomics of the manifold objectives of *Quadragesimo Anno*'s political economy. Its twin goals of full employment and a living wage, when overlaid with subsidiarity as a third aim, make vocational groupings a rational economic response to the social issues of its day.[5]

The writing of *Quadragesimo Anno* is well documented. In his twilight years, Oswald von Nell-Breuning (1986) acknowledges principal authorship of the encyclical. This admission is made even more significant in view of his earlier book-length commentary (1937) on *Quadragesimo Anno* soon after the publication of the encyclical. Hence, materials are readily available that shed light on the appropriate hermeneutics of the encyclical.

In what follows, I will first examine the historical context of *Quadragesimo Anno*, with particular emphasis on the social question of its time and on the key foundational teachings of *Rerum Novarum* that it expands further. The final section of the chapter is an assessment of the microeconomics of its proposals.

Historical Context

Written forty years after *Rerum Novarum*, Pius XI publishes *Quadragesimo Anno* at a time of great economic stress. He is concerned with the worsening relative inequality seen in the great concentrations of economic and political power held by the few amidst the destitution of the many (Freemantle 1956). Adding fresh urgency and weight to the encyclical's apprehensions are the turn of events by 1931. Marxism is no longer merely an abstract nineteenth-century idea but has become a well-established historical movement (USSR). The Great Depression only serves to make even more alarming the claims of an ideology that is bent on actively promoting its centralized political economy as a more attractive and viable alternative to a then-faltering Western capitalism. After all, laissez-faire's liberalism carries the seeds of its own destruction within its competitive dynamics and its logic of survival of the fittest where a starting point of many buyers and sellers eventually ends up as a market of a handful of powerful sellers facing many buyers.

Vocational Groupings

Quadragesimo Anno echoes *Rerum Novarum* in its unbending disapproval of extreme socialism. Like Leo XIII, Pius XI seeks to correct the imperfections of a market economy instead of dismissing it outright as an unworkable social arrangement. *Quadragesimo Anno* reiterates, affirms, and expands the same principles of equity for a just economic order proposed earlier by Leo XIII. This is particularly true on the issue of labor-management relations and on the proper distribution of output between capitalists and workers. In both cases, the goals are full employment, humane working conditions, and a living wage (von Nell-Breuning 1937; MM #10–40).

In response to the increasingly uneven concentration of economic power and wealth that threatened the competitive structure of the market economy, *Quadragesimo Anno* (#81–98) proposes the establishment of industry-level vocational groupings of employers and employees as venues for cooperation in critical areas of mutual concern such as wage setting.

> The aim of social legislation must therefore be the re-establishment of vocational groupings. . . . [T]he demand and supply of labor divide men on the labor market into two classes, as into two camps, and the bargaining between these parties transforms this labor market into an arena where the two armies are engaged in combat. To this grave disorder which is leading society to ruin, a remedy must evidently be applied as speedily as possible. But there cannot be question of a perfect cure, except this opposition be done away with, and well-ordered members of the social body come into being anew, vocational groups

namely, binding men together not according to the position they oc-
cupy in the labor market, but according to the diverse functions they
exercise in society. For as nature induces those who dwell in close
proximity to unite into municipalities, so those who practice the same
trade or profession, economic or otherwise, combine into vocational
groups. These groups, in a true sense autonomous, are considered by
many to be, if not essential to civil society, at least its natural and spontaneous development (QA #82–83).

Von Nell-Breuning's (1937) chapter 11 and its addenda provide excellent discussions of the motives, the mechanics, and the understanding
of such kind of corporatism.[6] A distinct preference for appropriating
some of the positive characteristics of medieval guilds is evident in this
proposal (Postan, Rich, and Miller 1963; Renard 1918). As Pius XI describes it:

> At one period there existed a social order which, though by no means
> perfect in every respect, corresponded nevertheless in a certain mea-
> sure to right reason according to the needs and conditions of the times
> (QA #98).

The incongruity of *Quadragesimo Anno*'s conception of industry-
level associations cannot be ignored. In the first place, it opens itself to
criticisms of being anachronistic. Moreover, its proposal appears to be
inconsistent with its anxieties. After all, the encyclical is highly critical of
economic and political concentrations that seem to be the hallmarks of
unfettered market operations. It is ironic that Pius XI's proposal to transfer responsibility for wage setting from the market to these industry-wide
associations is itself a concentration of power, although this time in the
hands of workers.

An anthropological premise animating corporatism is the belief
that the individual is radically self-centered and that vocational groupings hold in check the pursuit of selfish interests detrimental to the rest
of the community (Palazzini 1962, 331–33). A more benign reading of
Quadragesimo Anno, however, could ascribe to the encyclical a deep-
seated optimism in the capacity of the human person to use power for
good. After all, Pius XI could have taken the easier way out by simply
urging governments to take the lead, through antitrust action, in correcting the harmful effects of economic concentration and domination.
There is substantial working experience by the 1930s on the requisite
mechanisms both for the enactment and the enforcement of laws that
can mend the self-ruinous tendencies of competitive markets (such as
the Sherman Act of 1890). Rather than take this easier and quicker juridical route to address the social question, *Quadragesimo Anno*
chooses the more roundabout course of letting workers and owners of
capital take responsibility themselves for outcomes in economic life

through their individual and collective conscientious exercise of power. *Neither the state nor the market has the final say, moral agents do.* This underlying confidence in the human person is reflected in an unspoken conviction that these industry-level associations will be characterized by cooperation instead of an adversarial competition with each other. Power can be exercised responsibly for the common good, rather than for preying upon other economic agents. Indeed, the encyclical's call for a social reconstruction can be viewed as an affirmation of its trust in the fundamental capacity of *homo oeconomicus* to go beyond self-interest.[7]

Vocational groupings can be viewed as a leveling of the playing field. It is balancing one concentration of power (the capitalists') with another agglomeration, the collective power of unions. This is evident in von Nell-Breuning's (1937) conclusion to his discussion of vocational groupings. Commenting on corporatism and capitalism, he observes:

> Corporate order . . . eliminates from the separation of capital and labor that side which makes it so unbearable at present; *it makes full-fledged and fully qualified professional members of those who by their labor* add to production, and thus to the common contribution to the welfare of society; thereby it restores them to the nation; *it assures them of their standing in society, something that had been lost.* Thus it restores true national order (von Nell-Breuning 1937, 233, emphases added).

In terms of reducing relative inequality by breaking up concentrations of economic power, it is most likely so much easier, less complicated, and far more efficient to simply rely on government antitrust legislation rather than embark on a drastic, massive overhaul of the economy's organizational infrastructure along vocational groupings. However, Pius XI has the distinct goal of ensuring that workers do for themselves what they are capable of accomplishing on their own. Great value is attached to preserving the principle that people ought to do what they can do for themselves. In such vocational groupings, workers would still be able to exercise their collective private initiative, albeit at a higher level of aggregation.

The importance accorded to economic agents taking responsibility for their own affairs is evidence of a continuity in vision. In particular, take note of the parallelism between *Rerum Novarum*'s staunch defense of voluntary associations (unions) as a key mechanism for achieving balance and *Quadragesimo Anno*'s proposal of vocational groupings. Both are founded on the pivotal premise of safeguarding the liberty of people to work for their own welfare and to conduct their own affairs freely within the common good. *Quadragesimo Anno* (#79) articulates the guiding rule in what has now come to be known as the principle of subsidiarity:

[J]ust as it is wrong to withdraw from the individual and commit to the community at large what private enterprise and industry can accomplish, so too it is an injustice, a grave evil, and a disturbance of right order for a larger and higher organization to arrogate to itself functions which can be performed efficiently by smaller and lower bodies. This is a fundamental principle of social philosophy, unshaken and unchangeable, and it retains its full truth today. Of its very nature, the true aim of all social activity should be to help individual members of the social body, but never to destroy or absorb them.

While the spirit of the principle of subsidiarity is already very much in evidence in *Rerum Novarum*'s defense of unions and private property ownership, it is Pius XI who formulates it in a precise working definition.

The difficulty of implementing vocational groupings does not escape von Nell-Breuning. In the introduction to his commentary, he directly addresses the widespread skepticism regarding the practicality of such a reordering of society:

[L]et us frankly admit that frequently the reason for the great interest in learning what a vocational order would look like is not so much zeal to begin immediately with this realization, but doubt whether the Holy Father's noble ideas are really possible and practicable. Some fear that Pius XI may have become the victim of visionary ideals (von-Nell-Breuning 1937, 6).

In numerous sections of his book, von Nell-Breuning repeatedly affirms the value of self-help and cooperation at the lowest possible level of aggregation without immediately running to government for relief and remedy. Hence, it is not surprising that he titles the chapter devoted to industry-level associations, *Corporate Co-operation*. Moreover, von Nell-Breuning views self-help as one of the most distinctive accomplishments in the forty years since *Rerum Novarum* (see his chapter 4). *Quadragesimo Anno*'s political economy of vocational groupings stands in sharp contrast to the more state-driven variants of the corporatism of its time[8] because its animating principle of subsidiarity is at the heart of the entire process of improving the welfare of the workers.

Roundabout Affirmation of the Market System

Quadragesimo Anno is written at a time of great economic distress, uncertainty, unemployment, and poverty. This state of affairs is believed to have been largely caused by the undue concentration of wealth resulting in widespread economic inequalities. The scope for individual economic action and decision (the very essence and lifeblood of free exchange) is increasingly absorbed and restricted by larger corporate bodies that have thrived well in the generous liberties afforded by the market. This is viewed with alarm and is taken as a warning sign of an economic order on the verge of self-destruction. Pius XI responds by restating (1) the incompatibility of the socialist and the Christian approaches to correcting the market for its flaws, (2) the necessary boundaries of market operations, (3) the attendant obligations to private property ownership, (4) the notion of superfluous income, and (5) the legitimate claims of both labor and capital and their dual individual-social character. The 1931 encyclical is a recapitulation of a fundamental point made by *Rerum Novarum*: The market performs an important function, but there are limits to its operations.

Quadragesimo Anno goes further to offer its own distinct insight through its articulation of what is already implicit and nascent in *Rerum Novarum*'s championing of the right to form associations: the need to protect and nurture private initiative. It is unfortunate, however, that commentators (and the subsequent social documents) closely associate this principle only with the counsel against the state overreaching and arrogating to itself what properly belongs to the private realm, thereby casting it within the context of a state-versus-private-sector conflict. This is only a partial reading of the original statement of the principle, which seeks to defend the scope of individual action not only from an overextended state but also from the threat emanating from within the private sector itself in the form of the larger corporations' insatiable appetite for expanding and absorbing smaller entities. The latter concern is, of course, at the heart of Pius XI's proposal of vocational groupings.

This broader interpretation of the principle of subsidiarity must be stressed to give full justice to the essence of *Quadragesimo Anno*'s contribution to political economy. Whether by design or not, its principle of subsidiarity is, in effect, a ringing endorsement of the market per se whereby due recognition is accorded to the central role and importance of people working for their own gain, their own mutual benefit, and their own advancement, whether singly or as a group. Indeed, this is the very rationale of market operations. The principle of subsidiarity is about protecting and nurturing creative private initiative and freedoms for which the market serves as an essential channel for expression and development. It guards not only against an overzealous state but also against excessive economic domination and monopolies within a fully operational market slowly being smothered by the weight of its own success.[9]

The social question of the day was the perceived threat of an undue concentration of economic power and wealth. Laissez-faire liberalism denies any such problems; socialism uses it as a validation of its prediction of capitalism's expected demise; pragmatic, economic policymakers would have merely resorted to antitrust legislation, thereby conveniently handing over to the state the responsibility of preventing economic monopolies. True to its belief in the importance of nurturing individual responsibility, action, and initiative, *Quadragesimo Anno* subscribes to none of these approaches but applies its principle of subsidiarity to the social question on hand. Pius XI seeks to address the problem of economic domination with a corporatist approach–avoiding one form of economic concentration through another concentration of economic power, this time in the hands of the industry-level vocational groupings of employers and employees.

Quadragesimo Anno follows the lead of Leo XIII in affirming the central task of improving worker welfare, but always within the market-place. However, it adds its own original contribution to our moral reflection on market operations by highlighting the critical importance of protecting individual economic liberties and action from being unduly absorbed either by the state or by private monopolies. In effect, whether intentionally or unintentionally, Pius XI affirms private economic initiative as the wellspring and foundation of a political economy's vitality and viability. He validates the marketplace without entirely embracing laissez-faire capitalism through his critical acknowledgment of the need to impose prudent limitations and oversight on market operations.

The appendix provides a more technical assessment of the economic merit of Pius XI's proposed vocational groupings in the context of the social question of his time. From a purely economic point of view, his suggestion carries both attendant opportunities and risks. In the first instance, a case can be made that this unusual solution is, in fact, a rational response to the microeconomic requirements of the social issue. In particular, these vocational groupings provide an avenue for satisfying simultaneously the triple objectives of maintaining full employment, securing a living wage, and preserving the principle of subsidiarity.[10] However, the same microeconomic assessment would show that *Quadragesimo Anno*'s vision of a reconstituted social order also brings with it significant risks of engendering a monopoly-monopsonist industry. This is not even to mention the welfare losses imposed on the economy.

SUMMARY AND CONCLUSIONS

What can be said about *Quadragesimo Anno*'s corporatism given the benefit of hindsight? The empirical arguments for or against vocational groupings can be partly gleaned from an examination of wage-labor markets. The United States has less regimented factor markets compared to Europe and is consequently believed to be more nimble in responding to dynamic changes in the economy. It has consistently enjoyed lower unemployment rates (relative to Europe) through its ability to create more jobs (Baddeley, Martin, and Tyler 2000; Card, Kramarz, and Lemieux 1999; see also Simonazzi and Villa 1999). Critics argue, however, that these new jobs are mostly low-paying service work without health care or other benefits. Moreover, they point to the wider income disparities in the United States compared to Western European nations with stricter oversight on labor-management contracts (Bettio and Rosenberg 1999). What does all this mean for Pius XI's corporatism? Even if vocational groupings were to succeed in reducing income inequalities, they would severely dampen economic dynamism because of the attendant rigidities that industry-level governance brings in its wake. Thus we are back to the classic tradeoff of having to choose between better growth or more equity.

The shift in the preferred primary institutional vehicle of reform from *Rerum Novarum*'s voluntary associations (unions) to *Quadragesimo Anno*'s industry-level vocational groupings is an excellent illustration of a gradual move up the rungs of intermediate human associations of ever greater aggregation. In the forty years between these two social documents, it is apparent to Pius XI (and the drafters of the encyclical) that unions, acting singly and independently of each other, are unable to promote effectively the welfare of their membership. Hence, there is a pronounced switch in the later encyclical toward industry-level bargaining units. Intermediate levels of aggregation in human associations are exhausted first before appealing to the state's fiat in ironing out conflicts in worker-management relationships or in breaking up economic concentrations. *Quadragesimo Anno*'s version of corporatism can be better understood and appreciated in the face of the three objectives that it seeks to achieve in the labor market: full employment, a living wage, and the principle of subsidiarity.

Perfect competition is founded on price-taking behavior and, as argued in the appendix, improving the marginal product of labor is the best long-term solution to achieving full employment at a living wage even while promoting the exercise of private initiative. Such an improvement in productivity can be effected principally through a deliberate effort to keep on upgrading skills development and training. Unfortunately, this can take a long time because it relies on a trickle-down mechanism that is itself a function of income distribution and the network of forward and backward linkages within the economy. Vocational groupings allow for the satisfaction of all three goals simultaneously within a reasonable period of time. *Quadragesimo Anno*'s corporatism may seem to be anachronistic, what with its guild-like characteristics. However, one can also view it as an imaginative, rational economic response to achieving a stringent set of triple objectives during a very unsettled and unsettling period of economic malaise.

Notes

1. This study is limited to the major papal, conciliar, synodal, and pontifical commission documents. Episcopal teachings (McGoldrick 1998) are not included since they are generally addressed to region-specific constituencies. See Novak (1984) and Massaro (1998) for earlier studies on Catholic social thought and political economy.

2. *Rerum Novarum* (#7) fails to make a critical distinction between different kinds of socialism regarding private ownership. There are variations that span a wide spectrum from an outright ban on all private property ownership to restrictions limited only to the means of production, to state ownership of critical industries, and even to a full recognition of ownership rights. It becomes immediately apparent in reading Leo XIII's staunch and spirited defense of the right to private property ownership that he is addressing the more radical type of socialism that bans all forms of such proprietorship.

3. See Charles (1998) and Waterman (1991) for a more detailed history of the larger backdrop against which Leo XIII writes the encyclical.

4. Readers unfamiliar with the various principles of the modern papal social tradition may want to take a quick look at the definitions and derivation of these principles in chapters 12 and 13.

5. A living wage is one that permits workers and their dependents to become propertied, middle-class families. See RN #65–66 and QA #63–75.

6. Addendum 1 is especially important. See also Cramer and Leathers (1981) for a description of *Quadragesimo Anno*'s corporatism.

7. There is even more reason to adopt such a benign interpretation after weighing the potential risks of such vocational groupings, as is done in the appendix.

8. See, for example, Jessop (1979) and Winkler (1976). See also Cramer and Leathers (1981, 753–60) for a description of corporatism within a social class theory.

9. It is perhaps this appreciation for the essence of markets that leads *Quadragesimo Anno* to qualify Leo XIII's teachings on the living wage with a word of caution. The encyclical is clearly concerned with the delicate balance in the internal workings of the market as is evident in its prudent approach to wage setting. In spite of the great and urgent importance given to remunerating workers with a living wage, *Quadragesimo Anno* (#70–75) is keenly aware of the tradeoff between the provision of high wages and employment opportunities. In qualifying the teaching on the provision of a family wage with other considerations, such as the exigencies of the common good and the state of the business and the general economy, Pius XI exhibits an apparent respect for what the market can and cannot accomplish. No matter how well meaning and noble moral norms are, there are limits to what may be realistically imposed on the market without irreparably impairing its fundamental function of lending order to the common productive endeavor. Moral principles and norms work within "laws" intrinsic to economic life.

10. Dempsey (1958) is an example of the continuing search for that elusive "third" alternative political economy that has the right combination of subsidiarity, market operations, and equitable economic outcomes.

Chapter 2

AGRICULTURE AND THE IMPORT-SUBSTITUTION STRATEGY

INTRODUCTION

U nless set against the larger backdrop of the economic history of its time, the full weight of *Mater et Magistra*'s contributions (Calvez 1964) to social ethics will most likely be underappreciated. In particular, it is worth noting John XXIII's extended discussion of the conditions in the rural sector to the point of being described as the "agricultural encyclical" (O'Rourke 1963). David O'Brien and Thomas Shannon (1977, 48) view the encyclical's lengthy section on agriculture as a noticeable departure from the practice of previous social documents, while Riga (1966, 117) considers it to be the "most important as well as the best informed in the whole letter." The degree of specificity with which policy prescriptions are advanced, ranging from changes in credit allocation to infrastructure development, is unusual for encyclicals in this tradition because the difficulties of delving into specific solutions to social problems are well acknowledged (OA #3–4).

Why does John XXIII devote so much attention to the rural sector? Why is he so precise in his policy proposals? The literature has been silent in this regard. Unlike von Nell-Breuning's (1986) "The Drafting of *Quadragesimo Anno*," nothing is available on the writing of *Mater et Magistra*. A solution to this lacuna in the literature is to examine the larger historical backdrop of the encyclical. After all, just like Leo XIII and Pius XI, John XXIII is writing a theological reflection with specific social problems in mind.

15

The object of this chapter is to retrieve the economic history and development thought of that era and to show how these can provide a frame of reference for a better appreciation of John XXIII's lengthy exposition on the plight of the rural sector. The theory and practice of the development economics of his era suggest that John XXIII may have in fact been advancing a moral commentary on the import-substitution strategy earnestly pursued by many developing countries. *Mater et Magistra*'s policy prescriptions bear a close resemblance to the measures that have been consistently advocated by both economists and policymakers to correct for the excessive push to industrialize that has inadvertently nurtured an antiagricultural, antirural bias.

THE ECONOMIC MILIEU

Four economic phenomena are well underway by the 1950s. First, growth and development lead to a spontaneous structural shift that reduces the relative weight of farming in the country's total output. Empirical evidence from nations that have completed the various stages of the Industrial Revolution suggests that agriculture loses its dominant place in economic life in favor of industry and services. The rural sector declines both in its contribution to the national income and as a proportion of the labor force (Kuznets 1966). After all, a distinguishing feature of the modern economy is its industrial character in contrast to the agrarian nature of medieval economic life.

A second phenomenon of the period is the pronounced growth bias in economic thinking and policy. A tremendous appetite for ever more industrial goods and services is generated by massive postwar reconstruction, the release of pent-up demand held back by the war effort, the surge in family formation and its accompanying "baby boom," a freer global trade, and the creation of new products and wants from advances in science and technology. Moreover, this demand is backed up by real purchasing power from the accumulation of surplus, another exceptional aspect of the modern economy. The post–World War II era has the highest sustained growth rates in all of economic history (van der Wee 1987).

A healthy respect for the potential benefits of a direct and active government role in the conduct of socioeconomic life is a third relevant development. Undergirded by the theoretical work of John Maynard Keynes (1936), this new appreciation for the role of the state in the economy is validated and strengthened by successful government interventions in addressing pressing needs and problems, such as the U.S. federal programs during the Great Depression, the impressive overnight transformation of entire nations into wartime economies, and the effective targeted assistance rendered through the Marshall Plan. Keynesianism becomes the dominant school of economic thought in the three decades following the end of World War II.

Finally, the big push for industrialization in many developing countries replaces the colonial systems that crumble after the war. Former colonies emerge as newly independent nations, and the economics of colonization gives way to development economics. The wide disparities in living standards between the erstwhile peripheral territories and the developed world become even more apparent, and industrialization seems to offer the most promising path for narrowing the gap. After all, the principal lesson from nineteenth-century Western history is clear: Modern industry is the engine of sustained economic growth. Thus, for poor countries, the establishment of a vibrant industrial base is the unavoidable starting point in emulating the developed world.

This daunting task is matched by a confidence that full industrialization is attainable within the span of a few decades. Such optimism is not completely unfounded. The timing is propitious given an international economy that is growing rapidly and, more importantly, increasingly open to trade (McPherson 1994, chapter 8). Moreover, these newly independent countries do not have to go through the time-consuming and expensive process of developing the requisite technologies of an industrial sector. These are readily available and can be purchased off-the-shelf from the wealthier countries, which are more than eager to create new markets for their capital goods. Both of these factors make the prospects of industrialization quite enticing and encouraging. Not only could the poor nations emulate the developed countries, but they could do so within a shorter period of time. What took Western nations several decades to build could now be accomplished in less than a single generation.

Two other considerations make a compelling case for turning this massive push for industrialization into the centerpiece of most governments' economic blueprint. First, population pressure leads to an insatiable need for ever more jobs. The demographic transition[1] has been particularly dramatic in the Third World. Job creation takes on immediate urgency, and industry is better at this given the exhaustion of available arable land for agriculture.

The unfavorable long-term secular decline in the terms of trade of primary goods is a second cause for why industrialization becomes the preferred path for the newly independent countries (Love 1980). The price of manufactured goods tends to rise faster than that of raw materials. Quality improvements due to technological advances can command ever higher prices for finished goods, while the price of primary goods is subject to the vagaries of the weather and the uncertainties of supply and demand. This is not even to mention the downward pressure exerted by the increasing availability of synthetic substitutes. At any rate, this is an added incentive for former colonies to shift from being merely primary producers to becoming manufacturer-exporters of finished goods. Poor countries benefit more from their rich natural resources when they process these into finished products, thereby generating for themselves even more income from the higher value-added content of their exports. An industrial base is essential for this goal.

Industrialization is not merely a tantalizing prospect for these poor countries, it is also a necessity for them. Post–World War II economic conditions and events converge on what has now come to be known as the import-substitution strategy to economic development.

THE PROMISE OF THE IMPORT-SUBSTITUTION STRATEGY[2]

If the nation is to develop a viable industrial base, outlets must be found for its manufactured goods. For developing countries, this is a major, though not insuperable, hurdle. Markets must be found or developed and guaranteed as a necessary first step to industrialization.

At first blush, the global market seems to be a ready and ideal answer considering its size and nations' increasing openness to trade, in contrast to the nationalistic protectionism of the inter-war period. However, the international marketplace is an exacting and unforgiving place for suppliers, especially for new entrants like underdeveloped countries. These emerging nations have to compete against well-entrenched, long-established name brands whose parent firms (in the First World) are well poised to best any new competitor given their years of accumulated experience and vast financial reserves. Selling in the international market exacerbates what is an inherently difficult task to start with for emerging nations. Not only do they have to work out the birth pangs of their new industrial sector, but they also have to do so while simultaneously matching the price and quality of manufactured goods coming from the multinational firms. There is little time to master the learning curve. Consequently, markets have to be found elsewhere and are indeed found right there at home–their own domestic markets!

The most logical place to look for a ready market to make a local industry viable is among domestic consumers. All that has to be done is to replace imports with locally manufactured goods. However, newly established, inexperienced local enterprises would still fare poorly against foreign competition even in their own domestic markets given the quality of these imports and the marketing expertise and competitive pricing of foreign firms who enjoy the advantage of economies of scale from their global operations. As a result, restricting foreign access to domestic markets using traditional "infant industry" arguments becomes the first order of the day for governments.

Restricting foreign sales in domestic markets is too attractive an option to forego. First, it is a politically expedient decision as it is viewed as keeping jobs at home instead of sending them abroad (via imports). Second, as people buy from local manufacturers, more jobs are generated, giving the general population even more purchasing power which, in turn, creates an even bigger market for the emerging industrial base. It becomes a self-perpetuating benign cycle where the growth of the industrial base is fueled by domestic spending which then generates even more industrial jobs that pay relatively much higher wages than agriculture. The multiplier effects are substantial. Third, the domestic market provides local entrepreneurs with sufficient breathing space and time to go through the learning curve and build up the experience, discipline, and financial reserves necessary to enter and compete successfully in a wider field of even greater promise–the international marketplace. Related to this is a fourth benefit in which the human capital of the nation is developed in a process of learning-by-doing where the industrial sector becomes the training ground for the acquisition of new skills. Fifth, much-needed investments are limited by domestic savings and the available foreign exchange. These two gaps can be mitigated by restricting imports, thereby allowing governments to conserve their scarce foreign reserves and channel them toward the purchase of job-creating, wealth-producing capital equipment, instead of nondurable consumption goods.[3] Sixth, backward and forward linkages ultimately create a web of light, medium, and heavy industries. What starts out as an effort to industrialize by replacing imported consumables can progress eventually to an industrialization where the nation produces the very tools and equipment necessary to manufacture these consumer goods.

These advantages give the import-substitution strategy an aura of economic rationality: protect nascent industries until such time that they can compete against foreign imports. Such protection usually comes in the form of quotas, tariffs, or other informal trade barriers that keep imports out of the domestic market. There is an added benefit that makes these policies particularly attractive for cash-strapped bureaucracies. Tariffs, licensing fees, and quotas generate windfall fiscal revenues at a time when these national governments also happen to be short of funds.

Unfortunately, tariffs, quotas, and other restrictive practices that keep imports out of the nation also translate into higher prices for everyone else in the community. While benefitting local industrialists, more expensive consumer goods crimp the real purchasing power of farmers. But this reduction in real purchasing power is only the first of many other burdens rural residents are made to bear.

Restricting access to domestic markets is only one dimension of the import-substitution strategy. In addition to carving out a secure market for local enterprises, governments employ a wide array of measures designed to accelerate the establishment of industrial firms. Numerous incentives and direct assistance are offered to unleash the energies of local entrepreneurs. Among the most common forms of support are agricultural price ceilings, an overvalued exchange rate, heavy infrastructure investments in urban areas, and preferential credit for the industrial sector.

Agricultural Price Ceilings

Price ceilings are imposed on agricultural goods to keep the price of basic staples down. This shores up the real purchasing power of industrial wages. Assuring workers' access to cheap basic necessities indirectly shields industrialists by preempting union demands for higher nominal wages.

A price ceiling on basic staples for the benefit of urban dwellers weighs heavily against the interests of the agricultural sector. Farmers, unable to get a good price for their produce, find it more difficult to generate the necessary surplus for re-investment in improving their farms. Worse, it also takes away the incentive to improve their productivity. These price ceilings are de facto hidden taxes imposed on the agricultural sector. Farmers, in effect, subsidize factory wages as real resources are transferred from the agricultural to the industrial sector.

John XXIII observes that "the price of rural products is more a recompense for farmers' labor than for capital investment" (MM #138). In other words, agricultural prices are about people's livelihood. The encyclical highlights further the importance of prices by suggesting that the state stabilize agricultural prices given the volatile fluctuations in farm prices. However, prudence must be exercised in balancing the competing claims of farmers and consumers. *Mater et Magistra* suggests that the following circumstances be considered in pricing policies: the unpredictable nature of farm production, the importance of agricultural goods for basic-needs satisfaction, and the injustice of compelling farmers to bear the full brunt of feeding the country by sacrificing their own purchasing power (MM #137, #140–41).

Foreign Exchange Overvaluation

The foreign currency exchange rate is overvalued to make it cheaper (in terms of the local currency) for entrepreneurs to import industrial equipment, expertise, and raw materials. This overvaluation (or a two-tier exchange rate with preference given to imports of capital goods) hurts farmers. The overvalued rate that makes it cheaper for industry to import its needs also means that exports (generally raw materials and agricultural goods) are now more expensive for foreign buyers. As a result, rural producers lose their competitive edge in the international marketplace.

Physical and Social Infrastructure

Investments in social and physical infrastructure are heavily concentrated in the urban areas. A viable industrial sector requires cheap, plentiful, and steady supplies of power and water in addition to excellent communications and transportation facilities such as ports, airports, and roads. Housing for industrial workers must also be available and complemented by social infrastructure, schools, and hospitals.

Given their eager drive to industrialize, governments pour enormous sums into key urban centers. Since newly independent countries generally find themselves in a chronic state of fiscal deficits, rural investments in social and physical infrastructure are neglected. This exacerbates an already unsatisfactory situation and spawns a self-feeding cycle of decline: deteriorating living conditions lead to a further lack of interest in agrarian affairs on the part of bankers and even of rural dwellers themselves.

This neglect and unequal treatment precipitate other intractable problems. The resulting heavier migration to the cities adds even more pressure for ever greater investments in the social and physical infrastructure of cities in order to accommodate this large and unrelenting influx of people seeking a better life. This massive rural out-migration into the already crowded urban centers gives rise to new and even more pressing dilemmas: crime-ridden slums without access to electricity, sewage, and potable water; unemployment and underemployment; and overburdened urban health and education systems. These, in turn, tend to rend the social fabric as labor becomes restless and the poor resentful and frustrated over the worsening bias in wealth outcomes.

John XXIII acknowledges what is fairly well established and accepted in development thinking by then: that economic development is accompanied by structural changes where the population's center of gravity gradually shifts from the rural to the urban areas (MM #124). However, he sees no reason why the rural sector should be so impoverished without any seeming hope for the future. Policy reforms designed to hasten social progress and improve economic productivity and living conditions must be introduced in the rural sector. This includes upgrading marketing facilities and providing a minimum level of essential public services such as drinking water, medical services, housing, transportation, and schooling. Furthermore, the rural population must have access to the furnishings and equipment essential for a dignified farm life (MM #127).

Given the disproportionate attention and social resources funneled into the industrial sector, it makes absolute sense for John XXIII to come up with a long and specific list of what effective measures must be taken on behalf of a largely forgotten and unappreciated rural sector. The encyclical calls for organizing rural industries, service establishments, artisan enterprises, and cooperatives that are instrumental in enhancing the value added by farmers through produce preservation, processing, and transportation. These entities supplement household incomes, create new employment opportunities, and secure farm earnings on a more stable and predictable foundation (MM #141). Besides, these small-scale industries, cooperatives, and artisan enterprises serve as conduits for people to contribute to the community in their own creative ways of producing new wealth. The state, therefore, is justified in encouraging these ventures through preferential measures in education, taxes, credit allocation, social security, and insurance (MM #84–90).

The viability and stability of the farm household are a function of its money income. *Mater et Magistra* calls for additional steps to assure the rural family of such an income, to wit: assistance with increasing and marketing their output; continuing basic education, technical instruction, and training for farmers on new developments and scientific advances; mutual-aid societies and professional associations; and proper representation in the administrative and political bodies of public life (MM #143). In addition, land ownership for farmers is essential as this is constitutive of rural dwellers' self-determination, that is, the right to be the agents of their own development and destiny (MM #144).

Credit

Preferential and generous credit terms are provided to industrialists as a way of encouraging risk taking. Governments make credit lines available, serve as co-signers for foreign loans, and even subsidize the cost of borrowing. Given the choice of lending to a farmer or to an industrialist, bankers would much prefer to lend to the latter. The risk of default or loss from agricultural loans is far greater due to the inherent uncertainties that come with working the land. Crop failures can easily result from blight, disease, and sudden shifts in weather patterns. Besides, government-subsidized credits are usually available for industrial loans. Given that it is more lucrative and safer to lend money to industry, it should not come as a surprise to see credit dry up for the agricultural sector. Thus, it becomes even more expensive for farmers to secure much-needed funds, if they are available at all.

John XXIII is sensitive to these dynamics as he calls for provisions for capital financing and for the establishment of banks to provide capital to farmers at reasonable rates of interest. This special effort is viewed as a necessary counterpoise to the general preference of investors for nonagricultural activities, thereby forcing farmers to pay ever higher interest rates in financial markets (MM #134).

Related to this, John XXIII also endorses crop insurance in view of the vagaries inherent to farming. In addition, farmers and their families need some form of social insurance to deal with sickness, old age, or unemployment. It is ironic that those in the service and industrial sectors, who already enjoy more stable and considerably higher incomes in the first place, are covered by better social security and insurance benefits relative to those in the farms (MM #135–36).

The assorted array of measures taken by governments in their quest for higher economic growth comes with a heavy cost imposed on the agricultural sector. The earnest national drive to industrialization is a laudable, sincere effort to overcome poverty. Unfortunately, there are unseen and unintended consequences as governments vigorously pursue an import-substitution strategy to industrial development. They inadvertently impose undue burdens on the rural sector. In a world of scarcity where a zero-sum phenomenon is operative, pro-industrial government policies have antiagricultural, antirural bias as a mirror image.

It is not surprising, therefore, to see John XXIII's alarm at the glaring imbalance between industry, services, and agriculture, with the latter trailing far behind the other two. Related to this is the distressing disparity in the living standards of rural and urban dwellers as a result of differences in their productivities (MM #125, #135). This state of affairs can be attributed partly to the indifference or insufficient attention paid to improving the lives of the rural populace.

Other measures proposed by the encyclical include promoting greater equity. *Mater et Magistra* appeals for the provision of key public services and infrastructure that improve living conditions and also enhance the earnings capacities of the poor. Rational policies are to be instituted in order to increase employment, stimulate private initiative, and improve the productive and efficient use of local resources (MM #150–51). Nongovernmental poverty-alleviation programs are to be set up as supplementary avenues of assistance.

John XXIII suggests that the application of recent technical improvements in mechanical equipment and advances in biology, chemistry, and the other sciences be extended to the farming sector, which should not be allowed to lag behind the other two sectors in this regard (MM #128, #145). In levying taxes, special consideration ought to be given to the peculiar nature of agriculture where farm residents face greater risks, get delayed or seasonal incomes, and experience a shortage of much-needed capital (MM #133).

Two observations must be made regarding *Mater et Magistra*'s exposition on the agricultural sector. First, these policy prescriptions are not original as they are readily found in the literature on agricultural development and the community-participation approach to development (Meier 1995). In fact, these policies are now believed to have been the critical policy decisions that account for the economic success of East Asia compared to Latin America. John XXIII's ease in writing about these issues suggests an awareness of the debates swirling around the development thinking and policy of that period.

Second, what truly stands out in John XXIII's discourse on the ills besetting agriculture is the degree of detail in the policy prescriptions proposed. Other modern Catholic social documents rarely discuss a particular issue with such specificity and sustained effort because the variations and fluidity in local conditions make proposing detailed prescriptions a hazardous, if not futile, venture. *Mater et Magistra* could afford to be so precise and concrete in its discussion of the plight of rural life because John XXIII has a specific socioeconomic problem in mind. That the encyclical's policy proposals are geared toward mitigating an antirural, antiagricultural bias could only suggest that *it is addressing the confluence of economic events of its time in the import-substitution strategy in development thinking and practice.*

CONTRIBUTIONS TO ECONOMIC ETHICS

Mater et Magistra advances our understanding of market operations through its formulation of the principle of socialization and its illustration of what fairness in market outcomes and processes entail.

First Contribution: Principle of Socialization
(or Principle of Subsidiarity, Part II)

The occasion that gives rise to the fuller specification of the principle of subsidiarity is John XXIII's concern that the increasing intervention of public authorities in the economic order is both a symptom and a cause of the "socialization" of society. "Socialization" is defined as the increasing complexity and multiplication of social relations and a greater interdependence among people (MM #59–60). Thus, there is need to balance individual economic freedoms with rightful and necessary government intervention (MM #66).

The most controversial part of the encyclical is the acknowledgment of the need for and the legitimacy of an ever larger role for government in economic life in the face of "socialization." Society is increasingly bound by more complex interdependencies where many areas of social life are beyond the scope of individual competence, thereby requiring collective action in some form or another. This prompts John XXIII to acknowledge an augmented, valid, and active role for government in socioeconomic life. But John XXIII does not stop at this. He is fully aware of the unique and tremendous opportunities for government to accomplish much good in countless lives.

> Indeed, as is easily perceived, recent developments of science and technology provide additional reasons why, to a greater extent than heretofore, it is within the power of public authorities to reduce imbalances,

whether these be between various sectors of economic life, or between different regions of the same nation, or even between different peoples of the world as a whole. These same developments make it possible to keep fluctuations in the economy within bounds, and to provide effective measures for avoiding mass unemployment. Consequently, it is requested again and again of public authorities responsible for the common good, that they intervene in a wide variety of economic affairs . . . in a more extensive and organized way than heretofore . . . (MM #54).

Such an acknowledgment of the obligation of higher bodies highlights the complementary parts of the principle of subsidiarity first formalized by Pius XI in *Quadragesimo Anno*. The principle of subsidiarity is commonly understood and stated as a "hands-off" approach on the part of government with respect to private initiative. What is not commonly known or acknowledged, however, is that paragraph #79 of *Quadragesimo Anno* is only one of two parts to the principle of subsidiarity. There is a second half to it, the unspoken, implicit segment that stresses the obligation of higher bodies to perform what lower bodies cannot accomplish for themselves for the sake of the common good. *Mater et Magistra* (#51–53) deserves credit for making this explicit:

> At the outset it should be affirmed that in economic affairs first place is to be given to the private initiative of individual men who . . . pursue their common interests. But in this matter . . . it is necessary that public authorities take active interest, the better to increase output of goods and to further social progress for the benefit of all citizens. *This intervention of public authorities that encourages, stimulates, regulates, supplements, and complements, is based on the principle of subsidiarity as set forth by Pius XI* . . . (emphasis added).

Mater et Magistra strengthens the principle of subsidiarity by noting that, together with a healthy respect for the realm properly reserved for private initiative, higher bodies are obligated to furnish assistance to floundering lower bodies (MM #53, #65). The foundational premise undergirding this claim is the encyclical's understanding of the nature of community. The end of community, indeed the purpose of any and all social activity, is to facilitate the individual's attainment of a full and perfect life (MM #65, #74; QA #79). In addition to this, *Mater et Magistra* complements Pius XI's formulation of the first half of the principle of subsidiarity by providing another critical foundational premise, this time on the nature of the human person. Despite the expanding complexity and increasingly intense interdependence of "socialization," the human person is still morally and ultimately accountable for these social processes and outcomes (MM #62–63).

The significance of this strong affirmation of the moral agency of the human person cannot be taken lightly because of the following implications for the conduct of political economy. First, a convenient argument used to absolve the individual of moral accountability for market out-comes and processes is to point to the nature of a perfectly competitive market where the atomistic economic agent is merely a price taker who cannot substantially affect market results (for good or for ill). *Mater et Magistra* (#62–63) disagrees with this position; the marketplace is not governed by the amoral, immutable workings of economic "laws" that are completely autonomous of human moral choices.

Second, providing the opportunity to exercise human freedom is not good enough; it has to bear the seeds for substantial and productive in-teraction with others. Hence, we have *Mater et Magistra*'s explicit speci-fication of the second half of the principle of subsidiarity where the community (state) is obligated to assist individuals grow as moral agents by providing the necessary environment that is conducive to growth in personal moral agency and individual perfection. For this reason, John XXIII defines the common good as the sum total of those social condi-tions that allow people to live more fully (MM #65).

Second Contribution: Principle of Participation

Mater et Magistra's affirmation of personal moral agency leads to an im-portant norm that flows from the principle of subsidiarity. Since the human person is held accountable for social processes and outcomes, people should be able to participate in a substantive manner in socio-economic life (the right of participation). This meaningful participation consists of:

1.   helping community members learn and grow in responsibility by providing the necessary opportunities for the exercise of such charge.
2.   respecting people's right to be the artisans of their own destiny, that is, to give individuals a wide berth in developing through their own efforts (norm of self-help).

In other words, personal accountability carries with it the right and obligation to discharge that moral agency through the derivative right to participation. This provides an additional rationale for the first half of the principle of subsidiarity, *Quadragesimo Anno*'s call for the protec-tion of private initiative.

Great caution must be exercised by government in carrying out its obligation of providing the ideal social conditions for the attainment of the common good. Unless done with care, government policies can cause more harm than good as seen in the woeful neglect of agriculture precipitated by the damaging effects of the unintended, de facto antirural bias of the import-substitution strategy to development. John XXIII em-phasizes this repeatedly in stressing the need for a balanced growth for industry, agriculture, and services. This articulates a useful yardstick for evaluating government interventions in economic life: whether they result in a more equitable distribution of burdens and benefits in community life.

Deficiencies in the treatment of the agricultural sector, especially when set against the larger backdrop of the import-substitution strategy to development, highlight a principle that can be inferred from *Mater et Magistra*: the principle of participation. In calling attention to the plight of the agricultural sector, John XXIII underscores the importance of being inclusive in social life. However, it is equally important to ensure that such participation is substantive and equitable. Participation is meaningful when individuals are able to secure for themselves (without undue hardship) the means to flourish in life. It is an equitable participation when there is a proportionate sharing in the burdens and the benefits of the collective effort. Neither of these are in evidence in rural life. The cost of developing an industrial sector for the country falls disproportionately on the shoulders of the farmers.

Third Contribution: Balanced versus Unbalanced Growth

Mater et Magistra's exposition on agriculture serves as a commentary on another development policy question of the time. There is debate in development theory on the choice between a balanced and an unbalanced approach to growth. The balanced-growth strategy argues for an economy-wide spurt in capital investment. The objective is to inject life and activity in as many sectors of the economy as possible. Such growth, occurring along a wide front, has the advantage of creating new complementary markets for each other's products, thereby assuring the viability of these new activity-generating investments. Proponents of this strategy see the lack of demand (the smallness of markets) as the principal obstacle to economic growth in less developed countries (Rosenstein-Rodan 1943; Nurkse 1953).

Critics argue that it is unrealistic to pursue such a strategy because it requires a tremendous infusion of capital, which is precisely the bottleneck and the principal scarcity faced by poor countries. If they had the necessary capital to pursue a balanced-growth strategy, they would not be poor at all in the first place. Furthermore, there is a minimum optimum size for capital investments. In the rush to achieve an economy-wide investment spurt, there is the danger that most projects will be undersized or inefficient due to undercapitalization. Critics recommend an unbalanced-growth strategy instead. In the first place, capital investments inevitably cause imbalances in the economy because of shortages in critical factors of production and know-how. The key, then, is to manage these shortfalls and to concentrate on "growth points" that can create a snowball effect and pull the other sluggish sectors along with it. The necessary task at hand is to encourage and make room for the innovation and entrepreneurship that would identify and develop these "growth points" (Hirschman 1958; Scitovsky 1959).

It is fairly obvious where John XXIII would stand in this debate. He deems it improper to achieve unusually high rates of growth by making certain sectors of the economy suffer.

> It often happens that in one and the same country citizens enjoy different degrees of wealth and social advancement. This especially happens because they dwell in areas which, economically speaking, have grown at different rates. Where such is the case, justice and equity demand that the government make efforts either to remove or minimize imbalances of this sort. . . . [I]t is precisely the measures for advancement of the general welfare which civil authorities must undertake. *Hence, they should take steps, having regard for the needs of the whole community, that progress in agriculture, industry, and services be made at the same time and in a balanced manner so far as possible* (MM #150–51, emphasis added).

> Accordingly, efforts should be made to ensure that improved social conditions accompany economic advancement. And it is very important that such advances occur simultaneously in the agricultural, industrial, and various services sectors (MM #168).

Given its repeated call for equity across all sectors, it is very likely that *Mater et Magistra* falls within the ambit of the balanced-growth strategy. An untrammeled pursuit of an unbalanced approach to development imposes a disproportionate share of the cost on a few. The burdens of a contractual relationship should not unduly fall only on one of the parties. John XXIII is emphatic in noting that it is patently unjust to deliberately put a class of citizens in an inferior socioeconomic position for the benefit of another class.[4] The benefits of the economic order are meant for all. Besides, a balanced-growth strategy is consistent with the principle of subsidiarity.

The choice of this balanced-growth strategy would enable the agricultural sector to better absorb output from the other two sectors, help keep inflation down by providing essential consumer needs for the economy, and provide adequate training and skills to rural workers displaced by farm modernization. All these lead toward a more orderly and easier transfer of labor to the industrial and service sectors (MM #129–30). Other scholars of dual economies essentially make a similar observation that agriculture provides not only the markets for consumer goods but also the finances and the workforce in the national effort to industrialize.[5] These arguments stressing the importance of agriculture are not new and have been presented all along both in the balanced-growth and the dualistic surplus-labor literature (Lewis 1954; Fei and Ranis 1964; Paauw and Fei 1973).

Mater et Magistra shares many points of convergence with development economics on agricultural development and the balanced-growth strategy. The encouragement of mutual-aid societies, credit unions, and artisan cooperatives is standard fare for poverty-alleviation programs. Both have an appreciation for the key role that cottage-industry operations play in spelling the difference between success or stagnation for emerging economies; both see the need to actively set conditions in the social order that would be conducive to the establishment of these small-scale enterprises (MM #84–90). Both argue for a cessation of the common practice of imposing hidden burdens or "taxes" on the agricultural sector to finance industrial expansion through pricing policies for commodities, capital funds, and foreign exchange. Both acknowledge the importance of enabling farmers through extension programs and education.[6]

Fourth Contribution: Nature of Equity in Market Operations

In leaning toward a balanced-growth strategy and in criticizing the import-substitution policies that discriminate against the agricultural sector, *Mater et Magistra* conveys an understanding of the *nature of equity* as fairness in both access-opportunities and outcomes. This is evident in his alarm over the imbalances in socioeconomic processes and outcomes on a sectoral (among agriculture, industry, and service sectors), regional (between urban and rural areas), and global (between developed and developing countries) scale. *Mater et Magistra*'s prescriptions for addressing these imbalances consistently encompass the obligation of the rich and the strong to help the poor and the weak within a spirit of participation that provides the necessary assistance and occasion for people to be the agents of their own development. Its notion of equity as fairness in access and opportunities is reflected in its constant appeal to the norm of self-help in the principles of subsidiarity and participation. Equity as fairness in outcomes is also very much in evidence as the encyclical repeatedly emphasizes the inadmissibility of government policies that fail the standard of proportionality in the distribution of burdens and benefits. The cost of development should not be borne by selected sectors of the economy (as in the case of agriculture in the import-substitution strategy), just as the benefits cannot be reserved only for a few. In living amicably and justly together, the community has to distribute burdens according to people's ability to bear them, just as benefits derived must also be consistent with the burdens borne.

In summary, *Mater et Magistra* advances our understanding of morality in the marketplace. First, it argues that the principle of subsidiarity is not merely about the affirmation of free market operations through the protection of private initiative, but also the community's obligation to ensure that the market provides the necessary opportunities for meaningful and productive participation for all consistent with the promotion of the common good. Second, *Mater et Magistra* shows that equity in market operations involves both fairness in access and outcomes.

FURTHER WORK

What does this exercise of linking *Mater et Magistra* to the import-substitution strategy add to the literature? What new ground is broken by this chapter in showing that John XXIII's agricultural policy prescriptions match those of policymakers and scholars who are concerned with this one-sided effort at industrialization?

There is nothing in the early or later commentaries on *Mater et Magistra* that provides a point of reference or context for this encyclical's section on agriculture. Commentators observe the lengthy treatment accorded to the rural sector and the specificity of the policy proposals advanced; these are unusual even for such a social encyclical. However, no explanation has yet been provided for these features of the document.

In painting the larger economic milieu of the time and in bringing to the fore the widespread development thinking and practice of the era, this chapter suggests that *Mater et Magistra*'s extended discussion of detailed policies to ameliorate the plight of farming families is a response to the antirural, antiagricultural bias of the import-substitution strategy. These policy recommendations are similar to those in development thinking on the correction of imbalances caused by an inordinate drive to industrialize. None of the commentaries in the literature that deal with John XXIII's section on agriculture mentions the import-substitution approach to development.[7] This is odd considering the economic conditions of the time. This gap in the literature may be reflective of a failure to cross disciplines and to see what economic history and economic development have to offer.

Definitively establishing the link between *Mater et Magistra* and the import-substitution strategy lies beyond the scope of this chapter and requires access to archives that reveal more about the writing of this encyclical. If and when materials become available, it would be well for future historians to examine the import-substitution strategy to development as a frame of reference for part III of the encyclical. In the meantime, reading *Mater et Magistra*'s vivid exposition on rural conditions within the larger backdrop of the economic history of its era allows one to have a better appreciation for John XXIII's exposition on agriculture.

Notes

1. A rapid increase in population is precipitated by the rapid decline in death rates (due to medical advances) without an immediate, corresponding change in fertility rates.

2. The literature on the import-substitution development strategy, both in its theory and practice, is enormous. This section is a nontechnical exposition written for a wide audience. For further readings on the nuances and intricacies of this strategy, see Prebisch (1979), Hirschman (1968), Bruton (1970, 1989), Chenery (1960), Iglesias (1992), Grabowski (1994a, 1994b), and Krueger (1997). Credit for the seminal thought behind this autarkic strategy to growth and development is generally accorded to Raul Prebisch and the Economic Commission for Latin American (ECLA) of the United Nations.

3. For an exposition on "two-gap" models, see McKinnon (1966). Yergin and Stanislaw (1998) devote an entire chapter describing the heavy government involvement in economic life in most developing nations during the three decades following World War II. By taking the "commanding heights" of the economy, governments hope to reduce the "savings gap" of the nation through state ownership of critical resources and industries and through inflation-induced savings.

4. *Mater et Magistra* #69 observes: "It happens in other places that excessive burdens are placed upon men in order that the commonwealth may achieve within a brief span, an increase of wealth such as can by no means be achieved without violating the laws of justice and equity."

5. Note what W. A. Lewis has to say: "[T]he most important item on the agenda of development is to transform the food sector, create agricultural surpluses to feed the urban population, and thereby create the domestic basis for industry and modern services" (cited by Meier 1984, 421).

6. See, for example, Austin (1981) and Harper (1984).

7. See, for example, Calvez (1964, 56–63), Riga (1966, 117–41), O'Brien and Shannon (1977, 44–49), O'Rourke (1963, 238–49), McCormack (1963, 128–30), McLaughlin (1994, 26–27), and Boland (1994, 585).

Chapter 3

DEVELOPMENT AND SOLIDARISTIC EGALITARIANISM

INTRODUCTION

A characteristic feature of the post–World War II era is the increased attention accorded to the Third World. This is reflected in the "internationalization" of the social questions addressed by the documents of the period. Aside from the expanded scope of the subject matter, there is also a pronounced turn toward activism within this tradition. Prior to the Second Vatican Council, these social documents are few and far in between. Thus, it takes forty years before *Quadragesimo Anno* follows the lead of *Rerum Novarum* and another thirty years for *Mater et Magistra* to continue this body of teachings.[1] In contrast, there is a rapid succession of major social documents issued every few years since John XXIII.

These theological reflections on development and international affairs should not be read as a complete nor closed system. After all, they are not intended to be academic treatises. Their value lies in the insights that can be gleaned from their teleological reasoning and from the principles and norms undergirding their appraisal of particular aspects of global political economy. Some of these contributions are examined in what follows: the concept of development as primarily a moral phenomenon, a stricter egalitarianism, and the obligations of solidarity in international relations.

The postconciliar documents are heterodox in their economics and contest the classical liberal belief of leaving markets alone. They are activist in shaping market processes, even with correcting market outcomes. These documents are reflective of a keen desire to restore justice in the sinful structures of society through personal renewal and collective action.

CONCEPT OF DEVELOPMENT

Development as a Moral Phenomenon

Issued barely two years after the promulgation of *Gaudium et Spes*, *Populorum Progressio* seeks to dispel the prevailing thinking among Third World countries that progress is about emulating the wealthier nations' high levels of consumption. The encyclical's principal contribution to political economy is its critique of the conventional belief that development is purely, if not chiefly, economic in nature. Together with the subsequent social documents of its period, *Populorum Progressio* argues that *genuine human development is primarily a moral phenomenon* with significant ramifications for both the constitutive elements and the requisite processes of such advancement. Economic growth need not necessarily lead to human well-being. Growth, per se, is premoral because its ultimate value is determined by how it is achieved and for what purpose it is pursued (PP#19). The distinctive moral dimensions of development discussed in the next two sections lay the groundwork for the participative egalitarianism advanced in chapter 10.

Necessary content of authentic development

These social documents propose three tenets on the necessary content of development: that it is primarily geared toward the human person's perfection, that it is holistic, and that no one is excluded from it. Paul VI states it succinctly:

> Development cannot be limited to mere economic growth. In order to be authentic, it must be complete: integral, that is, it has to promote the good of every man and of the whole man.[2] (PP #14)

The human person is both the subject and the end of development economics especially since this subfield is about the improvement of the quality of life in impoverished countries. The common association of human welfare with economic growth alone is incompatible with this social tradition.[3] There are two objections to viewing human well-being exclusively in terms of material prosperity. In the first place, such increase and accumulation need not automatically benefit all. A skewed distribution of output and entitlements can prevent sizable segments of the population from benefitting from such an expansion. Second, even if everyone had a fair share, there is no guarantee that the resources made available will redound to genuine human welfare. After all, human perfection goes well beyond the satisfaction of material needs.[4]

This is not to say, however, that economic growth should not be given the attention that it deserves. Economic growth and the procurement of material goods, while not sufficient conditions for authentic development, are indispensable.[5] They facilitate the enjoyment of a wider range of choices and liberties, from assuaging hunger and averting disease to the higher liberating human experiences such as the enjoyment of culture and an education that allows people to deal with and change the world around them (Schultz 1980). The satisfaction of the more basic necessities becomes the springboard for the subsequent fulfillment of more profound needs.

If development is to be authentic, however, there has to be an advance in the corporal, intellectual, cultural, social, and spiritual realms of a person's life. Social development must accompany economic growth; there has to be an effort to overcome not only destitution but also all forms of servitude (PP #34, #47). Progress is more than just a quantitative phenomenon; it is principally a qualitative order where ennobling human relationships and participation in social life are just as important as the availability of material goods (OA #41a; JW #15). This makes development a richer, albeit a more complex, process than is presented by economic models.

Nonexclusion is another necessary condition of genuine progress and flows from the judgment that inequities in social, political, and economic spheres tear away at the very woof and warp of societal cohesion. No one can be left out of the development process. As repeatedly argued within the tradition, individual good can only be achieved within the common good; both are distinct but inextricable from each other. There is both a personal and a social character to development, and its necessary first step is a healthy respect for the value of every and all persons (SRS #33e).

This social dimension also means that the desire for progress should go beyond national boundaries. In fact, the tradition's horizon in referring to development covers not only the perfection of the individual or of the nation alone but also extends to the community of nations.[6] Indeed, the social question addressed in the seminal document *Rerum Novarum* has become international in scope, due in large part to *Mater et Magistra*'s phenomenon of "socialization," where an increasingly intense and complex interdependence among peoples and nations is fueled by rapid advances in science and technologies. Just as the social good is a necessary condition for individual well-being, the good of the entire community of nations is also a necessary condition for the welfare of each individual nation.

Process of development

Development is not an automatic nor a limitless process that can only move forward. It is a reversible process; hard-earned gains can be lost. Moreover, it requires thoughtful effort. *Justice in the World* takes issue with deterministic notions of progress, be it the Marxist view of the inevitable evolutionary self-destruction of capitalism or of laissez faire's "invisible-hand" dynamics.

That right to development is above all a right to hope. . . . To respond to such hope, the concept of evolution must be purified of those myths and false convictions which have up to now gone with a thought-pattern subject to a kind of deterministic and automatic notion of progress (JW #16).

The endeavor to improve human life is one of constant struggle and deliberate hard work; it consists of courageous and concerted action. It is a long and complex process because of the "frailty of human resolutions" and the "mutability of circumstances" (SRS #38a, #27a, #30f; PP #55). Consequently, the tradition is not sympathetic to the claim of neoclassical and laissez-faire adherents that the system can function with minimal oversight; it sees a legitimate role in economic life for the state and other intermediate bodies and associations. Development is a purposeful activity that requires planning and intervention within the spirit of the principles of subsidiarity and solidarity. It cannot be left entirely to the workings of an individual self-interest that is believed to reflect back to the common good. The vestiges of original sin preclude such complete trust in the self-healing powers of the economic order espoused by the classical school.

Deterministic notions of progress are also ultimately reductionist in that moral responsibility is taken away from the person. The primary agent of development is the human person who is the principal efficient cause behind societal institutions and processes. Consequently, development is both a right and an obligation for the person and the community.

Distinctively Christian Contribution

The preceding notion of development—humanistic, holistic, social, international, and nondeterministic—is an inevitable offshoot of spiritual values. However, such conception should not be mistakenly thought of as belonging exclusively within the domain of faith since it can be also found in nonreligious advocacy.

The *Human Development Report 1990* of the United Nations Development Programme speaks simply, but eloquently, of the human person as the end which economics serves. It sets the advancement of personal growth as the object of economic life.[7] Development is multifaceted and goes beyond mere growth in gross national product (GNP). Economic well-being is only one dimension of a complex set of needs and is merely a means toward achieving many other noble values in the quest for human perfection.[8] Innate gifts and talents are to be developed; the provision of the necessary avenues for their use and expression is important.[9] The social dimension of development is very much a concern where the focus is not limited to the individual alone but is also extended to the community.

The *Human Development Report*'s view is shared by many development economists. There is consensus that "quality of life" is a better measure of the human well-being that development is supposed to effect. This is clearly evident in the burgeoning literature on the quest for appropriate development indicators.[10] Measures such as life expectancy, child mortality, literacy, and access to basic necessities have long been used to supplement gross national product (GNP) in gauging country performance.[11] The term "development" has been used with greater caution.[12]

This comparison would be incomplete without mention of the kindred spirit that Catholic social thought's differentiation between *having* and *being* finds in economist Amartya Kumar Sen's *functionings*. In speaking of human perfection, the tradition assigns cardinal importance to *being*, rather than *having*, since the person "is more precious for what he is than for what he has" (GS #35; PP #19; SRS #28). Material wealth cannot be an end in itself because of its intrinsic instrumental character. In a similar vein, Sen views the true measure of development to be the freedom and the ability of people to become what they would like to be.[13]

Culmination in the transcendent end

In spite of these similarities, there are major differences between this theological tradition and development economics in their conception of human advancement. *Populorum Progressio*'s principle of integral development is a more nuanced notion of progress that is centered on the transcendent nature of people; they enjoy a destiny that reaches far beyond themselves to the Absolute. Thus, the process of development is necessarily accompanied by growth in moral comprehension on the part of individuals. This consciousness manifests itself in the freedom to act selflessly for the welfare of others. After all, the originality and contribution of this social tradition are grounded in its ethical examination of key contentious issues and not in a scientific description of deficiencies in the social order. For this reason, it asks more and expects more from the development process than economics does: nothing less than charity with all its concomitant possibilities for self-sacrifice and service.

> [T]rue development must be based on the *love of God and neighbor*, and must help to promote the relationships between individuals and society. This is the "civilization of love" of which Paul VI often spoke (SRS #33h).

This goes beyond Sen's (1979) *commitment*.

Limits to consumption

To further illustrate the difference that a theological dimension makes, let us examine the reasons given for why material accumulation is not a good measure of progress. For development economists, pecuniary measures are not satisfactory because there is no definitive correlation between earnings and human well-being. This is due either to a faulty distribution or to an inefficient use of such incomes for meeting basic and social needs (UNDP 1990). Hence, supplementary social indicators are used as "quality-of-life" measures.

In the case of Catholic social thought, income measures alone are unsatisfactory for precisely the same reasons given by development economists. However, it offers the additional insight that an inordinate focus on monetary gain puts personal growth at risk by encouraging avarice, excessive materialism, and self-interested behavior. The *homo oeconomicus* model is an unsuitable formulation because it does not acknowledge limits to consumption. In fact, consumer theory assumes insatiability for mathematical convenience. For this theological approach, overindulgent consumption, like destitution, is an obstacle to personal development. Destitution encumbers people in accessing the gifts of nature vital to sustaining life; excessive consumption is a hindrance because it prizes accumulation and immediate gratification to the detriment of integral human development. Beyond the limits set by prudence and moderation, the consumption of material goods can be counterproductive for human development.[14] Human virtue is essential to the process of development both as a means and as an intrinsic good. Moral life is rarely discussed as part of the development process, and if it is, only its instrumental role in ensuring the smooth functioning of society is underscored (see, for example, Fitzgibbons 1995). An exclusive preoccupation with material profit would most likely lead to a stunted development.

Structures of sin and personal conversion

Personal and social sin hamper authentic development and cause enormous suffering. The Second Vatican Council poignantly describes the dilemma as a paradox of contradictions and imbalances (GS #8–9). Never before have people uncovered so much of nature's secrets; never before have they enjoyed so much control over their living environment. Yet, this newly gained power has brought with it the ironic loss of freedom as technology takes the upper hand in shaping lifestyles. Never before have the likes of such material prosperity been enjoyed; yet, many are trapped in impoverished existence. Never before have so much innovation and beauty been seen in the ingenious uses to which the gifts of nature have been put. Yet, the cost inflicted on the fragile balance of its ecology has been enormous. The Council attributes these contradictions to the human failure to use properly the forces and the powers of development that have been unleashed.

This dilemma has been aggravated by institutions that perpetuate and fuel such incongruities and imbalances. *Sollicitudo Rei Socialis* (#37d) refers to these as the "structures of sin" because they are the social manifestations of the effects of original sin. At the root of these systemic ills is personal sin; the selfishness and avarice of individuals overflow into society and seep into every facet of community life. The institutionalization of such failures in turn makes it even more difficult for the individual to overcome evil and self-centeredness at a personal level. Shortcomings in discharging individual duties to society are diseconomies that impede development. Such disexternalities can be extensive in their effects and may even last well beyond the life span of the person(s) responsible for them. Personal and social sinfulness mutually reinforce and feed off each other.

This cycle could only be broken through individual personal conversion (SRS #38c). Obstacles to development can only be addressed by economic remedies rooted in moral decision and action. There is need for a fresh appreciation for the teleology of economic life; material goods serve to promote the fullness of people's transcendent vocation. And even in this, there is a hierarchy of values where some goods have relatively greater relevance and importance in promoting human thriving. The profit motive is replaced in preeminence by "the demands deriving from the order of *truth* and *good* proper to the human person" (SRS #33h, emphasis in the original).

Solidarity and mutual responsibilities

The ethical dimension of development requires a spirit of solidarity, that is, the obligation of empathic concern for and action on behalf of other people and nations, particularly those who are least able to fend for themselves. Nations have a responsibility to assist poorer economies in direct proportion to their ability to help. Contributive justice calls for a concern of all for all.[15]

In summary, the concept of development cannot be cast merely in terms of material accumulation. To do so would be to impoverish the whole process itself and to fail to do justice to the other facets of life that provide it with richness and meaning. Because it deals with matters that affect human well-being in a substantive manner, the practice of development economics cannot be isolated from moral considerations. More importantly, it is not the immutable laws of economic science that determine the trajectory of human progress; rather, advancement is shaped by people exercising moral agency properly and intelligently in taking responsibility for each other's good and for societal processes.

SOLIDARISTIC EGALITARIANISM

Each new social document is invariably prefaced with an examination of the economic conditions of its time. Each consistently laments and invites attention to worsening inequalities in wealth outcomes, earnings capacities, and the exercise of power. The impressive growth rates of the post–World War II era have kindled high expectations that poverty can be finally eradicated within a generation. However, these hopes have proved to be premature as poor countries languished, even during an unprecedented time of global economic expansion (JW #10). Despite significant achievements in improving the human condition in many parts of the world, there are still sizable pockets of the most dire forms of destitution where even the most elementary needs of water, food, and shelter are lacking. One of the most telling signs of failure has been the disparity between those who have and those who have little or nothing at all.

The imbalance between rich and poor countries is observed in both wealth outcomes and rates of progress. In addition, this widening gap occurs across a broad front beyond economic matters to include the social, cultural, and political realms. These inequalities are also prevalent within national borders given the incidence of unemployment, underemployment, and homelessness even in developed countries. Inequity seems to be a persistent phenomenon in the modern economy, distinctive in its pervasiveness throughout the entire social order both domestic and international. The manifold causes believed to engender poverty in the Third World include the unsustainable growth in population, agricultural neglect, the primitive state of industry, and the massive outflow of people from the rural sector into the urban centers.

How do we assess the market in the face of such destitution and disparities? It may be that the unfettered "invisible hand" is intrinsically unable to guarantee that the benefits of growth trickle down to the fringes of society. Pareto optimality, after all, has no mechanism for keeping relative inequality within limits since distribution is not addressed at all in this criterion. Alternatively, market failures may be preventing the "invisible hand" from delivering its much-touted advantages. In either case, there is need for the "visible hand" of other institutions to supplement the market.

The post–Vatican II era marks a significant period for modern Catholic social thought on distributive justice given its turn toward a strong egalitarianism that serves as the prism through which social affairs are examined. For Drew Christiansen (1984, 656), the crisis of inequality is the central social question of Paul VI's pontificate. The principle of relative equality takes center stage as the patristic standards of economic equity are retrieved. The theological reflections of this period make "egalitarian distribution a cardinal principle of magisterial social ethics" (653). Furthermore, Christiansen is quick to add that this desired relative equality is not merely one among many other social principles. It is a fundamental rearrangement in the tradition's approach whereby egalitarian distribution becomes *the* social strategy from which flows all other reflections, principles, and norms.

Christiansen offers two key characteristics of this era's principle of relative equality. In contrast to its weaker version, this solidaristic egalitarianism calls for an equality of resources and opportunities. Furthermore, it assigns to government both the right and the obligation to intervene in market operations for larger societal goals. This, of course, is related to strong egalitarianism's acknowledgment of positive rights (and, therefore, of positive obligations) in contrast to the libertarians' view of rights and obligations as negative, that is, limited to noninterference (Berlin 1969).

This solidaristic equality has harmony as its proximate goal. The operational intent of postconciliar egalitarianism is to provide a basis for maintaining concord within the community.

> [T]he basic thrust of the norm [relative equality] is that the distance between any set of groups ought to be curbed so that their ability to act in a fraternal/sororal way toward one another is not subverted (Christiansen 1984, 666).

This proximate goal of peaceful coexistence serves the larger end of actualizing solidaristic unity within the community. This formulation is consistent with Paul VI's famous maxim that "Development is the new name for peace" (PP#76). It advances our understanding of distributive justice by highlighting one of its necessary fruits—peace.

> Peace cannot be limited to a mere absence of war. . . . No, peace is something that is built up day after day, in the pursuit of an order intended by God, which implies a more perfect form of justice among men (PP #76).

Put another way, harmony presents itself as a practical, observable standard for how well a community works out distributive justice in the context of its time and place. The presence or absence of concord and the quality of that peace are convenient diagnostic tools.

The high value accorded to amicable cooperation is reflected in the underlying attitude and pace to changing the structures of sin—with all haste, but prudently. Paul VI (PP #32) recognizes the urgency of the reforms he espouses, especially in matters concerning equity. However, he is also keenly aware of an equally important responsibility not to unduly worsen human suffering through the disruption, chaos, and disequilibrium that may arise from too hasty and drastic an overhaul. Such would be recklessness. This approach of prudent haste is evident in some of his policy prescriptions. For example, in implementing agrarian reforms and industrialization programs, he cautions against rashness that sweeps aside beneficial practices and structures in the process (PP #29). While appreciating the value of equity and equality of opportunity, he is also realistic in conceding that there are cases where these can only be successfully and peacefully achieved when done gradually at the margins. There is a willingness to wait patiently and to accept the likelihood that setting the stage for a more equitable distribution of outcomes in the future may be more feasible than overhauling present entitlements immediately.[16] The tradition advocates the introduction of much-needed reforms without delay while keeping in mind that such dispatch in action should not aggravate or even create new divisions. It is willing to work with patience and within an extended time frame, if necessary. Prudence is the key to maintaining such balance.

As in the case of the import-substitution strategy, the heavier emphasis on government intervention must be viewed within the larger history of the time, lest too much be attributed to this turn toward radical egalitarianism. This is an era of Keynesianism triumphant in Western political economy. The inability of classical, self-healing markets to account for the deep and prolonged Great Depression becomes the occasion for the signal contributions of Keynes's *General Theory* (1936). This provides the intellectual underpinning of an activist macroeconomics that becomes staple for the post–World War II fine-tuning of the economy through government action (Yergin and Stanislaw 1998). Postconciliar egalitarianism is a reflection of a larger milieu that coincided with a turn toward a more sociohistorically oriented method of theological reflection.

The restrictions on private property ownership, the acknowledgment of a rightful larger economic role for government, and the acceptance of positive rights are not unique nor original to the Paul VI–era social documents. Issues of equity have been major concerns even for the pre-Vatican II documents. The desire for greater relative equality has always been an integral part of the tradition, although the methods and the complexity of ameliorative solutions proposed are different. Earlier social documents employ a larger set of standards besides strict egalitarianism. For example, even as Leo XIII is alarmed at the growing disparity between workers and capitalists, he does not focus on redistribution, whether of wealth, of incomes, or even of the means of production. Instead, he calls for remedial measures (such as the right to form unions) that strengthen the position of workers in fending for themselves in a market economy. Pius XI is concerned with the strange admixture of great concentrations of political power and economic wealth amidst a vast sea of poverty. Thus, he proposes a reorganization of society along vocational groupings to improve relative equality by providing comparable bargaining power to both labor and capital. John XXIII's *Mater et Magistra* devotes an unusually lengthy and detailed exposition on the disadvantaged rural sector relative to the rest of the population. He calls for a necessary balance in development across all sectors of the community. Indeed, the maldistribution of economic resources and roles has always been a concern since the earliest days of the modern tradition, although there are differences in the degree and the manner by which equality is to be pursued. Christiansen is correct in observing a perceptible change toward a greater sense of urgency attached to the issue and a shift toward stricter standards of equity in distribution. Solidarism is the "deep theory" undergirding postconciliar egalitarianism. The impact of such solidaristic egalitarianism is evident in the choice of the principle of solidarity as the primary prism with which to examine the ethics of the social question's internationalization.

INTERNATIONAL ECONOMIC RELATIONS: TAKING RESPONSIBILITY TOGETHER

Principle of Solidarity as Animating Spirit

Populorum Progressio's notion of integral human development undergirds the conviction that development is primarily a moral, rather than an economic, phenomenon. *Sollicitudo Rei Socialis*, the ensuing commemorative document, also has its own distinctive contribution appropriate for its own period: calling attention to the principle of solidarity as the moral touchstone for much of international relations.

Neither the expanded scope of the social question nor the concept of solidarity is original to *Sollicitudo Rei Socialis*. John XXIII (MM #200–202), the Second Vatican Council (GS #77ff), and Paul VI (OA #43b) had already come to the conclusion that the nature of social issues has undergone such a sea change since Leo XIII, so much so that international cooperation is no longer merely an option but a necessity. Satisfying the demands of justice, even for domestic affairs, is increasingly beyond the scope of individual nations' capabilities and can only be accomplished in collaboration with other countries. The complementarity of nations has long been recognized and acknowledged.

Solidarity has also been very much a part of the earlier documents. *Gaudium et Spes*, part I, explores the tradition's anthropological basis through a theological reflection on the nature of the human person and the community. *Justice in the World* and *Octogesima Adveniens* already use the term "solidarity" to describe the proper bonds that should exist among nations.

The originality of *Sollicitudo Rei Socialis* lies in its making explicit what has always been operative in the background: the use of the principle of solidarity as the overarching framework within which intractable problems of global political economy can be resolved justly. Referring to the growing empathy of peoples for each other, John Paul II notes:

> It is above all a question of *interdependence*, sensed as a *system determining* relationships in the contemporary world, in its economic, cultural, political and religious elements, and accepted as a *moral category*. When interdependence becomes recognized this way, the correlative response as a moral and social attitude, as a "virtue," is *solidarity*. This then is not a feeling of vague compassion. . . . On the contrary, it [solidarity] is *a firm and persevering determination* to commit oneself to the

common good . . . because we are *all* really responsible *for all* . . . a commitment to the good of one's neighbor . . . (SRS #38f, emphases in the original).

The solidarity that ought to govern relationships between individuals is the same principle that should enliven nations in their dealings with each other. This transposition should not come as a surprise, for as *Gaudium et Spes* (#83) observes, the root causes of conflict in an unsettled and unjust international order (envy, distrust, pride, avarice, and the lust for power) are ultimately traceable to the human heart. Thus, solidarity provides the fundamental datum with which the other principles (such as universal access, socialization, subsidiarity, and primacy of labor) are used to appraise global economics.

Universal access principle

As part of post–Vatican II egalitarianism, the application of the universal access principle is expanded into the international arena.

> The same criterion is applied by analogy in international relationships. Interdependence must be transformed into *solidarity*, based upon the principle that the goods of creation *are meant for all*. That which human industry produces through the processing of raw materials, with the contribution of work, must serve equally for the good of all (SRS #39c, emphasis in the original).

The universal access principle calls for a reevaluation of the affluent lifestyles of developed nations. The *Human Development Report of 1998* notes the disturbing asymmetry in the use of global resources between the wealthy and the poor countries and appeals to developed nations to curtail their excessive consumption (United Nations Development Programme 1998). Every social document since *Mater et Magistra* has pointedly observed that the First World must be willing to sacrifice its high standards of living as part of the needed restructuring of the international economy. Moreover, its disproportionate use of scarce natural resources and the resultant damage to the environment go against the principles of equity and stewardship. The object of this longstanding criticism is the developed world's consumerist ethos.

A second challenge posed to the First World pertains to living up to the just-use obligation that comes with the universal access principle. Paul VI (PP #48, #49) argues that both charity and justice impose a moral obligation on developed countries to provide assistance to poor nations by putting their superfluous income at the service of the latter. They are urged to be mindful that the fruits of their economic activities are meant not only for their own people but for the rest of humanity as well. Thus, the Synod of Bishops (1971) endorses the Second Development Decade's call for a firm commitment on the part of wealthy nations to set aside a percentage of their income as aid to poor countries. Their document *Justice in the World* (#66) lauds this form of graduated income tax on an international scale as a first step toward the pursuit of a global socioeconomic plan. The bishops also support the goal of providing trade concessions to less developed countries by way of better prices for raw materials, more open markets, and preferential treatment of manufactured exports.

A third implication of an internationalized universal access principle is the need to weigh seriously the morality of spending huge sums for implements of war, while those who suffer extreme destitution are left untended. Thus, Paul VI (PP #51) appeals for the establishment of a World Fund, a pool of monies to be set up from funds that would have otherwise been spent on armaments but which could be designated instead for aid to poor countries.

Primacy of labor

Just like the universal access principle, *Laborem Exercens*'s primacy of labor principle can also be transposed in an international context. *Sollicitudo Rei Socialis* notes:

> *Solidarity* helps us to see the "other"–whether a *person, people or nation*–not just as some kind of instrument, with a work capacity and physical strength to be exploited at low cost and then discarded when no longer useful, but as our "neighbor," a "helper" . . . to be made a sharer, on a par with ourselves . . . (SRS #39e, emphasis in the original).

There is need for a just price for goods coming from the Third World. *Gaudium et Spes* (#86b) already anticipates this challenge, while Paul VI makes it even more personal in *Populorum Progressio* (#47) when he directly asks First World consumers whether they are "ready to pay a higher price for imported goods so that the producer may be more justly rewarded."

Socialization–subsidiarity nexus

Perhaps the most interesting effects of solidarity in an international setting come from the principles of socialization and subsidiarity balancing out each other and defining the permissible range of global social action. Socialization defines the obligations of the developed world and multilateral agencies in furnishing assistance to poor nations. Subsidiarity, on the other hand, highlights the obligation of every nation to be the architect of its own development.

Sollicitudo Rei Socialis (#16b; #39a and 39d) notes that both developed and developing countries share in the blame for poverty in many parts of the world–the former for their negligence and indifference to the plight of the poor, and the latter for their own mismanagement. Both groups owe it to themselves and to the community of nations to set their own houses in order. After all, there is an inseparable connection between international and domestic harmony. This becomes even more evident as the web of cross-border interdependence grows more intricate and intense. Moreover, stronger nations should have a sense of responsibility for the welfare of their weaker neighbors, while the latter should contribute to the commonweal of nations in the measure they can.

Socialization The moral imperatives of an "internationalized" primacy of labor and universal access principles are reinforced further by the principle of socialization (the obligation of the strong to help the weak). Populorum Progressio (#44) notes that aid to poor countries stems from a threefold charge: the duty of solidarity, the duty of social justice, and the duty of universal charity. Similar to domestic interactions within the nation, international relations must be marked by "mutual respect and friendship, interdependence in collaboration, [and] the betterment of all seen as the responsibility of each individual" (PP #65). The manner by which aid is provided is therefore important. Mater et Magistra (MM #171, #173), for example, reminds donor countries that they must never try to impose their own cultures on the aid recipient. Assistance should always be disinterested aid, not for political leverage or gain nor for domination in any form or manner.

Paul VI also notes that assistance must always be respectful of the cultural and historical identities of all peoples given the fundamental equality of everyone. Thus, he (PP #71–73) repeats verbatim the Second Vatican Council's (GS #85b) admonition that in sending experts and missions to these countries, great care must be taken that such expatriates do not adopt a lordly or a condescending attitude. Rather, they should view their local counterparts as coworkers, true to the sprit of solidarity's disinterested love. In this connection, Paul VI observes that in assisting impoverished nations, an ongoing program is better than occasional ad hoc aid packages dependent on the generosity of the donor. Ideally, aid should be based on the actual need and absorptive capacity of the recipient country, rather than on the goodwill of the donor country alone. Such practice is more consistent with the teaching on the right use of superfluous income. It is important to have close communications and careful planning between donors and beneficiaries (PP #50, #54; cf. GS #88c).

Multilateral agencies are also important institutions within which to discharge the obligations of socialization. *Gaudium et Spes* (#83ff) and *Justice in the World* (#68) endorse the efforts of regional and international bodies in dealing with poverty-related issues such as agrarian reform, agricultural development, and basic-needs satisfaction. These organizations render great service to the community of nations but need constant reevaluation and redirection. These processes should neither be manipulated nor corrupted for national ambitions and ideologies; instead, they should merit the cooperation of everyone, for the benefit of all. It is through these transnational bodies that the international community fulfills its obligation of promoting development and of ensuring that resources set aside for such purpose are distributed equitably and used appropriately. In any multilateral or bilateral aid, less developed countries must be treated as full partners and share in decisions concerning priorities and investments.

Subsidiarity Accompanying the constant calls for assistance to poor countries is the perennial reminder that the principle of subsidiarity must be upheld. The poor need occasion to build up their confidence at basic self-determination and develop an identity in the process. This includes fostering their initiative in working for their own betterment. Thus, *Mater et Magistra* (#175–77) urges extreme care in safeguarding that Western secular values do not destroy or supplant the recipient country's heritage of values, especially its appreciation for spiritual values. This entails a sensitivity to the preservation and promotion of the rich hierarchy of values enjoyed by recipient countries. *Gaudium et Spes* (#86a) reminds developing nations that the object of assistance should always be the fulfillment of the human person, using the country's own resources to the fullest extent possible and accomplished within its own traditions.

Populorum Progressio (#65) argues that all peoples have the right and the obligation to work toward their full development in accord with their own culture. After all, they are the principal agents of their own development, the "artisans of their destiny." Because of the right to self-determination, they should also enjoy freedom from interference from donors in matters related to domestic policies and goals (PP #54). Referring to the value of literacy programs, Paul VI (PP #35) notes that the genuine, primary agents of development are those institutions whose object is to empower communities to act for themselves.

Justice in the World (#17, #71) invites developing countries to value and to put to good use their innate capacity for self-determination. *Octogesima Adveniens* (#43b) observes that the morality of development aid can be summarized as assisting the poor country to help itself without taking advantage of its vulnerability. Finally, *Sollicitudo Rei Socialis* (#44a) captures the essence of subsidiarity in development assistance by noting that self-help and initiative are the keystones of development. This encyclical provides a succinct description of the delicate balance that has to be maintained between the principles of socialization and subsidiarity:

> In order to be genuine, development must be achieved within the framework of *solidarity* and *freedom*, without ever sacrificing either of them under whatever pretext. The moral character of development and its

necessary promotion are emphasized when the most rigorous respect is given to all the demands deriving from the order of *truth* and *good* proper to the human person (SRS #33h, emphasis in the original).

In dealing with international economic relations, especially with the question of aid, there is a critical mix that must avoid the two extremes of breeding dependence (the failure of the principle of subsidiarity) or of precipitating indifference to the plight of the poor (the failure of the principle of socialization). Both principles must be operative.

Taking Responsibility for Societal Structures of Sin

Another distinctive theme of the post–Vatican II era's social documents is the forceful call to action–the need to take responsibility for the social structures of sin. This is aptly summarized by the 1971 Synod of Bishops' bold proclamation:

> Action on behalf of justice and participation in the transformation of the world fully appear to us as a constitutive dimension of the preaching of the Gospel, or, in other words, of the Church's mission for the redemption of the human race and its liberation from every oppressive situation (JW #6).

The rapid advances in technology, the heightened sensitivity to the finitude of resources and the irreversible damage wrought on the environment, the swelling clamor for a better life in poor countries, and the greater regard for human rights all serve to accentuate the failings of the international order. The pervasiveness of international events intruding into domestic affairs and the severity of their impact on developing countries underscore the need to reform international "structures of sin" that foster inequities in global political economy.

Sollicitudo Rei Socialis (#16c, #35a) notes that existing economic, financial, and social mechanisms often take a life of their own and beget a momentum that perpetuates the flaws of the social order. People are eventually conditioned to accept these systemic lapses as unalterable or are unwilling to take the burden of reforming such structures. This requires both an effective political will and moral courage. John Paul II echoes Paul VI's (OA #43b) observation that the challenge of reform is to remove obstacles to global harmony and development. Only then can we satisfy the principal demand of justice: that of affording each country the ability and the freedom to work for its own development in a spirit of cooperation without any fear of domination. Such an effort requires reformulating working arrangements among nations, especially the networks pertaining to production, exchange, money, profits, and supranational organizations.

The need for reforms is particularly acute in the area of trade. *Populorum Progressio* provides a sustained, searing criticism of unfettered markets and calls for the end of free trade because it has failed to satisfy the most elementary requirements of equity. Paul VI (PP #58, #61) argues that unrestricted trade is intrinsically unreliable given countries' unequal bargaining power and the wide disparity in the economic conditions of these countries. Moreover, markets are unable to cull out, on their own, outcomes that are inequitable. He goes on to note that existing trade arrangements have aggravated poverty in many Third and Fourth World countries and have widened even further the gap in the opportunities open to developed and less developed countries.

Paul VI (PP #57) addresses a particularly contentious debate in development thinking on the terms-of-trade problem.[17] He notes that free trade works, but only between developed countries, and not between rich and poor countries. Wealthier nations export manufactured goods and capital equipment that enjoy a high and increasing value from incorporating advances in science and technologies. On the other hand, less developed countries are heavily reliant on cash crops and other primary exports whose prices have been subject to wild fluctuations in response to fluid demand and supply conditions. In addition, their earnings potential is sluggish (relative to manufactures) because of the low value-added component of such products and the growing availability of synthetic substitutes. Consequently, the export revenues of poor countries have been unpredictable, at best, and insufficient for procuring much-needed and increasingly expensive capital equipment. There is a terms-of-trade problem in the exchange between rich and poor countries because the former can buy cheap and sell expensive, to the detriment of the latter. The result is an ever widening gap both in wealth outcomes and, more importantly, in earnings capacity.

Free trade is founded on the axiom of unrestricted competition; its justification is rooted in the benefits that it is supposed to bring in its wake. In arguing for an end to unfettered exchange in the international marketplace, Paul VI (PP #60) remarks that not even developed countries themselves subscribe to the tenets of untrammeled competition in their own domestic economies. This is particularly true in their extensive farm subsidies to protect their agricultural sectors from unfavorable or disruptive price swings. These extra-market interventions are also evident in their financial, fiscal, and social support to key industries that are floundering. Paul VI (PP#61) observes pointedly that it is a double standard for developed countries to preach the benefits of free trade and leave the resultant international imbalances unaddressed, while at the same time intervening heavily in their own domestic markets to preserve balance and societal harmony.

Populorum Progressio is adamant that completely free markets foster greater inequities and worsen poverty. The duties of solidarity and socialization (the strong coming to the aid of the weak) and of universal charity (a readiness for self-sacrifice for others) require that such inequitable trading arrangements be corrected. At the very least, it falls under the obligation of social justice. Moreover, bilateral and multilateral efforts to provide financial and technical assistance to less developed nations will be offset and rendered useless if no reforms are forthcoming in international trading arrangements.

Paul VI's position is not alien to the tradition since the moral warrants for his criticism are already found in the earlier documents. *Rerum Novarum* (#63) observes that natural justice takes precedence over the sanctity of the contract; *Quadragesimo Anno* insists that neither party should bear a disproportionate share of the burdens of exchange and that both parties should enjoy parity in bargaining power; and *Mater et Magistra* appeals for appropriate market interventions that ensure meaningful participation for all within the principle of socialization.

The *Wall Street Journal* is said to have described *Populorum Progressio* as "warmed-over Marxism" (O'Brien and Shannon 1977, 311). Lest we be carried too far in thinking that Paul VI is advocating a socialist, centralized control of the economy, it is important to note that the encyclical appreciates the value of the competitive market and does not seek to do away with it altogether.

> Without abolishing the competitive market, it should be kept within the limits which make it just and moral, and therefore, human. In trade between developed and underdeveloped economies, conditions are too disparate and the degrees of genuine freedom available too unequal. In order that international trade be human and moral, social justice requires that it restore to participants a certain equality of opportunity. This equality is a long-term objective, but to reach it, we must begin now to create true equality in discussion and negotiations (PP #61).

Paul VI merely proposes extra-market mechanisms that ensure fair and humane outcomes. International commodity agreements that establish norms for stabilizing prices, guarantee the supply of certain types of products, and encourage new industries are important first steps. This proposal is not original to Paul VI and has in fact already been implemented (in varying degrees) in commodities such as coffee, tin, sugar, wheat, cocoa, olive oil, tea, jute, sisal, bauxite, and bananas. The record is a mixture of failure and limited success, as seen in Morton and Tulloch's (1977, 338–41) summary of post–World War II international commodity agreements, including their dates of establishment, membership, objectives, methods, and current status.

Paul VI emphasizes full and equal participation in decision making for less developed countries in international agencies. Such an arrangement is their only leverage and protection against the undue concentration of economic power among the developed countries. This appeal to empower poor countries as equal participants is reminiscent of similar concerns that prompt *Quadragesimo Anno* to call for the reorganization of the domestic social order along vocational lines. The critical point of intersection between these two documents, separated by four decades of impressive economic achievements, is their common foundation in the principle of subsidiarity: ensuring that people are involved in the decisions that affect them and not to leave their fate at the mercy of the vagaries and impersonal operations of the market.

In the same spirit of subsidiarity, *Sollicitudo Rei Socialis* (#45) suggests that regional self-help accommodations go a long way toward assisting poor countries achieve autonomy, development, and self-determination. Developing countries within geographic proximity of each other can accomplish much among themselves to improve their economic positions. They can jointly pursue development programs, and coordinate investment, production, and trade decisions. Regional common markets for their products and services would create a larger market, thereby lessening their dependence on the First World even as they complement each other's productive base.[18] This cooperation should also extend to financial affairs. Regional organizations among Third World countries can serve as channels in promoting the ideals of equality, freedom, and participation. John Paul II is, of course, referring to the regional groupings of developing countries for purposes of greater economic integration and cooperation that have already been tried with mixed results, to wit: Latin American Free Trade Association (LAFTA), the Central American Common Market (CACM), the Andean Common Market (ACM), the Caribbean Community (CARICOM), the East African Community (EAC), and the Association of Southeast Asian Nations (ASEAN). Examples of more specialized groups include the Asian Development Bank (ADB) and the African Development Bank.[19]

Change toward greater equity in the structure and rules of the international community–this is the distinctive theme undergirding the social documents of Paul VI's pontificate. It is important to note that his concerns reflect the simmering dissatisfaction within the global political economy of his day. This groundswell of discontent eventually finds expression in the New International Economic Order (NIEO). There are many similarities in the language and in the policy prescriptions of the Paul VI–era social teachings and the NIEO literature.[20] Compare, for example, the following summary of NIEO objectives with the post–Vatican II social documents:

> [T]he New International Economic Order (NIEO) involves: the regulation and stabilization of international primary commodity markets and the creation of a Common Fund for this and other purposes; improved access to Northern markets for the exports of Southern countries and

appropriate adjustments in Northern economies to facilitate the expansion of Southern shares of global manufacturing industry; international
monetary reform; the regulation of the activities of transnational corporations and the creation and enforcement of a code of conduct governing the international transfer of technology; the promotion of economic
cooperation among developing countries; increased resource flows to
developing countries; and in general, the alteration of existing institutional mechanisms and structures so as to support the objectives of development in the Third World (Helleiner 1982, 1–2).

It would be a mistake to conclude, however, that the postconciliar
social documents are merely echoing the emerging NIEO lock, stock,
and barrel. The root principles governing modern Catholic social
thought on international relations go much deeper and are much older
than this movement. Note, for example, the wartime Christmas messages of Pius XII that deal with the necessary conditions for restoring
justice to the international order. NIEO policy proposals that spring
from the turbulent and unsettled international environment of the 1970s
find a natural fit with the basic principles long held and taught by this
theological social tradition–the need for participation, self-help and
self-determination, solidarity, and equity; the evil of economic domination and of uneven, burdensome contracts; the limitations of markets;
the importance of a just price and a just wage; an option for the poor
and greater protection for the weak; universal access to the goods of the
earth; and the principle of subsidiarity. As the web of global interdependence becomes more complex and intense, the principles and norms
employed to address social questions at the national level inevitably
find extension in the community of nations (Thanawala 1998). The
transposition of moral principles from a domestic to an international
setting is an apt example of John Paul II's emphasis on the continuity
and adaptability that should characterize Catholic social thought's approach to new problems if it is to be a living tradition.

> [C]ontinuity and renewal . . . [t]his twofold dimension is typical of her
> [the Church] teaching in the social sphere. On the one hand it is con-
> stant, for it remains identical in its fundamental inspiration . . . in its vital
> link with the Gospel of the Lord. On the other hand, it is ever new be-
> cause it is subject to the necessary and opportune adaptations suggested
> by the changes in historical conditions and by the unceasing flow of the
> events which are the setting for the life of people and society (SRS #3).

In summary, the post–Vatican II social documents bring the practice of development and international economics to a moral plane that
is enlivened by solidarity, justice, and charity. *Populorum Progressio*'s
key contribution is the notion of development as primarily a moral phenomenon; *Justice in the World* and *Octogesima Adveniens*, the call to
action; and *Sollicitudo Rei Socialis*, the obligations of solidarity in an

international setting. Most importantly, by emphasizing the moral dimension of authentic development, the post–Vatican II social documents underscore the unavoidable consequence of moral agency: having to take responsibility not only for personal actions but also for the sinful structures of society, whether national or global. Moreover, one embarks on living up to this responsibility *together* with others. All this entails the simultaneous use and mutual reinforcement of the principles of solidarity, subsidiarity, universal access, primacy of labor, socialization, and, most of all, integral human development.

The success of taking responsibility together for societal outcomes and processes ultimately devolves upon every individual's willingness to assume responsibility as an *indirect employer*.[21] *Laborem Exercens* (#77) defines this as one who "substantially determines one or other [*sic*] facet of the labor relationship, thus conditioning the conduct of the direct employer when the latter determines in concrete terms the actual work contract and labor relations."

Notes

1. There are, of course, Pius XII's wartime Christmas addresses, his 1941 *Pentecost Address*, and his speeches to various professional groups in the 1950s that touched on social issues.

2. In the absence of a gender-inclusive translation of the social documents, the use of "man" or of male pronouns must be read to mean both male and female.

3. It is not alone in holding these views. Observe what Lewis (1955, 429) has to say in addressing the question of whether growth is desirable: "Economic growth is only one good thing among many, and we can take it to excess. Excessive growth may result in, or be the result of, excessive materialism, excessive individualism, excessive mobility of population, excessive inequality of income. . . ."

4. Again, note what Lewis (1955) observes: "The advantage of economic growth is not that wealth increases happiness, but that it increases the range of human choice. It is very hard to correlate wealth and happiness."

5. SRS #28h remarks: "*[D]evelopment* has a *necessary economic dimension*, since it must supply the greatest possible number of the world's inhabitants with an availability of goods for them 'to be,' . . ." (emphasis in the original).

6. SRS #17a observes: "[D]evelopment either becomes shared in *common* by every part of the world or it undergoes a *process of regression*. . . . This tells us a great deal about the nature of authentic development: Either all the nations of the world participate or it will not be true development." See also SRS #9d.

7. UNDP (1990, iii) notes: "[W]e are rediscovering the essential truth that people must be at the centre of all development. . . . What makes them and the study of the development process fascinating is the entire spectrum through which human capabilities are expanded and utilised."

8. UNDP (1990, iii) states: "The purpose of development is to offer people more options. One of their options is access to income–not as an end in itself but

as a means to acquiring human well-being. But there are other options as well, including long life, knowledge, political freedom, personal security, community participation and guaranteed human rights. People cannot be reduced to a single dimension as economic creatures."

9. UNDP (1990, 1) notes: "[T]he process of development should at least create a conducive environment for people, individually and collectively, to develop their full potential and to have a reasonable chance of leading productive and creative lives in accord with their needs and interests. Human development thus concerns more than the formation of human capabilities. . . . It also concerns the use of these capabilities. . . ."

10. UNDP (1990); Morris (1979); Streeten (1981); Nordhaus and Tobin (1972); Seers (1969, 1972); Sen (1980).

11. The statistical appendices of the World Bank's annual *World Development Report* is a good example.

12. For example, Meier (1984, 5) notes: "[I]t should be recognized that economic development is not equivalent to the total development of a society . . . '[N]ational development' is a term that encompasses, at a minimum social and political development, as well as economic development."

13. Sen (1988b, 15–16) observes: "People value their ability to do certain things and to achieve certain types of beings (such as being well nourished, being free from avoidable morbidity, being able to move about as desired, and so on). These 'doings' and 'beings' may be generically called 'functionings' of a person. . . . The well-being of a person can be seen as an evaluation of the functionings achieved by that person. . . . What is being pointed out here is the importance of judging development in terms of functionings achieved . . ." (emphasis in the original).

14. PP #19, #14; GS #31b; SRS #28, #46d.

15. SRS #26e remarks: "[T]he good to which we are all called and the happiness to which we aspire cannot be obtained without an *effort and commitment on the part of all*, nobody excluded, and the consequent renouncing of personal selfishness" (emphasis in the original).

16. For example, note MM #61: "Every effort, therefore, must be made that *at least in future* [*sic*] a just share only of the fruits of production be permitted to accumulate in the hands of the wealthy, and that an ample sufficiency be supplied to the workingmen" (emphasis added). PP #61 observes: "In order that international trade be human and moral, social justice requires that it restore to the participants a certain equality of opportunity. This equality is *a long-term objective*, but to reach it, we must begin now to create true equality in discussions and negotiations" (emphasis added).

17. See, for example, Lewis (1952) and Bairoch (1975, chapter 6).

18. Compare this with Stewart (1976, 98–99) who notes: "Consumption patterns among South (i.e., developing) countries should be much more similar to each other than those of North (i.e., developed) countries: the sort of goods . . . developed for one country in the South should be more appropriate . . . to other South countries than to North products they currently import . . ."

19. For a summary description of these groupings, see Morton and Tulloch (1977, Table 8.2, 305–08). Meier (1984, 566) lists the literature that evaluates these regional efforts. Ul Haq (1980) has a good discussion of the issues involved in the setting up of such initiatives.

20. United Nations General Assembly (1974); UNCTAD (1977).

21. LE #78 notes: "The concept of indirect employer is applicable to every society. . . . [I]n the present system of economic relations in the world there are numerous *links between* individual *States*, links that find expression . . . in the mutual exchange of economic goods. . ." (emphasis in the original).

Part II

RETROSPECTIVE: EVOLUTION FROM SCHOLASTIC ECONOMIC THOUGHT

Much has been written on the contribution of scholasticism to the development of economic thought both in its normative and analytical aspects. However, there is little in the literature that examines the evolution of economic ethics from the scholastic doctors to the modern Catholic social documents.

In the development of Catholic social thought from the scholastics to the modern papal encyclicals, changes in normative economics reflect the transformation of an economic terrain from its feudal roots to the modern industrial economy. The preeminence of the allocative over the distributive function of price in the modern market breaks the convenient convergence of commutative and distributive justice in scholastic just-price theory. Furthermore, the loss of custom, law, and usage in defining the boundaries of economic behavior leads to a depersonalization of economic relationships that previously provided effective informal channels of protection for individual well-being. Hence, recent economic ethics has had to look for nonprice, nonmarket mechanisms for distributive justice. The scholastic just price, as the centerpiece of economic ethics, is replaced by the living wage (chapter 4). Moreover, attitudes shift from a medieval antipathy toward unions to the contemporary defense of organized labor on moral grounds. The greater attention to the issue of justice in social structures is in part a response to the transformation of the economy from that of precarious survival to one of bountiful and accelerating growth. This is accompanied by a change in the language of ethical discourse from obligations to individual rights (chapter 5).

Chapter 4

EXCHANGE-VALUE DETERMINATION: FROM SCHOLASTIC JUST PRICE TO THE MODERN LIVING WAGE

INTRODUCTION

E xchange provides an analytical lens with which to examine the evolution of scholastic economic thought to the modern Catholic social documents. Understanding the premises and practices surrounding the trading of goods and services is a necessary starting point in the study of economic ethics because exchange is a major, possibly *the* predominant, avenue of economic interaction among people–an interpersonal collaboration that supplies abundant matter for moral deliberation. As Odd Langholm (1992, 24) so aptly puts it:

> [E]xchange situations involve their participants in *a particular type of moral conflict.* . . . The moral reality is the individual person encountering his neighbour in the context of exchange, each possessing something which the other wants, each obliged, as a mere steward under God, to consider his neighbour's need. Focus on exchange . . . meant focus on the individual, in order to advise him on proper terms of exchange with his neighbour (emphasis in the original).

The adequacy and the fairness of the price at which goods and services exchange are perennial concerns in political economy. It is often a point of contention whether extra-market mechanisms are needed either to define the limits of the market or to supplement its impersonal operation with noneconomic goals. The ethical ramifications of this issue are of great interest to theologians and moral philosophers. Much scholarship has been done on the scholastic just price. However, hardly any work has been written on modern Catholic social thought on exchange-value determination. This is unfortunate as this collection of social documents offers a wealth of moral reflections and unconventional solutions to some of the most difficult economic problems of society.

Market prices[1] can be ethically unacceptable in one of two ways: They can either be set too high as to keep essential commodities beyond the reach of the consumer (as in the case of price gouging), or they can be set too low as to provide an insufficient income for the seller, producer, or worker. Modern Catholic social thought has dealt with the latter moral problem and has taught that economic agents have a moral responsibility to ensure that market prices generate an adequate livelihood for those who produce or who bring such goods and services to the marketplace. The concept of employer is expanded to include not only the immediate (direct) employer but anyone else who substantially affects and sustains such an employer-employee relationship even in an ancillary manner. *Laborem Exercens* (#77–81) refers to these as the *indirect employers* and affirms their share in the moral responsibility of underwriting the just treatment of workers. This definition of indirect employers is understood to include consumers (QA #72; PP #47, #57–58).

The object of this chapter is to probe this unexplored terrain by examining how the scholastic just price has evolved in the modern Catholic social documents in the face of an economy that has been so radically transformed from its feudal roots. To this end, the first three sections of the chapter present a summary of exchange-value determination in economic theory, in scholastic literature, and in modern Catholic social thought. The last two sections discuss the salient differences among these three approaches. The distinctive features of the modern Catholic position can be best appreciated when examined in the light of what the discipline of economics has theorized about pricing in a modern economy. For this reason, a brief survey of and comparison with economic models on pricing are necessary. The contribution of this chapter is threefold: (1) It sifts through what the modern Catholic social documents have to say about exchange value; (2) It situates these teachings within nineteenth-century economic thought; and (3) It compares modern Catholic social thought with scholastic just price by accounting for their differences and then explaining how and why these disparities have emerged.

EXCHANGE-VALUE DETERMINATION
IN ECONOMIC THOUGHT

Whether one views economics as the science of efficiently allocating scarce resources to competing uses or as the art of satisfying basic human needs, an inevitable starting point is the issue of how the price of goods and services is set. The modern economy, after all, is based on exchange among economic agents. The theory of value occupies a central role in the discipline because it influences all subsequent theorizing.[2] To understand the method of deriving value is to have a fairly good grasp of how the social order functions (or fails to function).[3] There are two fundamental models of exchange-value determination in economic thought: the classical school's cost of production and the marginalist school's consumer utility.

Classical School

Under the cost-of-production approach, price is nothing more than the cost incurred in manufacturing the commodity. This is a pricing method where manufacturers sum up the production expenses and add a markup for their profit.

Richard Cantillon is the forerunner of the classical theory of value. He regards value as the "measure of the quantity of Land and of Labour entering into its production" (Desai 1967, 344). Adam Smith sees labor as the ideal measure of value since toil represents the true cost of the work effort, is invariable, and cuts across all commodities.[4] This could be expressed in terms of either the labor embodied in the good or the amount of labor that the good can command when exchanged in the marketplace. Smith adopts neither the *labor-embodied* nor the *labor-command* view of value because of the difficulties they pose. For one thing, the labor-embodied notion of value can only apply to a crude economy before the accumulation of capital and the appropriation of land. Furthermore, he acknowledges insurmountable measurement problems because of the nonhomogeneity of labor arising from differences in skills and variations in the intensity and motivation of the work effort. It is extremely difficult to define or measure labor objectively (Pagano 1985, 21). In the end, Smith adopts a cost-of-production view where price tends toward the sum of the "natural" levels of wages, profits, and rent to which the economy gravitates in the long run given competitive conditions. He calls this the *natural price* (Smith [1776] 1937, I:48; Dasgupta 1985, 43).

David Ricardo believes that the labor-embodied view (more popularly known as the labor theory of value) is applicable to both the early and advanced stages of economic development, contrary to Smith's reservations. The use of capital in the advanced economy does not matter because, just like John Locke, he views capital merely as the accumulation of past labor.[5] With respect to the problem of nonhomogenous labor due to varying skills, Ricardo argues that the requisite training time for various skills is fairly well known and are stable. They can, therefore, be factored into the calculation of the labor content. In other words, skilled labor can be expressed in terms of unskilled-labor equivalents (Pagano 1985, 23; Desai 1967, 347). Ricardo is silent on the measurement problems arising from differences in work intensity and motivation. He does not consider rent to be part of the price because the land used at the margin is assumed to have no opportunity cost at all.

Both Smith and Ricardo do not completely ignore demand factors. In fact, both acknowledge their importance. If the good is to be exchanged at all in the market, it must be valued by the consumer for its use value in the first place. However, such value arising from utility, while admittedly a necessary condition, is not the determining factor behind price (Schumpeter 1954, 912, footnote #9). Smith distinguishes *market price* from his *natural price*. The former is the short-run fluctuation in the marketplace due to changes in demand conditions; the latter is the long-run equilibrium. Ricardo acknowledges that unfilled demand does affect price levels. He disregards this, however, because he believes that goods that derive their value from severe shortages are the exception, rather than the norm.

Karl Marx adopts Ricardo's labor theory of value but modifies it to distinguish between *necessary labor time* (that which enables workers to purchase the goods and services needed for their subsistence) and *surplus labor time* (the differential between the actual work time and the necessary labor time) (Lichtenstein 1983, 38–39). The latter is an illegitimate appropriation by the capitalists of what properly belongs to the workers. All value is produced by labor; capital is just *stolen labor.* Profit, therefore, does not have a legitimate place in value determination because it is merely residual income (Lichtenstein 1983, 20).

Other classical economists have theories of value that are variants of the above formulations. Thomas Malthus's view approximates the *labor-command* approach, as does W. Senior's *real costs*, Smith's *toil and trouble*, and John Stuart Mill's *equilibrium price* as the production cost (Pagano 1985, 40). The common thread in these classical formulations is that exchange value is cost determined.

Marginalist School

The principal exponent of the consumer-utility approach is the marginalist school, commonly associated with William Stanley Jevons, Leon Walras, and Carl Menger. This approach locates the source of value in the utility individuals derive from their consumption of goods. Hence, this methodology has sometimes been viewed as ultimately founded on mental constructs without any relation to real factors.

Hermann H. Gossen is the forerunner of this school. He combines the utilitarianism of Jeremy Bentham with a marginal-analysis methodology to derive a principle of marginal utility. This principle is in turn used to determine price and consumption levels. Gossen's major contributions are his two laws of utility. The first is the law of diminishing marginal utility where each additional unit of a good consumed yields ever decreasing increments of utility. In Gossen's second law, people maximize their utility by choosing a basket of goods in such a way that each commodity is consumed to the point where its marginal utility per dollar spent is equal to the marginal utility per dollar spent on other commodities. Jevons, Menger, and Walras follow along the same arguments. Value is derived solely from the satisfaction coming from consumption. The cost of production does not determine exchange value. The price of factor inputs is set only after the exchange value of the commodity has been determined; factor prices, therefore, are merely derived from the utility value of the goods. Exchange value is thus utility determined.

Marshallian Theory of Value

Alfred Marshall uses both the cost of production and consumer utility. His original contribution is the introduction of time as an important parameter in value determination. He proposes three time periods: the market time, the short term, and the long term. Market time refers to a very short period where supplies are fixed and price is determined subjectively by demand factors alone.[6] In the short term, it is possible for producers to increase the supply of goods, but only at a higher cost because resources cannot be readily shifted between industries given the time constraint. In this case, the supply curve is upward sloping, and both demand and supply factors determine the market price. In the long run, all factors of production can be moved across industries; there are no fixed costs as everything is variable. Consequently, value is determined chiefly by the cost of production, that is, the supply curve.[7]

SCHOLASTIC JUST PRICE

Not much has been written on exchange value by the early Church writers in spite of the rich heritage of social justice teachings from that period. The patristic era deals with the issue of exchange value only in an indirect way–through its unfavorable evaluation of the trading practices of merchants. Commercial activity is viewed with great caution, if not misgiving, given the common impression that merchants are motivated by cupidity and profit unconscionably from the needful plight of consumers (Baldwin 1959, 12–16). This dearth in patristic literature makes the scholastic period the proper starting point in any effort to trace the early roots of modern Catholic social teachings on normative value in exchange.

The heart of scholastic teaching on exchange-value determination is its notion of the just price. The demands of justice in exchange are satisfied when the contracted price is equal to the true economic value of the goods and services traded. Different types of goods are traded in *proportional reciprocation*, that is, in proportion to their economic value (Baldwin 1959, 72–73). The difficult task, of course, is finding out what constitutes this true economic value. Is this value determined by the cost of producing it or by the worth assigned to it by consumers given the satisfaction or use they derive from the good? There has been much debate about this.

Thomas Aquinas is generally acknowledged to be the reference point in any study of the medieval just price as evidenced by his influence on later scholarship on this issue. This is due to Aquinas's appropriation and extension of Aristotle and Albert the Great on the subject matter. Unfortunately, scholars are in disagreement over what Thomas Aquinas actually says about the method of arriving at the true economic value of goods. There are two principal opposing views, namely: (1) that the just price is none other than the market price, and (2) that the just price is the cost of production. A popular variant of the second position is the view that the cost of production pertains to the expenses necessary to maintain the social status of the producer, worker, or trader. This confusion is understandable since Aquinas's work is not meant to be taken as a complete treatise on price. Instead, his views on the just price have been taken from his commentary on Aristotle's *Nicomachean Ethics* and from his *Summa Theologiae*. In the latter work, the object of Aquinas is to discuss exchange value within the larger context of justice, rather than to show analytically how price is determined (Aquinas 1947/8, II–II, q.77).

Just Price as Cost of Production

Early scholarship links Aquinas's just price with the cost of production.[8] This cost of production is in turn embedded within the larger setting of a hierarchical medieval social order that has to be maintained and preserved for the sake of the common good. It would be appropriate to describe it as the social-status theory of the just price.[9]

The basis for this social-status theory is the principle of hierarchy where differences in function, rank, and role among the members of society are acknowledged and reflected in the requirements of both distributive and commutative justice (Spengler 1968, 224–27). These differences define the critical proportionality that governs relations of justice.

The primary end of the social-status approach is to ensure that economic agents are provided the necessary means to discharge their expected function in the hierarchical order. Preserving the cohesion and viability of the fragile social order is given paramount importance. However, the maintenance of this social order is dependent on the pattern of income distribution among its members according to the division of roles and responsibilities within the community. Consequently, the just price (i.e., the normative price at which goods and services are exchanged) is necessarily tied to social position. It stresses the distributive function of price (Worland 1967, 241–43; 1977, 506).

The social-status approach bridges the gap between the theory of pricing and the theory of income distribution. In this regard, Barry Gordon (1975, 228) suggests that the social-status technique to normative pricing lets "the structure of prices reflect the existing pattern of income distribution in the community."[10] Of course, an undesirable feature of such a method to pricing is that it locks the community into a set pattern of resource distribution. However, as seen in subsequent sections, this is a feudal economy of survival and its major concern is to keep the social order functioning by not upsetting a precarious status quo; income redistribution is accorded a lower priority, if at all considered.

Just Price as the Market Price

The starting point of the medieval theologians' writings on exchange value is the Roman and Canon law thinking that just price is the current price whether arrived at in the market or by regulation (Baldwin 1959, 70b, 71d). Both Aquinas and Albert the Great follow Aristotle in accepting want and human need as the primary determinants of exchange value. In fact, price is viewed as the numerical expression and measure of the good's ability to satisfy human wants. However, Aquinas and Albert the Great go further by adding a second set of factors that Aristotle never considers: labor (Baldwin 1959, 74–75). There has been much debate in the literature as to which has preeminence–the subjective (human need and want) or the objective factors (labor and other expenses of production).[11]

John Baldwin (1959, 77c–78) concludes that Aquinas views just price as the market price instead of the cost of production. He arrives at this judgment by noting that:

1. Aquinas's reference to the cost of production is in his earlier commentary on Aristotle's *Nicomachean Ethics*. Nothing more is mentioned about it in his later writings in the *Summa Theologiae* where only human need and want are presented as key to deriving the exchange value.[12]

2. Aquinas's discussion of labor and expenses is made in the context of justifying the commercial profits of merchants who by then are acknowledged to fill an important role in the economy by providing useful intermediary services.

The weight of recent scholarship favors Baldwin's position.[13] However, Aquinas's just price should not be equated with the liberal, laissez-faire competitive price because his acceptance of the market price is conditional. The requirements of the common good, prudence, and many other human virtues and values impose limits on this price (Bartell 1962, 368–72).

It is not the object of this chapter to take a position in this debate. It is sufficient to note, however, that these positions are not mutually exclusive. In fact, elements of both positions will come up repeatedly in dealing with modern Catholic social teachings on normative pricing.

EXCHANGE-VALUE DETERMINATION IN MODERN CATHOLIC SOCIAL THOUGHT

Modern Catholic social teaching (CST) uses two foundational notions to arrive at the key principle it deems essential to setting exchange value. First, it views the *telos* of all economic activity as the critical starting point in specifying the functional role of human work. Second, it distinguishes the two facets of work, defines their roles, and explains their hierarchical ordering. From these, a cardinal principle is derived for ensuring a just exchange value.

Work and Livelihood

A principal purpose of the economic order is to provide for the needs of the human person. It is meant to aid and facilitate human flourishing (GS #67). A fundamental feature of the modern economy is wage labor. Human services are exchanged for a contracted remuneration given either in cash or in kind. In a monetized economy, this wage-labor arrangement also serves as an important mechanism for the orderly distribution of society's output (besides gifts and transfers). In other words, wages have become the chief means by which people gain access to the goods of the earth (RN #62).

Individual access to these needed goods is dependent on how much people can produce and at what price they can trade their output in the marketplace. Thus, productivity and market price are two critical variables to consider. If the economy's end is to provide for the needs of all, exchange value should be set so as to amply compensate people's work effort given the level of their best productivity.[14] However, the exchange value of their output or labor must be at least sufficient to provide workers and their families with an adequate income. Herein lies the reason for modern Catholic social thought's interest in exchange-value determination. Prices at which goods and services are exchanged determine people's ability to meet their needs in two ways: through the income they receive (determined by the price their services or products can fetch) and through the purchasing power of that income (determined by the price of their consumption basket).

The Two Dimensions of Work

Laborem Exercens highlights the difference between the objective and subjective dimensions of work.[15] The objective character of work encompasses all the concrete manifestations of the work process such as the type and difficulty of effort, the factor inputs employed, the working conditions, the resulting product(s) or service(s), the production cost, and the technology employed. The term "objective" is used in the broadest sense of the word (LE #19). On the other hand, work has a subjective character because it is a human person that organizes and puts together all the aforesaid objective elements of work.[16]

This distinction highlights the diverse roles played by the factor inputs in the production process. In particular, it seeks to draw attention to the special role of the "human input." It is personal effort and ingenuity that initiate, plan, and implement the entire productive enterprise. Furthermore, it is the human element that bears ultimate accountability for the conduct and outcome of such activity. Consequently, whether in the form of brain power or of brute muscle, the worker enjoys a preeminent position over all the elements of production such as capital, machinery, and materials. These objective factors of production should, therefore, be viewed merely as instrumental, secondary, and subordinate to the human worker.[17] It is incorrect to refer to the worker as a factor of production; "subject of work" is more appropriate (LE #27).[18] Besides, the human person is the ultimate purpose of work. Thus, the subjective character of work takes precedence over its objective dimension.

Guiding Principle of Exchange-Value Determination

This modern theological tradition notes that even after accounting for differences in the objective content of work, exchange value has to be ultimately weighed in terms of how it affects the laborer.[19] The subjective dimension is both the fundamental and the ultimate basis for the value of work.

> *[T]he primary basis of the value of work is man himself*, who is its subject. . . . [T]he basis for determining the value of human work is not pri-

marily the kind of work being done but the fact that the one who is doing it is a person. The sources of the dignity of work are to be sought primarily in the subjective dimension, not in the objective (LE #27, emphasis in the original).

The provision of a living wage to the worker has been a perennial teaching of the modern Catholic social documents. While scholastic just price concentrates on fairness in exchange in the product market, this modern tradition devotes much attention to fairness in the exchange value of inputs, that is, the labor market. *It is a shift in focus from a just price for the work output to a just price for the work effort.* The latter is aptly described as a valuation by the subject of the work.

What are the implications of this objective-subjective distinction? Given the acknowledged equality in the dignity of all, does the preeminence of the subjective dimension mean that goods and services ought, therefore, to be valued merely on the basis of their labor content, a la Marx and Ricardo? Is there even a role for the market or for consumer demand in price determination? I am now ready to compare these theological reflections on this issue with the earlier economic models surveyed.

CONTRASTING MODERN CATHOLIC SOCIAL TEACHING WITH ECONOMIC THOUGHT

Classical Approach

In stressing the central role of labor in the work process, modern Catholic social thought (CST) appears to be no different from the labor theory of value espoused by Locke, Ricardo, and Marx.[20] Is this similarity more apparent than real? CST and Marxian theory both stress the importance of anchoring exchange value on something more fundamental and stable than the vagaries of the market.[21] This similarity, however, does not go much further than this. CST and Marxian views on value are diametrically and irreconcilably opposed to each other because:

1. While Marx holds that all value is created by labor and capital has no rightful place in the determination of value nor a proper share in output distribution, CST acknowledges the important contribution of capital in the work process and affirms its legitimate claim to a share in output. This is a constant theme of the tradition since *Rerum Novarum.*[22]
2. Marx's view that capital is stolen labor implies an inherent conflict between the working and capitalist classes. This is a claim that the economic order, as we know it, necessarily leads to an adversarial relationship. CST disagrees with this view and sees no inevitability in this class conflict. In fact, it finds such conflict to be an aberration, rather than the norm (RN #28).

There is a far greater affinity between these theological documents and Ricardo's labor theory of value than Marx's. Both CST and Ricardo see capital as accumulated past labor (LE #55–56) with an important role to play in production. Hence, both accept the rightful share of capital in output distribution. One major difference, however, is the question of wages. Ricardo and CST both speak of a wage floor. In the case of Ricardo, the wage floor is imposed by a "biological limit"–when it becomes impossible for the worker to survive at wages below the subsistence level. In the case of CST, the wage floor is imposed by a "moral limit"– when it becomes morally wrong to pay workers less than is necessary for them and their families to lead a full life. Naturally, this family wage is set at a higher level than Ricardo's subsistence wage. Furthermore, while Ricardo's law of iron wages[23] keeps the long-run wages at the subsistence level, nothing prevents wage levels from rising above the family wage. In conclusion, there are some points of similarity between CST's notion of value and the labor theory of value, but only in a limited Ricardian fashion, and certainly not in the Marxian sense.

Consumer-Utility Approach

Modern Catholic social thought is highly critical of the marginalist theory of factor payments where:

$$\text{wage level} = \text{price of output x marginal product of labor}$$
$$= \text{value of marginal product of labor}$$

Under perfect competition, the resulting income distribution ensures that each factor input receives a return equal to the value of its marginal product. This, it is argued, is an ethical outcome because the reward to each factor of production corresponds to its contribution to the social product (Clark 1899).

There are numerous objections to this claim. First, this conclusion is contingent on perfectly competitive conditions. Hence, for this to be truly operative, there must be at least complete information, frictionless mobility both for economic agents and resources, and no monopoly power. These requirements are not satisfied in practice (Landreth 1976, 254).

Second, the price of output is determined by how much satisfaction consumers get from the product. Hence, remuneration for the worker's effort is ultimately dependent on the utility derived by consumers. In effect, consumer utility becomes a decisive criterion in judging the contribution of a factor input to the social product. CST disagrees with this because there may in fact be a gap between real contributions to the good of society and the monetary rewards accorded by consumer satisfaction.[24]

Third, the marginal productivity theory of factor payments treats labor no differently from inanimate, material factor inputs. It does not distinguish the primary efficient cause (the human person) from the instrumental cause (all other elements of production) (GS #67). Consequently, it disregards the preeminence of the subjective dimension over the objective content of work for purposes of remunerating the various elements of the production process.

Fourth, should factor contribution be the only consideration? CST affirms the wisdom of linking factor payments to productivity. In fact, it asserts the importance and the need to weigh the productivity and contribution of workers in setting wage levels (GS #67; MM #71). However, the distributional outcomes arising from this criterion alone need not be automatically fair, not even under perfect competition as claimed by J. B. Clark (1899). After all, there is no guarantee that the workers' remuneration will indeed be a living wage.[25] The ethical standard is not simply whether the factor gets its due reward in return for its contribution, but more importantly, it must also consider whether labor gets paid enough to support a family. After all, this is the primary goal of the wage-labor economy. Distributive justice takes precedence over commutative justice; the latter gives way to the more urgent consideration of ensuring the physical well-being of workers and their dependents.

Modern Catholic social thought is opposed to a sole reliance on the marginal productivity method of factor payments because it does not provide for any safety net in the event that the resulting income is below the living wage. Productivity must certainly be taken into account. However, it cannot be the only nor the most important consideration. To do so, would be to leave the worker at the mercy of an impersonal market process that treats human labor as a market commodity. CST is adamant on this point.[26]

Fifth, the productivity of workers is a function of many factors such as the type of equipment used, the quality of technology employed, and the entrepreneurial competence available. Laborers should not be deprived of a living wage simply on account of management's failure to provide the proper conditions for a level of productivity that leads to the payment of adequate wages (QA #72).

Finally, the underlying dynamic behind the marginal productivity theory of factor payments summarized by equation A is the maximization of profits. This runs against CST's view that the primary end of economic activity is the promotion of both public and individual welfare by providing the necessary means for the proper growth and development of the human person. This is not to say that profits are unimportant. Profit is important, and CST acknowledges this (CA #35c). However, it cannot be the sole consideration. Special attention must be given to workers when it comes time to divide output from the common productive effort; unlike the objective elements of production, laborers need to lead a full life.[27]

Marshallian Approach

CST is keenly aware of the unique, essential, and timely service provided by the market in letting supply and demand determine the exchange value of goods and services. In setting wages, this theological tradition acknowledges the need to consider the manifold conditions that affect the economic viability of the business enterprise (QA #72; MM #71). It goes beyond partial equilibrium analysis to include the interrelatedness of prices and wages throughout the whole economy (QA #75). As it affirms the necessity of labor markets[28] and their links to the rest of the economy, CST is fully cognizant of economic realities and limitations when it comes to setting wage levels: The effort to provide workers with a living wage must be balanced against the risk of setting too high a wage level as to cause unemployment. It recognizes a tradeoff between wage and employment levels (QA #74). Indeed, the market is important. It can only be ignored at the risk of causing more problems. However, there are limits to unfettered market operations inasmuch as price outcomes are not necessarily equitable (PP #57–58). There is an important role for extra-market mechanisms in the economic order.

COMPARISON: SCHOLASTIC JUST PRICE AND MODERN CATHOLIC SOCIAL THOUGHT

Contribution of Modern Catholic Social Thought

The metamorphosis of theological economic ethics is evident in the shift from the scholastic goal of ensuring fairness in exchange in the product market to the modern concern over obtaining a just price in the labor market. Normative factor pricing is no longer viewed as an automatic consequence of normative commodity pricing.

Despite the claim that equity in distribution and exchange is the primary aim of scholastic economic teachings (de Roover [1955] 1974c, 166), scholars agree that the question of a just price and the issue of a living wage, much less the matter of labor cost, are never linked together as a single problem in medieval thinking. Aquinas does not address the relationship between market price and labor cost. In fact, cost is associated with price only in a peripheral way, that is, in the context of another question: whether merchants should be allowed to recover their cost for the usurious payments they make in the course of their trade. Aquinas is not interested in whether price is adequate to cover the labor cost, but he is concerned with whether this constitutes acquiescence to the moral problem of profiting from others' needs (Hollander 1965, 630–31). Consequently, he never explains nor proposes an economic mechanism to ensure that exchange value reflects the cost of production.[29]

Desire Barth (1960, 429) comes to the same conclusion that Aquinas does not link factor and product pricing together, not even in his *Commentary on the Ethics* where the cost of production is discussed. Gordon (1975, 228–29) agrees that aside from the social-status approach to pricing, a decided gap in scholastic thought is its failure to bridge the theory of pricing with the theory of distribution. Moreover, little attention is given to the valuation of labor in early scholastic thought. Wage payment is treated merely as a subset of the theory of pricing; it is governed by the same justice that applies to commodity exchange (Gordon 1975, 262). This omission is understandable, if not expected, since the medieval economy is not as heavily a wage-labor economy as it is today. Even Lessius himself, who is among the few who considers wage determination in any depth (Gordon 1975, 262–66), does not associate just price with the living wage, nor does he address the question of what happens if market price is below the necessary subsistence cost.[30]

Scholastics are not overly concerned with wage sufficiency in determining exchange value because of their implicit assumption that the market price gravitates toward the cost of production in the long run. The normative price has to settle around cost to ensure the long-term viability of the market price (de Roover 1958, 422). After all, people will not engage in their enterprise if they cannot earn a livelihood. It is presumed that the common estimation of exchange value properly compensates workers. Otherwise, people would not trade at all.

In a medieval production environment that is predominantly agricultural and employs family members or apprentices, the issue of wage adequacy is not a major social concern. In contrast, the modern era has had to deal with an economy that is essentially wage labor; people earn a livelihood by hiring out their services. Consequently, in contrast to scholastic social teachings, wages have always been at the forefront of moral reflection in contemporary economic ethics. In the wake of the modern economy's excesses and failures, these social documents repeatedly address the shortcomings of the wage-labor economy. In doing so, they have modified scholastic just price to include the issue of a living wage.

Nature of Cost

Before accounting for the causes of this development in teaching, it is necessary to explain first the nature of *cost* both in its scholastic and modern usages. It is clear from the social-status, cost-of-production approach that for scholasticism, *cost* is more than merely the Ricardian subsistence wage. *Cost* includes all that workers need to discharge their role in the social order. As discussed earlier, modern Catholic social thought's notion of cost is associated with the living wage–the income level that secures the basic needs of workers and their dependents in addition to providing them with sufficient savings both for emergencies and to purchase property. Thus, *cost* in both scholastic and modern usages pertains to more than just the necessities for physical survival; it includes the provision of goods necessary for a flourishing life.

The implication in both notions of cost is that actual wages can be at a level high enough to keep workers physically alive (a subsistence wage) but not good enough to provide for a decent livelihood (a living wage). Thus, remuneration can settle at a point between the subsistence level and the living wage and may in fact be the predominant condition for most people. This phenomenon clarifies a key difference between the scholastics and the modern social documents because the latter argue that market price may be chronically below the living wage, a condition that may linger into the long run unless corrected by policy.[31]

Accounting for the Differences:
The Medieval versus the Modern Economy

Scholastics see no compelling reason to combine the question of a living wage with the issue of the just price because they assume that price eventually settles at the cost of production in the long run. In fact, some scholars reconcile the two scholastic views of the just price by presenting the medieval position as: "value emphatically depends on utility" but "goods will not be produced below cost" (Worland 1977, 512; see also Baldwin 1959, 77a, 79a). This means that the just price automatically includes the necessary compensation for workers; otherwise such goods and services would not be exchanged at all as no one would be willing to supply them. In short, the medieval theologians believe that the market price (i.e., the just price) cannot be persistently below cost. Modern Catholic social thought concludes otherwise as seen in the disproportionate attention it devotes to the labor, instead of the product, market.

This disparity in assumptions stems from differences in the larger sociohistorical context of these teachings—the medieval versus the modern economy. The diverse features of the feudal and the modern economies account for the dissimilar approaches of scholasticism and CST. In particular, it is important to examine the expansion in the size and geographic scope of economic units and the change in the nature of products and their production processes.

Market size and geographic scope

The basic economic units of the medieval world stand in sharp contrast to the massive size and coverage of modern economic units that even now continue to grow in scale from the regional to the national to the global arena as a result of the rapid advances both in transportation and communications. This difference in size and scope between the feudal and modern economies affects exchange value in at least two ways: It influences the range of variations between the producers' cost structures, and it circumscribes the sellers' leverage in price bargaining.

Similarity in cost structures across suppliers In deriving the medieval price, Lessius confidently notes that "account has already been taken of the expenses which are *ordinarily and usually* incurred" (Gordon 1975, 261, emphasis added). In a world of relatively small economic units, the cost of production is fairly homogeneous across producers; what is "ordinarily and usually incurred" is easily ascertained. After all, suppliers face nearly the same manufacturing conditions, and the cost of production could not be dramatically different from one producer to the next. Consequently, once the market arrives at a common estimate of exchange value, vendors are able to recoup their expenses (principally their labor cost). It should not come as a surprise, therefore, that medieval theologians see no need to address the living wage as a separate question from the just price. The living wage is deemed to be automatically a part of the market price, the just price.

Such is no longer the case in a modern economy where suppliers are spread worldwide and face varying local working conditions in addition to employing different manufacturing technologies. The cost structure of producers of the same commodity may no longer be assumed to be alike. Expenses that are "ordinarily and usually incurred" can no longer be readily taken for granted. As a result, the final market price may be insufficient to cover the production expenses of high-cost regions. The alternatives for these suppliers would be to increase productivity, pare down the wages of its workers, or simply transfer their manufacturing facilities to low-cost areas. In the last two options, laid-off workers would be faced with a choice of either moving to where the jobs are (not always possible nor easy, especially in the case of overseas transfers) or accepting whatever jobs they can get, even if such employment opportunities do not provide an adequate livelihood. In other words, producers may be compelled to pay their workers subliving wages as a competitive, defensive measure in order to remain financially viable into the long run.

Ability to influence price levels Another consequence of the radically expanded geographic scope and size of economic units is the much greater degree of competition in the modern economy. In a social order of countless atomistic economic agents where the dissemination of information and the transfer of goods are more advanced, people are price takers for the most part whether as suppliers or as consumers. They cannot influence the price of goods and services at which they buy or sell. And even in oligopolistic markets characterized by imperfect competition, whatever control producers may exercise in pricing their goods is attenuated by the ready availability of competing brands or of substitute products that can increasingly be imported from almost anywhere in the world. In contrast, given the rudimentary transportation and communications in the feudal economy, sellers in the medieval market enjoy relatively greater leverage in ensuring that they do get a market price that covers their costs. This ability to influence exchange value is made even more secure through artisan guilds. Compared to their modern counterparts, medieval suppliers are in a better position to secure a living wage for their efforts. They are less of a price taker because of the rigidities that make competition in the feudal economy far more imperfect than in the modern era.

Nature of products and their production processes

Competition in factor payments Contemporary consumer and durable goods are more sophisticated and require more complex production processes. In the modern economy, most final products come only at the end of a long series of intermediate processes—a long sequence of exchanges. Herein lies another important difference between the medieval and modern economies.

In a simple cottage-type manufacturing activity, the functions of the manager, owner, worker, and salesperson are most likely performed by the same individual or by members of the same extended family. No distinction has to be made between profits and wages when it comes time to distribute the proceeds from the sale of the output. There is, consequently, a natural incentive for the worker-seller-manager to ensure that the selling price is high enough to produce a profit (the living wage). This identity of wages and profits in a medieval economy ensures that the vendor-manufacturer bargains for a market price above cost. As the medieval theologians assume, scholastic just price may in fact be already the living wage, given the simple feudal production structure.

In the complicated production processes of the modern economy, two major features are evident: the division of labor and the predominance of wage-labor arrangements. The responsibilities of ownership, management, production, and sales are now performed by different people, and as a result, sales proceeds will now have to be divided among different constituencies within the business organization as rents, wages, profits, and salaries. Competition for factor payments within the firm emerges. An increase in the selling price need not necessarily redound to the benefit of workers in the form of higher wages except for the self-employed and family businesses. In all likelihood, whatever higher revenues may be generated are funneled into higher profits or dividends rather than to wage increases. In a modern market economy, the distinction between who gets the profits and who gets the wages becomes even more important. There is neither a built-in incentive nor a direct link between a higher market price and the wages paid to laborers. Remuneration can in fact be below *cost* as defined and discussed earlier.

There is an asymmetry in a wage-labor economy. Workers share in the risks of the business; they suffer alongside the owners and managers when the business is floundering or is still working through its birth pangs. However, they need not necessarily share in the gains when the business succeeds and pays off handsomely. A difference between the simple family cottage-type medieval operation and the industrial, modern corporate business is the degree to which this asymmetry is encountered by workers. It is probably less likely and less severe of an experience for medieval workers given the simplicity of the work organization for the period and the strong ties of family, community, and religion that exert an informal moral suasion on how sales proceeds are apportioned into factor payments.

Factor mobility

Supply response Labor mobility is an implicit presupposition behind the scholastic belief that market price cannot be below cost since it would lead to the destruction of trades as suppliers move on to more remunerative ventures. Lessius, for example, measures the adequacy of wages by looking at the supply response of workers to the wages offered.[32] A positive supply response, that is, the availability of people willing to take the jobs offered, is indicative of the sufficiency of the wage payments made.

Following this line of reasoning, one would expect people not to put up with wages that do not provide for a decent livelihood in a modern era of greater factor mobility due to better communications and transportation. They would move to better-paying employment. This is a heroic assumption. In the first place, Lessius fails to see that the supply response generated may be flawed. In particular, the response may be the outcome of economic compulsion due to extreme need or the lack of better employment alternatives. Besides, the transactions costs associated with the psychological and financial burdens of moving may lead people to accept a cut in pay. Second, the inadequacy of wages may be mitigated by the willingness of workers to labor longer hours, get a second job, or even ask other members of the family to work. Third, labor mobility (and, consequently, the supply response) in the current economic order may in fact be overrated. The entry cost for meaningful participation in an increasingly knowledge-based modern economy is becoming steeper and requires new skills and longer years of schooling. And even with the requisite human capital, extreme specialization can wreak havoc in the form of higher structural unemployment as people with specialty skills find it difficult to secure alternative employment once the economy no longer has demand for their particular craft. While factor mobility has improved in the past two centuries of rapid economic growth and development, new forms of rigidities have emerged in the labor market.[33]

One should, therefore, not ascribe too much to labor mobility as a guarantee of living wages even for a modern economy, much less for the medieval world. It would be a mistake to accept uncritically a positive supply response as indicative of the adequacy of wage payments. That workers accept low-paying jobs should not be taken as conclusive evidence that wages provide a sufficient livelihood. The poor and the desperate accept whatever comes, since they can ill afford unemployment. Unlike a feudal era of strong social and religious ties where the clan or community serves as a fallback position, the modern economy provides no such guarantees to people who slip through the cracks in a large, impersonal market. As a result, the poor cannot afford to be selective in the jobs they get. Besides, the opportunities open to them may be severely restricted. Recent experience, even in the United States (acknowledged to be one of the most dynamic labor markets), confirms this as seen in the persistent existence of a class of working poor, that is, people who labor in service jobs even when the pay is insufficient to put them above the poverty line.[34]

Internalizing the future benefits of a living wage The degree of labor mobility influences the wage structure in a second important manner and accounts for another difference between the medieval and modern eras. Greater labor mobility may in fact decrease the likelihood that wages above the market rates will be voluntarily provided by employers. It is in the interest of a profit-maximizing business to ensure that its workers make an adequate livelihood. Well-paid employees presumably make for healthier and more productive workers both in the short and long terms.[35] However, businesses will find it in their interest to pay workers above-market rates only if they can capture some of the future benefits of an enhanced worker productivity arising from good wages paid in the current period. Otherwise, there will be no economic incentive to pay a living wage that is substantially above prevailing market rates.

The ability to internalize the future stream of monetary benefits of a living wage may be another important difference between the medieval and modern economies. Medieval work arrangements are more conducive to business enterprises benefitting from the future productivity of their workers. In addition to being bound by strong familial and social ties, medieval employers have relatively better economic incentives to look after the welfare of their workers. In contrast to frequent job changes in a dynamic modern economy, lifetime employment with the same employer is the most likely norm in a feudal order that is hemmed in by limited labor mobility (Tawney 1926, 26) and by a restricted range of occupational opportunities. Compared to their contemporary counterparts, medieval profit-maximizing entrepreneurs have greater reason to "invest" in the welfare of their workers. Modern work arrangements do not provide such an incentive in cases where dynamism and greater labor mobility encourage multiple job changes. Thus, from the strictly pecuniary angle of economic rationality, modern businesses have little inducement and a shorter time horizon than medieval employers when it comes to providing wages beyond prevailing market rates given that there is no guarantee of a long-term employer-employee relationship.[36] After all, they are unable to recapture the benefits of investing in the human capital of their workers.

Unfortunately, this is not to say that medieval producers actually paid their workers a living wage. The assumption here is that they would have, as rational profit maximizers. And even in cases where the artisan guilds functioned as monopsonies (due to the lack of labor mobility and competition), it would still be to the guilds' rational long-term economic advantage to provide living wages because of the enhanced productivity of workers.

To summarize this comparison, the issue for the modern Catholic social documents is not whether the just price is based on the current market price or the cost of production. Even if exchange value were based on the cost of production, CST would still not be satisfied because it does not assume (as the scholastics do) that the cost of production automatically includes a living wage for the workers. In many cases, it does not. Hence, even if the market price gravitates toward production expenses in the long run, workers may not necessarily be getting a livelihood conducive to a flourishing life. In fact, the provision of a living wage beyond prevailing market rates in a modern economy is made more difficult given the greatly expanded size and geographic scope of the basic economic units, the more complex production processes, and the inability of producers to internalize the future stream of benefits from a more productive workforce in the face of greater labor mobility. All these provide cogent reasons for modern Catholic social thought to modify scholastic teaching on exchange value by incorporating the issue of a living wage within the larger question of the just price.

In embedding the living wage within the just price, modern Catholic social thought is sensitizing the contemporaneous economy of growth to the requirements of social cohesion by calling attention back to the distributive consequences of the market price. It is, in effect, a reappropriation of the social-status approach, albeit in a modified and simplified form where the emphasis is now on the distinctive role of each person as the end of all economic activity. The focus is still on preserving the stability and integrity of the community, but not by way of preserving a hierarchical economic order. Rather, it seeks to establish a minimum base below which no one is allowed to fall. Human dignity is the more fundamental social status that these modern theological documents now seek to protect. It is an effort to recapture and reintroduce the solidarity and the community orientation of the small medieval economic units into contemporary market relations.

Moral reflection on exchange value has come full circle as we observe this important continuity between scholastic and modern thought. The medieval theologians' concern for the social status of the person in order to preserve society is matched by the modern social documents' conviction that the social order is viable and stable only to the extent that it defends and promotes the human dignity of each member of the community, especially the disadvantaged. In both cases, the distributional function of market price takes on greater, though not exclusive, importance.

FURTHER WORK ON UNRESOLVED ISSUES

Despite its keen awareness of the essential link between wages and prices and in spite of its repeated criticism of the inadequacies of the market, modern Catholic social teachings on pricing are limited to the labor market; they do not proceed further into an explicit and vigorous advocacy of a corresponding minimum moral price floor in the product market. After all, as can readily be seen from the above equation, an adequate wage for the work effort could be sustained into the long run if one gets an adequate price for the work output in the product market. This modern tradition only goes so far as to appeal for greater consumer sensitivity to the fairness of the prices at which people buy the goods and services produced by others in the community. It is left to the readers to infer that labor compensation ought to be *price-determining* instead of being *price-determined* (QA #72; PP #47). That CST should limit itself to the input market is most likely due to the enormous practical and ethical difficulties that a mandated just price (a moral price floor) in the product market would entail in the modern economy compared to the scholastic era.

Practical Difficulties

One of the greatest strengths of the market as an avenue for setting prices is the ease with which it can be administered. The enforcement cost of implementing a moral price floor is prohibitively high. Moreover, setting the appropriate minimum selling price is in itself a formidable problem. Given the dispersion of suppliers worldwide, how does one arrive at a living wage that takes into account a wide variety of living conditions? What factors should be included in calculating it? Should there even be a single living-wage rate? If this living wage were not uniform across the board, there would be differences in the mandatory minimum selling prices. How would one prevent high-cost regions from being priced out of the market without recourse to price-distorting quotas and tariffs?

Setting the moral price floor for the commodity requires data on its net labor content. Given the more complex production processes of contemporary goods, identifying and breaking down the net labor content for each commodity becomes an interminable task.[37] And as if these problems were not enough, all these calculations would have to be constantly redone in a dynamic setting as relative prices shift in response to new products, resources, markets, technologies, and work organizations.

What are the tradeoffs of this moral price floor with respect to employment generation and inflation? And how about the welfare losses and inefficiencies that are introduced into the economy as a result of suspending the price-setting function of the market below a certain threshold?[38] A moral price floor, just like the scholastic just price, would seem to be more feasible in a medieval than in a modern economy.[39]

Ethical Difficulties

Assuming for the sake of argument that such a price floor were practicable and enforceable, ethical difficulties still remain to be addressed. For example, it is not clear how moral accountability can be assigned since exchange involves the interaction of atomistic economic agents who exert no significant individual influence over market outcomes. Moreover, a wage-driven approach to exchange-value determination calls for more than just a de facto imposition of a minimum wage equal to the living wage. By tying the questions of a living wage and the just price together, the moral price floor regulates, in effect, both the labor and the product markets. A binding moral price floor leads to a mandated minimum selling price for goods and services to cover the living wage of workers.

This de facto regulation of the product market is an ethical dilemma in itself. Is there a moral argument for encumbering consumers with higher prices when inexpensive goods and services can be purchased from low-cost regions? Whose welfare should be protected, the worker's or the consumer's?[40] Imposing a price floor in a modern application of the just price requires working out the moral warrants for shifting burdens from the worker to the consumer. Moreover, its price-distorting effects must also be weighed against the argument that there is a moral obligation to be efficient in the use of our scarce economic resources (Piderit 1993).[41]

SUMMARY AND CONCLUSIONS

Scholastic teachings on exchange-value determination have evolved in modern Catholic social thought where the question of a living wage for workers is now incorporated as a separate and significant concern within the larger issue of a just price. The attention accorded to commutative justice in scholastic just price has shifted to a modern concern over distributive justice. Scholastics deal with the morality of exchange at a personal level, while the modern social documents assess fairness at an institutional level.

In writing about the just price, medieval theologians are concerned with averting fraud on the part of sellers who take advantage of the ignorance and need of buyers.[42] These theologians are critical of unequal exchanges and seek to arrive at proportionality in the value of goods and services. The object of the scholastics is to identify the bounds of commutative justice that make for a fair exchange.

In contrast, modern Catholic social thought is concerned with providing an adequate livelihood for workers. As noted earlier, people are price takers in a modern competitive economy; the risk of fraud where the seller takes advantage of the buyer is minimized given the inability of atomistic economic actors to influence the price. Rather, the immediate issues for the modern tradition have been the dismal working conditions for laborers, the inadequacy of wages, and the lopsided division of output in society given the imbalance in labor-management relations. It is concerned with the unequal exchange between workers and owners of capital in setting wage levels. Medieval theologians discuss these problems of exchange at the level of personal morality, while modern theological reflections examine them at the social level under the aegis of distributive justice where the adequacy of resources allocated to the workers is appraised.

A second shift can be observed in the allocative and enforcement mechanisms of the economy. This follows in the wake of the change in focus from personal to institutional morality and from commutative to distributive justice. In setting the communal estimate of the just price, the medieval economic unit is, in effect, also taking into account the social status of its members and the expenses they incur in discharging their function in the community. This communal estimation of the market price and the distribution of factor payments that flow from it are enforced through the informal channels of a social convention that is held together by religion, family, and community.

In an industrial society characterized by larger economic units and more complex production processes, the distribution of factor payments can no longer be based on sociocultural ties as in the feudal era. The modern economy has devised new mechanisms of distribution such as the wage-labor market and the marginalist approach to factor payments. Commodity and factor payments are no longer based on social status but on economic agents' contributions to the productive effort. More importantly, new channels of accountability have arisen in a modern economy where market outcomes are largely due to impersonal forces and where traditional bonds of community have been either lost or weakened. The informal manner of enforcing social convention through religion and blood relations has given way to formal, legal, and institutional directives such as minimum wage laws and other labor legislation protecting union activities and collective bargaining. Traditional social, personal, and moral forms of suasion have given way to the legal and impersonal safeguards of industrial society.[43] The next chapter examines these in greater depth.

Points of Continuity

In spite of the observed differences in the teachings on exchange value between scholasticism and the modern Catholic social documents, an important point of continuity remains, namely: the central role of the axiom of mutual advantage in validating any exchange. Medieval theologians develop the notion of a just price in order to ensure that all parties share equitably both in the burdens and the benefits of any trade. This is achieved when goods and services are exchanged at relative prices that reflect their proportional economic value.

Mutual advantage is also the animating principle behind the modern social documents' stress on the living wage. Market transactions, including the hiring of workers, must profit all economic actors: the consumers, the suppliers, the workers, and the owners of capital (QA #53–55).[44] The burdens and the benefits of exchange in the modern economy must be proportionately borne by everyone in the community. Consequently, mutual advantage for all parties in the transactions is the ultimate yardstick that morally validates the exchange.[45] This is an essential point of continuity between the scholastics and modern Catholic social thought on exchange-value determination. It should not be surprising, therefore, to discern a pattern of defending the disadvantaged party in both traditions. Medieval theologians seek to protect consumers from unscrupulous merchants who are considered to have the upper hand in trade in a feudal economy. Modern Catholic social thought, on the other hand, has championed the cause of workers who are viewed to be the weaker bargaining party in the modern wage-labor economy.

Another correspondence must be noted. There are similarities in the starting point and in the common opposition faced by scholastic and modern economic ethics. The medieval doctors argue against the Roman canonists in their claim that a price which results from a freely negotiated contract is morally and legally legitimate (Baldwin 1959). Modern ethical reflection faces a similar starting point: Laissez-faire adherents regard the mutual and voluntary nature of labor market exchange as sufficient grounds for assuming the moral validity of these transactions' outcomes.

In both cases, there is the implicit assumption that no exploitation can occur in markets because people will not enter into any exchange at all if they do not reap benefits from such trading. Consequently, a completed market transaction is prima facie evidence of mutual advantages for all parties concerned. The modern economy adds a further argument in support of this position: The enormous benefits of allocative efficiency from free market operations cannot be ignored. In both disagreements between scholastics and Roman canonists, and between Catholic social thinkers and laissez-faire proponents, the point of contention is the relative importance that should be accorded the social gains of an unfettered market compared to the larger social goals that could only be realized by curtailing its operations.

For the scholastics, there is moral validity to the transaction only when there is equivalence in exchange (commutative justice), when no one is exploited, and when all affected parties receive their due according to their social roles (distributive justice). The satisfaction of these conditions (i.e., the payment of a just price) takes precedence over whatever weight may be given to the freedom of contract. In the modern Catholic social documents, market outcomes and processes are subjected to scrutiny and are overridden whenever the economic structures undergirding the economy fall short of the standards of justice.

Notes

1. The terms "market price" and "exchange value" will be used interchangeably.

2. I use the common Smithian-Ricardian understanding of "value" as price or exchange value. This is in contrast to Marx who reserves the term "value" for the labor content of output and uses "price" to refer to exchange transactions.

3. As Ayres (1936, 233) puts it: "The economist engages in price analysis because he seeks a theory of economic order. From the distant past he has inherited the idea of a natural equilibrium of forces by virtue of which order obtains among men. . . . Among the forces which eventuate so felicitously are the inherent qualities of human nature: perception of pleasure and pain, wants and satisfactions, and so forth. Economic theory accordingly presumes that these wants and satisfactions are registered in price, and therefore that *price is the mechanism by virtue of which social order reigns*" (emphasis added).

4. Smith ([1776] 1937, 34–35) observes: "[T]he real price of everything, what everything really costs to the man who wants to acquire it, is the toil and trouble of acquiring it. . . ." He further notes, "[Labor is] the real measure of the exchangeable value of all commodities."

5. Ricardo (1971, 65) notes: "[N]ot only the labour applied immediately to commodities affects their value, but also that which is bestowed on the implements, tools and buildings with which such labour is assisted." He further notes, "Exchange values are in proportion to the labour bestowed on their production; not on their immediate production only, but on all those implements or machines required to give effect to the particular labour to which they are applied" (67).

6. The supply curve is strictly vertical. Hence, the demand curve determines the price.

7. Assuming a constant cost industry, the supply curve is strictly horizontal and value is determined solely by the supply curve.

8. See, for example, de Roover (1958, 418, fn. 1) and Barth (1960, 413, fn. 1) for a listing of works that subscribe to the theory that Aquinas's just price consists of the cost of production defined by the living expenses necessary to preserve the economic agents' status in society. Duns Scotus defines just price as that which "allowed [the] merchant to support his family adequately" (Gordon 1975, 223).

9. Spengler (1968, 226) observes that the social status of the economic agents easily melds into the cost of production especially in the light of the role played by the guilds where the exchangers are clearly grouped according to status.

10. Gordon (1975, 174–79) rejects the social-status approach to pricing because two different principles are operative: commutative justice for determining price and distributive justice for income distribution and the preservation of social status.

11. Gordon's (1975) chapter on "Price and Value in Scholastic Thought, 1300–1600" and de Roover ([1955] 1974c) examine the scholastics from 1300 to 1600 on this topic. These surveys find that Aquinas is a standard reference point; that the "common estimation" is given by the "market consensus" governed by utility and scarcity; and that there are occasions when direct price regulation is warranted in order to preserve justice. Most favor the utility-based reasoning, but some favor the cost-of-production approach with particular stress on labor cost.

12. Barth (1960, 414) agrees that outside his commentary on the *Ethics*, Aquinas does not use cost as a determinant to just price.

13. See Hollander (1965), de Roover ([1955] 1974c, 1958), Worland (1967, 1977), Barth (1960), and Gordon (1975). An exception is Wilson (1975). See Baldwin (1959, 76a) for various medieval theologians who follow Aquinas in equating just price with current market price.

14. I am assuming away shirking and other free-rider problems on the part of the worker.

15. A word of caution must be offered. Some authors use the terms "subjective" and "objective" to describe the two competing approaches to value determination in economic thought: the marginal utility approach for the former and the cost-of-production approach for the latter. See, for example, Lichtenstein (1983). As will soon become apparent to readers, *Laborem Exercens* uses these terms in a different sense.

16. LE #23 notes: "Man . . . is a person, that is to say, a subjective being capable of acting in a planned and rational way, capable of deciding about himself, and with a tendency to self-realization. *As a person, man is therefore the subject of work*. As a person, he works, he performs various actions belonging to the work process" (emphasis in the original).

17. LE #52 observes: ". . . [A] principle that has always been taught by the Church: *the principle of the priority of labor over capital*. This principle directly concerns the process of production: in this process labor is always a primary *efficient cause*, while capital, the whole collection of means of production, remains a mere *instrument* or instrumental cause" (emphasis in the original).

18. This has been one of the major points of continuity in the modern Catholic social documents and dates as far back as *Rerum Novarum*'s insistence that labor ought not to be treated as a mere commodity.

19. LE #27 remarks: "[D]ifferent sorts of work that people do can have a greater or lesser objective value. . . . [N]evertheless . . . each sort is judged above all by *the measure of the dignity* of the subject of the work, that is to say the person, *the individual who carries it out*" (emphasis in the original).

20. Note the following excerpt from *Rerum Novarum* (#15–16) as an example: "Moreover since man expends his mental energy and his bodily strength in procuring the goods of nature, by this very act he appropriates that part of physical nature to himself which he has cultivated. On it he leaves impressed, as it were, a kind of image of his person, so that it must be altogether just that he should possess that part as his very own and that no one in any way should be permitted to violate his right. . . . Would justice permit anyone to own and enjoy that upon which another has toiled? . . . [S]o it is just that the fruit of labor belongs precisely to those who have performed the labor." See also Fortin (1992).

21. Marx observes: "[V]alue was an *objective* property that had to be rooted in something more substantial than the 'superficial' market forces of supply and demand" (Hebert and Ekelund 1984, 52).

22. QA #55 & #68 note that the Marxist solution of giving the entire social output to workers exclusively is an unjust claim. Furthermore, there are numerous passages in the social documents that call for profit sharing with workers. Such a call is an implicit affirmation that profits have a legitimate place in the work order.

23. A sizable labor pool, continuously fed by population growth, ensures competition for the available jobs. This keeps wages down to the subsistence level, just enough to keep employed workers alive.

24. MM #70 notes: "It frequently happens that great, or sometimes very great, remuneration is had for the performance of some task of lesser importance or of doubtful utility. Meanwhile, the diligent and profitable work that whole classes of decent and hard-working citizens perform, receives too low a payment and . . . one that does not correspond to the contribution made to the community."

25. Furthermore, a factor payment such as wage income is the outcome of demand and supply interactions and is, consequently, the result not only of labor's productivity and contribution, but also of numerous other economic and sociological factors (Landreth 1976, 254). In addition, there is also the difficulty of disentangling and measuring the marginal product of a factor from all the other factor inputs (Taussig 1924, II, 213–14). Marshall notes that the marginal productivity postulate cannot be used as a theory of wages for the same reason: "This doctrine [referring to the marginal productivity theory] has sometimes been put forward as a theory of wages. But there is no valid ground for any such pretension . . . since in order to estimate net product, we have to take for granted all the expenses of production of the commodity on which he works, other than his own wages" (Marshall [1890] 1961, 518). It is a heroic assumption, therefore, to claim that factor payments in a competitive economy automatically lead to ethical outcomes.

26. RN #31 notes: "It is shameful and inhuman, however, to use men as things for gain and to put *no more value* on them than what they are worth in muscle and energy" (emphasis added). QA #83 observes: "Labor . . . is not a mere chattel, since the human dignity of the workingman must be recognized in it, and consequently it cannot be bought and sold like any piece of merchandise." MM #18 remarks: "[W]ork, inasmuch as it is an expression of the human person, can by no means be regarded as a mere commodity."

27. MM #18 argues: "For the great majority of mankind, work is the only source from which the means of livelihood are drawn. Hence, its remuneration is not to be thought of in terms of merchandise, but rather according to the laws of justice and equity."

28. QA #53 explains the rationale for labor markets in the following sequence of arguments: (1) There is a right order in God's plan for nature's gifts to satisfy the person's needs; (2) This right order entails "everything having its proper owner"; and (3) Therefore, for those without property on which to apply one's labor, an alliance must be formed with those who have, and just remuneration must be given. See also QA #64.

29. Neither does Aristotle.

30. Lessius does address the reverse case. He recommends nonbinding profit sharing in cases where productivity exceeds subsistence pay.

31. Market price can be below *cost* into the long term because it is the quality of life, not whether the worker lives or dies, that is at stake when exchange value (and consequently wages) is below what CST considers to be *cost*.

32. Lessius observes: "It can be established that it [the wage payment] is not below the minimum, from the fact that there are others who are willing to perform such work or office or service for the remuneration in question. That is a clear indication that such a remuneration, all circumstances considered, is not below the right value for that occupation" (cited in Gordon 1975, 263).

33. A necessary condition for allocative efficiency in perfectly competitive markets is the perfect mobility of factors that allows the employment of scarce resources in their most valued uses. Thus, capital controls, investment restrictions, and barriers to migration create market inefficiencies.

34. The destitution that constrains people to accept inadequate wages is a phenomenon acknowledged early on in *Rerum Novarum*. Leo XIII notes that mutual agreement alone does not make for the validity of wage contracts; the adequacy of the wage is also a necessary condition of moral legitimacy (RN #63).

35. This is a positive externality where the social benefits to society of having well-fed and productive workers are not captured by the wages offered in the labor market.

36. There may be empirical evidence to disprove this. For example, Kahneman, Knetsch, and Thaler (1986) find that a sense of fair play is an additional consideration of profit-seeking firms in the labor market.

37. I am back to Adam Smith's problem in using a labor-embodied approach to pricing in an advanced economy with capital.

38. The incentive and the discipline to innovate and be efficient that come with competition are lost. The economic ramifications of this are beyond the scope of this chapter but need to be addressed. Recent empirical evidence suggests that distortions can be counterproductive and impede long-run economic well-being and performance (World Bank 1991).

39. In spite of these unresolved difficulties, it must be noted that these concerns of Catholic social thought on price determination have been perennial issues in political economy. One only has to look at the longstanding terms-of-trade debate between developed and less-developed countries (Meier 1984, 502–03, 555–58). The moral qualms concerning the potential exploitation of cheap Third World labor by multinational companies is another example.

40. This moral problem is not a mere speculative academic exercise. The subsidies and protection accorded by the major developed countries to their farmers are examples where agricultural interests are put ahead of consumers'.

41. The foregoing analysis has been predominantly microeconomic in nature. From a macroeconomic angle, the provision of a living wage may have growth-dampening effects in the short term as resources that would have been devoted to investments in plant and equipment as reinvested profits are diverted into wage-goods consumption. However, this expected increase in consumption may lead to an improvement in human capital and enhance the long-term prospects for growth.

42. Observe another shift. In the modern economy, it is now the seller that is viewed to be the vulnerable party that needs protection from the relatively stronger position of buyers. This is particularly true not only in labor markets but also in the exports of Third World commodities. Thus, there is a perceived need to protect disadvantaged sellers in the modern era.

43. This is not to say that there are no provisions for price regulation in medieval social ethics. Scholastic thinkers have always accepted the need to regulate market prices especially of essential commodities such as food.

44. This point is emphatically made by *Rerum Novarum* and *Quadragesimo Anno* in their critique of ideological assertions that labor or the owners of capital have exclusive claim over the economic fruits of the modern economy to the total disregard of the other party. The tenet of mutual advantage is invoked by Leo XIII and Pius XI.

45. The problem here, of course, is choosing the criteria for what constitutes mutual advantage. This is similar to the problem of arriving at due proportion in the common good, which is briefly discussed in chapter 14.

Chapter 5

FROM ORGANIC HIERARCHY TO INDIVIDUAL RIGHTS

The evolution of the scholastic just price into the modern concern for a living wage is a reflection of a much larger shift toward addressing the systemic, rather than merely personal, injustices in socioeconomic life. Note, for example, the prevailing preference for rights language, the new appreciation for the exercise of private initiative for economic gain, and the change from the scholastic antipathy toward guilds to the contemporary defense of unions. Moreover, the scholastic silence on social justice contrasts vividly with a vigorous critique of sinful societal structures in recent economic ethics. It is puzzling that concern over unjust social institutions and the advocacy of unions do not arise earlier because glaring income and wealth disparities, state encroachment on private economic freedoms, and poor working conditions are not only already prevalent but probably even worse during the medieval era. Just like the metamorphosis of the scholastic just price, these changes in normative thought correspond to the shifting economic terrain as feudalism is transformed into the modern industrial economy. Economic history can shed much light on the evolution of economic ethics.

CALL TO ACTION: TRANSFORMING SINFUL STRUCTURES OF SOCIETY

From Personal Morality to Institutional Justice

The medieval doctors are interested primarily in the moral quality of individual economic behavior rather than the justness of economic institutions and processes. Scholastic economic ethics deals largely with interpersonal relations and personal moral accountability. Langholm, Jacob Viner, and Joseph A. Schumpeter all observe that hardly any thought is given to the interaction between individuals and economic institutions, or to the ways either can leave a lasting mark on the other. Even more rare is the topic of reforming existing social institutions.[1] After all, the medieval writers see themselves as confessors and spiritual directors, not as social activists.

> Primarily, however, and so far as their practical task was concerned, *it was not the merits or demerits of institutions that mattered to them*, but the merits or demerits of individual behavior within the frame of given institutions and conditions. More than anything else, they were directors of individual consciences or rather, teachers of directors of individual consciences. They wrote for many purposes but principally for the instruction of confessors (Schumpeter 1954, 102, emphasis added).

In contrast to the scholastics' nearly exclusive focus on personal economic behavior related to the honest exchange of goods and services (e.g., just price and usury), modern Catholic social documents examine economic processes together with their auxiliary institutions and instruments: labor-management arrangements (*Rerum Novarum*, 1891), industry-level vocational groupings (*Quadragesimo Anno*, 1931), government import-substitution development strategies (*Mater et Magistra*, 1961), and international political economy (*Populorum Progressio*, 1967, and *Sollicitudo Rei Socialis*, 1987). The term "social justice" is of recent vintage (Pius XI 1931; Muench 1948, 3327). Nowhere is this contrast more glaring than in these social documents' entreaties for individuals to take personal responsibility in shaping social institutions:

> It is up to the Christian communities to analyze with objectivity the situation which is proper to their own country, to shed on it the light of the Gospel's unalterable words and to draw principles of reflection, norms of judgment and directives for action . . . to discern the options and commitments which are called for in order to bring about the social, political and economic changes seen in many cases to be urgently needed (OA #4).

This shift in attention from personal to institutional sinfulness can be partly traced to the altered role of price in economic life. The repercussions of such a change go beyond the labor market (as examined in the preceding chapter) to encompass most, if not all, economic behavior.

Revisiting Scholastic Just Price

The scholastic notion of just price is often described as the value prevailing in the market, a formulation that implies that market operations determine medieval pricing. If we invoke "market operations" at all in reference to the feudal economy, we must do so only in the most carefully qualified way, for medieval markets do not exhibit today's broad private economic freedoms. As argued in the preceding chapter, the scholastic "market estimate" is ultimately founded on the social roles of the parties involved in the trade. Custom, law, and usage, not unfettered demand and supply, form the basis for the common estimation represented by the market price. These traditional mechanisms are manifested in various ways, such as the uniform pricing-production-sales standards of the craft guilds, the practice of passing on trades and craft membership from father to son, and the "customs of the manor" that govern the terms of exchange between the serfs' services and the manorial lord's protection (see North 1981; Postal et al. 1963; Vinogradoff 1957; and Renard 1918). This pricing by convention causes a convergence of commutative and distributive justice.

In a feudal world of isolated communities, animal husbandry is the main economic activity; production is consumed on the spot. The little trade that transpires between villages is predominantly an exchange for consumption, that is, a transaction between the final user and the producer.[2] The English economic historian William Ashley describes the thirteenth century as a time when "the great majority of articles in the daily use of the mass of the people are bought by the consumer from the actual maker" (Ashley 1925, I:138). Defrauding buyers and profiteering from the extreme needs of others are the principal concerns of the period. This is apparent in the two teachings that together take up most of the scholastics' and their commentators' attention–just price and usury.[3] Regardless of whether medieval just price is defined as the usual or the joint estimate of exchange value, Langholm (1987, 125) observes that its end is still the same: preventing the exploitation of any party to the transaction. Safeguarding the welfare of all requires equivalence in the value of goods or services traded (Baldwin 1959, part 4). For this reason, teachings on the just price are associated with the satisfaction of commutative justice, but this is only part of the story.

In addition to ensuring that nobody is victimized, scholastic just price has a second function: *just income formation*. The price at which goods and services are traded is the outcome of the community's collective estimation. The community believes that "the maker should receive what would fairly recompense him for his labour" and "what would permit him to live a decent life according to the standard of comfort which public opinion recognized as appropriate to his class" (Ashley 1925, I:138).[4] Consequently, equivalence in exchange is a function of the social roles of the parties engaged in the trade. While the proximate objective of scholastic teachings on just price is to prevent fraud or undue profits from others' needs, their deeper concern is distributive in nature: providing people with access to the goods or services essential to their social roles. The scholastics give preeminence to the distributive dimension of price: Equity in the allotment of societal resources is treated derivatively as the predictable result of just income formation achieved when people secure a just price for the work effort or output they bring to the market. This means that commutative and distributive justice are simultaneously satisfied in the medieval notion of just price. After all, equivalence in the exchange of goods and services between people is ultimately founded on what is owed to the person by the rest of the community. Commutative justice is a function of distributive justice.

Economic Metamorphosis: Price in the Modern Marketplace

As feudal society is transformed into the modern market economy, the economic and political spheres are separated from each other. In the medieval world, economic and political powers are exercised by the same institution. Thus, manorial administration is charged with governing its self-contained economic life, even as it dispenses justice within its own realm. The guilds in the urban areas prescribe standards of production and terms of sale (including price) within their crafts, even as they operate as vehicles for the sociopolitical participation of their membership in the larger community.

The emergence of an economic sphere autonomous from the political structure unleashes the private initiative that gives birth to the modern industrial economy. This new order is characterized by scale in operations and division of labor, in contrast to the autarky of medieval economic units. Population increase, the growth of urban areas, the emergence of technologies and institutions conducive to commerce, and the shift to the factory system break down the isolation of communities from each other and pave the way for greater economic interdependence. In other words, exchanging goods or services with others is no longer merely an option (as in the feudal manor); it becomes a necessity with exchange permeating every facet of life. The breathtaking expansion in the scale and the scope of economic activity in the past three centuries is evident in the intense trading of goods and services not only for consumption (end use), but also for production (intermediate goods, labor, capital, and land) and for distribution (wholesale and retail activities).

In contrast to the simple decisions undertaken by medieval economic agents who produce for consumption on the spot, their modern counterparts are besieged by the perennial need for calculation as an ever greater part of economic activity. Unlike their autarkic feudal cousins, modern economic actors have to answer the basic economic questions (what to produce, when, where, and with what) even while engaged in a long requisite chain of exchanges and interaction with others.

Economic decision making has to satisfy simultaneously the demands of product, place, and time utility with minimum expenditure. In other words, modern economic agents have to make the right calls with respect to specializing in the appropriate goods or services, producing them in the exact quantities required while employing least-cost methods and inputs, and then, exchanging them at the proper time and in the right place. The role of punctual, accurate, and useful data for such involved decisions takes on greater importance, and providing such can be adequately met by only one medium—the market price. Only price can convey information quickly, efficiently, and effectively over widely dispersed geographic areas to a large number of interested parties in a timely way. This is a service rendered by the modern market that no other institution or mechanism could yet replace.

Increasingly operating on the basis of exchange in all stages from production to distribution to consumption within an ever burgeoning menu of new and ever more sophisticated goods and services, the modern economic order's major task has been to ensure that scarce resources are put to their best competing uses. Langholm observes that in contrast to medieval just price, modern price "serves to *allocate joint social resources optimally*" (Langholm 1987, 125, emphasis in the original). This should not come as a surprise at all, considering that custom, law, and usage are simply unable to keep up with the dynamic and complex requirements of industrial economic decision making. This paves the groundwork for a major alteration in the function accorded to price. The feudal practice of setting exchange value by convention shifts to the modern reliance on the unfettered operation of demand and supply. Medieval pricing is set with an eye toward the equitable distribution of societal goods and roles. In contrast, modern pricing is concerned with matching demand and supply to achieve the most productive disposition of scarce resources to their optimum uses, that is, allocative efficiency.

An incongruity should be noted in this transformation. As we move away from self-contained communities and as exchange begins to encroach into many aspects of social life, one would think that an even greater emphasis would be placed on the distributive role of price since questions of equity become even more apparent and more contentious as markets expand. It is ironic that it is the allocative function that has taken precedence.

This comes with a cost—the loss of custom, law, and usage that have been instrumental and effective in defining the boundaries that ensure just processes and outcomes in economic life. Replacing them are suprapersonal economic institutions that are better suited for the pursuit of efficiency to the exclusion of other worthwhile societal goals. Why, then, do normative teachings such as modern Catholic social documents acquiesce to this shift in practice? They have no choice. They have to accommodate a radically transformed economy imbued with a breathtaking dynamism that produces more good, on the whole, than harm.

Shifting Terrain for Ethical Reflection

Even if the authors of modern Catholic social documents were to cling to the scholastic use of price for distributive (rather than allocative) ends, there is no way to reverse, much less to stop, the process that has been unleashed by the Industrial Revolution. Empirical evidence from the past two centuries attests to the tremendous improvement in the human condition brought about by the modern market economy. Even after taking the human cost of modernization into account, the industrial order has, on the whole, led to striking advances in the standards of living whether measured by economic or social indicators. Not only has the Malthusian specter been dissipated, but there has even been a sustained increase in per capita incomes; the economy can support more people, and richer people at that.[5] By providing the necessary economic incentives and releasing private ambitions, the economy has benefitted enormously from the technological advances and new organizational techniques that have, in turn, continuously advanced people's standards of living. Even in the face of pockets of extreme poverty that still exist today, ethical reflection cannot ignore the signal accomplishments in improving economic life most especially in the period since World War II (World Bank 1991).

Which function of price should take precedence–its allocative or distributive role? At the heart of this choice between the workings of demand and supply or the continued reliance on custom, law, and usage is the classic tradeoff between growth and equity. Should we concentrate our efforts on dividing the pie properly or should we rather expend our energies on making the pie grow bigger? The opportunity cost of adhering to the scholastic preference for the distributive over the allocative facet of price would simply be too prohibitive and counterproductive, indeed inappropriate, given the changed historical circumstances.[6] Not only have we seen the gains that industry can bring in its wake, but we have also witnessed the market prove itself as an incomparably effective vehicle for attaining allocative efficiency.

The problem of enforcement constitutes a second practical reason for accommodating this shift in the function of price. Even though there are difficulties with maintaining distributive justice in the medieval marketplace, people generally observe the doctrine of just price in practice. It is not easy to regulate price setting because private transactions can neither be fully nor constantly monitored. This difficulty is especially true in the isolated communities and fragmented markets of the feudal economy. Langholm (1982, 278) observes that "in the unruly societies of the Middle Ages exchangers were mostly left to their own devices, and moralists had to rely on precepts about just pricing enforceable only in the internal forum."

In spite of the inherent difficulty of ensuring compliance with moral teachings on private economic life, the scholastic just price has surprisingly effective enforcement mechanisms provided by the medieval ecclesiastical institutions. In his exposition on the economic doctrines of the scholastics, Viner observes that not only is the Roman Catholic Church able to assert its right to be involved in secular affairs with moral ramifications, but it also has within its means a vast array of formal and informal enforcement mechanisms for these moral teachings: the pulpit, the large number of clerics discharging various civil functions, papal governance of its states, ecclesial principalities and estates, the jurisdiction of ecclesiastical courts over many conflicts[7] of an economic nature, and sanctions of a social and spiritual nature that range from economic boycotts to excommunication and exclusion from the sacraments. And even if these are not enough, given the inability to oversee most economic transactions, there is recourse to yet another enforcement mechanism, this one in the internal forum: the confessional or deathbed absolution where restitution could be made a condition for pardon (Viner 1978, 46–47). W. Ashley (1925, I:132) comments on the depth and pervasiveness of clerical influence:

> They enforced them [referring to the criterion of just price and the prohibition against charging interest] from the pulpit, in the confessional, in the ecclesiastical courts; and we shall find that by the time that the period begins of legislative activity on the part of the secular power, these two rules had been so impressed on the consciences of men that Parliament, municipality, and gild endeavoured of their own motion to secure obedience to them.

Given the myriad channels through which religious teachings influence, indeed mold, societal values and practices, there is neither need nor urgency to reform unjust economic structures. The Roman Catholic Church is efficacious in influencing individual economic behavior because it is very much a part of the social structure. It wields effective moral suasion in both internal and external fora and could, consequently, monitor social life from the corridors of power. The loss of traditional ecclesiastical enforcement mechanisms in the modern period necessitates a more formal, separate, and vocal articulation of the theological vision of the right order in social structures. Religion now plays its role of guardian-protector of individual well-being from a much more circumscribed position in society. This is made particularly acute in economic ethics because the premier institution of modern economic life, the market, is principally concerned with optimality and efficiency rather than equity.

In summary, medieval thought and practice give preeminence to the distributive over the allocative function of exchange value. This can be deduced from numerous scholastic references to just income formation founded on social roles, from scholars' judgment that medieval just price is based on the cost of production rather than on consumer utility (Baldwin 1959), from the premodern practice of setting prices by convention, and from the simple observation that allocative efficiency is a modern concern. The scholastic notion of just price is a convenient vehicle for satisfying simultaneously the requirements of commutative and distributive justice. However, as the feudal economy gives way to the modern industrial economy, there is a reversal in the importance of the allocative and distributive dimensions; the former overshadows the latter and breaks the convenient confluence of commutative and distributive justice achieved in medieval ethics. Thus, unlike scholastic economic teachings, modern thought has had to look for nonprice, nonmarket mechanisms for securing distributive justice and has focused on the justness of social structures. This search has led to changes in the language of ethical discourse and to numerous teachings on alternative work arrangements.

FROM PRECARIOUS SURVIVAL TO ABUNDANT GROWTH: DEMISE OF ORGANIC HIERARCHY

The language employed by modern Catholic social thought has shifted from one of obligations to that of individual rights (Hollenbach 1979; Byers 1985; Hebblethwaite 1985, 264–84; Petrella 1972, 352–65). This is in part a reflection of the much larger epochal "turn to the individual" inaugurated by the Enlightenment. However, one can also make a case for the claim that the contemporary preference for individual liberties over the scholastic doctors' organic hierarchy is a necessary accommodation to the sea change from feudalism to the industrial market economy. The move from precarious survival to self-sustaining growth removes the economic justification for a rigidly structured society and provides greater freedoms to both individuals and communities. Rights become a way of retrieving the safeguards previously provided by custom, law, and usage that have now been rendered inoperable.

Medieval Caution

The hard conditions of feudal life provide a rational basis for the perceived need for a tightly regimented social life. Economic activity is predominantly agricultural based on animal husbandry, that is, production for consumption on the spot. The isolation of communities is not conducive to commerce that could have spawned a division of labor so essential for increased productivity. Output is low, tools are rudimentary, and little surplus could be accumulated. Not surprisingly, very little is left available for capital investments to improve crop yields. Small surpluses also deter the refinement of agricultural methods because experimentation in an agrarian setting requires sufficient reserves of basic necessities to cushion expected occasional failures that come with trying unfamiliar methods. Thus, manors set rules on what crops to plant, when to plant, and how to divide up the land into strips. Household activity is shaped by community decisions. After all, the manor is the basic economic unit with the overriding goal of achieving self-sufficiency for all its needs.

This reasonable aversion toward innovation is, unfortunately, compounded further by the weak incentives coming from the social structure itself. The era's ill-defined property rights give rise to the *problem of the commons* (Hardin 1968) where shared properties deteriorate from neglect as individuals see no reason to expend personal effort and care without reaping the full benefits from such improvements. Moreover, peasants have little protection from arbitrary exactions by the lords. Besides, there is little immediate use for monetary savings since trade is minimal, and travel is hard and dangerous.

The paucity of surplus, of much-needed innovative ventures, and of requisite incentives all converge to relegate the economy to long-term secular stagnation. The consequent deficiency in technological creativity leads to low output and a dismal productivity that, in turn, engender conservatism in the next rounds of economic activity.

The sensible response to such tenuous subsistence is to work toward the preservation of the status quo–that which has been handed down and has been proven to work for generations. Production does not, indeed could not, revolve around private economic gain as it is besieged with the urgency of cobbling together a viable cooperative effort to procure the material prerequisites of existence. It is the group that secures the most feasible opportunities for the individual. Tradition assigns people to their places and sets the expectations from such roles. People, in turn, assume their designated station in the community and contribute to the collective enterprise, with their private economic lives largely governed by the group. Occupations are, for the most part, predetermined; crafts and skills are passed down from parent to child. And as seen previously, scholastic just price is not based on satisfaction in consumption but is derived instead from the common estimation of the income required to sustain sellers in a lifestyle befitting their roles in community (Baldwin 1959). Medieval economic ethics is founded on an organic hierarchy model (Heilbroner 1975).

Modern Economic Individualism

Industrialization brings human experience from the edges of destitution to unbounded prosperity. This transformation precipitates significant changes that remove the need for strict regimentation.

Why no longer necessary?

Survival is the pragmatic end of medieval conventions that provide the means for coping with the insecurities and uncertainties of feudal economic life (Rosenberg and Birdzell 1986). In contrast, the modern age has witnessed breathtaking advances on a broad front: the adoption of the factory system as the primary mode of production, the introduction of market exchange in many spheres of life, and, of course, the lead taken by science and technology in pushing the frontiers of human capabilities in mastering the material world.

These remarkable strides overshadow the utility of an inflexible stratified economic life. Greater output opens new possibilities for experimentation and innovation in both production and organizational techniques. Better capital formation generates even more surplus, thereby leading to ever bolder initiatives in technical creativity. This secures greater predictability in the satisfaction of basic needs; the proximate collective economic goal is no longer the pressing end of subsistence but continued bounty.

Commerce serves as a cushion against unexpected natural or man-made disruptions. The expansion of markets across wider geographic areas creates an ever tightening web of interdependence both within communities and across borders brought about by advances in transportation and communications, growth in population, and a greater appreciation for the benefits of exchange. Trade enhances the ability of populations to weather and recover from unforeseen misfortunes. No longer isolated from each other, communities can recoup more readily from setbacks with relatively greater ease and speed than their medieval counterparts.

The improved capacity to produce, keep, and productively use surplus and the group's strengthened durability in the face of unexpected reversals are two key factors that allow a greater measure of freedom in the way the community is organized. Relieved of the exigencies and difficulties of securing the requisite material conditions for life, society no longer has an economic need for unbending established arrangements.

Why not even tenable?

The medieval organic hierarchy has been rendered an unviable option even had the modern era wanted to preserve it. First, the emergence of a commercial sphere independent of political institutions unleashes expansive private freedoms. In contrast to the feudal rigidities and constraints to movement across communities, across crafts and skills, and up (or down) the social ladder, the current economy provides a multidimensional geographic, social, and professional mobility. Economic agents select their occupation and can improve their social station and prestige through wealth accumulation. They have, for the most part, the liberty of choosing their place of domicile and their degree of participation in social life. These are taken for granted as fundamental human rights in the modern era; it would be unthinkable for the community to predetermine for individuals what trade they may or may not enter (cf. craft guilds) and what income they are to receive given their social standing (cf. medieval just price).

Related to this is a second reason for why a fixed social order is no longer defensible as an organizing principle. Faced with medieval uncertainties, the individual's best chances of thriving are to be part of an extended community. People have to depend on each other for protection against unforseen dangers, from the vagaries of the weather to the predations of roving bandits. By necessity, individuals have to rely on and be party to a wide web of religious, family, and communal ties.

In contrast, contemporary economic agents can strike out on their own, survive, and even prosper outside of traditional domestic circles. Compared to the feudal home-based producers, today's economic participants can sustain themselves by joining the contractual wage-labor market. Moreover, the modern welfare state undergirds this with a social safety net independent of customary support systems based on kinship. The means to social, professional, and geographic mobility are available to the individual who no longer has to be wedded to an extended network of familial and communal bonds for economic sustenance and advancement. Citizenship has provided viable alternatives to blood ties.

The inherent dynamism of the industrial economy is a third reason for why the fixed social paradigm is no longer workable. In a setting where change is slow and manageable, tradition lends itself very well as a convenient avenue for regulating the common productive effort and for dispensing roles and responsibilities. Unfortunately, this breeds an inertia and rigidity that could not supply the agility required by the new economic conditions.

Market pricing has proven itself to be much better than convention in responding to changes. Moreover, the industrial economy creates an unceasing stream of new demands and uses for society's limited means, thereby heightening even further the importance of flexibility in optimizing the use of common resources. The market has proven itself to be an efficient mechanism for this task.

A fourth reason has to do with the shift in attitudes on the immutability of public institutions. An economy of great uncertainty and low technological development that severely restricts human mastery over the environment readily spawns a sense of fatalism. Individuals and communities are easily conditioned to a resignation of working within, rather than changing, the social life that has been received.[8] The inauguration of a more expansive sphere of personal freedoms has provided the means, confidence, opportunities, and stimulus for the community, through private initiative, to recast and reshape social structures. Common life itself is no longer taken as unchangeable but is viewed as the object of legitimate individual and collective choices. Moreover, the incessant flux of contemporary economy provides innumerable occasions to reengineer social practices.

Economic Institutions

Modernity has given rise to the need for mechanisms that ensure the justness of social structures. Both the medieval and modern economies are self-reinforcing in their own way: a winding spiral of low-level output in the former and accelerating growth in the latter. The moral issues under these two regimes are vastly different.

Self-reinforcing growth provides more urgency and matter for moral reflection because its unceasing changes can create new instances of injustice or possibly even worsen existing unjust social conditions. In contrast to a static setting, more is at stake in a rapidly evolving environment where new competing claims clash given the ceaseless shifting of burdens and benefits across society. Moreover, there is need for even greater vigilance in the modern setting of abundance where appropriate accumulation can quickly turn into an inordinate acquisitive ethos characteristic of a Faustian ethics of greed. Given the surfeit of goods and services and the rapid increase in incomes, recent moral teachings consistently warn of a materialist consumerism that is just as, if not more, deleterious as destitution is to integral human development.

On a positive note, the vibrancy of the economy is also a matter of great interest to moral ethicists because of the unique opportunities it presents in alleviating poverty and rectifying injustices. For example, Pius XI and Paul VI see much promise in reforms that are gradually implemented so as not to disrupt the stability of community life, while laying at the same time the groundwork for a more equitable distribution of future streams of income (QA #61; PP #61, #29). There is a pragmatic acknowledgment that it is far easier to redistribute that which is yet to come compared to that which people already possess. Growth in the economy makes this approach a relatively more palatable and politically feasible avenue of amelioration.

In all these cases, the vigor and flux of the modern economy present theological ethics with a new challenge of delineating the continually changing boundaries between proper personal economic gain and rightful social obligations. This is by no means easy. Langholm (1992, 594) describes this tension well:

> [T]here is a development in economic thought, by which the focus gradually shifts from the individual to society, the size of the social product justifying inequalities and imperfections in distribution, pacifying and eventually perverting the sense of personal duty, until the economy comes to be viewed as a system of suprapersonal mechanisms. . . . [A]n element of utilitarian reasoning was reluctantly admitted but vigorously

circumscribed by a deontological element . . . and this incompatibility is the source of a dilemma which always troubled Christian social thought. It is a compromise. It grants the social benefits of man's avarice to a certain extent, while appealing, insistently and consistently, to his benevolence. It looses the reins on forces which it nevertheless desires to control. It admits that property ought to be private in ownership (because this furthers productivity), but insists that it should be common in use (for it is a Christian duty to share).

Given the major changes of the last two centuries, Christian economic ethics confronts a dilemma that is especially acute in the modern period: how to achieve simultaneously the protection of individual well-being while availing of the enormous benefits of a spirited market-driven economy that can improve the lives of people, but only at the expense of traditional institutions. A delicate balance has to be struck between private economic gains and larger community goals, even as we operate within both the promise and the liabilities of the market, the preeminent modern economic institution.[9] The limitations of the market are of particular moral concern given that it is unable to replace the safeguards previously provided by organic hierarchy.

Custom, law, and usage function not only to preserve society but also to protect individuals within the community, as in the case of scholastic just price and the prohibition of usury. In the evolution of the feudal to the industrial economy, the market replaces these protective channels that had so heavily regulated private pecuniary behavior (Polanyi 1944). This presents ethicists with a different set of problems.

The market—formal, institutionalized, and impersonal—cannot replicate the reciprocity and the wide berth that the personal, informal arrangements of conventions are able to make based on the familiarity nurtured by religious, family, and communal bonds. The limitations of the market are fairly well known: it allocates societal resources on the basis of consumer purchasing power without regard for other fundamental criteria such as need, merit, promise, and contribution; it ignores equity and does not make judgments on the propriety and morality of exchange in certain goods and services (such as child pornography and prostitution); it does not provide public and merit goods in sufficient quantities and cannot deal with market failures such as pollution; and it can exclude and marginalize people (Buchanan 1985). Economic institutions, the market in particular, can take a life of their own and crush, rather than ennoble, individuals. Abuses in the early phases of the Industrial Revolution provide vivid examples. Left to its own laws and momentum, the market is unable to weigh larger societal goals outside of maximizing growth. It is also incapable of making exceptions or of incorporating subtleties called for by particular human circumstances.

There is need to continue reaping the fruits of progress through the market economy, while affording, at the same time, avenues through which larger moral ends can be achieved. The dilemma confronting modern economic ethicists is how to avail of the promise of the market while mitigating its limitations. Put in another way, how does one continue to operate in a market setting while retrieving historic safeguards? The task is to find substitute mechanisms because the demise of organic hierarchy disallows the employment of custom, law, and usage *from within* the regular workings of the market. There has to be recourse to extra-market avenues and the articulation of clearly defined rules that set boundaries on what is acceptable in the processes and outcomes of the political economy. The shift (described in preceding sections) from the scholastic focus on the moral quality of individual exchanges to the modern preoccupation with the justness of social structures[10] is a response of theological economic ethics to this dilemma.

Normative Responses

Economic institutions ought to be evaluated according to how well they serve the person. This means having to deliberate on two issues: (1) the obligations owed by the community to the individual, and (2) the limits on what the community may ask of its members. The former is more difficult to implement as it entails the acknowledgment of positive rights; the latter merely requires negative rights (Berlin 1969).

From obligations to rights

The employment of a language of entitlements is necessary in a market economy. In particular, there is need to state explicitly economic rights such as the rights to gainful employment, food, clothing, and other basic necessities (John XXIII, 1963). In the feudal setting, these claims are accepted, indeed expected, because of the unspoken (but understood) informal, customary obligations of extended social ties that make the mutual provision of basic needs the norm of what it is to belong to an extended family and the local community. This is in striking contrast to the modern welfare state where the social safety network is underwritten formally by the government.[11] Thus, it becomes essential to specify precisely the basis, the nature, and the scope of entitlements.

Finally, one must remember that the medieval economy does not produce much of a surplus that would be the object of competing claims. Not so in an era that has been relieved of the Malthusian peril. Agreement on how to apportion superfluity is now a necessity.[12]

Principle of participation

In addition to a greater sensitivity to rights, a new appreciation for the principle of participation is evident.[13] There is less need for such a norm in the feudal community because "to belong" means just to be where you are supposed to be in the "nature of things" through membership in the extended household or the local village. Participation is taken as a *given*. Not so in the modern economy where the degree and quality of people's interpersonal engagement are determined by their ownership of socially valued assets. The greater latitude for personal action afforded by the new economic liberties of the market comes at the expense of a greater risk of isolation.

Shorn of the security provided by established religious, familial, and communal ties, individuals in a modern economy can find themselves completely bereft of any succor. Thus, there is need to specify minimum standards for what constitutes meaningful participation in economic life: gainful employment that provides opportunities for improving one's professional and social standing. The focus is on the person.

Relative equality

The equitable distribution of burdens and benefits across members of the community is another concern. In a feudal setting, inequalities are not only tolerated but are also expected as part of the "nature of things." Each person has a distinct role to fill and is remunerated accordingly through the scholastic just price.

In contrast to this fixed hierarchical division within the community, modern economic ethics views individuals as free moral agents, each sharing in a fundamental longing for a better life and deserving of the opportunity to satisfy such yearning. Inequalities are still deemed to be a normal part of social life, but there is a lower threshold for such legitimate disparities. This shift is best illustrated in the alteration of the understanding of superfluous income. Following the medieval formulation of St. Thomas Aquinas, Leo XIII describes superfluous income as that part of earnings not needed to maintain one's social standing in the community. In contrast, John XXIII defines superfluous income on the basis of others' relative needs (RN #36; GS footnote #10, chapter 3, part II; see also Christiansen 1984).

FROM ANTIPATHY TO ADVOCACY: UNIONS

Normative Shift

Scholars agree that the medieval ethicists are not enthused about unions, guilds, or other alternative work arrangements. On the few occasions these are mentioned at all, the treatment is either one of censure or wary accommodation. As de Roover observes:

> [T]he Doctors rarely mention the guilds and then only to reprove them
> for their monopolistic practices. I do not find evidence in their treatises

that they favored the guild system, which is so often pictured as an ideal organization for Christian society or is recommended as a panacea against the evils of modern industrialism (de Roover [1955] 1974c, 186; see also de Roover 1974b, 336–45 and Friedman 1980, 238–39).

This aversion is born out of a longstanding condemnation of monopolies (and by extension, of oligopolistic and monopsonistic practices) that dates as far back as Greek and Roman economic thought.[14] This is not to say that there are few instances of abused workers at that time. Nor could it be said that scholastics are unaware of these; they are (Kirshner 1974a, 26; de Roover 1974b, 340). But even in cases where there is a clear need for worker protection, forming worker associations as a defensive measure is not encouraged. Instead, the scholastics seek to redress these injustices by simply appealing to the moral sensibilities of employers.

> Employers were warned by Bernardine against exploiting workers by paying them less than the going rate; conversely, workers were warned against organizing in order to seek benefits and higher wages. . . . [T]he worker was so often eager for a job that he would accept a starvation wage (*Hungerlohn*) just barely adequate to support himself and his family. Antonine [St. Antoninus] pleaded with employers to pay a fair wage, but he was adamantly opposed, as were all the Schoolmen, to unionization (Kirshner 1974a, 26).

Even guilds themselves threaten to blacklist workers and artificers under their jurisdiction who attempt to organize labor unions.[15] There is a suspicion, if not outright disapproval, of anything that approaches rings or conspiracies that could disadvantage buyers, whom the scholastics view as the more vulnerable party in the medieval marketplace.

In contrast to the scholastic aversion toward organized labor, modern Catholic social documents have not only consistently championed the cause of unions but have also proposed alternative work arrangements. This 180-degree turn is most plainly illustrated by *Quadragesimo Anno*'s (Pius XI, 1931) call for a reconstituted social order with some features borrowed from medieval guilds (QA #88–98). How do we account for this shift from antipathy to advocacy? The change in economic arrangements dislodges the formal and informal safeguards for worker welfare embedded in the medieval economic order. In the modern economy, these lost protective structures have had to be replaced by nonmarket mechanisms.

Economic Explanations

Several factors account for this shift in attitudes toward organized labor. First, there is very little thought given to production in economic theory prior to the Industrial Revolution (Langholm 1987, 117; Schumpeter 1954, 101). Little is said about work arrangements and other labor issues. This lack of interest is understandable since production up to that point is primarily home-based and, therefore, traditionally organized and managed according to household customs. Economic thought and ethics concentrate primarily on exchange (and mostly on exchange for consumption) as this is the principal avenue for moral conflicts in economic life.

Second, in the little exchange for production that does occur, there is adequate labor protection through the guilds, the scholastic just price, and the more informal channels of moral suasion that minimize the abusive treatment of workers. There is no need to deal formally with work arrangements as a separate issue.

The shift from a feudal to a modern market economy leads to changes in these social conditions such that questions pertaining to production management and organization have to be directly and separately addressed. Traditional channels of safeguarding worker or producer well-being are lost and have to be replaced. The specialization and division of labor spawned by industrialization expand exchange for production (intermediate goods and services) and widen the distance between economic agents, with the consequent loss of informal channels (religious, familial, and communal ties) that have previously set boundaries for private economic behavior.

Loss of Formal Channels

The convergence of commutative and distributive justice in scholastic economic ethics means that fairness is simultaneously achieved in both the product and the input markets through the same instrument–the price. After all, the just price paid in the medieval product market is based on the common estimation of the income needed by producers (the labor market) to live up to their social role. The shift toward allocative efficiency in the modern market economy breaks this automatic link between factor and product market pricing. As a consequence, laborers now have to fend for a living wage for themselves separate from the product market even as the economy's objective moves away from equity toward efficiency. Achieving a living wage for workers while satisfying the requirements of growth and efficiency is a rare accomplishment in the modern economy. Unlike medieval workers, modern laborers cannot depend on the workings of product market pricing alone to assure them of such a wage.

In contrast to modern Catholic social ethicists, the scholastic doctors are not compelled by economic conditions to support the cause of unions or alternative work arrangements. After all, in spite of the moralists' misgivings about the legitimate role of organized labor in the social order, guilds do, in fact, relieve the scholastics of the need to address worker safeguards. These medieval associations fend quite well for their affiliates. Organized in terms of skills, crafts, and trades (analogous to modern-day labor unions), guilds are effective in protecting the common interests and promoting the economic well-being of their members (as are unions). Furthermore, they serve as self-help, mutual-aid alliances and as channels for sociopolitical participation and public service within the larger community (which are other ideal functions of unions). Finally, guild members are working for themselves (thereby addressing some of the modern proposals for co-management, co-ownership, and profit sharing in work arrangements). Guilds, even as they are viewed with great suspicion, paradoxically provide many of the features greatly sought today by social reformers. The demise of guilds as part of the evolution into the modern economy creates a gap in worker safeguards that modern economic ethics must fill. In discussing the value, functions, and rights of unions, *Rerum Novarum* and *Quadragesimo Anno* articulate a desire to gain back some of the positive attributes of medieval work organizations that have been lost with the change from feudalism to the factory system.

Loss of Informal Channels

Despite the modern reliance on demand and supply (instead of custom, law, and usage), it is still possible to preserve the end of scholastic just price theory (equitable income distribution) without recourse to formal methods of overriding the market. Mutual goodwill on the part of economic agents could lead to an adequate income for everyone. After all, the market price is merely indicative, not imperative; one may choose to pay more for goods and services out of one's sense of fairness, honor, or charity.

The nature and dynamics of exchange in the modern economy work against retrieving even these informal channels. The specialization and division of labor as part of industrial organization have put an ever greater distance between the producer and the end user. Unlike economic agents in the preindustrial economy, the consumer and the manufacturer in the modern era are separated from each other by multiple tiers of transactions with intermediate producers and distributors in between.

The medieval proximity between the end user and the producer works toward internalizing compliance with the principle of just price.[16] Where buyers and sellers deal with their own neighbors, friends, or relatives, the commercial transaction is merely a small (and most likely relatively insignificant) part of a much larger multidimensional relationship among people who depend on each other for support in many other spheres. Mutual dependence in medieval relationships most likely engenders a strong moral incentive to pay a fair price out of a sense of empathy or to avoid fracturing relationships or maybe just to save face. These incentives lend weight and efficacy to custom, law, and usage even when formal enforcement mechanisms are inadequate or absent. People know what is expected of them and what to expect of others.[17] This natural check is lost in a modern economy where exchange has become not only impersonal but also purely commercial. In the current global economy's cornucopia of goods, most consumers cannot empathize with, much less think about, the remote Third World workers who produce the shoes or the clothes they wear. Paul VI (1967, #47) expresses the crux of the matter well in asking First World consumers whether they would be willing to pay higher prices for imports to afford better pay for overseas workers. Formal nonmarket mechanisms of price supports have become necessary in the face of anonymous exchanges in modern economic life.[18]

The medieval treatment of employees, more as members of the master's extended household[19] than as strangers, is a second valuable informal channel of moral suasion that is lost with the shift of economic production from country cottages to urban factories. The medieval extended household is the basic unit of production, even in the proto-industrialization that precedes the modern economy. Home-based production means the unity of the household and the workplace. Whether in rural cottage industries or in the guilds, it is common for the master, the apprentices, and the journeymen to live in the same household, which doubles as the workplace. The move to factory-based production spells the demise of this household-workplace nexus; it also means that workers set up their own independent households (Rosenberg and Birdzell 1986, 152–53). The familiarity and the ties that come with living under the same roof are lost. This distancing between workers and employers accelerates the depersonalization of labor market relations. The association between workers and employers becomes a purely business transaction, thereby diminishing the chances of a greater solicitude of employers for their workers.

The loss of this informal channel is made worse by the regimen that the modern market imposes on the employer in rationalizing production for efficiency, a discipline that makes the workers' position even more uncertain and vulnerable. In medieval agrarian life, where land and labor are the two key factors of production, the role of labor is secure; its contribution is readily apparent. The treatment of workers may not have been always fair when it comes to dividing the produce between rent (landowner) and wages (workers), but all parties recognize that the land's bounty is clearly a function of labor. This changes.

In the modern economy, the factors of production are land, labor, and capital. Labor may not always be necessarily perceived as the crucial or the most productive factor. This role has often been ascribed to capital, with unfavorable consequences in the short term for the share of labor in social output. The standing of workers becomes more precarious in proportion to their diminished power in an economy where labor now faces competition from capital for the role of the most significant factor of production. In fact, capital has been pivotal in raising the productivity of workers in the modern economy. While there may be competition in the short run when it comes to the division of output, in the long run, capital is beneficial in improving standards of living. This is a key explanation to the industrial economy's ability to support more people and at a higher standard of living.

Consequences

These shifts in economic life require greater vigilance in ensuring gainful employment and decent working conditions for workers within the unfettered operations of the industrial economy. The atomization of the economic agent in the industrial era and the modern pursuit of private economic gain make it difficult for individuals to retrieve and internalize for themselves an ethos that values relationships in economic behavior. The personal touch is lost as interactions among economic actors become anonymous, institutionalized, and impersonal. This makes it easy to treat other economic agents as means (as factors of production), rather than as ends and as the subject of work (John Paul II 1981). Consequently, modern Catholic social documents have had to call repeatedly for a wide array of nonmarket measures to ameliorate the plight of workers that include minimum wage legislation, a living wage, government assistance, unionization and mutual self-help associations, industry-level vocational groupings of employers and workers as partners in decision making, and alternative work arrangements (profit sharing, co-ownership, and co-management of the means of production). Economic ethicists have had to find substitutes for the safeguards that had been provided previously by formal and informal mechanisms of the medieval economic order.

A TRANSFORMED TERRAIN FOR PRIVATE ECONOMIC GAIN

Earlier thinking on the place of private economic enrichment in moral life has been reformulated. It is understandable to see why patristic and scholastic writers frown on the pursuit of personal economic gain as this would mean leaving that much less for others in a subsistence economy. A logical extension of this is their antipathy toward trade which they deem to have no real contribution to society and is, therefore, undeserving of any remuneration.[20]

> To seek to enrich one's-self [sic] was . . . in itself unjust, since it aimed at appropriating an unfair share of what God had intended for the common use of men. . . . "If covetousness is removed," argues Tertullian, "there is no reason for gain, and, if there is no reason for gain, there is no need of trade." Moreover, as the trader did not seem himself to add to the value of his wares, if he gained more for them than he had paid, his gain, said S. Jerome, must be another's loss (Ashley 1925, I:128–29).

The end of economic activity is the sustenance of people in their station in life. Anything over and above this is immoral hoarding that deprives others of what is rightfully theirs.

> To the medieval theologian an "eagerness for gain," beyond that neces-sary to maintain a man in his rank in life, was in itself avarice. . . . But if the pursuit of wealth for its own sake was sinful, how were the ordinary activities of life to be justified? The answer to this question was given by another dominant idea of medieval thinkers—the ideal of status or class. Men . . . had been placed by God in ranks or orders, each with its own work to do, and each with own appropriate mode of life. That gain was justified, and that only which was sought in order that a man might pro-vide for himself a fit sustenance in his own rank. . . . With the canonists, this idea of class duties and class standard of comfort is either explicitly or implicitly referred to as the final test in every question of distribution or exchange. . . . [T]heir only just claim to their [referring to the lords of land] rents is founded on their fulfilling the duties of their class, and rightly governing and protecting those subject to them (Ashley 1925, II:388–93).[21]

The economic root of this moral teaching is obvious: severe scarcity in the medieval world. This is an example of how economics can shape ethical thinking. However, the reverse is also true where moral norms modify economic processes and outcomes. In particular, the patristic-medieval teaching of restricting economic gain according to one's station in life exacerbates the languid state of the premodern economy by cir-cumscribing the scope of private initiative. This holds back even further a frail economic life that is already hampered by the lack of tools, inno-vation, and mobility.

The central importance of private initiative today has altered norma-tive thinking on the limits and the ends of personal gain. In the first place, the scholastic standard of "what is needed to maintain one's sta-tion in life" has been replaced by choice in career selection and social status. The individual's place in society is no longer taken as a given but is itself the subject of personal decision that flows from the natural right of self-determination.

Second, an increase in one's consumption in the modern economy need not inevitably come at the expense of others' unmet needs. An ex-panding societal output can provide enough for all as seen in the greater numbers of people supported by the economy at a higher standard of liv-ing (Rosenberg and Birdzell 1986).

Third, in contrast to the rudimentary capital markets of the pre-modern era, the contemporary economy has many legitimate uses to which privately owned surplus can be used to benefit others in creating employment opportunities (QA #50–51; CA #36d). The growth in the productive uses of such funds, the availability of new instruments, and the continued integration of financial markets have established fresh avenues for living up to the *just-use* obligations of property ownership by making it easier to put privately generated surplus at the disposal and use of others. This shift is reflected in the new appreciation for the value and legitimacy of pursuing personal economic gain:

> *[T]he right of economic initiative* . . . is a right which is important not only for the individual but also for the common good. Experience shows us that the denial of this right, or its limitation in the name of an alleged "equality" of everyone in society, diminishes, or in practice absolutely destroys the spirit of initiative, that is to say *the creative subjectivity of the citizen* (SRS #15b, emphasis in the original).

> It is precisely the ability to foresee both the needs of others and the combinations of productive factors most adapted to satisfying those needs that constitutes another important source of wealth in modern society. . . . Organizing such a productive effort, planning its duration in time, making sure that it corresponds in a positive way to the demands which it must satisfy and taking the necessary risks—all this too is a source of wealth in today's society. In this way the role of disciplined and creative human work and, as an essential part of that work, initiative and entrepreneurial ability becomes increasingly evident and decisive (CA #32b).

The wide availability of economic opportunities in the wake of industrialization has turned the pursuit of personal gain and advancement into a real service for the rest of the community. In contrast to the earlier disapproval of trade and entrepreneurship, investment is now viewed as a moral decision that can produce much good.

> [I]t is not a matter of the duty of charity alone, that is, the duty to give from one's "abundance," and sometimes even out of one's needs, in order to provide what is essential for the life of a poor person. I am referring to the fact that even the decision to invest in one place rather than another, in one productive sector rather than another, is always *a moral and cultural choice*. . . . [T]he decision to invest, that is, to offer people an opportunity to make good use of their own labor, is also determined by an attitude of human sympathy and trust in Providence, which reveal the human quality of the person making such decisions (CA #36d, emphasis in the original).

SUMMARY AND CONCLUSIONS

Viner (1978, 49) has described the state of Catholic economic ethics at the time of the Industrial Revolution as "largely frozen in its medieval shell" with little movement in economic morality from the end of scholasticism to 1891.[22] *Rerum Novarum* and the legacy of the social documents it spawned articulate a new vision of a just Christian society attuned to the needs of the modern economy. In fact, Langholm's (1992, 565) description of the scholastic doctors' efforts may also be a fitting characterization of modern Catholic social documents: "By a common denominator we may perhaps describe the economic doctrines of the medieval theologians as a set of compromises, codes of economic conduct which must be operational while abandoning as little as possible of the Christian vision of society." This chapter has examined some of these adaptations, together with the causes that may have given rise to them.

The transformation of feudalism into the modern industrial economy is both a cause and an effect of custom, law, and usage relinquishing to suprapersonal economic institutions the role of setting prices. Price has a dual function, namely: (1) It provides timely information essential to the efficient allocation of scarce resources to their competing uses (its allocative dimension), and (2) It influences the distribution of factor incomes through the revenues that goods and services can generate (its distributive dimension). The medieval subsistence economy is more concerned with the distributional nature of pricing, evident in the social-status approach in scholastic literature. In contrast, the modern economy of growth has been preoccupied with the informational-allocative function of price both in theory and in practice. Thus, the convergence of commutative and distributive justice in the scholastic formulation of just price has, in effect, been broken.

In the circumstances of industrial modernity, distributive justice has had to find an avenue of its own outside of market processes. This search for nonmarket, nonprice mechanisms to safeguard distributive justice is one difference between scholastic economic teachings and the economic ethics advanced in modern Catholic social documents. Besides, medieval ecclesiastical enforcement mechanisms have had to be replaced by regulative strategies that ensure the justness of contemporary economic structures. While just price and usury are the leading concerns of scholastic normative economics, recent ethical thought has focused primarily on the morality of social processes and outcomes in the face of the Smithian *invisible hand.*

Joseph Finkelstein and Alfred Thimm (1973, 11) claim that it is not technological progress that precipitates the most radical modification of economic life from feudalism to modern industry. It is rather the transformation of our self-understanding of what it is to live as a community that has been the more decisive factor behind change: "the alteration of the view of society–from a world of harmonies within a harmonious universe to a world of Faustian competition." This chapter suggests otherwise. It is a radically transformed market-driven economic life that induces a shift away from the organic hierarchical vision of society.

Theological social ethics has had to keep pace and respond to the transformation of economic life by shifting its conception of social life from that rooted in an organic hierarchy to one that is steeped in rights language. In scholastic thought, everyone has an appointed, fixed function to discharge, and the emphasis is on the obligations attendant to fulfilling one's designated station in life. In contrast, modern social ethics employs a human rights model in according a great premium to purposeful participation, relative equality, and the protection of the individual from unjust social structures.

The medieval organic hierarchy is rooted in the experience of an economy of precarious subsistence. It is a static existence with little to spare; the overriding concern is survival where all are expected to do their share toward providing for the material needs of the community. The extraordinary growth and vibrancy of modern industry recast the fundamental economic problem with wide-ranging implications for moral reflection. The market economy of self-sustaining growth spells the death knell for the organic hierarchy paradigm. In a world of low-level stagnation and a precarious economic balance with not much cushion or surplus against unforseen setbacks, the medieval economy is principally concerned with achieving a modicum of stability and predictability within the given social order. Hence, the stress and focus are on ensuring a distribution of income that preserves the cohesion of the hierarchical order. In contrast, efficiency is the principal object of the modern economy of growth.

Changed economic conditions remove the need for such an inflexible conception of social life. The modern market is founded on individual freedoms, especially the liberty of pursuing private gain and improvement. It is rooted in an individual autonomy characterized by mobility—social, geographic, and occupational. Equally important, the means have now been furnished to nurture and sustain such individual autonomy. Surplus means relief from the pressing need to ensure personal and communal preservation; it paves the way for moving further toward measures that improve the quality of life including changing social structures and institutions. Economic history can go a long way in helping us better understand and appreciate the demise of the medieval hierarchical vision of the social order and its replacement by individual rights as an organizing principle of theological economic ethics.

Economic history cannot be taken out of its larger epochal context. In particular, one must note that the Enlightenment's "turn to the subject" fosters the modern confidence in the autonomy and power of human reason and radically changes attitudes regarding the mutability of social institutions. Consequently, the changes in economic terrain just examined cannot be viewed as the sole nor necessarily the most decisive factors behind the observed shifts in economic ethics. However, what this exposition on the transformation of the economy does accomplish is to present an analysis of why the scholastic just price is untenable in the industrial era. Moreover, it argues the case for why there are economic reasons for contemporary ethicists to be genuinely concerned about the ability of current socioeconomic institutions to fulfill the requirements of distributive justice. Economic history and theory can be employed fruitfully to enhance our understanding of the specific mechanisms by which ethical reflection evolves in its continuing accommodation of the rapid changes in economic life.

Notes

1. Viner (1978, 50) writes: "The Scholastics . . . recognized in some measure that virtue has social implications, but in the main they confined their discussion . . . [to] questions of commutative justice arising from transactions between individuals in the ordinary course of their worldly life. *They said almost nothing about the impact of individual behavior on social institutions, or the impact of social institutions on individual behavior, or the possibilities of deliberate or spontaneous remoulding of existing institutions"* (emphasis added). Langholm (1982, 271) observes that this is also true of patristic literature: "The idea that terms of exchange are determined by suprapersonal forces which extenuate moral blame on the individual level was essentially foreign to ethical thinking at least until well into the sixteenth century. The patristic focus, even in the case of issues carrying broad social implications, was on immediate personal relations." For further discussion of this stress on personal behavior rather than on social institutions, see Langholm (1992, 566), Tawney (1926), and Worland (1967).

2. I am treating the manor as the basic productive economic unit. One could, of course, view manorial life as a series of exchanges: the serfs rendering their labor (work week) and tithes to the lord of the manor in exchange for protection. Furthermore, there are also merchants who are engaged in the buying and selling of goods for commercial profit. Such trades are, however, a relatively small part of the predominantly subsistence nature of the medieval economy.

3. Even usury itself may be considered a subset of teachings on the just price. Since money is deemed to produce no value on its own, its price is set at zero. The shift and nuances in the teachings on usury are not addressed in this analysis since these have already been the subject of extensive analysis and debate in the literature. See, for example, Dempsey (1943) and Noonan (1957).

4. See also Baldwin (1959) and Worland (1967, 289, note 10 and chapter 8).

5. To avoid falling for the fallacy of division, one must qualify this generalization by acknowledging that aggregated statistics do not always present the complete picture. Parts of sub-Saharan Africa, for example, have descended into even deeper poverty in the past two decades (World Bank 1991).

6. In fact, Barone (1935), von Mises (1935) and Lange (1936/37) present theoretical arguments on the necessity of the allocative function of price even in a command economy.

7. A sample of such cases and an extensive bibliography on the role of such courts in economic life can be found in Viner (1978, 16).

8. Langholm (1987, 118) observes, "[T]here was a tendency in scholastic thought to accept the social order and invite poor and rich alike to view their God-given roles as opportunities to exercise Christian virtues: humility and self-denial on the part of the former, charity and compassion on the part of the latter." See also Hollenbach (1979, 54–55, 92–93).

9. Whether one can achieve this balance while holding on to an organic model is an issue that needs further examination. For example, Waterman (1999) notes the tension between the underlying organic vision of community within the tradition and the implicit assumption of spontaneous order under-girding markets.

10. See Langholm (1982, 271; 1992, 566), Schumpeter (1954, 102), and Viner (1978, 50).

11. This is not to downplay the significant role of private philanthropy today. The critical point being made here is the formalization of a substantial part of these traditional income transfers. Cipolla (1976, 20–23) estimates that transfers to the poor may have amounted to more than one percent of GNP in preindustrial Europe, a figure far higher than current levels.

12. Wealthier countries, on the whole, have well-developed, clearly defined and well-articulated entitlements in their welfare programs compared to struggling poor countries. After all, there is not much to distribute in the latter.

13. This is seen in *Rerum Novarum*'s fight for unions as venues of collective action for workers, in *Quadragesimo Anno*'s call for industry-level vocational groupings, in *Mater et Magistra*'s concern for farmers left out of the process of development, in the repeated calls for alternative work arrangements that give workers some say in the decisions that most affect them, and in the repeated appeals of *Populorum Progressio, Sollicitudo Rei Socialis,* and *Centesimus Annus* for overseas assistance that allows poor nations to be the agents of their own development.

14. The scholastics' wariness of monopolies is said to have carried over all the way to Adam Smith through the influence of Samuel von Pufendorf and Hugo Grotius. See Kirshner (1974a, 21–22).

15. Sometimes the punishment is even death. See de Roover ([1951] 1974a, 284–85).

16. Recall W. Ashley's (1925, I:138) observation that the bulk of medieval exchanges is between the consumer and the actual producer.

17. This is not to claim that such self-imposed restraints are always operative in the medieval economy. Numerous examples of local government regulation of prices, especially of necessities, suggest a problem of profiteering. Voluntary compliance obviously operates better in closely knit, smaller communities where economic actors could not disappear into the anonymity of the larger urban concentrations.

18. For example, there are agricultural subsidies and international commodity stabilization funds for some key Third World exports.

19. This, of course, is by no means always the case for the period. In fact, the increasingly severe subjection of workers ultimately leads to the decay and demise of the guilds (Renard 1918, 109–10).

20. St. Thomas Aquinas acknowledges that there are instances when merchants do provide valuable service for the preservation of the commonweal. See de Roover (1974b, 336–45).

21. See also Archibald (1949–50) and Viner (1978, 62–66). Viner questions this characterization of scholastic disapproval for individuals striving to raise their social status. He notes that there are few citations that directly support this interpretation of medieval teaching. According to de Roover (1974b, 340–41), Cajetan believes that individuals are not confined to their social status by birth. It

would not have been greed to advance to a rank in society commensurate with their virtues or achievements.

22. Schumpeter (1954, 73–106) describes scholastic economics as spanning from the ninth century to the seventeenth century, the eve of the Industrial Revolution.

Part III

CONTRAST WITH NORMATIVE MAINSTREAM ECONOMIC THOUGHT

Having examined the differences between the modern Catholic social documents and scholastic economic teachings in the preceding two chapters, I now turn to a comparison of this theological social tradition with the predominant strands of thought in economics. Are there grounds for comparing Catholic social teachings on political economy with contemporary mainstream economic thinking and policy? Positive and normative economics must be distinguished. These theological social documents do not claim to offer alternative, or even scientific, models with which to interpret, explain, and forecast economic phenomena. Rather, they are normative in advancing what they believe are the essential conditions for a just economic order. On the other hand, economic thought has both normative and positive content. W. Senior, John N. Keynes, and Lionel Robbins view economics as a strict science; ethics is not properly within the scope of the discipline. They stress the positive side of economics that provides a straightforward descriptive explanation, modeling, and prediction of economic outcomes.

The line between the positive and the normative is not always distinct, and readers are rarely advised when such separation is breached.[1] Economic theorizing that starts off as a descriptive exercise can and does end up as policy prescriptions. For example, Adam Smith's (1776) assessment of disparities in the sources of national wealth is ultimately a critique of mercantilism. Ricardo's abstract modeling eventually winds up as an argument for the abolition of poor laws.[2] The same is true with other schools of thought such as socialism's steadfast rejection of the right to private

117

property ownership and classical liberalism's insistence on a laissez-faire approach to conducting economic affairs. Other examples include Keynesianism in the immediate post–World War II era and the reemergent classical school in the Chicago economics of unfettered markets.

Of greater concern, however, is the claim that there is no purely positive economics because personal values influence the choice of questions to address, the dimensions to highlight, the data to measure, and the simplifying assumptions to use in modeling. Thus, it is difficult, if not impossible, to distinguish *what is* from *what ought to be*. For example, Malthus ([1798] 1958) offers a descriptive theory of the economic order. However, animating the dynamics of his celebrated theory of population is his view that poverty is self-inflicted through people's proclivity to procreate to the point of destitution. Not surprisingly, he is critical of poor relief laws. Other illustrations of this blurred distinction can be readily found in population and fertility studies. Are the poor destitute because of their high fertility rates, or are their large families a consequence of their poverty? In other words, is fertility properly an endogenous or an exogenous variable? The approach to these questions, fraught with sweeping policy implications, depends on one's views on the direction of causation (Schultz 1988). The difficulty of separating the descriptive from the normative is also evident in the management of the adjustment and stabilization programs in developing countries.[3]

This is not the place to rehearse the issues surrounding the question of whether there exists a purely positive economics or a completely value-free social science for that matter.[4] It is sufficient for our purposes to note that not only are there grounds for a comparative assessment of the normative content of economics, but there is also an identifiable body of literature that, by the discipline's own admission, lies in the normative realm: welfare economics.

And what are the warrants for Catholic social thought to put forth its vision of what ought to be? The same as everybody else's. As the economist J. N. Keynes puts it, what is seen in economic phenomena need not be accepted as immutable and inevitable. They are subject to deliberate change and modification on the part of economic agents.[5] In addition, most economists concede that the principles and propositions of economics require insights from the other human sciences before they can be put to practical application. Aside from proponents of economic determinism, few scholars accept the discipline as a complete explanation of economic life. Most admit that standard economic analysis is partial at best because it restricts itself to a vision of reality seen only through the spectacles of *homo oeconomicus*. This self-imposed limitation is accepted because of the belief that it is all that is required of the economist; other disciplines will have to pick up from where positive economics leaves off. Adam Smith, Mill, and Marshall, among others, acknowledge the importance of accounting for a wide variety of factors in explaining economic phenomena and in formulating appropriate policies for the promotion of society's interests (Flubacher 1950, 105–06, 140–41, 317). Even Robbins's ([1932] 1949) means-ends approach has to accept the incomplete nature of economics as a science since the selection of ends is believed to lie outside the scope of the discipline.

Catholic social thought is one such effort that brings to bear extra-economic considerations in the assessment of the economic order. In juxtaposing these church teachings with normative economic thought, I contrast the policy prescriptions and modes of behavior proposed by economic thinkers against theological insights on the human person's transcendent nature and end. Of course, such a comparison is also an opportunity to examine Catholic social teachings on the political economy against economic theory and history. Examples of this latter exercise are found in the preceding two chapters on the evolution of this tradition and in the appendix on the economic risks of *Quadragesimo Anno*'s corporatism.

In what follows, I use "mainstream economics" to refer to the standard economics that is widely taught as a science of means-ends (Robbins [1932] 1949) along the lines of instrumental rationality where the economic agent maximizes goals subject to constraints. Given a perfectly competitive market, a judicious, cost-efficient allocation of limited means leads to a Pareto optimality where no one can be made better off without rendering somebody else worse off (Ferguson and Gould 1975; Hargreaves Heap 1989). Chapter 6 is a quick overview of economic thought on the nature of the human person, and it is written for the noneconomist as a background preparation for contrasting modern Catholic social teachings and mainstream economic thought. Readers already familiar with the philosophical underpinnings of traditional economics may choose to skip directly to the comparison in chapter 7.

Notes

1. There is considerable disagreement over whether a purely positive economics is possible at all. See Weston (1994) for a quick survey of the question.
2. Flubacher (1950, 122–23, 129); see O'Brien (1975) for other classical economists and their normative prescriptions.
3. Fiscal and external balances are the primary criteria used for most adjustment programs in the Third World. Failure to account for extra-economic goals precipitates even greater suffering among the poor in many adjustment programs. See Cornia, Jolly, and Stewart (1987).
4. See Hausman and McPherson (1996) for a critique of the neoclassical claim of value neutrality.

5. J. N. Keynes (1891, 43) notes: "Economic phenomena depend upon the activity of free agents, whose customary behaviour may be modified not merely by legislative interference, but also by changes in their own moral standard, or in the social pressure brought to bear upon them by public opinion, and it follows that, in general, we are not justified in assuming finality in regard to concrete industrial facts, or in affirming that, in the economic world, *what is, must be*" (emphasis added).

Chapter 6

ANTHROPOLOGICAL PRESUPPOSITIONS IN ECONOMIC THOUGHT

INTRODUCTION

Examining the key differences between modern Catholic social teachings and mainstream economic thought requires a comparison of their premises on the nature of the human person. Economists themselves acknowledge that such suppositions have a direct bearing on economic theorizing and policymaking (Flubacher 1950, 219, footnote 165).

> [T]he science of economics was founded upon the assumption of a human nature so construed as to give rise to "truck, barter, and exchange," the division of labor, enlightened self-interest, . . . in short, a conception of human nature of which the pecuniary system seemed to be a natural expression. Any critical discussion of the classical principles of political economy must therefore take cognizance of the theory of human nature from which those principles emerged. . . . Whatever its form and preconceptions, economics is necessarily a description, an analysis, and even it may be a prediction of human behavior; and consequently it cannot avoid being affected by any important development in the study of human nature (Ayres 1936, 224).

These anthropological axioms determine the nature and direction of research and define the boundaries of the questions posed for examination.[1] They are foundational to the subject of economic analysis so much so that changes in the formulation of these postulates necessarily cause corresponding alterations in the discipline's theories and predictions.

121

The need to probe these premises also arises from the concern that these assumptions, originally meant to simplify economic analysis, can eventually become self-fulfilling in reshaping people's conduct.[2] What started as a positive, value-free exercise can and does end up altering the individual's set of values, desires, and behavior.[3] The modeling exercise of consumer maximization can lead people to adopt the simplifying axioms of *homo oeconomicus* as normative. Moreover, the classical school's anthropological assumptions have been described as a means of justifying the economic practices of its time as moral, particularly the institutions of private property and the free market.[4]

The perceived materialism and impersonalism of the social order flow partly from classical liberalism's role as the philosophical underpinning of modern economics. To understand contemporary mainstream economic thinking, it is necessary to examine its origins in the context of the Enlightenment. This is the intellectual milieu that fosters the emergence of the discipline as a legitimate autonomous field separate from moral philosophy. This period eschews natural law and metaphysical speculative deliberations in favor of the precise logic of science and mathematics. Moreover, its turn to the subject spawns a newfound confidence in the rational powers of the human person.

Paul Streeten (1954) submits that the three legacies from the classical school are (1) liberalism with its advocacy of laissez faire, that is, complete individual autonomy and freedom in economic life with a minimum of government intervention; (2) utilitarianism with its call for the maximization of social happiness; and (3) the harmony of interest doctrine with its belief that private and public interests coincide automatically. Within this school are the eighteenth- and nineteenth-century English economists such as Adam Smith, Malthus, Bentham, Ricardo, Mill, Senior, and J. E. Cairnes. Classical liberalism is sometimes referred to as old or early liberalism in order to contrast it with the later liberalism of the nineteenth century, which is more amenable to government intervention in the economy.

Mainstream economics situates the discipline within the mechanistic operation of a Newtonian world that lends itself to a scientific study devoid of normative considerations. Legacies from eighteenth- and nineteenth-century economic thought on the nature of the human person include self-interested behavior, the *homo oeconomicus* model, and utilitarianism. To a large extent, these philosophical foundations have shaped the view of the human person that has persisted throughout the evolution of economic thought, namely: that the individual is a rational calculating economic agent interested only in maximizing the satisfaction of personal preferences. This makes it easier to perpetuate the earlier association of economics with mere wealth accumulation and diminishes an appreciation for the place of equity and justice in the economic order.

SELF-INTERESTED BEHAVIOR

Adam Smith's invisible hand undergirds the market's much-touted unique capacity for generating allocative efficiency. Key to this, however, are two assumptions on human nature: the person's acquisitive drive and propensity to trade. Both of these are grounded, in turn, on self-interest. These have become foundational for modern economics.

1. *On the acquisitive drive*

[T]he desire for bettering our condition ... comes with us from the womb and never leaves us until we go to the grave. ... An augmentation of fortune is the means by which the greater part of men propose and wish to better their condition (Smith [1776] 1937, book II, chap. III, 324–25).

Every individual is continually exerting himself to find out the most advantageous employment for whatever capital he can command. It is his own advantage, indeed, and not that of the society, which he has in view (Smith [1776] 1937, book IV, chapter II, 421).

2. *On the propensity to trade*

[A] certain propensity in human nature . . . the propensity to truck, barter, and exchange one thing for another (Smith [1776] 1937, book I, chapter II, 13).

This individual self-love leads to the promotion of the public good through a "natural harmony of interests."

It is not from the benevolence of the butcher, the brewer, or the baker, that we expect our dinner, but from their regard to their own interest. We address ourselves, not to their humanity but to their self-love, and never talk to them of our own necessities but of their advantages (Smith [1776] 1937, book I, chapter II, 14).

These observations have led to the view that people are motivated principally by self-interest and, given free reign to act in such manner, individuals automatically promote the public good as well. This, of course, is nothing new since Bernard de Mandeville's *The Fable of the Bees* already argues that private vices such as pride, indulgence, and avarice are beneficial to the public at large in the way they build up the national wealth and foster social and economic development.

The association of Adam Smith merely with self-interested behavior and the unfettered operation of the market is a selective reading of his works. In the first place, he is cognizant of nonselfish motives in human behavior, having written at length on the subject of sympathy. Second, if one were to be a purist, Adam Smith does not fully meet the principal characteristics of a classical liberal economist. He has a metaphysical and theological frame of reference that is evident in his natural harmony of interests theory. He is not utilitarian, although he is strongly in favor of individualism. He sees the need to incorporate noneconomic considerations if economic principles are to be properly put into practice. At any rate, regardless of whether *The Wealth of Nations* has been read accurately or not, the self-interested behavior of atomistic economic agents in the modern economy is generally ascribed to Adam Smith.

Marx accepts the conception of the person as self-interested. However, he arrives at a completely different conclusion because unlike Smith, who held to a natural harmony of interests, Marx sees self-interest as destructive. Instead of leading to the promotion of the public good, self-interest inevitably results in immiserization.

Note that there are economic thinkers who take altruistic motives into account. Philip Henry Wicksteed sees no reason to limit economics to commercial transactions alone since the discipline lends itself to the analysis of anything that has to do with allocating scarce means and resources (including time) to achieve goals. Furthermore, he argues that economics need not be the science of selfishness since people enter into exchange transactions without necessarily having selfish motives. The only necessary condition for an economic relationship is to have an arms-length transaction, that is, for parties to pursue their own agenda, and not that of their trading partners. This can be anything, selfish or altruistic (Lutz and Lux 1988, 56).

Other economists question the realism of characterizing rational economic behavior as the pursuit of one's own interests.[5] Marshall's views on economic rationality are also a relevant contribution.[6] It is a common mistake to associate economic rationality with the promotion of self-interest. The only necessary condition of rationality is consistency in the choice of alternatives in the person's preference ordering. If A is preferred to B, which in turn is preferred to C, there will never be a case where C will be chosen in favor of either A or B, or B chosen in favor of A. Nonselfish motives can be accommodated in the basic economic tools of analysis.

Sen (1979) critiques even the concept of rationality as consistency of choices, which has become standard for traditional formulations of human behavior. Such notion implies that people have a single all-purpose preference ordering to which they strictly adhere without fail, in whatever circumstance they may find themselves and regardless of any new considerations they may have for the subject matter on hand. The person, in effect, does not recognize the need for making distinctions. "The *purely* economic man is indeed close to being a social moron" (Sen 1979, 102, emphasis in the original). Hence, the title of *Rational Fools* for Sen's classic contribution.

Sen argues for a new approach: allowing commitment on the part of economic agents instead of relying solely on egotistical formulations. Commitment goes a step further than sympathy; the latter refers to empathy and could be accommodated in economic analysis as an externality. Commitment, on the other hand, is where a person deliberately makes a choice that leads to an inferior personal welfare compared to the other available choices. In other words, commitment allows for self-sacrifice.

> [C]ommitment does involve, in a very real sense, counterpreferential choice, destroying the crucial assumption that a chosen alternative must be better than (or at least as good as) the others for the person choosing it . . . (Sen 1979, 96; see also 95–97).

This notion of commitment is significant because it strikes at the heart of traditional economic conceptions of human behavior where decisions and actions are assumed to be always self-serving.

> [C]ommitment . . . drives a wedge between personal choice and personal welfare, and much of traditional economic theory relies on the identity of the two. . . . The basic link between choice behaviour and welfare achievement in the traditional models is severed as soon as commitment is admitted as an ingredient of choice (Sen 1979, 97).

In spite of these criticisms and alternative models, the most commonly used formulation is still that of the self-interested economic agent. This is, in large part, due to the methodological convenience that such an assumption provides in avoiding the externalities in consumption that emerge once tuistic behavior is permitted (Hausman 1994).

UTILITARIANISM

Felicific Calculus and the Greatest Happiness Principle

Bentham's utilitarianism has two principal elements that are noteworthy for our purposes, namely: its calculus of pleasure-pain and its greatest happiness principle. The human person is a pleasure-pain calculating agent who maximizes happiness and minimizes pain. Writing in reaction to natural law and the contractual theories of social organization, Bentham sees his felicific calculus as a sufficient explanation of human behavior and interaction. Moral behavior is founded on the greatest happiness for the greatest number (Mill [1863] 1962, 257; 1965, 147).

Mill modifies Bentham's utilitarianism to account for differences in the quality of happiness. It is not sufficient to limit oneself to a comparison of the absolute amounts of gratification in choosing between alternatives. One must also account for variations in the inherent quality of different types of enjoyment.

Mill observes that people's motives are varied and complex. He recognizes the need to go beyond hedonism and to take into account the full range of human emotions. There are the simple types of pleasures like eating, and then, there are the "compound pleasures" such as the love of justice (Viner [1927] 1958a, 324). Mill faults Bentham for failing to consider other important factors behind the human person's conduct such as the desire for perfection, fidelity to conscience and spiritual beliefs, and the pursuit of high ideals.[7] Having said all this, however, Mill still takes the same narrow road as Bentham does in modeling the person purely in terms of economic motivation. Marshall calls this abstraction the *Economic Man*.

Hermann Heinrich Gossen ([1854] 1938), the precursor of the marginalist revolution, brings Smithian self-interest a step further by turning it into a divine principle where the maximization of individual pleasure over a lifetime (from both material and nonmaterial things) is seen to be the ultimate purpose in life, willed no less than by God. Economics, then, becomes the "science of pleasure" with good and pleasure becoming identical.

The Heritage of Utilitarianism: More Apparent than Real?

Many believe that the contribution of utilitarianism to contemporary economic thought is overstated. Marshall goes out of his way to disavow any inherent link between economics and utilitarianism. He gives a broad definition of satisfaction beyond hedonism to encompass even the higher and the nobler goals (Marshall [1890] 1961, footnote 1, p. 17 in I, II, section 1).

Schumpeter (1954) views utilitarianism as neither "necessary nor useful" for economic analysis. He sees the linkage of the marginal-utility approach to this pleasure-pain framework as unfortunate and the result of mere association rather than logic.[8] The marginalists do not claim the need for egotism in their formulation since they do not specify the nature of the wants and desires of their economic agent. The common association of the marginalists with utilitarianism is partly due to the misuse of language and terms. For example, Jevons calls economic theory a "calculus of pleasure and pain."[9] Gossen and F. Y. Edgeworth define utility as the quality of pleasantness accompanying consumption.[10] Robbins ([1932] 1949, 85, 95) argues that the determination of exchange value has neither a necessary nor an essential connection with psychological hedonism. A full spectrum of motivations can be accommodated to include even altruism.

Whether utilitarianism's contribution is more apparent than real, its influence is undeniably extensive. Viner ([1927] 1958a, 331) sees a real substantial influence of Bentham and Mill over subsequent liberal continental theorists in their economic analyses. Streeten sees utilitarianism as one of the three legacies from the classical school. J. Harsanyi (1982) notes the intellectual indebtedness and affinity of current economics to classical utilitarianism.[11] Even while denying the real contribution of hedonistic philosophy to the discipline, Schumpeter himself concedes the extensive use of the method of analysis afforded by utilitarianism. It cannot be simply brushed aside in economic debate.[12] It readily lends itself to welfare economics and has been closely tied with the advocacy of unconditional free trade (Schumpeter 1954, 398). Talcott Parsons (1968, 234) attributes part of this considerable utilitarian strain in economic theory to its advantages of malleability and simplicity, thereby readily lending itself to mathematical formulation and manipulation. Besides, it neatly fits another enduring legacy from classical economics: the view that people are self-centered with the goal of maximizing their own satisfaction. A final word to illustrate the perception of this extensive influence: As Erskine McKinley (1965, 37) notes in his study on the nature of the person in economic thought, "We are also given to looking down on utilitarianism as a philosophy, yet scratch an economist and find a Benthamite."

HOMO OECONOMICUS

The *homo oeconomicus* model conveniently serves the purpose of turning economics into a science and sets the stage for the common association of the discipline with mere wealth accumulation. Ricardo is the first classical economist to put the field well on its way to a self-imposed, restrictive view of economic phenomena. He portrays the operation of economic principles as a mechanistic action devoid of human will and ignores the extra-economic considerations of Smith. Labor is treated as a mere commodity, and the competitive and combative aspects of economic life are highlighted (Flubacher 1950, 125–28).

Mill is the "the father of the analytical abstraction of the economic actor" (Lutz and Lux 1988, 42; Nitsch 1983, 15). While Ricardo is remembered as the first classical economist to attempt a purely scientific exposition of economics, it is Mill who gives rise to what has now come to be popularly known as the *Economic Man*, an abstraction of the person where no consideration is given to other essential human motives or passions (whether pleasant or unpleasant) other than those that are directly related to work or wealth accumulation. In spite of his earlier acknowledgment of the richness of human motivations, Mill restricts his model only to the acquisitive aspects of human behavior and motivation.

> Political Economy . . . does not treat of the whole man's nature as modified by the social state, nor of the whole conduct of man in society. *It is concerned with him solely as a being who desires wealth.* . . . It makes entire abstraction of every other human passion or motive. . . . Political Economy considers mankind as occupied solely in acquiring and consuming wealth. . . . Not that any political economist was ever so absurd as to suppose that mankind are really thus constituted, but because this is the mode in which science must necessarily proceed (Mill [1836] 1948, 137–39, emphasis in the original).

Mill, in effect, compartmentalizes the human person, and in the process, he shifts the focus of economics (as a discipline) from the early classical concern for national wealth (e.g., Smith [1776] 1937) to the self-interested accumulation of personal material gain. He equates the discipline with the study of the human person as a maximizer of wealth.

Alfred Marshall criticizes Mill's abstraction of the economic agent as unrealistic. Nowhere is there a human person driven solely by pecuniary selfish gain. Not even the household breadwinner, working for the benefit of the family, would qualify as an *Economic Man* so defined.[13] Marshall expands and humanizes Mill's abstraction by changing the analytical framework to accommodate a greater range of human motives (Nitsch 1983, 17). He does this by introducing two distinct features in his framework: utility and economic rationality. Utility is defined as "the benefit derived from the satisfaction of *entirely subjective* drives, wants, desires and tastes, originating with the individual as the last, indivisible entity of the economic system" (Weisskopf 1973, 556). By using utility, a much broader range of human motives beyond wealth accumulation can be incorporated into economic analysis.

Senior subscribes to the Smithian view of likening the relationship of wealth maximization and economics to that of gravity and physics (Lutz and Lux 1988, 39). Senior acknowledges the need to supplement economic principles with extra-economic, nonpecuniary considerations. However, he sees this as outside the realm of an economist's responsibilities. After all, wealth for him is the sole subject matter of political economy; welfare properly belongs to the field of legislation (Flubacher 1950, 138).

Cairnes patterns economics after the physical sciences where phenomena can be explained as mechanical occurrences independent of the human will. He sees the discipline as a "science of wealth," and not of human welfare. The distribution of societal output ought to be governed by purely economic considerations (Flubacher 1950, 157–59).

The effort of classical economists such as Ricardo and Senior to isolate economics from ethical considerations is pursued with even greater vigor by the marginalist school. Marginalism opens even wider the avenues for associating utilitarianism with the new emerging discipline. In particular, value determination is linked to the personal preferences reflected in the consumer's utility and firmly entrenches economic behavior in the realm of the subjective (Flubacher 1950, 314).

Two observations are worth noting on the use of the *homo oeconomicus* model. First, many economists criticize it as inadequate for its narrow focus on a single dimension (the economic hedonistic psychology) of the human person.[14] Adam Smith himself would have found the model too confining as he has a richer view of the human person (Coase 1976). Vilfredo Pareto describes the multidimensional nature of the human person.

The same man, which I consider as *homo oeconomicus* for an economic study, I can consider as *homo ethicus* for a moral study, as *homo religiosus* for a religious study, etc. . . . [As] the physical body comprehends the chemical body, the mechanical body, the geometrical body, etc.; [so] the real man comprehends the *homo oeconomicus*, the *homo ethicus*, the *homo religiosus*, and so on (Pareto 1927, 18, cited by Nitsch 1983, 16).

Second, despite their criticisms, most economists still employ such a restrictive framework because of its advantages in simplifying economic analysis. Just as quickly as they concede the limitations of the model's assumptions, they justify its use by noting that such a supposition is not too far off from actual behavior if one were to talk of economic affairs alone.

Jevons and Edgeworth both follow Mill in acknowledging the richness of human motives, but they similarly limit themselves to accepting individual self-interest as sufficient for purposes of accounting for economic behavior.[15] Jevons ([1871, 1888] 1965, 23) sees economics as a strict pleasure-pain exercise where the end is to "maximize happiness by purchasing pleasure, as it were, at the lowest cost of pain." Schumpeter (1954, 131) observes that even after acknowledging the richness of human motivations, scholars still use the simplifying assumptions of the model for convenience.

Homo oeconomicus is the most commonly used framework in economic analysis. As McKinley (1965, 11) observes: "[I]t is this abstracting of one department of human affairs from all others that enables many economists today to criticize utilitarianism as a superficial and even contemptible philosophy, then diligently turn to using it under the guise of rational *homo oeconomicus.*" In spite of all the criticisms leveled against such self-centered formulations, mainstream economics still views the human person as one whose "chief aim is to acquire the greatest amount of wealth with the least possible effort" (McConnell, 1943, 72). The economic agent is a "totally selfish, single-minded marginal pleasure-versus-pain or gain-versus-loss calculator, insatiable satisfaction-seeker and wealth-accumulator at home" (Nitsch 1983, 16). Such a view is sustained in no small way by the image of the "'irrational' consumer of advertising psychology" characterized by pure subjective experiences, sensations, and "kicks" (Weisskopf 1973, 558). I am now ready to draw out some of the implications of these philosophical underpinnings and compare them with those of the modern Catholic social documents.

Notes

1. In talking of "well-defined questions posed with preselected assumptions which severely constrain the nature of the models that can be admitted into the analysis," Sen (1979, 91) observes that, "[a] specific concept of man is ingrained in the question itself, and there is not freedom to depart from this conception so

long as one is engaged in answering this question. The nature of man in these current economic models continues, then, to reflect the particular formulation of certain general philosophical questions posed in the past."

2. Weisskopf (1973, 547) observes: "[T]he history of economic thought abounds with statements and implicit assumptions which, put together, present an image of man. It was and is an image of how man should be in order to function in the economy. The economic image of man, although referring to actual economic behavior, has almost always a normative connotation: Man *should* be such and such in order to be an effective subject of the economy. Assumptions in economics about the nature of man, then, are rarely ever factual statements but value judgments—judgments how man ought to be, how the economy wants man to be, what he should want, will, think, and do so that the aims of the economy become his own aims." In contrast, da Fonseca (1991) finds that people's beliefs, rather than economists' discourse and language, shape actual economic behavior.

3. See, for example, Radin (1996), Anderson (1993), and OA #39 for a further exposition on such concerns.

4. Nitsch (1981, 21) notes, "[M]uch as certain theologians contend that 'man has always created God in his own image and likeness,' verily we can paraphrase that 'economists have always molded their men in their (discipline's) own image and likeness.'" Weisskopf (1973, 550–51) remarks: "Economics, in its academic as well as in its popular formulations, has tried to fulfill this need for moral justification of the economic system and of the behavior it requires from its participants. The growing use of mathematics, econometrics, and abstract model building has obscured this function and tended to repress the moral philosophy which is implied in economics. However, its concepts of human nature were chosen, consciously or unconsciously, to serve the purpose of moral justification."

5. See, for example, Lionel Robbins ([1932] 1949, 85, 95).

6. Marshall ([1890] 1960, 20–21) notes: "Now the side of life with which economics is specially concerned is that in which man's conduct is most deliberate, and in which he most often reckons up the advantages and disadvantages of any particular action before he enters in it."

7. John Stuart Mill ([1838] 1974, 100–01) writes: "Man is never recognized by him [referring to Bentham] as a being capable of pursuing spiritual perfection as an end; of desiring, for its own sake, the conformity of his own character to his standard of excellence, without hope of good or fear of evil from other source than his own inward consciousness. . . . Nor is it only the moral part of man's nature, in the strict sense of the term—the desire of perfection, or the feeling of an approving or of an accusing conscience—that he overlooks; he but faintly recognizes, as a fact in human nature, the pursuit of an other ideal end for its own sake."

8. Schumpeter (1954, 134, 408–09, 1056–57). See also O'Brien (1975, 25).

9. Schumpeter (1954, 134); Welch (1987, 772).

10. Georgescu-Rogen (1968); Welch (1987, 772).

11. See also Welch (1987, 772).

12. Schumpeter (1954, 134, 408–09); C. Welch (1987, 770, 772).

13. Marshall ([1890] 1961, Preface to the First Edition, p. vi) observes: "Attempts have indeed been made to construct an abstract science with regard to the actions of 'economic man,' who is under no ethical influences and who pursues pecuniary gain warily and energetically, but mechanically and selfishly. But they

have not been successful, nor even thoroughly carried out. For they have never really treated the economic man as perfectly selfish: no one could be relied on better to endure toil and sacrifice with the unselfish desire to make provision for his family. . . . But if they include these, why should they not include all other altruistic motives . . .?"

14. On the need to consider people in their totality (including their spiritual and intellectual dimensions) and to take their ultimate goals and values into account, see Marshall ([1890] 1961, book I, chapter 2, section 1, 17, 1st paragraph).

15. Jevons [1871, 1888] 1965; Edgeworth (1881, 16) notes: "[T]he first principle of Economics is that every agent is actuated only by self interest."

Chapter 7

FELICIFIC CALCULUS AND TRANSCENDENT END

oth Catholic social thought and mainstream economics[1] are teleological: the former, for its avowed end of bringing people to their
transcendent end, and the latter, for its goal of allocative efficiency
characterized by Pareto optimality.

Standard economic thought views the human person as a non-
tuistic, atomistic agent interested only in maximizing the satisfaction of
personal preferences. On the other hand, Catholic social thinking sees
the person as a rational social being imbued with a transcendent end.
This contrast in anthropological premises leads to wide disparities in
their views on economic life, especially with respect to the ends pursued,
the use of extra-market mechanisms, the criteria for equity and participation, and the appropriate treatment of individual economic agents.
Each of these is discussed in the following sections.

A CONTRAST OF ENDS

Mainstream economic thought seeks to promote allocative efficiency
with its choice of Pareto optimality as the appropriate evaluative criterion of market outcomes.[2] On the other hand, the social documents are
concerned with conformity to the natural and eternal laws that define
the innate moral structure of the human person. This human project is
summarized by *Quadragesimo Anno* and *Gaudium et Spes*:

> For it is the moral law alone which commands us to seek in all our con-
> duct our supreme and final end, and to strive directly in our specific ac-
> tions for those ends which nature, or rather, the Author of Nature has
> established for them, duly subordinating the particular to the general. If

this law be faithfully obeyed, the result will be that particular economic aims, whether of society as a body or of individuals, will be intimately linked with the universal teleological order, and as a consequence we shall be led by progressive stages to the final end of all, God Himself, our highest and lasting good (QA #43).[3]

Christian revelation . . . leads us to a deeper understanding of the laws of social life which the Creator has written into man's moral and spiritual nature (GS #23a).

Freedom and Free Choice

Catholic social thought's distinction between free choice and freedom accounts for its search for a more objective basis for gauging the ends and means of economic life beyond personal wants and desires. It has long been recognized that a benefit of economic progress is the expansion of the range of choices available to the person. The relatively greater control over the external world afforded by science and technologies, the greater productivity achieved in coaxing nature of her gifts, and the improvement in work organization have all led to the emancipation of the human person from extreme want and uncertainties. Consequently, W. Arthur Lewis describes economics as a process of expanding human choices (Lewis 1955). Many other economists view the expansion of choice in the consumption basket or in the opportunity set to be the very heart and defining characteristic of economic freedom (Laslier et al. 1998). Others go beyond this to include capabilities and functionings in their notion of economic liberty (Sen 1985a, 1985b, 1988a).

Catholic social thought acknowledges the necessity and importance of enhancing the range of human choices. But the expansion of the person's opportunity set brought about by economic progress is not in itself the object of economic life but is only one of many other means to a goal that is deeper and more profound than merely having a wide variety of options. Moreover, such an expanded choice set need not necessarily lead to an improvement in well-being since the latter is dependent on the content and quality of the choices made. Thus, *Centesimus Annus* notes that availing of such enhanced opportunities must conform to the objective standards of human nature and strengthen the person's relationship with God and neighbor. Free choice is not an end in itself but is only a means for reaching the heights of integral human development.

Happiness as an End of Economic Life: The Difference between Having and Being

The open-endedness of preferences and the common, longstanding association of wealth accumulation with the *homo oeconomicus* model partly account for economic thought's singular focus on *having* to the neglect of *being*.

Utilitarianism's amorphous happiness

Sen (1984a) notes that utilitarianism has three components: consequentialism (results determine the rightness of actions), welfarism (individual utility is the yardstick for evaluating the goodness of states of affairs), and sum ranking (the goodness of actions is determined by the sum total of individual utilities). What is the end of economic life? Utilitarianism's answer is *the greatest happiness of the greatest number*. Unfortunately, what is encompassed by this "happiness" is unclear.[4] Utilitarianism has been criticized for the circularity in the way it defines happiness as that which people desire because it leaves them content. The term is ill defined and is used at such a high level of abstraction so as to be completely malleable. Alasdair MacIntyre criticizes this "sievelike nature of the utilitarian concept of pleasure" as "a vacuous tautology."[5] Thus, economic life's purpose is left indeterminate.

A second related difficulty with utilitarianism is its failure to provide a more nuanced set of criteria for making choices. Mill refines Bentham's utilitarianism by accounting for differences in the quality of pleasures. However, this acknowledgment of a hierarchy of pleasures does not go far enough as it provides no principle for distinguishing the "higher" from the "lower" pleasures.

The resulting imprecision from these two difficulties is illustrated in a characterization of the marginalist school's use of utility in value determination:

> [T]he calculus of pleasures and pains . . . has been turned to account in the exposition of the economical notion of final utility in relation to Value. . . . The individual is not only the best but the only judge of his own interests, as of his own pleasures. *All desires are equally legitimate; all objects satisfying a desire (of whatever character the desire may be) are equally wealth* (Bonar 1893, 219, emphasis added).

Not only is the scale of "happiness" ignored, but the end itself is completely elastic and indistinct.

In welfarism, human well-being is founded on the satisfaction of individual preferences. Many deem the utilitarian roots of such an approach to be inadequate and unacceptable for purposes of establishing guidelines for a just order in economic life because these preferences are kept so expansive as to accommodate just about anything that the individual desires. Preferences are intentionally kept amorphous and their specification deliberately kept "thin" in line with Karl Popper's (1952) liberal pluralism. A much-revered strength of the unfettered market is that it avoids making substantive philosophical commitments on the notion of the good. The ultimate measure for ends and means is the individual's preferences. Daniel Hausman and Michael McPherson (1996) dispute the neutrality of Paretian principles because the de facto preeminence it accords to individual preferences (over rights, entitlements, capabilities, and other evaluative criteria) is in itself already a ranking of values. Moreover, it operates on the assumption of self-interest.

Jon Elster (1982) poses a fourth problem by asking why such a criterion for justice is based solely on personal wants. Utilitarianism is founded on shifting sand because these personal wants are subject to constant change in a dynamic process that is best described as adaptive preference formation arising from the agent's experiences. Moreover, the harmonious attainment of human values for the community under such a personal want-based criterion would require either of two things: (1) that individuals are moved by "well-understood interests" or enlightened self-interest or (2) a wise and selfless autocrat will have to determine what is the greatest happiness for the community to which all should conform. Consequently, Elster (1982, 219) asks, "why should the choice between feasible options only take account of individual preferences if people tend to adjust their aspirations to their possibilities?"

Schumpeter summarizes utilitarianism's dilemma well. The economic analysis of individual behavior does not require a hedonistic formulation; it could even incorporate religious beliefs and practices.[6] Despite this, however, Schumpeter himself is the first to concede that, in practice, this latitude does not really go that far.

> In consequence, defenders of that doctrine [referring to utilitarianism] have been to some extent successful in their attempt to redeem it from the allegation that has made human behavior turn on beefsteaks. But this success . . . was more apparent than real. For if we go very far beyond the grossest gratifications of the simplest appetites, we come dangerously near to identifying expectation of "pleasure" with all possible motives whatsoever . . . and then, of course, the doctrine becomes an empty tautology. . . . Thus, if we are to derive the conclusion *they* derived from their ideas about pleasure and pain, we have after all no choice but to adopt a definition of the latter that may indeed allow some freedom for going beyond beefsteaks, but only a limited one; that is to say, we have no choice but to adopt a theory of behavior that is at variance with the most obvious facts (Schumpeter 1954, 130–31, emphasis in the original).

Homo oeconomicus: economics as wealth accumulation

In spite of Mill's acknowledgment of a scale of happiness and despite Marshall's analytic contributions that allow economic tools of analysis to accommodate nonselfish motives, economic thought has been confined, for the most part, to the "lower" reaches of integral human development. It has focused on consumption and wealth accumulation, a satisfaction based on *having*. This materialistic cast hearkens back to the philosophical premise of classical economics that associates the well-being of *homo oeconomicus* with material affluence. Note, for example, how Mill defines political economy as the science of the individual as a wealth maximizer.

Confining economics to the study of wealth accumulation conveniently dovetails and solves utilitarianism's indeterminacy in specifying what it means by happiness and satisfaction. Thus, the quest for material affluence and consumption has come to be the central preoccupation and goal of *homo oeconomicus*. In contrast to the richness of Adam Smith's conception of the economic agent, later economists focus their attention solely on the person's gain and enjoyment. Needless to say, this encourages the common belief that the end of economics is pecuniary in nature where human well-being is equated with material abundance. Not surprisingly, C. B. Macpherson (1962) characterizes it as *possessive individualism*.

The association of economics with wealth accumulation and of human well-being with consumption readily fills the lacuna in utilitarianism's happiness.[7] This is unfortunate because human flourishing is more than pecuniary gain alone according to the principle of integral development. In addition, such a claim does not acknowledge the possible tradeoffs between working for material benefits and achieving other worthwhile human goals.

The modern Catholic social documents have been highly critical of the resultant lifestyle of materialism and economism[8] that has been engendered by the economic order (SRS #28). An attitude of consumerism is prevalent where immediate and personal gratification is regarded as *the* essential and primary value. Artificial needs are created through the improper use of media advertising, and a culture of waste and unrestrained consumption is fostered within an economic life that is viewed principally and solely as an avenue for consumption-profit maximization. This outlook is also reflected in government policy where the term of reference for economic progress, until recently, has been gross national product (GNP) growth. External adjustment and stabilization have been cast merely in terms of balancing macroeconomic accounts with little sensitivity to the human cost incurred (Cornia, Jolly, and Stewart 1987).

Economism has given short shrift to the more primary needs of the human person: the development and use of personal gifts and potential, the opportunity to blossom in a full life steeped in the practice of virtues, and the requisite growth in the fundamental values of truth, friendship, justice, and charity. These are not viewed as relevant issues in the *homo oeconomicus* model nor are they important in the gain-loss calculus of utilitarianism. Besides, standard analysis insists there is no value-free way of distinguishing needs and preferences.

Catholic social thought has a richer definition of economics than the mere efficient allocation of scarce resources to competing needs. Hence, even as it acknowledges the achievements and the greater output afforded by the industrial economy, this social tradition does not readily conclude that such superior yields automatically promote the common good. After all, human well-being is multidimensional. It goes beyond the widespread view that the end of economics is the provision of greater choices for the individual. As discussed previously, even Marshall ([1890] 1961) himself acknowledges the richness of economics beyond the traditional conception of wealth accumulation. Rather, the end of economics is to free individuals from material want and uncertainty so that they may have the opportunity to work for higher and more profound human values and needs. Economic activity is meant to be promotive of the development and exercise of authentic human freedom. It works not only for the material welfare of people but also for their complete well-being.

Despite Marshall's ([1890] 1961) acknowledgment that preferences can accommodate altruism and sympathy, most economists still frame *homo oeconomicus* as concerned solely with private profit, trucking, and bartering. In contrast, these social documents have a greater kinship with the Aristotelean *homo oeconomicus*, a household manager engaged in the prudential art of supplying the needs of the family and making the household self-sufficient.[9] Economics is viewed more as an art (rather than as a precise science) requiring prudence and, consequently, virtue and character development. This is far more compatible with a holistic view of human development and growth, where production and commerce are but parts of a much larger set of activities in the person's life. Thus, *homo oeconomicus* is an inappropriate compartmentalization of the human person. To deal with the individual as *Economic Person* alone, separate from the *Ethical Person*, the *Religious Person*, and others, is not to deal with the human person at all. Not the least of these misconceptions are the definition of economics as the "science of self-interested behavior" (Lutz and Lux 1988, 54) and the reduction of the person's dominant activity to a single dimension, the technological (OA #29–30).

As seen both in chapter 3 on the historical context of the postconciliar social documents and in the proposed conceptual framework of part V, this social tradition views individuals as indivisible in their various dimensions and, thus, deserve to be treated accordingly. Material well-being is not the end but is merely a means for the ultimate good; the material is subordinated to the transcendent.[10] What is important is not how much individuals consume, but how well they embody fundamental human values in the way they earn and use material gains. Thus, integral human development calls for the advancement of nothing less than the total person: body, mind, and spirit.

The priority given to *being* rather than *having* emphasizes *Populorum Progressio*'s and *Sollicitudo Rei Socialis*'s point that economic development is primarily a moral phenomenon in the way it assists human activity to focus on advancement in character and the attainment of nonmaterial, qualitative human aspirations such as fellowship, empathy, equality, and participation. These are key human goods that are not traded in the market and, therefore, hardly dealt with in mainstream economic thought. Economic life can provide the setting for the inculcation of virtues such as honesty, hard work, creativity, temperance, and friendship.

Two other differences in these theological documents' approach to political economy are worth noting. The stress on *being* rather than *having* changes the points of reference in other ways. First, harmony in society, rather than merely economic growth, becomes a foremost concern. For example, *Quadragesimo Anno* (#81–87, #95) proposes its syndical corporations not for their economic efficiency, but rather for the framework of cooperation they engender. Second, there is a longer time horizon considered as a normal part of decision making for current economic activity; there is a sense of responsibility to future generations by examining long-term consequences.

In summary, welfarism is open-ended and does not and cannot specify an ultimate end for economic life. The subjective nature of utilitarianism, rooted as it is in personal wants and desires, leads to imprecision and vagueness in defining its notion of happiness. The maximization of consumption-profits conveniently fills the gap left by an undefined end. Thus, the perceived materialistic cast of the socioeconomic order may in large part be due to the confluence of utilitarianism's amorphous conception of happiness and of *homo oeconomicus*'s acquisitive mode.

In contrast, Catholic social thought regards union with God as the goal of all human action. Not only does it have a "thick" notion of the good, but it also sketches the terrain of proximate means that lead to this good, such as the inculcation of virtues. Furthermore, there is a hierarchy among these means; primary values and needs take precedence and regulate the satisfaction of the secondary values and needs. This is an ordering based on the natural and moral structure that comes with personhood and its transcendent end, rather than on the individual's subjective preferences. As a result, it is exacting in its expectations of human acts. The disparity is highlighted by comparing the stress on *having* and wealth accumulation in economics as against Catholic social thought's focus on *being*.

EXTRA-MARKET MECHANISMS AND THE HARMONY OF INTERESTS

Economic Thought on the Harmony of Interests

The marginalization of people can be mitigated to a large extent by appropriate government action. Whether such intervention is forthcoming or not, however, and to what extent it is pursued are entirely dependent on the stance taken with respect to the legitimacy of a governmental role in economic life. Mainstream economics is not homogeneous in this regard. There is a full spectrum of views ranging from the new classical economics and monetarism (classical liberalism) that argue for a minimalist approach, to the other end of the spectrum that subscribes to activist state fine-tuning as in the case of Keynesianism and welfare economics (social liberalism). Catholic social thought leans toward the latter. Thus, in the following sections that describe the positions for or against extra-market mechanisms, I limit my comparison to those strands of mainstream economics that still subscribe to the early classical aversion to government participation in economic affairs and not to the much later social liberalism.

Wherever one may fall within this continuum, the justification for such a policy position is ultimately founded on the premises one accepts on the natural harmony in the social order. Preference for laissez faire is based on the assumption of a natural harmony of interests in economic life. In other words, left to themselves, atomistic economic agents in the marketplace will bring the economy to the point of Pareto optimality; there is an inherent, unseen mechanistic plan that brings about this orderliness.

Streeten (1954) observes that the harmony-of-interest view is one of the three legacies of contemporary economics from the classical school. The Physiocrats view the economic order as intrinsically stable and harmonious. This is reflected in François Quesnay's *Tableau Economique* that explores the smooth workings and the interrelationship of the various segments of the economy. An even more famous proponent, of course, is Adam Smith with his conclusion that letting individuals pursue their own interests automatically leads to the promotion of the public good via an *invisible hand*.

> [E]very individual . . . intends only his own gain, and he is in this, as in many other cases, led by an invisible hand to promote an end which was no part of this intention. Nor is it always the worse for the society that it was no part of it. By pursuing his own interest he frequently promotes that of the society more effectually than when he really intends to promote it (Smith [1776] 1937, book IV, chapter II, 423).

Smith believes that the self-interested, acquisitive nature of the human person, far from causing anarchy, actually leads to a thriving social order.[11]

Resolving whether there is indeed a natural convergence of private and public interests is important for utilitarianism and its common association with laissez faire. There are two poles in utilitarianism that have to be reconciled. On the one hand, individuals are perceived to pursue their own interests and to use a pleasure-pain calculus to gain the most happiness. On the other hand, we have the *greatest happiness principle*, which says that human action ought to be directed toward the maximization of the community's total happiness. The implicit assumption behind these two philosophical premises is that there is a coincidence of individual and community interests. Take away this assumption and there is a problem of reconciling these two postulates. The dilemma is how one can make a credible leap from the first premise of individual self-interest to the second premise that views these same individuals behaving in such a manner as to promote the public welfare, linking in effect their own happiness to that of the community's. It is not clear how the transition is made from *what satisfies me* to *what benefits everybody*.[12]

This "randomness of ends" has been dealt with in various ways (Welch 1987, 773). The problem could be assumed away, a *deus ex machina* could be brought into the picture, or one could just admit that there is need to take an extra step of reconciling divergent interests. Adam Smith resolves the problem both by recourse to Providence (as do others such as Jevons, Richard Whately, and Quesnay) and government intervention.[13] Edgeworth (1925, II, 102–03) simply assumes that over the long haul, individuals realize that of all the courses of action available to them, the promotion of the general welfare assures them of their own maximum happiness.

Justification for the claim that utilitarianism assumes a coincidence of individual and social interests is not clearly presented. Textual evidence can be presented to support both sides of the issue. On the one hand, Bentham and Mill acknowledge that frictions between what the individual desires and what is good for the public do arise. In such cases, they suggest the use of sanctions, censures, and legislative measures to ensure the promotion of the public good. Mill himself sees the need for readiness on the part of individuals to sacrifice their own happiness in favor of the community's (Sidgwick [1886] 1968, 243, 245–50). On the other hand, there are also views to the effect that it is inconceivable for individuals not to find their own happiness in that of the general public's. Note, for example, Sidgwick's description of Bentham's views on this point:

> [I]n the *Deontology* . . . it is distinctly assumed that, in actual human life as empirically known, the conduct most conducive to general happiness *always* coincides with that which conduces most to the happiness of the agent . . . (Sidgwick [1886] 1968, 244, emphasis in the original).

This ambiguity serves to strengthen the observation that the classical authors hardly establish a convincing link that shows how and why individual agents, by advancing the general happiness, in effect work for their own personal happiness.[14] Mill himself admits that there is no particular reason why one should work for the well-being of others except that it reflects back onto one's own happiness (Flubacher 1950, 149). This inability to provide a stronger and more definitive connection between individual and community happiness is understandable. It is a handicap that utilitarians take upon themselves in rejecting any notion of the natural law. After all, the argument for the coincidence of individual and public happiness is not new; it is reminiscent of the natural harmony of interests view of the Physiocrats and of Adam Smith.

Viner ([1949] 1958b, 316) is not surprised at the absence of any discussion of a natural harmony theory in Bentham's works because of the latter's avowed denial of the natural law. To go around the problem, Bentham acknowledges that there is neither an assured nor an automatic concord between private and public interests. There is need to harmonize these either through an appeal to the individual's sense of sympathy, altruism, and justice; through education or religion; or through government sanctions.[15] As a result, Streeten (1954, 346–47) distinguishes two types of natural harmony, to wit: (1) the crude version where there is no need for government intervention because of the assumption of an automatic convergence of interests, and (2) the modified harmony version where impediments such as ignorance require government intervention and where "harmony may have to be engineered."

Scholars have taken pains to correct the common misperception that classical economists are doctrinaire and unbending in their advocacy of laissez faire.[16] There is general agreement that the classical school does acknowledge flaws in the natural order and accepts the need for both legal and nonlegal means to bring about harmony in the economic order. Their stance toward government intervention can be described as pragmatic, relativist, and conditional.[17]

Adam Smith is closely associated with the call for laissez faire in the conduct of economic life. He is most remembered for his vigorous advocacy of individual freedom and autonomy, believing that the pursuit of individual interests leads to the promotion of the commonweal. Two qualifications must be said about this, however. In the first place, Adam Smith is not completely against any government intervention. He concedes that there are flaws in the natural order.[18] Harmony does not come automatically as a consequence of growth, nor is it ever completely achieved. He acknowledges that self-interest and excessive competition can be harmful, and he is amenable to a "wide and elastic range of activity for government."[19] In fact, he sees the need for intervention in certain areas of economic life such as the protection of labor and the prevention or correction of abuses. He notes that working for one's self-interest is subject to the limitations imposed by the demands of justice. Second, the vigor with which Adam Smith champions laissez faire in the conduct of the economy must be taken in its historical context. Just like the Physiocrats, he writes in reaction to the prevalent mercantilism of his day and its heavy-handed use of stifling and extensive government controls in the economy that favored merchant classes, monopolies, and other vested interests.[20]

Bentham himself views the governmental role in economic life as more than just police duty. He sees it as setting the proper conditions conducive to prosperity (Viner [1949] 1958b, 317). Early Mill should be distinguished from late Mill. The later Mill is a good example of the shift from old liberalism to an activist approach that recognizes a legitimate role for government. He is open to state intervention in order to curb abuses under laissez faire. He considers inequality to be intolerable and is sympathetic to the idea of the public ownership of the means of production. The later Mill belongs to the transformed new liberalism of the late nineteenth century.[21]

The question is not whether classical economists reject any government role in the economy; rather, it is a question of how much state intervention they are willing to accommodate. Note that their acceptance of a government role is considerably qualified and is determined by their perception of the extent of disharmony in the economy. Bentham, for one, is said to view sanctions as applying more to the juridical and political fields, rather than to economic life, since he sees a greater and more spontaneous harmony in the latter (Viner [1949] 1958b, 316). Thomas Sowell (1974, 22) presents the stance of classical economists well by describing it as a "general" policy of laissez faire.

The classical school's aversion to the unnecessary expansion of the governmental role arises from the latter's perceived inefficiency and vulnerability to manipulation by vested interests. Furthermore, such a concentration of power is viewed as fertile ground for the danger of imposing the majority's preferences on the minority (Sowell 1974, 23). D. P. O'Brien (1975, 276, 278) cites certain types of intervention that the classical school avoids: price fixing, oversight of industrial processes, protectionism, food-price caps, monopolies, and the regulation of working hours. Streeten (1954) makes a distinction between distribution and production. Classical economists are willing to intervene in distribution for purposes of equity; they are less inclined, however, to interrupt the market in matters concerning production because of its presumed smooth and efficient functioning.

Catholic Social Thought on the Harmony of Interests

Where does this social tradition stand on the harmony-of-interest theory? How does its position on this question affect its expectations of the individual and the government with respect to the promotion of the common good?

Unlike Marx, this theological tradition concurs with the classical and neoclassical schools in viewing the economic order as intrinsically harmonious. Adam Smith illustrates this idea well in saying that there is a "natural" price, profit, rent, and wage level. Beneath the utilitarian belief in the coincidence of individual and public happiness is an unspoken assumption of such a harmony of interests.

Another similarity is these social documents' acknowledgment that the human person is a calculating rational being strongly inclined toward self-interest. The individual has preference for certainty and stability and responds to incentives regarding enterprise, initiative, and wealth creation.[22] Furthermore, the tradition also shares the observation that individual self-interest can, within reasonable limits, lead to greater output.[23]

This social tradition and Smith also hold comparable views on the innate goodness of the person, in contrast to Calvinistic and Hobbesian claims of a deep-seated depravity. This is an essential element of Smith's natural harmony of interests. Just like Locke, Smith believes that the person "is naturally good; his natural instincts and his reason do not inspire vicious behavior" (Weisskopf 1973, 553).

These similarities, however, should not be taken as an endorsement of the laissez-faire policy of untrammeled self-interest and individualism with minimal oversight from the government. One only has to read the numerous and repeated admonitions of the Catholic social documents against self-interest (described on different occasions as ungodly, evil, selfish, sinful, and harmful to the common good) to dispel this impression. Two reasons for this disparity in views regarding self-interest should be examined. In the first place, Catholic social thought believes that individual self-interest need not and, in fact, does not often lead to the promotion of the public good; there are no automatic links between social welfare and individual satisfaction.[24] Second, this social tradition maintains that people bear within themselves the effects of original sin, which can potentially cause undesirable outcomes in social life. However, people have the benefit of grace and a transcendent end and are, therefore, capable of going beyond their own narrow interests. While individuals do exhibit egotistic motives, this should in no way preclude the possibility of selfless behavior.

Not automatic

This theological tradition believes that while the system is intrinsically harmonious, this does not necessarily mean that it will always be so. Markets do not always self-adjust smoothly, nor do they always lead to desirable outcomes. In this, there is agreement with Keynes who believes that the equilibrium can settle below the optimum. The economy is not always predisposed toward full employment as the classical school holds. There should, consequently, be a readiness to let government intervene in order to achieve full employment. Both share the common judgment that laissez faire does not always work for the good of all, and that capitalism has to be regulated if it is to survive.[25]

There is also agreement with Marshall on this point. Both Marshall and this social tradition see value in capitalism in spite of its problems related to equity in distribution. Marshall is open to an active state role in correcting the system of its deficiencies, although this must be limited and well defined in order to preserve the integrity of what properly belongs to the private realm (Dasgupta 1985, 117–20). Both favor capitalism because it is conducive to technical efficiency and because competition enhances economic freedoms and provides the best environment for unleashing individual enterprise, energy, creativity, and initiative. A reform of the system will be sufficient to address its accompanying problems of inequity.

In all this, it would seem that Catholic social thought holds the same position as the classical forerunners of contemporary mainstream economics: There is room for both government intervention and laissez faire. Their differences lie in the mix of these two policy postures. Their willingness to resort to government intervention in economic life is a function of their perception of just how readily this harmony of interest comes about. Classical economists concede that there are flaws in the natural order that require government action. Two observations can be made in this regard for purposes of comparison.[26]

First, classical economists are averse to interventions in production that they view to be smoothly functioning. Hence, they are reluctant to regulate price and working conditions.[27]

Second, one must recall that the classical school's willingness to allow government intervention is conditional, pragmatic, and relativist; it is a strictly qualified acquiescence.[28] As a *general rule*, it is averse to government participation (Sowell 1974, 22–23), believing that the mechanistic feature of the economy takes care of itself. Market forces are seen to lead to an orderly socioeconomic life, for the most part. While there is a readiness to bring in the government, such occasions should be understood to be the exception rather than the rule.

Catholic social thought goes farther than the classical school with respect to the areas and the types of intervention it deems appropriate for government. For example, one only has to look at its teachings on state involvement in wage and price setting and on legislation concerning working conditions. These fall in the realm of production.

Agency and the harmony of interests

The more activist position of Catholic social thought on government participation in economic life suggests that it sees relatively more disharmony in the socioeconomic order than the old liberalism of the classical school. This social tradition believes that personal interest and the good of the public have many points of divergence in practice. Accepting this as an unavoidable constraint in social life is a necessary first step. It paves the way for a conscious effort on the part of individuals to shift their attention to activities that are in harmony with the public good (CA #25c). Such an admission of areas of conflict and friction leads to the search for channels that promote cooperation. Besides, the wounded nature of people and their capacity for envy, pride, avarice, and self-centeredness are factors that must be considered. To give free reign to self-interest is surely to give rise to some of these disordered passions that are harmful to others and the general welfare.

This brings to the surface the next logical difference between classical liberalism and Catholic social thought regarding the manner by which the public good is achieved: a fortuitous, unintended externality for the former and intentional for the latter. This theological tradition holds that promoting the common good is not accidental nor is it a mere byproduct of securing one's self-interest as Smith proposes. Rather, achieving the common good entails deliberate effort.

An appreciation for the social nature of economic life is a necessary condition for a just order. The commonweal does not come about as easily as most classical liberal economists would like to think. After all, the social good needs the firm foundation of justice and the vitality of charity; both require enormous effort and constant struggle as seen in the principle of solidarity. This means that in addition to economic thought's focus on commutative (e.g., marginal productivity theory of factor payments) and distributive justice (e.g., development economics), Catholic social thought also stresses contributive justice, that is, individuals' contribution to the common good in the measure they can.

Under the principle of solidarity, individuals ought to put the interests of the larger community ahead of their own both in their deliberations and actions. This paves the way for self-sacrifice and service to others. Catholic social thought views individual self-interest as inevitably resulting in disorders. Unbridled self-interest cannot be sustained in the long run as it goes against an essential feature of personhood, a social being that can find fulfillment only by acting within community and for others. Other-centeredness is a sine qua non for personal growth and development. The goal of economic development is said to be the expansion of human choices and freedom. Yet, freedom for this theological tradition is authentic only when it is oriented toward human service and the responsibilities of social life (GS #31b). To be exclusively and primarily self-interested, therefore, is to subvert the goal of economic life. Hence, there is a premium placed on cooperation, a linchpin of any sustainable just social order. Analytically, this means that the individual ought to have an interdependent utility function where personal satisfaction is affected by the state of others' well-being. After all, the principle of solidarity is a call on the individual to treat others as another self (GS #27a).

One other difference will become increasingly evident to the reader: Catholic social thought attaches a personal and social dimension to almost everything in the economic order. For example, the disposition and use of incomes and properties are always weighed against this dual character. Compared to mainstream economic thought, these theological documents have a greater sensitivity to and a stricter notion of the common good.

This social tradition believes that the unfettered competition of the marketplace cannot be the sole means of promoting the commonweal in economic life. Extra-market mechanisms such as cooperation and state intervention are necessary. The need to complement competition with cooperation is not foreign to mainstream economists. Observe what Kenneth Arrow (1979, 157–58) himself has to say in this regard:

> The market is a very important coordinating mechanism but it is by no means the only one; in the social sphere as a whole it is simply one among many. . . . [W]e can take it for granted that for society to operate at all, to function successfully in any sense, we must have an ethical code, that is, some sense of justice. Conduct of an economy of even the most self-interested type requires a degree of recognition of others, or it will not function on its own terms.

Sen (1979, 100–01) provides other examples where such cooperative behavior is necessary.

The principle of solidarity finds its closest affinity in Sen's notion of commitment and sympathy. Also worth noting is Harsanyi's (1955) dual structure where agents take into account ethical preferences in addition to their subjective preferences. Harsanyi treats ethical preferences as individuals' social considerations, in contrast to subjective preferences that reflect their personal interests. This dual structure allows economic analysis to accommodate the dual nature (i.e., the personal and the social character) of almost everything such as labor, capital, private property, the gifts of nature, and even the individual's talents and behavior. Both Sen's and Harsanyi's approaches are innovative and converge with this social tradition's own view that personal choice and personal welfare are not necessarily coincident, contrary to standard analysis. This makes room for the operation of charity and self-sacrifice.

In summary, both Catholic social thought and the forerunners of contemporary mainstream economics hold to the view of a natural harmony of interests. Both see the need to mix laissez-faire operations with government intervention. However, this theological tradition takes a more activist stance. Early classical economists believe that, as a general rule, the *invisible hand* transforms the fulfilment of individual self-interest into the promotion of the common good. In contrast, this theological tradition believes that this harmonious order is better achieved by encouraging individuals to internalize the social consequences of their actions. This social consciousness does not come about automatically, much less easily, especially when the individual's only frame of reference is self-interest. An other-centeredness is more conducive to virtuous and selfless living and is, consequently, more likely to contribute to societal good and harmony. After all, it is the striving for the good and the true that is in line with natural law and, thus, preserves the inherent harmony of the economic order. This results in cooperative behavior with others in the promotion of both personal and public welfare. The logical conclusion of this, of course, is that in the classical liberal school's framework, only the individual good need to be consciously pursued; for this social tradition, both the individual and the common good need to be actively promoted all the time. I return to this in the next chapter when I compare the operational goals set for the economy. The need to be deliberate in promoting the good of others is consistent with this social tradition's perennial point on the importance of owning up to personal moral agency in economic life.

IMPERSONALISM, RELATIVE EQUALITY, AND THE COMMON GOOD

Mainstream economic thought has been criticized for nurturing an ethos of impersonalism.[29] Such inadequate appreciation for the dignity of the human person is manifested in various ways as in the exclusion of whole segments of the population from socioeconomic life, the insufficient assistance provided to the destitute, the treatment of the individual merely as a consumer, and the use of human labor as a factor of production no different from inanimate commodities. This impersonalism may be rooted in the philosophical underpinnings inherited from the discipline's nascent period in the eighteenth and nineteenth centuries. In particular, there is the heritage of (1) an individualism where the point of reference is self-interest and (2) a utilitarianism that does not acknowledge natural rights and which is based solely on the *greatest happiness principle*. Preferences are entirely subjective without any objective foundations for shared ends.

An implicit operating assumption of utilitarianism is that public happiness is merely the summation of individual happiness (Schumpeter 1954, 131). In effect, the community is perceived to be merely the sum of individuals and suggests a particular understanding of the nature of the individual, the community, and the delicate balance that has to be maintained if the extremes of individualism and collectivism are to be avoided. Four implications for purposes of our discussion arise from this "additive view" of the common good: (1) It espouses an economic individualism; (2) It is open to the exclusion of some people from the social order; (3) It views the community as tangential to the essential nature of the human person; and (4) It does not require symmetry and balance in the individual and community's relationship to each other.

Individualism

Economics emerges as a separate field from moral philosophy at a time when greater importance is being accorded to individuals and their rights. Clearly articulated individual liberties replace the community-status mentality and the duty-bound orientation of the medieval social order. It is not surprising, then, that much of the key economic thinking of the period is steeped in the individualism characteristic of the Enlightenment.[30] Steven Lukes (1973) views the personal freedom from institutional regulation as the distinctive feature of economic individualism.

The innate individualism of utilitarianism may not be immediately apparent from a first reading of the history of economic thought. Most of the authors I have been considering profess a universal utilitarianism[31] where the object is the promotion of the happiness of all.[32] However, Guy Routh sees an individualism in Benthamite utilitarianism despite its *greatest happiness principle*.[33] The regard accorded to others is essentially motivated by the advantages the individual hopes to gain in the process.[34] Bentham's ultimate frame of reference is still the individual's interest.[35]

Mill calls for the subordination of individual to general happiness (Sidgwick [1886] 1968, 245). The manner by which the principle is posed, the greatest happiness for the greatest number, gives the impression of a primacy accorded to the community. However, the animating motive beneath this seeming concern for the public good is still individualism. The common good is promoted only because it serves individual self-interest. For example, Mill's willingness to let government intervene in setting the length of the workday arises not out of a sense of justice nor from an appreciation for the dignity of the person. Rather, it stems from his desire to set up the most favorable conditions "to aid the greater number of individuals in achieving what they consider to be their self-interest, and which could not be achieved without the aid of the state" (Flubacher 1950, 149–50). Schumpeter (1954, 131) characterizes the "total happiness" of utilitarianism as eventually being resolved into "individual sensations of pleasure or pain, *the only ultimate realities*" (emphasis added). The common good is understood to be the total of this collection of individual happiness.

Finally, one must recall that utilitarianism is not merely a philosophy of life. Equally important for economic thinking is its method of analysis (Schumpeter 1954, 134). The essential feature of this approach is the satisfaction of personal wants and desires independent of other people's welfare.

To claim that public happiness is nothing more than the summation of individual happiness is to assume that sympathy and commitment are either irrelevant or unimportant. This additive view implies that personal satisfaction is unaffected by other people's state of happiness. Individuals are largely viewed as independent of each other or unconcerned about each other's welfare. Most are deemed to be indifferent to the plight of others and are intent, to a large extent, on pursuing only their own preferences. Such economic individualism is, thus, another factor that contributes to the impersonalism of the social order. One must note, however, that this non-tuism is a methodological necessity to avoid the externalities of interdependent utilities; they are assumed away for convenience (Hausman 1992).[36] There is no place for the principle of solidarity in traditional economic thought. This need not necessarily be the case since many have argued that selfishness is not intrinsic to the theory (see preceding chapter). Moreover, Gary Becker's (1974) framework for social interactions lends itself well to incorporating altruism in economic modeling, albeit at the cost of losing the simplicity of the basic microeconomic model. Having noted this, however, one must also acknowledge that the maximization exercise of economic analysis is commonly associated with the promotion of self-interest, and sometimes even selfishness.[37] Many also think that such behavior is what economic rationality is all about. No doubt, Smith's ([1776] 1937, book I, chapter II,14) oft-quoted description of the pursuit of self-advantage by the butcher, the brewer, and the baker contributes to this widespread impression.

Exclusion, Relative Inequality, and Rights

The philosophy behind utilitarianism and individualism can imbue an economic order with a tolerance for, if not an acquiescence to, the de facto marginalization of segments of its population and the treatment of the person as a mere consumer or factor of production.

As already noted, for utilitarianism, morality is measured by how well it promotes the greatest happiness of the greatest number. This requires an interpersonal comparison of individual happiness and tailors actions and decisions toward achieving that maximum level of happiness (Streeten 1954, 348). Implicit in Pareto optimality is the rule of equity where a person's happiness counts as much as anybody else's; a strict rule of equality is operative in the interpersonal comparison of individual happiness.[38]

There is a well-known deficiency, however, in that utilitarianism does not have a principle of justice in distribution. Would a situation of maximum happiness be acceptable if a few enjoyed vast "quantities" of pleasure at the expense of the pain suffered by many? Would maximum happiness be admissible where the majority enjoyed pleasure at the cost of imposing an uneven share of the cost on a minority? Where does one draw the line? There is no principle of equity or justice on how the gain-loss, pleasure-and-pain, or even preference satisfaction of this maximized "happiness" is to be distributed across individuals despite Mill's ([1863] 1962, V) claims that utilitarianism incorporates justice in its considerations (Frankena 1973, 41–42).

Underlying this deficiency is again utilitarianism's rejection of natural rights; Bentham is writing in reaction to natural law. In spite of his avowed rejection, many authors see Bentham's utilitarianism as a natural-law system in approach, methodology, and results. In fact, Schumpeter (1954, 132–34, 428–29) himself calls it the last of the natural-law systems. The harmony of interests implicit in Bentham's jump from a positive description of the individual pursuit of self-interest to the normative call to promote the public good has some elements of natural law in it.[39]

Whether Bentham's utilitarianism is a natural-law system or not, what is important is that he rejects the notion of a natural law[40] and, consequently, does not acknowledge natural rights. For Bentham, all rights are legal, created by positive law; there are no inalienable or nonlegal rights (Hart 1982). Thus, utilitarianism has been criticized for the narrow and impoverished base of its anthropological assumptions that give little regard to duties, virtues, and the human need for self-respect, commitment, and values (Welch 1987, 774). Utilitarianism's denial of any innate rights and its lack of a principle of equity and justice for the distribution of final outcomes contribute to a mind frame that does not nurture an acute sensitivity to the plight of those who may bear a disproportionate share of the "pain" or who may be left out of the social order.

To sum up, impersonalism (evidenced in the marginalization or exclusion of peoples from socioeconomic life and in the treatment of the individual as no more than a mere consumer or a factor of production) is engendered to a significant degree by the philosophical underpinnings of individualism and utilitarianism in prevailing economic thought. Utilitarianism not only contributes much to the reinforcement and promotion of individualism, but it also suffers from the absence of a principle of equity and justice in the distribution of final outcomes. This is not surprising since it does not acknowledge any innate or inalienable rights. All this contributes to the building of an economic order that fails to bestow unique importance to every member in its ranks. Thus, utilitarianism defines the common good as the mere sum of individual happiness in society.

While giving a qualified assent to the need to call on government to intervene in the economic order, the classical liberal forerunners of mainstream economics subscribe to a viewpoint of keeping it to a minimum, especially in the areas believed to operate efficiently on their own such as production. The preference for a laissez-faire approach in the conduct of economic life restricts a readily available avenue (government action) through which the marginalization of people can be mitigated, if not completely avoided.

A nonselfish appreciation for the uniqueness and worth of each person is a sine qua non for an economic order that excludes no one. Thus, Catholic social thought not only acknowledges the centrality of natural rights, but it also uses them as building blocks for a just economic order (Hollenbach 1979). For example, it recognizes immanent rights in economic life such as the right to the satisfaction of basic needs. This right is inherent to the person and must be respected regardless of the individual's productive contribution and regardless of market outcomes. Many other rights branch out from this, such as the rights to gainful employment and a just wage. Unlike Pareto optimality, this theological approach also appraises the manner by which final outcomes are distributed.

> [T]he economic prosperity of any people is to be assessed not so much from the sum total of goods and wealth possessed as from the distribution of goods according to norms of justice, so that everyone in the community can develop and perfect himself (MM #74).

No one may be excluded from having a share of that "total" level of social happiness. Rights and obligations must be observed. These logically follow from the principles of nonexclusion to be discussed in part V, such as the principles of participation, relative equality, preferential option for the poor, and universal access to the goods of the earth. Everybody counts, and not only when the sum of societal happiness is being tallied as in the utilitarian methodology. For this reason, this social tradition defines the common good as "the good of all and of each individual" (SRS #38f). The concern is for both the good of the community and of each *particular* individual. Thus, not even the promotion of the good of the majority justifies the infringement of the rights of minorities (CA #44b). This also explains why the social documents strongly criticize economic arrangements that treat the individual as a mere consumer or factor of production.

The attendant inherent rights from the person's transcendent end will have to be accepted in their totality and according to their relative importance. A selective acknowledgment of these immanent rights is not good enough. For example, extreme laissez faire embraces the right to economic freedom and initiative and the right to private property ownership. At the same time, however, it fails to acknowledge the primacy, much less the existence, of the right to universal access to the goods of the earth and its correlative rights such as the right to the satisfaction of basic needs and the right to gainful employment (CA #4b–c). Hence, there is value in articulating conceptual frameworks (as will be done in the last three chapters) that afford an integrated presentation of the essential conditions that must be satisfied in order to arrive at a just social order.

Nature of the Community

If this additive view of happiness were to be accepted and the common good were to be seen merely as the sum of individual good, what does this say about the whole? To claim that the community is merely the sum of its component individuals is to say, in effect, that the individual is the only ultimate reality; the community is not real in its own right and is merely a creation of mutual agreements struck among individuals. Catholic social thought disagrees with such methodological individualism (Lukes 1973) where data concerning individuals are the only valid basis for explaining social phenomena.

This theological approach does not view the community as the mere sum of individuals nor merely as the result of a Hobbesian social contract. Community life is not accidental to the individual in the Aristotelean sense of being peripheral to the person's nature. It is an essential dimension of personhood rooted in a transcendent reality. Right from the beginning at creation, the human person lives in the company of others; man and woman provide fellowship to one another and work together in exercising stewardship over the goods of the earth. This bond has been further strengthened in the course of human history, culminating in the Incarnation and the redemption effected by Christ as He unites Himself to every person, thereby forging a unitive bond among people, and between God and the human person. In the eschatology, Christ will present a completed *Kingdom*, a community of men and women freed from all stains and imperfections (GS #39d). Indeed, the frame of reference whether for the past, the present, or the future is always that of a communion of persons, a family. Community life cannot be merely tangential to the human person because the Blessed Trinity is the model of life, an essential union of love with and for others. In examining the gift of each other as part of integral human development, this union is seen as an indispensable feature of the human person's transcendent dignity and self-understanding. These social documents view the unity of and relations within the human family to be just as real as the individuals who constitute such a family.[41]

That the community is more important than the *greatest happiness principle* can be inferred from the requirements it (the community) imposes. *Centesimus Annus* (#47b) notes:

> [C]ommon good . . . is not simply the sum total of particular interests; rather it involves an assessment and integration of those interests on the basis of a balanced hierarchy of values.

This hierarchy stems from the natural and moral structure constitutive of personhood. Points of conflict between individual and public interests must be subordinated to this ordering of values. Particular actions must be undertaken only within the larger setting of the community. This means that personal happiness cannot be independent of the state of other people's well-being, as an additive methodology suggests. The good of the community is not so amorphous as to accommodate just about any Pareto-improving action that adds to the stock of total happiness. Not just about any addition is good enough; it has to be respectful of the values that come with community.

It is worth noting a point of discrepancy in utilitarianism. Bentham's and Mill's universal utilitarianism calls for individuals to behave in such a manner as to promote the good of the community. They consider this to be so important as to acknowledge the pivotal role of religion, education, and legal sanctions in ensuring that individuals are imbued with "enlightened self-interest" or "well-understood intentions." This call and concern for other-centeredness is contrary to an additive view of the common good because it requires interdependent preferences. One way to avoid this inconsistency is to assume a radical and complete interior conversion where the individual fully internalizes what the good of the community requires, a heroic assumption at best. Of course, mainstream theory goes around this by assuming that *homo oeconomicus* has well-informed and well-formed preferences.

Balance and Symmetry

All this stress on the communal aspect of living, however, should not be taken to mean that Catholic social thought falls in the other extreme of a Hegelian absorption of the individual by the collective. This social tradition affirms the importance and uniqueness of each person whose well-being is the end of all social institutions. The common good is meant to assist the individual achieve perfection (MM #65; GS #26a). Moreover, note that even within collective action, these social documents are adamant that it is still the person who is the subject. In fact, people are seen to be capable of transcending the social forces that shape and influence their formation and growth. Such importance accorded to the individual is also seen in the repeated stress to remove obstacles to universal participation and to people's exercise of their moral agency. Catholic social thought avoids both the contractarian individualism of Locke and Hobbes, on the one hand, and Hegelian organicism on the other. It is appreciative of the distinctive worth of both the individual and the community. Its view of community can be called organic but only in the following sense: (1) that each part is essential to the functioning of the whole, (2) that parts are interdependent and need each other for their own well-being and proper functioning, and (3) that the whole is more than just the mere summation of the parts. Thus, as Hollenbach (1994, 146–47) observes:

> The blending of rights language and common good language in recent Catholic thought is not a result of conceptual confusion. It is the consequence of a clear-eyed vision of the human person whose dignity is social through and through.

The tradition straddles the best of both liberalism and communitarianism by emphasizing the social character of the medium that nurtures human self-actualization.

A healthy appreciation for the right balance is important if the extremes of individualism and collectivism are to be avoided. The view that public welfare is merely the summation of individual happiness raises the danger of thinking that the relationship between the individual and the common good is asymmetric in terms of importance and contribution. This risks giving rise to the impression that the person can be expediently sacrificed for the community, for the sake of a "greater good." Both are necessary conditions to each other (GS #25a; CFL #73d; see also Maritain 1947).

In summary, utilitarianism views the community as merely the sum of its individual membership. Catholic social thought, on the other hand, has an organic notion of community that arises from its transcendent view that all human persons are called to share in a common divine life and belong to a single family of humanity. This is not to say, however, that this theological tradition embraces a Hegelian organicism where individuals lose their unique identity and importance as they are completely absorbed by the collective. The principles of subsidiarity and participation, the numerous teachings that are supportive and protective of the individual, and the theme of human dignity that undergirds these social documents are indicative of the value and uniqueness given to the individual. The delicate balance exercised by Catholic social thought in this regard can be seen in its juxtaposition of the principles of solidarity and subsidiarity. Furthermore, it is also evident in the way it deals with individuals in the fullness of their talents, their gifts, their behavior, and their very being and *always* according to their dual dimension of *the personal and the social*.

TREATMENT OF PERSONHOOD

One way of evaluating anthropological premises is to examine their appreciation for the personhood of the economic agent. This can be discerned by perusing differences with respect to their rationale for properly treating other individuals, the issue of participation, the notion of moral agency, and the question of determinism.

Rationale for the Proper Respect of Other Individuals

Economic thought calls on atomistic economic actors to treat other individuals on the basis of their equality in the rights they share, whether such equality arises from a social-contract view of community or from universal utilitarianism's implicit rule of equal weights for summing people's happiness. On the other hand, Catholic social thought calls for the appropriate respect and treatment of every person in the socioeconomic order because each individual is the visible image of the invisible God. The transcendent basis for CST's treatment of the person leads to two points of divergence from mainstream economics: (1) the acknowledgment of human rights independent of work and social outcomes and (2) a rationale for virtues and selflessness.

In the principles of nonexclusion described in chapter 13 (participation, relative equality, preferential option for the poor, and universal access), individuals enjoy rights that come with their personhood, even prior to their contribution to the productive effort of the community (CA #11c, #34a). Other rules of equity, such as contribution, talent, rights, and purchasing power, are secondary to the more fundamental equality of sharing the same filiation with God.[42]

Second, respect for the personhood of another individual merely on the basis of an equality of rights cannot account for selfless sacrifice. To respect others as children of God, however, is motivation and reason enough to ask for selfless acts where personal choice may not necessarily lead to an improvement of personal welfare. This is a distinctive Christian characteristic. In contrast, observe the difficulties utilitarians have in providing a link between personal and social happiness. Recall that Mill could not account for why individuals ought to aim for general happiness except for the assertion that therein lies their own greatest happiness (Flubacher 1950, 149). This is not a difficulty for these theological documents even as they concede that, in practice, individual and public interests may not always coincide and may in fact be at odds with each other. The tradition harmonizes these interests through the principle of solidarity where people deliberately behave in such a manner as to consider the well-being of others and the general public. But what are the grounds for such selflessness? How can we show that such behavior on the part of individuals brings them closer to the attainment of their end? The key lies in Catholic social thought's understanding of authentic human freedom. As seen in chapter 12, the dynamism of authentic human freedom's growth and development lies in the self-diffusiveness of the person's participation in the goodness of God. This is in line with the divine unity of charity in the Blessed Trinity that is presented to the individual as the paradigm worthy of emulation in community with others. Thus, this social tradition insists on setting higher standards of equity than most schools of thought in political economy. The diffusiveness of such goodness also accounts for the documents' confidence that such a difficult undertaking can indeed be successfully, freely, and intelligently achieved.

Participation

Catholic social thought criticizes Marxism in its treatment of the individual as a "cog in the machine" and in its willingness to sacrifice the individual's rights and freedoms for the sake of the collective's productive effort. People are "completely subordinated to the functioning of the socioeconomic mechanism" with their subjectivity effectively transferred to the collective. They are reduced to a mere set of social relations with severe restrictions on their ability to make decisions affecting important areas of their own lives (CA #13a; QA #118–19). Genuine participation and self-determination are severely impaired.

The social documents appreciate the market economy for the liberty on which it is founded. However, ensuring genuine universal participation is also a major problem for this system. Purchasing power is a prerequisite for the enjoyment of this freedom, as wealth and power serve as de facto entry requirements for incorporation into the stream of economic life. The market allows for the participation of all, but only in theory. In practice, segments of the population are excluded by their lack of human capital or purchasing power, or both (CA #33a). The market's inability to deal with this shortcoming can be attributed to its utilitarian foundation which, as already mentioned, has no principle of justice or equity in the distribution of final outcomes.

The tradition's principles of nonexclusion, rooted in the unique value given to each person, call for nothing less than the actual involvement of everyone in the community. Furthermore, not any type of participation is good enough. It has to be authentic in the sense that it provides for the development of the person's full potential for intelligent human interaction. Token participation in economic life from the fringes of society is insufficient. The social documents' advocacy of extra-market mechanisms of allocation is meant to ensure that the market's theoretical universal participation is translated into practice, and a meaningful one at that.

Moral Agency

Related to the question of nonexclusion is the issue of moral agency. An important anthropological postulate of these documents is the subjectivity of people. By virtue of their intelligence and freedom, humans are moral agents. They are fully capable of making decisions for themselves, especially in those areas affecting their future and well-being. Moreover, the innate and derived rights they enjoy carry correlative obligations. Rights and duties necessarily give rise to accountability. As a consequence, they cannot act arbitrarily and their behavior is measured against an objective standard.

Liberalism and socialism err in different ways but arrive at the same end result, a diminution of the person's moral agency. Socialism restricts individual freedoms that are fundamental to the exercise of moral agency. Liberalism causes individuals to relegate part of their moral responsibility to the marketplace by advocating laissez-faire operations; people become purely price takers, unable to affect, on their own, economic outcomes and processes. Catholic social teachings severely criticize socialism for transferring the individual's subjectivity (the ability to make free choices as a subject) to the collective through the state's exercise of its all-encompassing powers; such action vitiates the person's agency (CA #13). A laissez-faire market does this as well. Given free reign, the market has the definitive word on final outcomes in economic life regardless of the human cost. Utilitarianism is asymmetric in that while it champions individual autonomy and freedom, it does not have a well-developed sense of accountability to duties and responsibilities to others and, in particular, to the community.

In both socialism's "subjectivity" of the collective and classical liberalism's laissez faire, outcomes are left to the determination of social institutions and processes. There is the implicit assumption that the good of individuals can be achieved without these people exercising their freedom themselves and taking responsibility for their own development. Their uniqueness as an autonomous subject, needing to grow and develop further in the responsible exercise of reason and freedom, is neither adequately nor properly supported. This theological tradition takes the subjectivity of the individual seriously. Closely related to this is the question of determinism.

Determinism

There are risks involved in using models and methodologies that do not present the totality of the human person (OA #38–39). The use of *homo oeconomicus* as a frame of reference is a good illustration. The materialist tack of economic thought and this theological tradition's transcendent views lead to differences in judgment as to who or what ultimately shapes the socioeconomic order. The materialist approach reduces the human person to the sphere of economics and to the mere satisfaction of material needs. Worse, there is a deterministic cast in that it is economics that shapes the human person, not the other way around. The person is treated not as a subject, but as an object, the result of economic and production processes (LE #61). An extreme formulation of this is most clearly seen in Marx (1904, 11).

> The mode of production in material life determines the general character of the social, political and spiritual processes of life. It is not the consciousness of men that determines their existence, but, on the contrary their social existence determines their consciousness.[43]

The immutability of the "economic laws" flowing from the mechanistic, Newtonian backdrop of mainstream economic thought is not too far off from Marx's radical economic determinism (CA #19d). The aversion to market intervention and the view that such interferences are useless and only cause more harm are reflective of the early classical school's confidence in the self-correcting powers of the unfettered economic order.

Catholic social thought acknowledges that social institutions, processes, and outcomes do condition the human person. They can help or impede full personal development and growth. They can enhance or frustrate the person's chances of developing and exercising authentic human freedom. The environment certainly makes a critical difference in the person's well-being. However, this theological tradition goes further than the materialist approach and repudiates its economic determinism by stressing that the individual is still fully capable of transcending difficulties no matter how formidable they may be. People can be conditioned by external influences, but they cannot be determined by them.

> The human person receives from God his essential dignity and with it the *capacity to transcend every social order so as to move toward truth and goodness.* But he is also conditioned by the social structure in which he lives. . . . These elements can either help or hinder his living in accordance with the truth (CA #38b).

> [T]he manner in which the individual exercises freedom is conditioned in innumerable ways. While these certainly have an influence on freedom, they do not determine it; they make the exercise of freedom more difficult or less difficult, but they cannot destroy it. Not only is it wrong from the ethical point of view to disregard human nature, which is made for freedom, but in practice it is impossible to do so (CA #25b).

Thus, in talking of transforming sinful social structures, this theological tradition sees personal interior conversion as an indispensable first step.

Interpersonal relationships are necessary given the social nature of people and the stewardship of the gifts of the earth they hold in common. Conflicts arise given the wounded nature of the person. Resolving such differences with the use of superior purchasing power in the market or through force to promote one's own interests is always an enticing option. However, only the use of reason and truth will allow for a just and long-lasting settlement of these conflicts. Catholic social thought believes that people are fully capable of this. Individuals not only can transcend their social condition and environment, but they can also rise above their wounded nature because of the sustaining grace they receive from Christ (SRS #40b, #47b).

To model people as egotistic in their behavior is to say, in effect, that people are completely helpless against the effects of original sin. This is contrary to Catholic theology and its view that there is a continuing struggle for the human heart between good intentions and ideals, on the one hand, and concupiscence, on the other. The common misassociation of *homo oeconomicus* with egotistic behavior is a de facto concession of the outcome of such struggle[44] and closes off the possibility of an unselfish regime as the norm, rather than as the heroic exception. The dismal nature of such a conception diminishes the person's promise for choosing the selfless, the good, and the noble.[45]

In summary, Catholic social thought disagrees with the determinism and reductionism that render the person subordinate to the economic order. Determinism and reductionism are not merely about the atomization of the economic agent (in being unable to affect the economic equilibrium with individual decisions); they are also an atomization of the person's moral agency in taking primary and ultimate responsibility in determining the way common life, including the market, is organized and lived. The exercise of this moral agency is an essential part of personhood.

Notes

1. As noted in the introduction to part III, I use "mainstream economics" to refer to the neoclassical synthesis that is standard fare in most undergraduate introductory courses in the discipline. It is important to be aware, however, that there are various strands of thought even within this "mainstream" as is seen in the fierce debates surrounding the proper role of government in markets. In what follows, I will note such substantive differences whenever relevant.

2. See Sen (1984a) and Hausman and McPherson (1996) for other competing criteria such as equity, needs, powers, personal liberty, rights, and entitlements.

3. See also CA #38a and GS #16a.

4. "Happiness" has been interchangeably used with "pleasure" and "good."

5. MacIntyre (1966, 238, 240). See also O'Brien (1975, 25) and Viner ([1927] 1958a, 325).

6. An example is Hollis (1981) who argues that the *homo oeconomicus* model is inadequate. It is contrary to Hume's observation that it is the passion, not reason, which animates the rational person. Original sin and its effects such as pride need to be incorporated into the model.

7. Schumpeter (1954, 407–08) seems to suggest that utilitarianism has an innate affinity to materialism. He notes that while "unsurpassably shallow as a 'philosophy of life,' it [referring to utilitarianism] fitted to perfection the streak of *materialistic* (antimetaphysical) rationalism that may be associated with liberalism and the business mind."

8. *Materialism* is used in the following sense: a "devotion to material needs and desires, to the neglect of spiritual matters; a way of life, opinion or tendency based entirely upon material interests" (*Oxford English Dictionary* 1933). *Economism* is the "belief in the primacy of economic causes or factors" (*Supplement to Oxford English Dictionary* 1982).

9. For a succinct description of the Aristotelean model, see Nitsch (1983, 13–14).

10. MM #175, #176, #210–11, #243–44, #246; LE #60; SRS #29d.

11. A major difference between Smith and Marshall is their treatment of the dynamics of the economic system. Smith relies on the natural harmony of interests to prevent individual self-interest from degenerating into anarchy. On the other hand, Marshall has no need to rely on the invisible hand argument to ensure order

in the community. While it is true that behavior is based on individual utility, economic rationality allows people not only to work out the consequences of their decisions but also to choose a consistent set of actions that would maximize their utility gains *over the long term*. This rationality is the guarantee that a purely subjective utilitarian approach does not end up in anarchy.

12. Routh (1975, 215–16); Welch (1987, 772); Streeten (1954, 349). Simon's (1962) understanding of authority is one way of bridging individual freedoms and public order. Solidarity is another avenue for reconciling the two, though in a teleological, rather than a deontological, mode.

13. McKinley (1965, 19, 27) observes that Adam Smith also gets around the difficulty by assuming a basic "sameness in human endowment" and universal rational economic behavior. See also Routh (1975, 215–16).

14. See Sidgwick ([1888] 1968, 245–47), Flubacher (1950, 149–50), and MacIntyre (1966, 232–44).

15. Welch (1987, 772); Streeten (1954, 346); Viner ([1949] 1958b, 312–13, 319).

16. Viner ([1927] 1958a); O'Brien (1975); Streeten (1954); Sowell (1974).

17. Viner ([1949] 1958b, 330); O'Brien (1975, 24, 272).

18. Viner ([1927] 1958a, 228–30) lists some of the flaws.

19. Viner ([1927] 1958a, 244). See also Sowell (1974, 21).

20. O'Brien (1975, 273); Flubacher (1950, 76–109, 111).

21. Flubacher (1950, 140–43, 150); Sibley (1970, 498).

22. RN #12, #22, #26; MM #229. See also John Paul II (1991, chapter 4).

23. RN #66: "For when men know they are working on what belongs to them, they work with far greater eagerness and diligence. . . . [T]his willing eagerness contributes to an abundance of produce and the wealth of a nation."

24. OA #26: "[N]or can he [referring to the Christian] adhere to the liberal ideology . . . considering social solidarities as more or less automatic consequences of individual initiatives, not as an aim and a major criterion of the value of the social organization."

25. Other similarities include the concern for the marginalized and relative inequality. See Oser (1963, 99, 330–31). Like Bentham, and later Mill and Pigou, Catholic social thought acknowledges the inability of laissez faire to bring about maximum welfare because of market failures, such as the inability to take social externalities into account. See Hebert and Ekelund (1984, 53).

26. Again, readers are reminded of the differences between the old and the new liberalism within the classical school.

27. O'Brien (1975, 276, 278); Streeten (1954).

28. Viner ([1949] 1958b, 330); O'Brien (1975, 24, 272).

29. *Personalism* is used in the following sense: "a view of social organization that places primary emphasis on the person and his involvement in it rather than on the material means necessary for achieving such organization" (*Supplement to Oxford English Dictionary* 1982).

30. Schumpeter (1954, 887–88) notes that the individualism of the period is reflected in its political, sociological, and methodological frameworks. Political individualism referred to the "laissez-faire attitude in matters of economic policy."

31. This is in contrast to an egotistic utilitarianism (hedonistic utilitarianism) of the Hobbesian variety of pure self-interested behavior.

32. For example, take note of Mill (1965, 147): "I merely declare my conviction, that the general principle to which all rules of practice ought to conform, and the test by which they should be tried, is that of conduciveness to the happiness of mankind, or rather, of all sentient beings: in other words, that the promotion of happiness is the ultimate principle of Teleology."

33. Schumpeter (1954, 429) considers utilitarianism as individualist but does not elaborate further. See also Routh (1975).

34. Routh (1975, 213–15). See also Bentham (1954).

35. Bentham (1907, 313), cited by Flubacher (1950, 113).

36. In the presence of externalities in consumption (i.e., with interdependent utility functions), perfect competition does not lead to Pareto optimality. See Quandt and Henderson (1980, 296–98). Wicksteed (1910) defines "non-tuism" as market behavior that is driven by self-interest. See also Giersch (1991, 26).

37. Experiments have been conducted to see if students of economics are more self-interested than those of other disciplines; the results are mixed. See Carter and Irons (1991) and Frank, Gilovich, and Regan (1993).

38. There is an enormous literature regarding the propriety and the feasibility of interpersonal utility comparisons. This is beyond the scope of this study. See, for example, Robbins ([1932] 1949).

39. Viner ([1949] 1958b); Streeten (1954, 346, 348–39); O'Brien (1975, 25).

40. Streeten (1954, 345) observes: "Bentham no longer had Adam Smith's faith in the natural order. *For him the ends which the economic system pursues are the ends of men, not of Nature.* The market is a mechanism (not an organism) designed by men to serve their will" (emphasis added).

41. As to the question of primacy between the person and the community, Maritain (1947) provides an excellent exposition on the difference between the "individual" and the "person." The community takes precedence over the "individual" but not the "person." After all, the end of the community is the perfection of the human person.

42. Hence, even while the infirm, the disabled, the old, and the very young may have minimal contribution to the work effort, if at all, they are still entitled to share in the produce of society by virtue of their personhood.

43. Furthermore, Marx, in differentiating his approach from that of Hegel observes: "To Hegel, the life-process of the human brain . . . is the demiurgos of the real world, and the real world is only the external, phenomenal form of 'the Idea.' With me, on the contrary, the ideal is nothing else than the material world reflected by the human mind, and translated into forms of thought" (Marx [1867] 1906, Preface to the second edition, p. 25).

44. This implies that the graces won by Christ are ultimately ineffective and useless.

45. Lutz and Lux (1988, 53) observe: "Marshall . . . proceeded to treat the consumer . . . as a self-interested utility maximizer who interacts with a basically profit-maximizing businessman. And he did so confessing his faith that 'progress chiefly depends on the extent to which the *strongest* and not the *highest* form of human nature can be utilized for the increase of the social good.' By this Marshall was expressing the belief . . . which can be traced to Hobbes and then Machiavelli, that the higher aspects of human nature were largely ineffective in curbing the much more powerful human *passions.* . . . Virtue could not override vice; only another vice . . . could be made to overrule the destructive vices" (emphasis in the original).

Chapter 8

TWOFOLD OBJECTIVES

DUAL GOALS

The character of an economy is revealed in the priorities it sets, in the way it resolves competing claims, and in the objectives it pursues in the various facets of its operations. In examining closely the modern Catholic social documents' vision of a just economic order, economists will readily observe prescriptions and suggestions that seem to move economic life in opposite directions. Take their labor policies as an example. These social documents unanimously call for the creation of employment *for all*. At the same time, however, they also invariably advocate policies that are generally believed to be harmful for employment generation. In particular, one can cite the call for co-ownership of the means of production, co-management, profit sharing, unionization, collective bargaining, and the provision of a living wage. These extra-market mechanisms are believed by many to adversely affect the allocative efficiency of the market with dire consequences for growth and job creation.

Another seeming inconsistency is the tradition's high regard for the benefits brought about by the market, only to be juxtaposed with an array of efficiency-distorting controls on market processes.[1] It is not a surprise, therefore, that competing schools of thought are able to point to different texts of the tradition as endorsements of their own political philosophies. The tradition disavows any pretensions to offering the third way between capitalism and Marxism (CFL #74e). Its self-proclaimed task is to encourage people, in the spirit of subsidiarity, to examine injustices through the principles of reflection, norms of judgment, and directives for action that spring from the Gospel values (OA #4; SRS #3; CFL #72).

These seemingly dissonant positions of Catholic social thought on political economy form a distinctive pattern that emerges from a close examination of the just economic order it espouses. In particular, one can discern the pursuit of a series of twofold objectives. To highlight what is distinctive with some of these patterns, the following sections compare these goals with those of classical liberalism or Marxism.[2] This theological social tradition often takes a much harder and more ambitious road by setting higher expectations and standards for the conduct of economic life. Unfortunately, it says very little about the practical requirements of implementation, nor does it examine these proposals against empirical evidence.

Private and Public Interests

Social ethics inevitably deals with the question of whose good ought to be actively promoted. Classical liberalism argues that allowing individuals to pursue their private interests is sufficient to ensure the stability and prosperity of the economic order. The only good that has to be actively and consciously promoted is that of the individual since the "invisible hand" cobbles these disparate interests into the public good. Individual interests are the entry point to the commonweal. The economic order should, therefore, be primarily aimed at providing people with the most favorable conditions for the pursuit of their own interests. In particular, it calls for individual autonomy in economic affairs. On the other hand, Marxist economics takes the opposite approach. It is the good of the collective that has to be actively pursued since individual good is derivative from such. The rights and liberties of individuals and groups are subordinated to those of the collective.

Related to the preceding issue is the question of who should be the lead agent of development. In contrast to late nineteenth-century liberalism, classical liberal economics sees private initiative as the principal impetus behind the growth, development, and stability of economic life. It has a minimalist accommodation of the state whose intervention is seen to be counterproductive and too intrusive for individual freedoms.[3] Marxism, on the other hand, views the state as the lead agent of development.

Both classical liberal and Marxist approaches are unacceptable to this theological tradition because they unduly emphasize one to the detriment and sacrifice of the other. Both the individual and the common good must be actively pursued at the same time. There is no automatic mechanism that would lead one to the other. Even as these two goods are integrally related to each other, they are not so closely linked as to make the attainment of one lead to the other. While they are necessary conditions to each other, neither is a sufficient condition for the other. Both must be deliberately and actively promoted *together*.[4] It is in this sense that the inseparability of the individual and the common good ought to be understood. The significance of this becomes even more apparent as the web of interdependence among people intensifies.[5]

Utilitarianism's only concern for outcomes is the maximization of the overall sum. This theological tradition's principles of nonexclusion incorporate an important additional constraint: equity in the sharing of societal and institutional outcomes. In contrast to a Benthamite greatest good for the greatest majority, these social documents insist on serving the good of all, with no one excluded. After all, the common good is defined as "the good of all and of each individual" (SRS #38f).

With respect to the promotion of interests, the utilitarianism of mainstream economics is individualistic at heart. Its promotion of general happiness is a function of its underlying and more fundamental concern that individuals be afforded the most favorable conditions to pursue their own happiness and self-interest to the fullest extent possible. On the other hand, this religious tradition's principles of solidarity and subsidiarity call for a requisite simultaneous effort in pursuing both the individual and the common good. They do not subscribe to the assumption that the pursuit of private interests automatically redounds to the promotion of the common good as a general rule. In fact, there will be occasions when personal sacrifice is necessary.

Catholic social thought's anthropological presuppositions differ radically from those of economic thought. This social tradition does not believe that the human person can be compartmentalized as *homo oeconomicus* and be viewed solely as self-interested and acquisitive. It is true that individuals do behave in such manner, but this is not universal, nor is it necessarily always the case, nor is it a permanent condition, nor should it be normative for what is commonly and mistakenly viewed as economic "rationality." Rather, people have a transcendent dignity arising from their likeness to God. It is an end brought to completion when individuals fulfill their obligations to community and when they face up to the challenge of overcoming selfish inclinations to reveal the goodness within themselves. Therein lies personal perfection and fulfillment.

A distinctive characteristic of Catholic social teaching on the economy is its acknowledgment of the importance and the need for the state to play an active role in socioeconomic life. Private economic agents and the state are viewed as co-developers of society, and there is no inherent contradiction between authority and individual freedoms, between personal initiative and solidarity, and between unity and fruitful pluralism (GS #74k). Both state activity and private initiative are viewed as necessary conditions for the proper and just functioning of the economic order. There is room for both, although roles must be clearly defined and understood. The state has a part to play, but it is instrumental in character. This means that it is charged with facilitating the development and exercise of private economic initiative, which bears the primary, though not exclusive, responsibility for the conduct of economic life (CA #11b, #48).

It is difficult and counterproductive to specify a precise formula for arriving at the proper balance between these two. There is no ready rule of thumb as the context and particular circumstances will have to be considered. The most that can be offered, however, in weighing and balancing simultaneously the requirements of the individual's good with that of the commonweal, are the principles of solidarity, socialization, and subsidiarity. These principles are a good starting point from which to examine the competing claims between private interest and the public good. Individuals are entitled to all the necessary assistance in developing their full potential and in enabling them to live a full life (principle of subsidiarity). They must keep in mind, however, that others too are entitled to the same assistance. Hence, there is need for a sensitivity to the demands of the common good and for a readiness to harmonize one's own desires with the welfare of others and of the larger community (principle of solidarity), even to the extent of letting higher bodies intervene (principle of socialization).

The task of balancing the demands of private initiative and the obligations of the state begins with an appeal to and examination of the requirements of both the principles of subsidiarity and socialization. Both principles affirm the existence of a realm specific to the individual and the community. Private initiative is the principal engine of growth (principle of subsidiarity). However, the wounded nature of the human person and the need for public goods both give rise to a requisite oversight on the part of the state (principle of socialization).

Material and Spiritual Development: An Integral Approach

Normative economics has to address the issue of what type of development ought to be pursued. Welfarism with its underlying utilitarianism views people as calculating economic actors. In contrast, Catholic social thought sees human beings in the light of their transcendent end and treats them in accord with their manifold dimensions as moral agents, as social beings, and as stewards of the goods of the earth.

A central criterion of utilitarianism is whether individual choices contribute toward the greatest happiness of the greatest number. On the other hand, this theological approach's operational goal is conformity to the intelligible moral structure that the human person gleans from natural and divine laws. Consequently, in terms of moral accountability, utilitarianism relies on its gain-loss calculus; it is subjective in that its moral judgments are ultimately based on personal wants and preferences. Catholic social thought, for its part, acknowledges both the duties and the innate rights that come with the aforesaid structure; the human act is weighed against objective standards.

With respect to the end of economic life, utilitarianism calls for the promotion of the happiness of the whole. However, its notion of happiness is so ill-defined and so abstract as to mean just about anything that the person desires. This arises from the lack of any objective measure for distinguishing various types of pleasures, gains, happiness, or preferences. On the other hand, the social documents have a clearly defined final end, accompanied by a hierarchy of needs and values that are instrumental in attaining this ultimate goal. Moreover, they have a vision of equity in distribution, while utilitarianism does not.

Both classical liberal and Marxist economics share the same materialistic view of development. Progress and well-being are measured principally in terms of consumption and affluence. Catholic social thought finds these insufficient, even deleterious when carried to excess, because they do not serve people in their totality (OA #41, #38–39). The task of economics goes beyond the satisfaction of material needs to include those in the cultural, social, and spiritual spheres (GS #64). Personhood requires taking full account of all human needs beyond the physical. This includes needs relating to the formation of personality, such as the fundamental human values of culture, religion, and history. While both liberalism and Marxism limit development merely to the material realm, this social tradition requires the full development of the human person.

The balancing principle for these material and other "higher" needs is, of course, the principle of integral development that provides the rationale and the necessary motivation to go beyond material well-being. Furthermore, this principle resolves conflicts that arise with respect to the satisfaction of needs, at least in theory and not necessarily in practice. It recognizes a hierarchy of values where the material is subordinated to the transcendent. In other words, the more fundamental human values and needs take precedence over the satisfaction of secondary human wants.

Rightful Ownership and Use of Property: Private Rights versus Public Claims

A perennial point of contention has to do with how the right to private property ownership and use ought to be regulated. In general, classical liberalism subscribes to strong property rights. On the other hand, Marxism frowns on this right as it holds such to be the root of all societal ills. Legitimate ownership belongs exclusively to the collective.

Catholic social thought makes a distinction between the right to private ownership and its just use (CA #30b–c). The use of nature, a gift to the human person, carries with it the right to appropriate parts of it as one's own for purposes of satisfying essential needs. This is the right to the private ownership of property, even those of a productive nature; it is part of natural law. Note, however, that the end of this right is not the sheer accumulation of wealth. Rather, the right is for the specific purpose of aiding individuals provide for their needs. Furthermore, it is not an absolute right but carries with it a correlative obligation of not impeding another economic right that is far more basic and takes precedence: the right of all to have access to the goods of the earth to satisfy their basic needs (MM #43).

Rightful ownership carries with it the obligation to use such properties in a manner respectful of the more primary right of everyone to enjoy the means necessary to sustain and enjoy the fullness of life; it is an obligation to use such properties with an eye toward contributing to the good of the larger community (GS #69a). The wounded nature of the human person makes the proper exercise of this right to ownership and use even more difficult (SRS #30c). Hence, this religious tradition sees the need to subject property ownership and use to the oversight of duly constituted authorities to ensure that such a right does not self-destruct through abuse (principle of socialization). In short, the right to own property is inviolable; however, its use is governed by the demands of the common good (RN #35–36; QA #47–48). By making this distinction between rightful ownership and the just use of private property, the legitimate concerns of both classical liberalism and Marxism are addressed.

The key balancing principle to this, of course, is the principle of the universal destination of the gifts of the earth. Thus, even as the right of private ownership is respected, the use of such properties is bound by the obligation to ensure that others are also able to satisfy their needs through the proper employment of such possessions. It is only after satisfying this that the *just-use* obligation, attendant to just ownership, is fulfilled.

A related question is how output ought to be distributed between labor and capital. When it comes to the distribution of factor payments, Marxism reserves no legitimate share for the owners of capital; only labor is entitled to the output. On the other hand, a laissez-faire market approach that operates primarily according to ownership claims of property rights tends to favor economic agents who hold the upper hand in bargaining position and leverage, a de facto bias in favor of capital. This is not even to mention the advantage that capital may have in enjoying a higher marginal productivity than labor.

Catholic social thought emphasizes the importance of both capital's and labor's contributions to the productive effort; such position dates as far back as the seminal document of the modern tradition in *Rerum Novarum*'s defense of the right to ownership. While affirming the priority of labor over all the factors of production, capital included, the social documents defend the propriety of setting aside part of societal output as just compensation for the use of capital. Profits are necessary in any business undertaking (CA #35c). It not only provides just compensation for human effort and work, but it also ensures the viability and stability of economic activity and unleashes human creativity. However, profits, important as they are, should not be the only criterion governing economic decisions and behavior. The other requirements of integral development and equity must be considered as well, especially the welfare of workers who depend on capital for their livelihood.

The common understanding of rational economic behavior on the part of the firm (or the consumer) is the attainment of an optimum equilibrium that provides the greatest profits (or consumer-utility satisfaction). A profit-maximizing strategy configures economic life to the unbridled pursuit of private interests, the preferential treatment of capital over labor, a macroeconomic strategy of growth-efficiency, unfettered competition, minimal state intervention, strong property rights, and an understanding of economic life cast exclusively in terms of wealth accumulation. *Satisficing* replaces this maximization-optimization mind frame with the acknowledgment of other important nonpecuniary considerations besides profits or consumer satisfaction (Simon 1959). This movement away from a conventional profit-oriented mode of thinking is readily discernible from the tradition's twofold objectives. The tradition's series of twofold objectives demonstrates a clear preference for satisficing, rather than simple profit or utility maximization. The proper mix of satisficing between profits and other nonpecuniary goals is ushered in by the principle of integral development and its distinction between *having* and *being*.

Both workers and the owners of capital have a rightful share. A useful guide to resolving competing claims in the division of output is for the burden to fall on those who are most able to bear them (SRS #47c). This rule of thumb is consistent with the preferential option for the poor and with the just-use obligation of the universal access principle. Besides, the goods of the earth, capital, science, and technologies are all instrumental in character; their primary function is to assist in the human person's quest to live a full life. After all, labor is the subject of work. Hence, the primacy of labor principle and its norms provide much guidance on this question.

Growth, Efficiency, and Equity

Traditional mainstream understanding of economic processes is one of "scarcity-choice-harmony" (Lichtenstein 1983, 11). Economic agents are assumed to behave rationally and in a self-interested manner. Faced with competing wants and desires, the market ensures that these disparate choices result in an efficient allocation of scarce resources. Unfettered competition (and free trade by extension) and secure property rights are necessary conditions to assure the smooth functioning of the market. The objective function is Benthamite in character: providing for the maximization of preferences for the greatest number. While allocative efficiency is the microeconomic goal, the overriding concern of macroeconomics is growth, rather than equity. These ends of microeconomic efficiency and macroeconomic growth feed off each other because allocative efficiency is a necessary condition for a superior growth trajectory. Equity is a subsidiary concern since the trickle-down mechanism ultimately brings benefits to everyone from a growing economic pie. The singular focus on growth-allocative efficiency and the prevalent view that economics is solely about wealth accumulation reinforce each other. Besides engendering impersonalism, this approach leads to a failure to appreciate the nonmaterial needs of people in their cultural, social, and spiritual context (PP #19). In contrast, Marxism is concerned with equality and is heavily reliant on extensive centralized planning, intervention, and control.

Catholic social thought calls for a dual strategy of growth-efficiency and equity (MM #74) and relies on both competition and cooperation through the use of market and nonmarket mechanisms. It seeks to reap the advantages of competition even as it is concerned that such competitiveness stays within the bounds of what is healthy and beneficial. This is accomplished by fostering cooperation among economic agents.

These social documents are interested in the good of all (principles of nonexclusion); growth considerations must necessarily be accompanied by a concern for equity.[6] Without the latter, the economic order runs the risk of self-destruction as the social fabric is torn asunder or weakened by conflicts arising from an unbalanced growth path. This concern for equity is readily evident from the full spectrum of Catholic social thought's prescriptions described in the first three chapters, from the resolution of labor-management conflicts, to the incidence of public burdens, to the need to pursue a balanced-growth strategy in all sectors of the economy, and, finally, to the conduct of international trade. Furthermore, this goal can also be discerned in the tradition's advocacy of a strong middle class through broadening the base of property ownership, a task that it envisions to be within the realm of the body politic (MM #115).

The dual-track approach to labor policy (CA #15e) is another example of combining equity and growth. This social tradition pursues equity-oriented measures (such as the provision of family wages, co-ownership, co-management, and profit sharing) at the risk of dampening investments. Yet, it also calls for the protection of individual enterprise and the generation of sufficient economic growth to ensure the continued creation of employment opportunities for all.

Growth is viewed as an important objective if the whole social order is to be stable and viable into the long run.[7] Providing all with the necessary means to self-development requires sustainable growth in the economy. This obligation compels this theological tradition to hold higher expectations for the economic order in providing for *both* growth and equity (JW #18). Post–Paul VI social documents do not focus exclusively on equity, especially in the aftermath of the Soviet implosion. This is especially evident in *Centesimus Annus*. The tradition's appreciation for the need for growth is seen on various occasions too, from Leo XIII's criticism of the "absurd" equality advocated by Marxists (which it describes to be nothing but a sharing of destitution), to Pius XI's reminder of the grave obligation to provide employment, to John Paul II's acknowledgment of the vital service provided by private economic initiative.

In pursuing simultaneously growth-efficiency and equity, this theological tradition is opting for a development strategy that requires decisiveness and sustained effort. Economic history suggests a seeming incompatibility in this strategy of growth-efficiency, on the one hand, and equity, on the other.[8] Only a handful of countries have been able to achieve both, such as the newly industrialized countries of the Pacific Rim. And even in these cases, there is considerable concern over the tradeoff between prosperity and the sacrifice of freedoms to an authoritarian regime.[9]

Helpful diagnostic principles in achieving balance between growth and equity are the principles of participation, solidarity, relative equality, and universal access. However, there is very little in the literature that defines specific thresholds for what distinguishes permissible from unacceptable relative inequality.[10]

CONTRIBUTIONS TO ECONOMIC ETHICS

Wherein lies the distinctive contribution of this social tradition to normative economics? Catholic social thought challenges the classical liberal paradigm to reach for higher standards on two fronts: (1) to recognize that the end of economics goes beyond the mere efficient allocation of scarce resources, and (2) to provide not only for the greatest majority, but for all. Moreover, it exhorts standard economic thought to go beyond its positivist cast and build an economics anchored in normative commitments. On the other hand, it also criticizes the Marxist model by upholding the importance of private economic initiative and freedoms and by stressing equity, not absolute equality.

Catholic social thought critiques both classical liberalism and Marxist collectivism as unacceptable (GS #65b; OA #26, #31–37). It disagrees with the anthropological presuppositions of the former for its utilitarianism, materialism, and individualism. From these flow liberalism's reliance on the profit motive as the principal engine of economic progress, its advocacy for unfettered competition as the key economic law, and its call for property rights with minimal social accountability or oversight.

Marxist collectivism is also untenable for its materialism, economic determinism, and its subordination of individual freedoms to the expediency and dictates of the collective. It is deemed even more problematic than liberal individualism because of the worse harms it inflicts in dominating the public and private lives of people, including their beliefs and ideas.

Catholic social thought embarks on a much harder path of pursuing simultaneous twin objectives:

- of actively promoting both the individual and the common good,
- of defining progress in terms of both the material and spiritual development of the human person,
- of affirming both the right to private property and its accompanying obligation of just use,
- of stressing the role of both the state and the private sector as active agents of development,
- of recognizing and protecting the legitimate claims of both capital and labor to a rightful share in output,
- of setting both growth-efficiency and equity as operational macroeconomic goals,
- of employing both market and nonmarket mechanisms for allocating entitlements,
- and of relying on both cooperation and healthy competition.

Managing the economy is complicated when there is need to juggle multiple objectives.[11] This is especially true when there is an apparent trade-off between goals and when policy requirements point to opposite directions; the choice of a course of action is not always clear. Prudent judgment will have to be made, and there is need for a greater measure of compromise and courage, both moral and political.

The mechanics of many of these twin objectives have yet to be worked out, and, more importantly, their claims have yet to be subjected to critical examination with the use of empirical evidence. A weakness of the modern Catholic social tradition is the untested nature of many of the norms that flow from its principles. It is uncertain whether the specifics and dynamics of how to get to its vision of a just economic order are compatible with observed data. Even as theological reflections suggest a theoretical inseparability and consistency across manifold desiderata, there are no clear seamless connections between many of these goals in practice. The economic analysis of *Quadragesimo Anno's* corporatism (see appendix) is a good example of how an optimistic view of the human person must be balanced with an analytical assessment of its microeconomics. Nevertheless, one must remember that this social tradition advances only the overarching principles and norms and does not purport to present specific solutions to particular problems. Its comparative advantage lies in the former and not in the latter. After all, the tradition itself acknowledges both the need to adapt its principles and norms to local conditions (OA #4) and the importance of incorporating insights from various human sciences for such an effort (MM, part IV; GS, part II). The potential contribution of these twin objectives, no doubt judged utopian or naive by some, may very well lie in their articulation of the underlying key principles that argue for why there is no a priori basis for thinking that these objectives are intrinsically incompatible with each other.

Notes

1. See, for example, John Paul II's (1991) *Centesimus Annus*.

2. I do not suggest that pure, unadulterated classical liberal or Marxist economies exist. What we see in practice is a full spectrum of mixed economies with varying degrees of liberal and socialist policies. In comparing Catholic social teaching with these two schools of thought, my intention is to put in sharper relief what is distinctive about this theological social tradition.

3. As noted earlier, one must distinguish classical liberalism from social liberalism. The latter is amenable to relatively greater state intervention in economic life. Thus, I refer only to the classical strands of mainstream economics (new classical economics, monetarism, etc.) in the comparison that follows regarding the appropriate role of government in the economy.

4. CA #25c. See also GS #63a; OA #24; CFL #73c.

5. GS #25a notes: "Man's social nature makes it evident that the progress of the human person and the advance of society itself hinge on one another. For the beginning, the subject and the goal of all social institutions is and must be the human person, which for its part and by its very nature stands completely in need of social life."

6. See, for example, Finn (1998).

7. GS #64 observes: "Today more than ever before attention is rightly given to the increase of the production of agricultural and industrial goods and of the rendering of services, for the purpose of making provision for the growth of population and of satisfying the increasing desires of the human race. Therefore, technical progress, an inventive spirit, an eagerness to create and to expand enterprises, the application of methods of production . . . must be promoted."

8. See, for example, "The Uneasy Triangle," in *The Economist*, 9, 16, and 23 August 1952. For a discussion of other difficulties related to achieving full employment, refer also to Viner ([1950] 1958c).

9. See "Freedom and Prosperity" in *The Economist*, 29 June 1991.

10. A word of caution is in order before I conclude this section. There are many strands of thought within both classical liberal and Marxist political economy. Space constraints do not allow a more nuanced differentiation of the positions held by these varying schools. It is important to note, however, that there are many points of convergence between Catholic social thought, on the one hand, and the more interventionist strains of mainstream economics and the more moderate forms of socialism, on the other.

11. The analytical demands of this can be illustrated in the maximization of the social welfare function. Catholic social thought would impose restrictions in the choice of arguments for the objective function and would require the satisfaction of many more constraints in the maximization process.

Part IV

POSTINDUSTRIAL SOCIAL QUESTIONS: PARTICIPATIVE EGALITARIANSM

Just like scholastic economic ethics, the modern Catholic social teachings will have to evolve to accommodate the increasing complexity and intensity of human interdependence in the postmodern economy. The principal base of wealth creation in society has shifted from natural resources to human knowledge. This phenomenon adds important new economic dimensions to the social nature of the human person. In particular, relative inequality may worsen given the dynamics of a globalized, knowledge-driven economic order.

The principle of participation becomes even more important in the face of this postindustrial transformation. The central role of human skills in the information age leads to corresponding alterations in what it takes to flourish in life. These, in turn, shape the nature and the strength of the universal access principle's claims on behalf of integral human development. The following three chapters weigh the changes in these obligations and rights.

Chapter 9

MARKET-DRIVEN REDISTRIBUTION OF BURDENS AND BENEFITS

GLOBALIZATION AND THE INFORMATION ECONOMY

At the heart of the globalized, knowledge-based economy is a ceaseless reshuffling of burdens and benefits across sectors and across populations. Freer trade and technological change both share a common consequence: The gains are widespread and enjoyed by many, while the costs are concentrated and borne by a few (Mokyr 1990, 178–79).

By its nature, the unimpeded flow of goods and services in free trade pits two groups against each other. On the one hand are the consumers who benefit from trade through an increase in their real incomes and an expansion of their consumption opportunity set. Exporters likewise benefit from a broader revenue base. On the other hand, some will suffer— those whose livelihoods, lifestyles, and even political power are jeopardized given the influx of goods and services that are cheaper and, perhaps, of better quality. Among the most often-cited recent examples are the workers in the "disappearing" industries in many First World countries due to price competition from low-cost developing nations.[1]

Technical change produces a similar pattern of gains and burdens. The exponential growth of production that we have come to expect as the norm is eloquent proof that not only have advances in technology been beneficial for the most part, but that these gains have been expansive.[2] However, there are often human costs attendant to the modernization of techniques, such as the overnight obsolescence or redundancy of once highly paid skills replaced by machinery, the need to migrate, the decline in social status, the involuntary change in careers, and the painful process of job retraining in midcareer.[3] Just like free trade, the fruits of innovation are enjoyed by many while those who bear the brunt of such technical changes are relatively smaller in number and may even be concentrated in readily identifiable sectors of society (Landes 1969; Rosenberg and Birdzell 1986).

Globalization and technical change have redistributive effects on their own and, given their synergy in the postindustrial economy, we are unable to fully determine a priori how the incidence of costs and gains will change, or even whether they will cancel out each other's effects. These are matters reserved for empirical investigation. However, it is possible to partially sketch an overview of some of their expected consequences given what we already know at this point about their processes. Enough is understood to describe four features of this globalized, information economy, namely, an accelerated dynamism, a revolution of expectations (especially among the poor), a dynamic comparative advantage, and ever higher investment requirements. Each of these raises troubling questions peculiar to their specific areas, but all four converge on the pivotal role of knowledge and the prospect of a worsening relative inequality that carries significant ethical consequences.

Accelerated Dynamism

Information technologies improve market operations through a better approximation of the essential conditions of perfect competition. As information becomes plentiful, complete, and easier to access, interpret, and use, economic actors are able to act and respond much better and much more quickly. Combined with major strides in transportation, the ready availability of cheap and timely information lowers transactions costs, increases factor mobility, eliminates many barriers to entry, and leads to an ever larger number of buyers and sellers. Markets move ever closer to ideal frictionless, "instantaneous" adjustments. A good foreshadowing of what is to come in a mature, global information-driven economy are the burgeoning financial and foreign currency exchanges where developments unfold so rapidly and misfortunes so suddenly befall the unsuspecting and the unprepared. The move toward a more perfectly competitive market tightens even further the relationship between wealth creation and economic agents' agility in response time.

This acceleration in the dynamism of the marketplace imposes at least two new demands on economic actors if they are to participate successfully in the market. They must have the means (material, intellectual, and emotional) to deal with constant change, and they must be able to respond promptly. The turnaround time keeps getting shorter as information handling improves. And herein lies the nub of the problem.

In his pioneering work, T. W. Schultz (1975) observes that the capacity to deal with disequilibria is a function of human capital. This means that those who are trailing badly to begin with (most likely because of inadequate skills) will fare even worse and be left farther behind in subsequent rounds of economic activity because they are the ones who are least able to deal with constant change. Furthermore, one must remember that accelerated dynamism works both ways; it can hurt but it can also open new opportunities for gain and advancement. It is most likely that those who have the requisite personal assets and the flexibility afforded by human capital will profit and improve their relative standing from such volatility. The prize goes to the quick and the nimble. Consequently, an information economy may effect a regressive redistribution where the cost of change falls precisely on those who are unable to deal with it. Put in another way, those who are least able to avail themselves of the fresh opportunities for advancement will be left even farther behind.

The frequency, degree, and speed of necessary economic adjustments work against the lagging sectors of the economy thereby aggravating relative inequality. For those who have had the benefit of human capital development, their experience will be a common "climb to the top" or a "neoclassical convergence" where income disparities are reduced (Williamson 1996; Epstein, Crotty, and Kelly 1996). In contrast, people who do not have the requisite skills will flounder and become statistical evidence for the claim that globalization is a "race to the bottom," where progress is so unevenly spread across sectors and across populations (Froble, Heinrichs, and Kreye 1980; Barnet and Mueller 1975).

Revolution of Expectations

The Industrial Revolution's bounty has been matched by a comparable revolution in consumption for the common person. Goods and services previously accessible only to the most privileged are made available in great quantities to the general populace. Industrialization is rightly associated with mass consumption as it has precipitated a sharp drop in the cost of production stemming from the productivity gains from new technologies and organizational techniques (Landes 1969; Braudel 1967).

This era of mass consumption is giving way to a new momentum—a revolution of expectations. The costs associated with information gathering, storage, and dissemination have dropped dramatically. This has been followed by an unabated pace in the mass consumption of information-based goods and services, even those that used to be nontradables.

Another genre of inequality is generated by this revolution of high expectations in a globalized information age that condenses both space and time. The dramatic increase in the exchange of information amplifies the demonstration effect that in turn leads to ever higher expectations for those who are trailing. It spawns a dawning awareness that a better standard of living is indeed possible. The growing ranks of the newly industrialized countries (such as Korea, Singapore, Hong Kong, and Taiwan) and the impressive speed with which they have kept pace with the First World only serve to affirm for the poor both the promise and the feasibility of such improvement. The greater awareness of how others live in a shared world necessarily shapes the threshold of what is deemed to be permissible inequality and what the standards of measurement should be. The demonstration effect that tells the poor that they are no different from the rich is an empowerment that finds expression in these higher expectations that inevitably move the world community to less tolerance for inequalities. Unfortunately, these surging hopes may far outstrip real productive capacities and may go unfilled. Relative inequality is, thus, perceived to be made even worse because expectations that were raised so high could not be met.

Dynamic Comparative Advantage

Free trade is justified on the grounds of comparative advantage. In an industrial economy that is dependent on natural resources for wealth creation, nations trade with each other on the basis of which goods could be produced most efficiently (Ricardo) or on the basis of which goods are most intensive in the use of their abundant factors of production (Hecksher-Ohlin). In either event, the case for exchange in an industrial era is founded on *natural* comparative advantage.

This has changed in the shift to an economic order where knowledge has overshadowed natural resources as the engine of wealth generation. Nations "create" their comparative advantage by producing high-technology products and services through human ingenuity. Needless to say, such created comparative advantage is a function of human capital. This can be likened to a ladder where the lower rungs represent the range of natural comparative advantage, with the higher rungs reserved for the open-ended nature of created comparative advantage (Meier 1995, 455–58). And herein lies an ethical ramification of a global, knowledge-based economy. Nations that are endowed with a good and rapidly improving human capital base will be able to climb the ladder of dynamic comparative advantage even faster and leave laggards that much farther behind.

Higher Entry Costs

Related to the new regime of created comparative advantage is the steeper entry cost of developing the requisite social infrastructure for information-driven economies. The outlays for research facilities, higher-level education, engineering know-how, and other requisite support institutions are even more substantial in the postindustrial epoch because more advanced science is needed. There is greater need for interdisciplinary input and collaboration, which are time- and resource-intensive. More sophisticated and expensive equipment and tools are needed. A lengthier time from a more roundabout process is needed before desired results are produced.

This, again, is a case where those who are unable to keep pace with investments in such infrastructures will find themselves relegated to the fringes. The difference between stopping in the plane of natural comparative advantage as against moving freely in the upper reaches of created comparative advantage determines whether one is consigned to the export of primary commodities and low-end manufactures, or whether one becomes an established exporter of high value-added goods. The ability to acquire, manage, and use information largely accounts for this disparity.

REVISITING POST–VATICAN II EGALITARIANISM

Given the likelihood of a worsening postindustrial relative inequality, what does the Catholic social tradition have to offer that will be helpful for sorting through these issues of distributive justice? Are the goals, content, features, methods, and dynamics of the solidaristic egalitarianism of the era of Paul VI appropriate for a globalized, knowledge-based economy? Which parts of it are applicable and which are dated?

The social documents of Paul VI's pontificate provide insights on bringing about distributive justice in a mature industrial and globalizing economy. Casting relative equality in the language of solidarity, setting harmony as the proximate goal and fruit of egalitarianism, and embedding theological reflection within the context of its time and place–these are important concepts and practices with which to shape allocative fairness in a rapidly evolving economy. However, much work remains to be done. In addition to adapting the social documents to the fresh challenges of a transformed economy, there is need (1) to translate principles and norms from their abstract moorings into concrete practicable measures, (2) to examine the economic ramifications of redistributive policies, and (3) to approach social injustices from a broader front.

An Abstract Egalitarianism

At the heart of communitarian equality is a process of periodic redistribution aimed at keeping disparities within an acceptable range. This is accomplished through activist, extra-market oversight and intervention.

> Relative equality is the normative, distributive principle which articulates how solidaristic equality is to be realized in a social system. Regular

redistribution to redress differences between groups is necessary to preserve and foster human community. . . . *[I]t points to a situation in
which inequalities are held within a defined range set by moral limits.*
Within that range, differences of income etc. are determined by the in-
terplay of a variety of norms: need, contribution, hardship, the common
good. But *limits are set on the permissible differences by the cardinal
norm of communitarian equality with its aim of sustaining and enhancing the bonds uniting people to one another.* In the Catholic context, the
ultimate goal of this norm is that men and women treat one another as
brothers and sisters, and the restriction it places on other norms is that
they should not diminish the possibility for such treatment (Christiansen
1984, 653–54, emphasis in the original).

This dynamic is inadequate because not enough guidelines are provided for policymakers who are charged with formulating and implementing specific rules and measures. In particular, even as solidaristic
egalitarianism calls for redressing wide variances, it is unclear what relevant factors ought to be appraised for such differences. There are many
spheres of human experience, each with their peculiar needs, characteristics, and rules of justice (Walzer 1983). And even if we are able to identify specific spheres such as those defined in the Yale Task Force's (1974,
102) synthesis of *Pacem in Terris*, is there a ranking of urgency or priority in rectifying these imbalances? How are they to be measured? What
decision rules are to be followed in the face of inevitable conflicts between and within spheres? For example, in talking of the economic
rights pertaining to human work, which issue deserves immediate attention: reducing disparities in wages, ameliorating working conditions, or
creating employment opportunities? The unending and unresolved arguments over minimum wage legislation (a higher minimum wage narrows
income disparities but at the cost of widening differences in job opportunities) is an apt illustration that such tradeoffs are not merely dry, sterile
academic musings. Identifying which gaps to keep within acceptable
limits is not easy, as seen in the literature in political philosophy. Debate
has been intense over competing responses to the question of *equality of
what* (Dworkin 1981a, 1981b). Catholic social thought has much un-
tapped potential in examining this fundamental issue in egalitarianism.

A second difficult question concerns the degree of equality to be pursued. The tradition does not call for a strict, absolute mathematical
equality. It is proportional equality that is the object of its remedial measures. And herein lies the problem. What does ethical theory have to
offer in setting the maximum tolerable limits of inequality permissible?
What are the "moral limits" that Christiansen refers to but does not develop in depth? Postconciliar egalitarianism's standard of fraternal and
sororal harmony is not good enough as there are varying grades of concord. Harmony is a relative term. Are there other measures that readily
lend themselves to an easier and a more objective observation?

A third important question left unanswered is the manner by which such redistribution is to be administered. The tradition offers much in this regard: Hollenbach's (1979) three strategic imperatives, the patristic standards of allotment (Avila 1983), the scholastic notion of the just price (Baldwin 1959), and the preferential option for the poor (Dorr 1983). All these, however, do not advance enough guidelines for evaluating the justness of various methods of redistribution within the context of time and place. Moreover, there is the issue of proportionality in the harshness of methods employed relative to the inequality to be addressed. Surely, even within a social crisis of inequality, justice itself imposes limits on the various means that may be employed. This leads us to another collateral question that needs further work: the ramifications of redistributive policies on the rest of the economy.

An Uncritical Egalitarianism

A second criticism of the tradition's teachings on equity is particularly important in the context of the need to have a growing economy. This tradition has been taken to task for being naive in focusing only on redistribution without a corresponding appreciation for the equally important flip side of the issue–producing that which is to be divided.

> Regular redistribution to redress differences between groups is necessary to preserve and foster human community (Christiansen 1984, 653).

The dynamics of postconciliar egalitarianism rests on its constant redistribution. Unfortunately, the tradition stops at this and offers no assessment of the impact of such measures on the rest of the economy. It is not surprising, then, that the Catholic social documents have often been viewed as being uncritical in their pursuit of equity. P. T. Bauer (1984) describes it as a legitimization of envy. Milton Friedman (1987) laments the U.S. bishops' pastoral letter on the economy for its unmistakable collectivist strain and for the incompatibility of its laudable ends and inappropriate means (National Conference of Catholic Bishops 1986). The Lay Commission on Catholic Social Teaching and the U.S. Economy (1984) also expresses deep reservations over the meliorative methods and venues advocated by the bishops.

The core argument for these criticisms is legitimate. Normative economics and policymaking are about shaping the incentives faced by individual agents in an effort to change their behavior toward goals society has set for itself. Redistribution may give rise to incentive-distorting effects such as free-rider problems with adverse intertemporal consequences. Furthermore, there is ample evidence in both theory and practice that whatever happens in one part of the economic structure has wide-reaching ripple effects on the rest of the system. This characteristic interrelatedness is an essential insight dating all the way back to the Physiocrats' *Tableau Economique*, considered to be the starting point of economics as a science precisely because of its analysis of the economy as a single unit (Rima 1996, 64–82). To ignore the hard empirical evidence of distributive policies is to be selective in reading the signs of the times; it is to be engaged in a truncated sociohistorical method.

Much has been said about why there is a need to redistribute and what has to be redistributed, but only lately has there been consideration given to how to produce or how to ensure that there is a continued production of that which is to be distributed.[4] There is a difference in the egalitarianism of the era of Paul VI compared to the pontificate of John Paul II. In the latter, the fundamental drive toward relative equality is still present and is evident in the even greater stress on alternative work arrangements to wage contracting, such as co-management, co-ownership, and profit sharing (*Laborem Exercens*). However, even as he reiterates the tradition's longstanding criticism of the ills of economic liberalism in economism, materialism, consumerism, and individualism, John Paul II moves toward a more moderated egalitarianism by acknowledging and affirming the indispensable role of private initiative, investments, and profits in production. In acknowledging the value of markets and entrepreneurship, John Paul II mitigates the radical egalitarianism of the period of Paul VI. This, no doubt, is a reading the signs of the times in paying heed to the failed experimentation with the centralized, nonmarket approach of the former Soviet bloc. Where does this leave us in a trade-driven, information-based social order, and how do we apply distributive justice?

The lead provided by *Centesimus Annus* suggests an important direction in the future development of teachings on equity, namely, a more balanced egalitarianism that complements distributive concerns with an appreciation for the ethics and economics of production. This is consistent with another emerging change in the tradition: the extension of the principle of stewardship beyond conservation or preservation to include the optimum, efficient use of such gifts from creation.[5]

A Cure-all Egalitarianism

The postconciliar strategy to achieving distributive justice is founded on the belief that redistribution is the panacea for societal ills. Inequality is viewed as the "fault line" and becomes the prism with which to examine all other social problems.

> This radicalization represents not just a shift in emphasis but rather a change in the Church's social strategy. In the teaching of the past two decades, the correction of inequality is not just another theme added to a long list of concerns. . . . Rather, *correction of inequality becomes the key to the social strategy of the Church*, realigning other principles of

justice and conceptions of right in its wake. Egalitarian redistribution becomes the means of redressing many injustices. Injunctions are laid for the redress of inequality in the expectation that egalitarian policies will lead to surer measures for the elimination of poverty and other elementary injustices than the complicated system of social principles which had been utilized even as late as John XXIII's *Mater et Magistra* (Christiansen 1984, 655, emphasis added).

Is retrieving this strategy the proper approach for dealing with the new demands of the transformed economy?

Postconciliar egalitarianism's failure to consider the impact of its redistributive policies on production is an example of its deficiency in responding to the needs of a changed economy. Relative equality cannot be the sole nor necessarily be the lead principle around which all other norms are to be construed and applied. In the first place, social problems are multidimensional and complex in their requirements. Second, as seen in chapter 3, the postconciliar approach assumes that inequality is the root cause of social problems. This, however, has yet to be conclusively established in the literature. The most that theological reflection can claim is that there are moral limits to inequality. Theology cannot go beyond this claim and ascribe to inequality the blame for all social issues. This is an empirical question that needs to be explored including an assessment of the direction of causation.

There is need to retrieve a broader social strategy of relying on a multifaceted approach to social ethics in lieu of postconciliar egalitarianism's aversion to employing a complicated structure of principles and norms. As will be argued in the conceptual synthesis proposed in the last three chapters, social principles complement each other. Used together as a single analytical framework, the tradition's complex set of principles and norms prevents abuses, misuses, or extremes to which such teachings can be carried when used singly without reference to other relevant moral dimensions. Besides, justice has many facets, and inequality, although admittedly important and maybe even pivotal, is merely one of many other relevant factors and consequences that need to be weighed in a critical manner.

TAKING STOCK OF TEACHINGS ON EQUITY: FURTHER WORK ON UNANSWERED QUESTIONS

The limitations of postconciliar, solidaristic egalitarianism should not lead one to conclude that Catholic social thought is ill equipped to deal with a worsening postindustrial relative inequality. There is much previous work to stand on to begin with, as seen in the contributions of Leo XIII's superfluous income criterion, in John XXIII's human rights, and in Hollenbach's strategic imperatives.

Superfluous Income Criterion

Various criteria have been offered for the distribution of the goods of the earth. These include supply and demand, merit, contribution, skills, promise, and need (Rescher 1966). Need has always been the primary and the ultimate criterion of distribution in the Catholic social tradition, whether viewed from Scriptures (Gospel of Luke), patristic literature (Avila 1983), medieval scholasticism (Baldwin 1959), or modern thought (see chapter 11). This is made clear as Leo XIII rearticulates the superfluous income criterion in elaborating on the just-use obligation attendant to private property ownership.

The specification of a superfluous income criterion does not bring us far in providing guidelines for the practical application of this norm or of the more general just-use obligation. The tradition's longstanding teaching on *need* is increasingly inadequate, especially in a knowledge-based economy. In the first place, even in their original formulation, the just-use obligation and the superfluous income criterion leave many unanswered questions as to make them impracticable as workable standards. In particular, they do not address how one balances obligations to a needy neighbor at the present time against the intertemporal duties owed to one's heirs (such as paying for a college education or leaving a bequest). Furthermore, prudence–in fact justice to one's family–requires saving for a rainy day. And yet, how much savings is enough before it becomes superfluous and therefore subject to use for the welfare of one's less fortunate neighbor? This question is greatly compounded by uncertainties regarding unseen needs that may yet arise down the road.

A second difficulty has to do with the inadequacy of the tradition's standard of *need* as it currently stands. It is easy to see how the satisfaction of basic needs for the vast majority of the population becomes the primary concern in an economy of precarious survival, as in the preindustrial era of the Sacred Scriptures and the patristic and scholastic doctors. The moral sensibilities of most people should make it relatively easy to reach a consensus on this point. Many would even find it self-evident. However, in the current economy of flowing abundance where most competing claims on scarce goods are not about the satisfaction of basic needs for survival and primary health, the notion of *need* has to be recast. This redefinition is fraught with difficulties because needs become more subjective as they move farther away from survival and basic health. Economic analysis avoids this conundrum by not distinguishing between needs and wants and, then, allocating resources on the basis of consumer purchasing power. Catholic social thought, or economic ethics for that matter, cannot avoid making this distinction and must grapple with the difficulties of arriving at standards. Chapter 11 is a contribution along these lines.

John XXIII's *Pacem in Terris*

Human rights are an unavoidable consideration in any discussion of distributive justice because they provide the foundational warrants for the scope, strength, and nature of rules that will govern what individuals and communities may or may not expect from each other. In his extended presentation of rights, John XXIII's *Pacem in Terris* clearly spells out the basis for affirming and promoting the dignity of human personhood. The Yale Task Force on Population Ethics (1974, 102) [reproduced in Hollenbach (1979, 98)] provides an excellent diagrammatic synthesis.

The value of these works can be better appreciated by noting the abuse and the confusion surrounding the use of rights language (Glendon 1991). John XXIII's *Pacem in Terris* represents an advance on the perennial difficulty of implementing the notion of distributive justice. In particular, a number of conceptual and practical contributions must be noted from *Pacem in Terris* and the Yale Task Force's schematic diagram. In the first place, John XXIII discusses the philosophical foundations for egalitarianism regardless of whether it is formulated in its strong or weak versions. The fundamental equality of all human beings is rooted in a natural law that affirms the shared experiences of contingency and need that are characteristic of human existence. It is this common humanity and its accompanying demand for respect that provide the basis, indeed the starting point, and the matrix for discourse on *why it is we live together* as a community. It is this foundational parity that imbues distributive justice with its claim of primacy of place in determining the minimum essential conditions of *what it is to live together and how we are going to live together* as a community.

A second contribution pertains to the better and more concrete specification of *Mater et Magistra*'s all too general and abstract "sum of living conditions" essential for the promotion of the common good (MM #65). The manifold facets of communal and personal life are highlighted along distinct bodily, religious, sexual, familial, economic, associational, and political needs. These various dimensions provide a ready reference of categories, whether it is in examining the quality of equity within a community, or whether it is in assessing the impact of distributive policies. Distributive justice, then, will have to respect the holistic nature of human existence discussed at length in *Populorum Progressio* (chapter 3) on integral human development. We cannot focus on only one sphere of life to the exclusion of others inasmuch as human needs come in variegated ways. This is relevant, for example, for the question of tradeoffs between economic and political rights. The issue of which has precedence is not the right question to ask since both types of rights are constitutive of human dignity.

The distinction among personal, social, and instrumental rights is a third contribution that opens the door to a more nuanced application of distributive justice. After all, rights and obligations vary in the strength and content of their claims. In other words, not all rights and obligations are equal. Personal, natural rights take precedence over derivative rights. Awareness of such a sliding scale in the strength of rights is essential for resolving competing claims. Furthermore, differentiating the varying grades of rights is necessary for purposes of understanding the correlative obligations they impose and the assignation of such duties on their addressees. On top of this, the social and instrumental rights specify the obligations owed by the community to the individual. In other words, personal rights define the proximate goals of applied distributive justice while social and instrumental rights specify the means.

More work needs to be done in making rights language even more efficacious in applied distributive justice. In particular, the question of competing claims needs to be addressed. How do we resolve apparent conflicts between two spheres of life? For example, how do we deal with the case of providing employment opportunities but only at the expense of curtailing the right to engage in political action for mutual protection? This is a case where the personal right to work (economic sphere) clashes with the personal rights to social interaction and self-determination (associational and political rights). This is not merely a theoretical question, as seen in the choices faced by some developing countries in having to trade political and civil rights for economic entitlements. Note, for example, the justification for a more authoritarian governance for the sake of economic prosperity (Douglass 1994).[6] In theory, both spheres of life are important; in practice, choices between these are sometimes made in the face of scarcity and pressing contingencies.

There is also the question of conflicts within the same sphere of human experience. For example, how does one satisfy simultaneously the right to a living wage with the right to employment opportunities? Theory and empirical evidence are inconclusive on the relationship between wage legislation and the creation of new entry-level jobs, the kind of employment that most likely provides immediate relief to the marginalized (e.g., Bhaskar and To 1999). The same issue on balancing claims arises in dealing with the tradeoff between vibrant job creation (economic sphere) and alternative work arrangements such as co-management, co-ownership, and profit sharing (political and associational rights).

Social and instrumental rights may also clash across the different spheres. For example, China's one-child policy goes against the social right to found a family and procreate (sexual and family rights) but is justified by the state as necessary if it is to provide adequately for the infrastructure to service the social right to food, clothing, shelter, rest, and medical care (bodily rights) and the right to education (communication rights). Are these real or merely apparent tradeoffs? If the former, what guidelines are available? Unlike personal rights, can social and instrumental rights be ranked a priori without reference to the context of the time and the place?

Living up to positive obligations and positive rights is not easy as they generally require scarce resources. Thus, it is difficult to acknowledge economic rights in practice, even as they are appealing in theory. When it comes to actual implementation, choices will have to be made on which economic rights to satisfy first, whose economic rights take precedence, and to what degree these are to be satisfied. This is true even among the wealthiest nations. Scarcity requires not merely allocating resources but also apportioning the extent to which different economic rights or resource-using rights are to be filled. What criteria will be used for such decisions?

The need for all this additional work should not diminish the distinctive contributions of *Pacem in Terris* in clarifying both the positive and the negative rights and obligations in the key spheres of human experience. John XXIII's exposition on human rights is an advance not only conceptually but also in practical terms as it provides distinctions that are essential for the concrete application of distributive justice.

Hollenbach's Three Strategic Imperatives

In his *Claims in Conflict*, Hollenbach (1979) examines the modern Catholic social documents from a human rights perspective. To facilitate the application of rights in policy and in order to deal with competing claims, he suggests three concrete rules (p. 204):

> [T]he societal effort to implement and institutionalize rights should adopt the following three strategic moral priorities:
>
> (1) The needs of the poor take priority over the wants of the rich.
>
> (2) The freedom of the dominated takes priority over the liberty of the powerful.
>
> (3) The participation of marginalized groups takes priority over the preservation of an order which excludes them.

These normative standards provide a more detailed specification of Rawls's (1971) second rule in his vision of justice as fairness where inequalities are permitted only as they benefit the most disadvantaged in the community. Hollenbach identifies the specific areas that bear watching for purposes of measuring advantage or disadvantage: needs, freedom, and participation. However, more conceptual work needs to be done. In particular, we have to be able to distinguish needs from wants, and we need to come up with methods to measure them. Moreover, we also have to define the scope of the consumption basket for each of these two categories. In the case of the second rule, we encounter the same limitations seen in John XXIII's *Pacem in Terris*. There is need to specify further the concrete elements of liberty and freedom. This necessarily includes guidelines for dealing with conflicting claims within and across the various spheres of life. Decision rules will have to be laid out that rank these spheres in their order of importance, to the extent possible.

The third rule presents the most difficulties and requires the most extensive further work. What kind of participation is required and how will it be measured and evaluated? Is there a minimum threshold for social interaction that will be guaranteed? How does one distinguish degree and quality of participation? On top of these difficult questions is the need to understand the ripple effects of preserving, as against modifying, existing practices within the community. Changing the status quo in itself raises manifold issues such as the justification of the new order chosen among the various alternatives available to society. Moreover, while these three rules are not mutually exclusive and, in fact, overlap in many cases, how do we resolve conflicts and prioritize among these three rules in the event of a tradeoff in practice? These unanswered questions and difficulties should not draw us away from the conceptual contributions of these three rules in incorporating human rights within existing socioeconomic structures and practices.

SUMMARY AND CONCLUSIONS

A globalized, information-based economy will most likely worsen relative inequality. Having surveyed some of the concepts, norms, and principles of distributive justice in the modern Catholic social documents, where do we go from here in developing an approach to equity that responds to the ethical challenges expected from a radically evolving socioeconomic order? It is clear that postindustrial egalitarianism could learn from the deficiencies of the social documents of the past hundred years by avoiding:

- an uncritical egalitarianism that fails to account for the inseparability of wealth-income creation from its distribution.
- an all too-general, abstract egalitarianism that does not provide sufficient concrete particulars from which to draw guidelines.
- an ahistorical egalitarianism that disregards the peculiar requirements and challenges brought about by the context of actual human experience.
- a cure-all egalitarianism that examines social questions only in terms of inequity in the distribution of shared resources and outcomes.

These considerations ought to be incorporated in any further development of Catholic social thinking on equity even while preserving and building on the strengths and contributions of the tradition, both modern and premodern. The changed nature of property, observed as early as *Mater et Magistra*, suggests a convenient framework of analysis along its twofold division of the material and the immaterial. This is especially timely in light of the dawning information age. We can sharpen our thinking and approach to distributive justice by examining equity in the access to and ownership of both tangible and intangible properties. The next chapter advances the thesis that the further development of the principle of participation is the key to equity when it comes to intangible property. Equity in the distribution of tangible property, on the other hand, can benefit from distinguishing three different intermediate ends to which goods of the earth can be employed. These distinctions are examined in chapter 11.

Notes

1. Modern economic history is replete with examples of how acrimonious debate has come to be an expected rite of passage for any nation that moves toward free trade. Note, for example, the tension over the Corn Laws between the landowners and the textile manufacturers just as the Industrial Revolution is taking root in early nineteenth-century England (Bairoch 1989). More recently, we have seen the difficult and often contentious negotiations in General Agreement on Tariffs and Trade (GATT) and the World Trade Organization (WTO) over unrestricted trade in farm goods.

2. As is commonly known, it is technological change that continues to disprove the dismal Malthusian prognosis. Not only has the modern economy been able to support more people, but it has sustained this larger population base with an even higher standard of living, testimony to technology's possibilities for serving human welfare.

3. Economic history recounts examples of resistance to innovation as in the case of medieval guilds, the Luddite riots, and the intense antimachinery lobbying that sought legislative relief from the English Parliament in an effort to halt mechanization in the early days of the Industrial Revolution (Bairoch 1989).

4. It must be noted, however, that both *Rerum Novarum* and *Quadragesimo Anno* temper their exposition on the right to an adequate wage by referring to the need to assess adverse ramifications on employment opportunities (RN #65–67; QA #63–75).

5. See, for example, Piderit (1993).

6. See also ""Freedom and Prosperity" in *The Economist*, 29 June 1991.

Chapter 10

THE UNIVERSAL ACCESS PRINCIPLE: ITS EVOLUTION AND ROLE IN A KNOWLEDGE-BASED ECONOMY

INTRODUCTION

The universal access principle states that *the primary finality of created goods is the service of all regardless of how titles of ownership are assigned.* This tenet has been instrumental in underscoring the key ethical issues in the social questions of the past century. The pivotal role played by this principle is understandable since competition over scarce material resources has been a major source of conflict in the modern economy.

The universal access principle must be viewed within the context of an industrialization that is intensive in its use of the goods of the earth. On the other hand, the postindustrial era is a major transformation away from a heavy dependence on natural resources to one that is knowledge based and skill driven in its value creation. Given this sea change in the relative importance of intangible knowledge over material goods, what modifications are necessary in our formulation, understanding, and application of the universal access principle? This is the question that this chapter seeks to address.

Before I examine the changed role of the universal access principle in the globalized, information economy, it is necessary to examine first the precise nature of this principle. What needs does it address? What obligations does it create or expand? Why is it necessary? What are its moral claims? What has been its function, and how has it been used in the modern Catholic social documents? The next section traces how this principle has evolved and become axiomatic in this tradition. Even while devoting an entire chapter to the universal access principle and even after acknowledging the increased importance of knowledge in the social order, *Centesimus Annus* does not explore in depth the ramifications of such an economic metamorphosis on this pivotal canon of the tradition. What follows is an attempt to bridge this gap.

It is astonishing that there is hardly anything in the secondary literature on the universal access principle despite its indispensable role in weighing many of the social questions of the past century. This lapse may be due to its close association with the right to private property ownership and worker rights–norms that have attracted most of the scholarship by virtue of their greater visibility and more controversial nature.

ITS EVOLUTION AND USE

Much has been written on the discontinuities of modern Catholic social thought. This includes shifts in its anthropological bases, philosophical methodology, and theological warrants.[1] A distinct uniformity, however, can be found in its teachings on the principle of universal access. In fact, this principle is often viewed as the common thread that undergirds many of the tradition's economic policy prescriptions. Regardless of differences in the issues of the times, the immediate, overriding task for modern theological reflection on the political economy remains the same: configuring the social order to conform to the larger moral order in its allocation of scarce resources to competing uses. The following exposition traces how the wide variety of social concerns in the past century provides an invaluable avenue for the further development and refinement of the universal access principle.

Rerum Novarum: Articulating and Justifying the Principle

Rerum Novarum addresses the conflict between workers and capitalists in the wake of the Industrial Revolution's excesses. Its task is made more urgent given the alarming, continued alienation of workers, enticed in large part by the claims of Marxism. As a result, a substantial part of the encyclical is devoted to disabusing people of the assertions and solutions offered by radical socialism through Leo XIII's staunch and vigorous defense of the right to private property ownership. However, the encyclical also notes that there are limits to ownership rights in the face of scarcity. In many ways, *Rerum Novarum* succinctly captures the whole project of political economy when it observes:

> For God is said to have given the earth to mankind in common, not because He intended indiscriminate ownership of it by all, but because He assigned no part to anyone in ownership, *leaving the limits of private possessions to be fixed by the industry of men and the institutions of peoples* (RN #14, emphasis added).

A principal task of political economy is to delineate the limits of the right to private ownership. Herein lies the modern genesis of the universal access principle that is to see development and refinement in the next hundred years of Catholic social thought. The heart of *Rerum Novarum*'s contribution, to what comes to be known later as the principle of universal access, is found in paragraphs 14, 35, and 36. This encyclical lays down the fundamental features of the principle upon which subsequent documents build.

In the first place, Leo XIII situates the principle within its proper theological setting: All creation, including the human person, comes from God. The fruits of the earth are meant to assist the person in preserving and maintaining the gift of life from God. The human person is held accountable for the use of these gifts.

Second, the natural right of private property ownership is not absolute. The goods of the earth are meant for the common benefit of all, even as the titles of ownership are assigned and respected. In the face of scarcity, this means that goods of the earth are governed by limits both in their ownership and in their use. Furthermore, there is an important distinction between just ownership and just use.

Third, *Rerum Novarum* defines "just use" in terms of a wider diffusion of benefits accruing from private properties. There is a twofold responsibility stemming from the principle of stewardship underlying just use, namely: the obligation to self (obligation to preserve and maintain life) and the obligation to others (because of the common destination of the goods of the earth). Unfortunately, this formulation gives rise to even more unanswered questions. For example, what is the right mix of benefits to oneself and to others? Are they even commensurable at all? Does this mean that property can never be exercised for one's exclusive enjoyment? Is a social component to the use of property always a necessary condition? The encyclical fails to address these difficulties although it provides some guidelines through its *superfluous income criterion.*

Fourth, Leo XIII implicitly acknowledges a hierarchy of moral claims by assigning priority to two fundamental rights undergirding the principle of universal access, namely: the right and obligation to preserve life and the right to the common use of the goods of the earth. Both of these are deemed to take precedence over the right to private property ownership. These prior claims limit the right of proprietorship and regulate its use. These two basic rights also supersede both the contractual arrangements and operations of the free market. Leo XIII (RN #63, #57) observes that the validity of a contract lies not only in the free and mutual agreement of its parties, but also depends on its satisfaction of the fundamental precepts of natural justice. In particular, contracts pertaining to wage rates are morally valid only if they provide for a truly human life for the laborer. Thus, the principle of universal access can override the liberties undergirding private economic activity and initiative.

Fifth, *Rerum Novarum* stresses the indispensable three-way link between the right to life, the principle of universal access, and human work. These three elements are distinct but inseparable. So tight is this connection that in subsequent documents, the universal access principle is sometimes referred to as the right to life. Universal access finds its theological grounding in the belief that the goods of the earth are a gift from God in order to sustain life. Philosophically, this principle is based on the natural right to preserve life.[2] The realization of this natural right, however, presupposes the availability of two necessary elements–the goods of the earth and human labor. In other words, the goods of the earth can fulfill their function of preserving and maintaining human life and health principally through human labor.[3]

Human labor is an intrinsic part of the principle of universal access. In fact, work is *the* principal avenue that bridges the natural right to preserve human life and the principle of universal access. People toil on the earth in order to obtain the necessities that they need for basic survival and health (RN #14–15). This close and necessary connection between human labor and the principle has two important consequences. In the first place, access to work becomes another essential right (PT #18–20). Labor is both personal and *necessary*. It is necessary because it is the primary means through which people appropriate the goods of the earth for their family's sustenance. It is the principal way by which the person satisfies the natural obligation of preserving and maintaining life. Thus, another consequence of the close link between human labor and the principle of universal access pertains to the right to adequate wages (RN #61–63). Wage labor[4] is, for most, the only means of access to the essential goods of life, the latter being a fundamental right of all.[5] It is important to note that the basic right to the means of life leads to two other derived rights, namely: the right to have a job and the right to a living wage for that employment.

Sixth, in addition to affirming the right to private property ownership, Leo XIII observes that there is an obligation to have this right enjoyed by as many people as possible. After all, widespread property ownership is another critical mode for implementing the universal access principle in the social order.

Quadragesimo Anno: Individual and Social Character of Labor and Capital

Quadragesimo Anno comes at a time when there is still apprehension over the contentious issues dividing labor and capital. However, this labor-management friction is overshadowed by broader conflicts arising from inequities in the socioeconomic order. In particular, Pius XI criticizes the moral failings of an unfettered capitalism that has engendered economic domination and an increasingly intolerable disparity in the living conditions of the rich and the poor. This larger tension in the social order is made even more acute by the seeming inability of capitalism to provide gainful employment for many during the Great Depression.

Quadragesimo Anno affirms *Rerum Novarum*'s defense of the right to private property ownership and also follows the lead of Leo XIII in counterbalancing this right with a reiteration of the conviction that the earth ought to provide for human "needs in an orderly and stable fashion" (QA #56). However, Pius XI develops this norm further.

First, *Quadragesimo Anno* sees a twofold personal and social nature to ownership. These must be balanced to avoid the extreme claims of collectivism and individualism (QA #45–46). Both dimensions are necessary, and there is an ideal mix between the two. This desired mean, however, is not defined and is left to prudential judgment as it necessarily varies according to historical circumstances.

Second, Pius XI develops further the distinction between just use and just ownership by associating them with different virtues. In particular, the acquisition and transfer of private property ownership are governed by commutative justice; the just use of such privately owned properties, by charity. This differentiation is important in defining the limits of just use and of just ownership. In fact, the encyclical remarks that the misuse or nonuse of private property does not forfeit the right per se. Use and ownership do not operate under the same moral limits and rules (QA #47).

Third, even as it adopts Leo XIII's Thomistic formulation, *Quadragesimo Anno* extends the moral obligations surrounding superfluous income. While acknowledging that the use of excess earnings is still properly within the realm of charity, Pius XI refers to it as a "grave obligation" where the use of superfluous income is "not left entirely to his [the individual's] own discretion" (QA #50). Furthermore, Pius XI suggests that superfluous income ought to be used to generate employment opportunities. It is also important that these jobs be a genuine contribution to society by producing commodities that are useful (QA #51).

Fourth, just as it does for property ownership, *Quadragesimo Anno* ascribes a twofold personal-social character to human work. Labor has a social dimension to it because human work is not accomplished in isolation from others. By its nature, economic life is a cooperative venture, and unless there is regard for both its individual and communal aspects, human labor "can neither be equitably appraised nor properly recompensed according to strict justice" (QA #69). Unfortunately, the encyclical does not pursue this insight further and fails to delve deeper into why or how the social aspect of human work affects the question of equity in compensation. It is only much later in *Laborem Exercens* and *Centesimus Annus* that these issues are addressed.

Pius XII: Primacy in the Hierarchy of Claims

The 1941 *Pentecost Address* of Pius XII commemorates the fiftieth anniversary of *Rerum Novarum*. It restates the fundamental right of every person to make use of the goods of the earth and highlights the salient features of the principle that are deemed to be of central importance.

In the first place, Pius XII explicitly affirms the primacy of this principle in the hierarchy of values and claims, and he describes the right to the use of the goods of the earth to be so basic as to precede all "other clear and undisputed rights over material goods," including the right to private property ownership, the right to individual economic initiative in the free exchange of goods, and the right of the state to oversee and regulate both of the aforesaid institutions of private property and markets (Pius XII 1941, 221). Pius XII takes this a step further by asserting that these latter rights are, in fact, meant to serve and promote the more primary right of using the goods of the earth.

Second, Pius XII observes that compliance with the principle of universal access is a precondition for the attainment and preservation of harmony and prosperity in the social order. Third, he maintains that this principle is not an end in itself but is merely a means to a higher end. The use of the material goods of the earth is meant solely to facilitate the human person's fulfillment of moral duties and obligations. The principle is fundamentally instrumental in character and cannot be separated from the human well-being that it seeks to promote.[6]

The 1942 *Christmas Message* affirms the right to the use of the goods of the earth as a natural foundation for serving the dignity of the human person. Hence, a necessary feature of a just social order is a wide diffusion of property ownership where people are given the opportunity to acquire the means of production. Pius XII (1942, 53) sees this as a basic obligation (see also MM #114).

Mater et Magistra: A New Kind of Property

Mater et Magistra reiterates the earlier formulation of the principle as an implicit obligation for broadening private property ownership because property has a functional role in enabling individuals to provide for their families' needs. Like his predecessors, John XXIII still views the social responsibility of private property more as a matter of humane action and Christian charity, rather than of strict justice (MM #120). *Mater et Magistra* reaffirms the purpose of the principle of universal access, namely, to support the human person to achieve perfection in both the natural and supernatural orders. This proper hierarchy of order is deemed to be an essential part of the principle (MM #246).

Mater et Magistra's distinctive contribution is its recognition of the shift in the wealth-generating capacity of the social order. John XXIII argues that livelihoods are derived not only from working with natural resources but also from professional skills. This transformation has been accompanied by a changing attitude whereby income from labor is increasingly held in greater esteem than revenues from property ownership. This is seen as a regular part of the advance in civilization (MM #106–67). Unfortunately, John XXIII fails to pursue further the moral implications of this extended concept of private property. For example, the question of access to this alternative form of asset holding is not addressed. It is not until forty years later in *Centesimus Annus* that this phenomenon is brought up again with some of its moral implications highlighted.

John XXIII's *Pacem in Terris* casts the moral claims of the universal access principle in the language of human rights. Using a schema of interlocking personal, social, and instrumental rights (Hollenbach 1979, 98), this principle provides the warrants for the economic and bodily rights of the encyclical.

Gaudium et Spes: Raising the Standards

Gaudium et Spes is important for our understanding of the principle because this pastoral constitution summarizes and synthesizes the teachings on universal access up to this point. It recasts the principle as a "right of having a share of earthly goods sufficient for oneself and one's family" (GS #69a) and as the "law of the common destination of earthly goods" (GS #71e). The theological foundation of this principle is founded on the understanding that God intended created goods for the use of all.

Vatican II secures the scope (nonexclusion) and the end (holistic development) of the principle of universal access by specifying vital imperatives in applying the principle to economic life:

1. The end of economic activity is not a mere increase of goods or profit but service to the human person (GS #64a).
2. The purpose of this service to the human person is a well-rounded development that encompasses the material as well as the intellectual, moral, and spiritual dimensions of personhood (GS #64a).
3. No one may be excluded from the benefits of the created world and its economic activity (GS #64a).
4. The principle requires the provision of gainful employment, that is, employment opportunities at a living wage (GS #70), since labor is the avenue by which universal access to the goods of the earth fulfills the obligation to preserve life (GS #67b).
5. A crucial two-dimensional balance has to be maintained in applying the universal access principle. In providing for the necessities of all, an appropriate proportionality must be observed

(a) between the interests of both the individual and the community, and (b) between present and future generations (GS #70).

6. The essence of the just use of any private property is that it should benefit not only the owner but others as well (GS #69a). There is a social character that cannot be separated from the private nature of its ownership (GS #71e).

7. There will be differences in societal arrangements across communities in regulating private property ownership and use. Regardless of these variations, however, these institutions are ultimately subject to the principle of the universal destination of the goods of the earth (GS #69a).

An original contribution of *Gaudium et Spes* to the evolution of this principle is its treatment of superfluous income. Leo XIII and Pius XI follow St. Thomas in defining superfluous income as the residual earnings not needed to maintain the individual's station in life. Vatican Council II takes a different approach by embracing John XXIII's understanding that superfluity is determined not by one's social status but by the needs of others (see GS #69a, fn. 10). This change in orientation is emphasized by reference to similar teachings on property ownership found in patristic literature (GS #69a). Furthermore, there is a greater sense of urgency attached to the principle. In *Rerum Novarum* and *Quadragesimo Anno*, superfluous income is governed not by justice, but by the virtue of charity. By the time of *Gaudium et Spes*, however, this obligation is no longer seen as a matter of charity but of justice. This shift is also evident in the application of this principle to the misuse or underutilization of private property. For Pius XI, these failings do not warrant nullifying the right itself (QA #47). In contrast, *Gaudium et Spes* sees justification in the expropriation of misused or underutilized lands (GS #71f). Another shift in application is on the question of alternatives to contractual labor agreements such as worker co-management, co-ownership, and profit sharing in business enterprises. Worker participation is increasingly presented as a moral imperative (GS #68a).

Whether for superfluous income or the expropriation of underutilized properties or greater worker participation, the boundaries imposed by social life on private property ownership and use have become increasingly restrictive given a more urgent sense of extreme need. There is a marked shift toward a more stringent interpretation and application of the principle, away from the scholastic social-status approach to superfluous income in favor of the stricter standards of the patristic doctors. The relative unmet needs of others, rather than one's social standing, become the point of reference for determining excess income within the universal access principle. The principle is now viewed through the spectacles of justice as perfected by charity (GS #69a).

Populorum Progressio: Personal Growth and Development

Populorum Progressio defines the crux of the social question as the need to establish balance between what is rightfully private and what is properly social. However, even as it acknowledges conflicts between private rights and community interests, the encyclical fails to pursue this issue further by providing concrete guidelines on how such frictions ought to be resolved. Conscious of the unique historical, geographic, and cultural grounding of such problems, Paul VI confines himself to a general statement on the obligation of public authorities to find a solution in cooperation with all the parties involved.[7]

Paul VI refers to the principle as the "universal purpose of created things" (PP #22), thereby posing the principle in terms of its end (the preservation and maintenance of human life) and highlighting an instrumental role of the gifts of the earth in the process. He also emphasizes that the primary finality of created goods is the provision of the individual not only with a livelihood but also with the means for personal growth. People have the right to use what is necessary for their survival and development. The close links between the universal purpose of created things and human labor is underscored once again.

Addressing the hierarchy of claims, the encyclical restates the primacy of the universal access principle over the right to private property and the rights related to the operation of the free market. It also embraces *Gaudium et Spes*'s more stringent standards as in the acceptability of expropriation as a necessary meliorative measure (PP #24). However, *Populorum Progressio* goes beyond *Gaudium et Spes* by noting that even the proceeds from such expropriation are not to be left to the discretionary use of the owners as there is still a social obligation attached to these funds. In particular, capital flight is viewed as morally reprehensible. Paul VI firmly places the use of private property within the purview of justice, rather than of charity, and adopts the Council's choice of relative need, rather than social standing, as the benchmark for guiding the individual's use of private property.

Laborem Exercens: Access through Labor

Laborem Exercens describes universal access as "the first principle of the whole ethical and social order" (LE #89; see also LE #64, #65). In an extensive discussion of the spirituality and dignity of labor, this commemorative encyclical lays the groundwork for the claim that *being* is a function of both *having* and *doing*. In other words, human work is important not only because it provides the means necessary for survival and health, but also because work itself is constitutive of character, personality, and quality of life. Human labor can either add to the perfection of one's existential *being*, or it can create obstacles and difficulties that reduce the quality of one's experience of *being*.

A principal argument of *Laborem Exercens* is the priority of labor over capital or any other factor of production for that matter.[8] Using the preeminence of labor over capital, John Paul II develops in greater detail the interrelatedness of human labor, the principle of universal access, and the right to life. This close link can be summarized as follows:

1. The priority of labor can be justified from its necessary character: that it is principally through labor that the person gains access to the goods of the earth. After all, it is through human work that the gifts of the earth are appropriated for human use (LE #53). Hence, John Paul II criticizes the error of economism in treating labor as a mere factor of production that puts it on a par with inanimate inputs. The priority of labor stems from human flourishing as the primary finality both of the goods of the earth and of all economic activities.

2. Human labor is also personal because it is essential for the individual's growth and development. Labor per se is not for the sake of pecuniary gain; rather, material accumulation is for the sake of labor and the fulfillment of its (labor's) ends. Material goods are central to providing people with the "workbench" that facilitates their efforts. These goods are merely instrumental in helping individuals earn a livelihood through their labor. The principle of universal access assures each person a "workbench" whether for human labor as a livelihood (work as necessary) or as a means of building and perfecting character and personality (work as personal). These two dimensions are best captured by the encyclical when it observes that the worker "takes them [referring to private property] over *through* work and *for* work" (LE #53, emphasis added).

3. Labor serves as a natural distributive mechanism that apportions access to the goods of the earth in an orderly fashion. Consequently, it is essential for the market to provide both employment opportunities and a living wage.

Laborem Exercens highlights yet another dimension of the social character of labor. It rejects claims for near-absolute rights to ownership and use on Lockean grounds that private property is nothing but the just desserts for the people who invest themselves in making nature plentiful in its yields. John Paul II rejects this argument by noting that the fruitfulness of capital, or any property for that matter, also comes about because of the labors of earlier generations. Current levels of productivity and skills have been facilitated in some way by the efforts of those who had contributed to the production and accumulation of present stocks of tools, technology, and know-how. Hence, human work is never done in isolation and always stands on the shoulders of others. There will always be a social aspect and character to property. This is key to appreciating the social nature of property ownership, especially of the means of production. Consequently, excessive proprietal claims can be avoided by viewing property through the prism of the earlier labor embodied in the tools, the technology, and the materials that make contemporary work so bounteous.

Sollicitudo Rei Socialis

Sollicitudo Rei Socialis echoes what has been taught earlier on the primary finality of economic activity–service for the needs of all. Both the gifts of the earth and the fruits of personal labor are imbued with a communal dimension flowing from the social character of labor. The right to property ownership is meant to facilitate universal access. It is this latter principle that instills a social character to property (SRS #42e).

Centesimus Annus: Full Circle Completed

It is in *Centesimus Annus* that we see a significant advance in our understanding and application of the principle of universal access. As early as 1891, there is already an appreciation for the wide range of divine gifts that include not only the earth's abundance but also personal skills. Unfortunately, *Rerum Novarum* and the subsequent social documents focus exclusively on the fruits of the earth as the principal object of the universal access principle in developing public policy. It is only in *Centesimus Annus* that attention is finally accorded to that signal gift in creation– the person as a gift to self and to each other.

> Indeed, besides the earth, man's principal resource is man himself (CA #32c).

> Not only has God given the earth to man, who must use it with respect for the original good purpose for which it was given to him, but man too is God's gift to man (CA #38a).

In an entire chapter devoted exclusively to the subject of private property and the universal access principle, John Paul II broadens the latter's scope by including human skills and knowledge as part of the entire range of gifts from God subject to the principle (John Paul II 1991, chapter 4). He also notes a critical defining characteristic of the postmodern economy: the source of the wealth-generating capacity of economic activity has been shifting away from natural resources and moving toward human capital. This encyclical expands on what has already been apparent as early as *Mater et Magistra*, that there is another form of property ownership, one that is nonmaterial: human skills and know-how.

> Whereas at one time the decisive factor of production was the land and later capital . . . today the decisive factor is increasingly man himself, that is, his knowledge, especially his scientific knowledge, his capacity for interrelated and compact organization . . . (CA #32d).

The enhanced role of human capital[9] in economic activity changes the moral implications of the universal access principle in ways that, unfortunately, are not explored even in a preliminary way in *Centesimus Annus*. How different are the demands of distributive and legal justice in a knowledge-driven social order compared to one that is natural resource based? What changes in obligations and rights are necessary in social, economic, and political arrangements? These are the questions reserved for the next section.

Summary: Universal Access Principle in the Industrial Era

Even as the original social question has expanded in scope over the past century from labor-capital conflicts to the international North-South friction, there has been continuity and development in the tradition's understanding of the universal access principle. This fundamental postulate has also been referred to as the principle of the common use of goods (LE #82), the right to life and subsistence (LE #82), the law of the common destination of earthly goods (GS #71e), the universal purpose of created goods (PP #22), and the principle of the universal destination of goods and the right to their common use (LE #65). It is considered to be *the* cornerstone for resolving competing claims to the point of being described as "the characteristic principle of Catholic social doctrine: [that] the goods of this world are originally meant for all" (SRS #42e). This is the wider context of most other rights in the social order, a core right that other derivative rights must seek to preserve, protect, and serve (LE #64).

Common to the modern social documents is the understanding that the principle's moral claim is that every person has a right to the means that are essential to human life. The theological warrant for this claim is rooted in the conviction (1) that human life is a gift from God and is accompanied by the obligation of preservation and development, and (2) that the earth's fruits are given by God for achieving the ends of human life. Consequently, every person is a holder of the right to access the means necessary for life, understood in its broadest sense from physical survival to integral human development.

This access is gained by means of three non–mutually exclusive avenues: through private property ownership, wage labor, or gifts and transfers (including government entitlements and assistance in cash or in kind). These channels provide the person with the necessary purchasing power to procure the requisite goods of life through the marketplace.

In agrarian and industrial economies, such access is keyed to a livelihood. This, in turn, requires tangible property (whether others' or one's own, such as land or industrial capital) as a necessary complement to human work. Human labor toiling on the gifts of the earth, with the aid of tools furnished by the earth itself, has been the primary mode by which people have acquired the material necessities for sustenance. Hence, we have the affirmation of the right to private property ownership, even of the means of production, based on the argument that such properties ease the burden of the daily human task of providing for oneself and one's dependents (RN #7–23).

For those who do not own employment-generating property, participation in the labor market is an unavoidable route. Given the central importance of property as a requisite complement if human labor is to be fruitful, the propertied become the addressees of the obligations defined by the principle. The nature of their responsibility can be found in the attendant "just-use" duties that come with ownership, that is, using these properties both for one's own welfare and for others' well-being. This finds expression in the *superfluous income criterion* and the mandate to create employment opportunities at a living wage. These worker rights and employer obligations have been perennial teachings throughout the tradition, finally culminating in the systematic exposition of John Paul II in *Laborem Exercens* and summarized concisely in the principle of the primacy of labor.

Gifts and transfers, established through custom, law, and usage, are the safety net of last resort if wage-labor contracting fails as a viable option. In this case, the preferential option for the poor, the principle of solidarity, and the principle of socialization provide the essential spirit in the implementation of such protective mechanisms.

The three channels through which the person procures the means necessary for life create the close and integral complementarity between the universal access principle and the other principles and norms of the tradition, especially the primacy of labor principle and private property ownership. They are distinct from each other, yet inseparable. After all, access to the means of life is premised on access to working with some property. These properties are instrumental in providing the necessary purchasing power to be able to participate in the market, either directly (through the returns from or the productive employment of one's own property), or indirectly (through wage earnings from working with someone else's property), or both.

KNOWLEDGE ECONOMY: CHARACTERISTICS AND ETHICS

The foundational premise of the universal access principle stands unchanged through its evolution in the past century: the provision of the means necessary to subsistence and human flourishing. However, the context of such human thriving has changed. It now remains to examine the postindustrial epoch and the changes it is expected to effect in the principle's content, claims, and addressees.

Characteristic #1: Beyond Subsistence Rights

Unlike feudalism or the early modern period, the information age is no longer an economy of tenuous survival but is one of accelerating abundance.[10] This shift provides a good occasion to revisit hard questions on the universal access principle that have never really been satisfactorily addressed in the literature. In particular, is this principle only limited to the right to subsistence? Or does access extend beyond mere survival and basic health to include a right to avail of the goods and social resources (roles, services) that are necessary for human thriving? The answer to this determines the nature and the strength of the moral claims that flow from this principle. After all, the requirements of human flourishing are obviously more time- and culturally-conditioned compared to the biological requirements of survival and basic health. The scope of the claims is different. Furthermore, this question has much bearing on the debate over economic rights inasmuch as a more expansive interpretation of the principle leads to a more generous assignation of rights and their corresponding obligations.

Is the universal access principle limited to basic subsistence rights?[11] An examination of the spirit of the principle would be helpful in this regard. One must remember that the proximate issue leading to the articulation of the principle in its earliest form is the conflict between the capitalists and the workers of a maturing Industrial Revolution. The principle is pivotal in allowing Leo XIII to accept as legitimate the claims of both the capitalists (the right to own and benefit from their ownership of the means of production) and the workers (the right to decent working conditions and a living wage). The principle is used by Leo XIII to remind the owners of capital of the concomitant obligations to their ownership.

Given the kind of assistance called for by the tradition for the poor, the intent of the principle goes beyond provisioning for mere basic survival and health. It includes providing the means that are necessary for excelling in various facets of life. Thus, Leo XIII speaks not only of giving workers a livelihood for basic sustenance, but he also calls for jobs and an adequate wage that allows them to become property owners themselves and move upward in society. This broad scope is echoed by the subsequent documents in their use of the principle on questions of relative inequality. The continued evolution of the universal access principle across the social documents of the tradition provides ample arguments to support the claim that the principle is still operative and binding even in an economy of plenty. After all, the principle's end is not human survival or basic health alone, but integral human development.

Characteristic #2: Heightened Subjective Dimension

A knowledge-based economy strengthens even further what *Laborem Exercens* (#22–27) describes as the *subjective dimension* of work and accentuates the instrumental role of human capital. The differentiation of the industrial from the knowledge-based economy is probably better and more accurately described as a shift in the *degree*, and not of substance or direction, to which economic life is a function of human capital. After all, the pivotal contribution of technical change and innovation to modern industrialization has been documented and discussed extensively (Landes 1969; Mokyr 1990). Empirical studies attribute a substantial part of growth to intangible human factors (Denison 1962).

This signal human role in economic productivity becomes even more pronounced in an information age. Human capital has eclipsed natural resources even further in creating value.[12] The even greater stake of personal labor in the information economy, on top of what is already a formidable contribution to begin with, only serves to provide even greater empirical support for the importance accorded by *Laborem Exercens* to the subjective dimension of work. This shift toward a skill-dependent economy makes it that much easier to justify the provision of a living wage, even by the neoclassical standards of the marginal productivity theory of factor payments (Clark 1899).

What are the implications of a heightened *subjective dimension* of work to the universal access principle? In a natural resource–based economic order, the object of the principle is access to the tangible goods of the earth. However, in a skill-driven order, the scope of the principle is expanded to include access to the skills and knowledge that are indispensable for the subsequent procurement of the other goods of life. To use the language of Walzer (1983), these skills have become the "dominant goods" that now hold the key to participation in the many other spheres of life. Thus, human capital can be viewed as a legitimate object of the universal access principle. Just as the goods of the earth are said to be for the common benefit of everyone, the same can be said of human capital. However, there is an important difference between natural resources and human capital as an object of the universal access principle. Unlike material goods, *human skills and knowledge are not merely instrumental but are also constitutive of human perfection.*[13] On the basis alone of their being integral elements of human thriving, requisite growth in personal talents and knowledge justifies moral claims to the means necessary for their development. The increased importance of their *instrumental role* only serves to add even greater moral weight, urgency, and imperative to nurturing human gifts and to ensuring access to the necessary means to do so.

The center stage that human ingenuity has taken (relative to material goods) in economic life accents two facets of human development:

1. The intrinsic value of human capital development as a *bonum honestum*, that is, as a quasi-end desired in itself.
2. The instrumental value of human capital development as a prerequisite to a meaningful life, that is, as a *bonum utile*, given its central role in determining access in a knowledge-based economy.

As argued in the conclusion of this chapter, the increased prominence and appreciation for the instrumental value of human development present both opportunities and hazards for realizing the teleology of economic life.

Characteristic #3: Intensified Socialization

A knowledge-based economy intensifies and expands further what John XXIII describes as the *socialization* of the social order. The prodigious growth in the scope of human knowledge and its increased sophistication highlight the greater importance of specialization, cooperation, and division of labor. Human interaction and collaborative effort become even more essential in creating and utilizing information and data. Consequently, John Paul II's observation that human labor is essentially work *with* others and *for* others carries even greater relevance in a postindustrial order (CA #32b). As the economy becomes more knowledge based, individuals move toward ever greater dependence on each other in acquiring, developing, and exchanging requisite information. An individual's knowledge and skills interact with others' human capital either as an input, an output, or maybe even both. The further development of knowledge is in large measure heavily reliant on the legacy of others' previous efforts. Human learning is a function of the critical mass with which it interacts; it is, for the most part, incremental in nature and builds on earlier and concurrent works. Human skills are gained and honed primarily through actual doing, the instructions of others, or participation in the larger community. Ethical implications follow in the wake of such an intensified and expanded "socialization," both in the general processes of social life and in the acquisition of the factor (human knowledge) responsible for the vibrancy of the transformed economy.

The paradox of John XXIII's "new" kind of property

A justification for private property ownership of material goods is the way they provide the individual with autonomy, freedom, and security in meeting recurring needs amidst the uncertainties of life (RN #7–23). In many ways, the same claim can be made for John XXIII's "new" kind of property: human skills and knowledge (MM #106–07). In fact, one may even cast this claim in stronger terms since skills and knowledge are internal in nature and provide the individual with an even greater degree of freedom and security, since they are not subject to the vagaries of weather, accidents, or theft unlike land or other tangible properties.

This greater autonomy, however, is true only up to a certain point. There is a paradox in this intangible "new" kind of property in that it introduces a different type of uncertainty and dependence. Given the nature of knowledge creation and application, the individual has lost some measure of autonomy because of a resulting greater dependence on the human capital of others. In many cases, such skills and knowledge are so specialized as to be productive only when used in conjunction with a significant amount of input from others' skills and knowledge and complemented by a substantial amount of material capital input. The requisite "workbench" has become even more complex and sophisticated in a knowledge-based economy with a consequent ironic loss of some individual autonomy. This serves to highlight even more the social character of human toil.

An amplified social character of human labor

The metamorphosis of economic activity into one that is knowledge-based expands the social character of human capital. After all, people have to interact even more intensively and extensively with the larger community both in their contribution to the pool of shared knowledge and in their demand for inputs from this same stock of human capital.

Quadragesimo Anno (#45–48, #69, #110) discusses the social character not only of capital but also of labor. The claim that there is a social mortgage to tangible property in a natural resource–based order has been argued repeatedly (Phan 1984; Johnson 1981; Wheeler 1995). The emergence of a skill-dependent economy provides a timely opportunity to examine in greater depth a similar mortgage for intangible property.

"Just-use" obligations attendant to personal toil and skills

Are there obligations that follow in the wake of the social character of human work? The "just-use" obligations attached to tangible property are well established in the tradition. Thus, John Paul II describes investment as a moral decision (CA #36d). Paul VI echoes the call for land reform and even sees justification in expropriating misused or unused land that could benefit the poor (PP #24). Pius XI calls it an act of liberality to use one's superfluous income in the creation of employment opportunities for others (QA #51). And, of course, there is also Leo XIII who, writing against the backdrop of a still predominantly agrarian order, views human toil as primarily organized around the bountifulness of the land. Thus, he considers it a moral obligation to allow nonowners both to work on the land of the propertied and to share in its fruitfulness (RN #14). The moral claims of the universal access principle are not a peculiarly modern phenomenon. One only has to look at Old Testament gleaning laws (*Deuteronomy* 24:19–22; *Ruth* 2) and the Jubilee law (Leviticus 25:8–55) to understand that this principle is not original to the modern Catholic social documents.

The heightened social dimension of human labor occasioned by a skill-intensive economy raises the question of whether a case of a "social mortgage" on personal gifts, skills, and talents can be made comparable in scope and degree to that made on tangible private property. After all, human labor entails people's investment of their very selves, personality, and sweat that turn such effort into a most personal activity. Does the just-use obligation apply to intellectual property as well, and by extension, to personal skills and gifts? Is there a comparable obligation on the part of individuals to let others benefit from their personal skills and knowledge? Are skills and knowledge "common" in the way the gifts of the earth in a natural resource–based economy are common?[14] Rawls (1971) includes inequalities even in personal endowments as subject to the rules of his *justice as fairness*.

Examining these questions is beyond the scope of this paper. However, there is enough in the tradition to provide a preliminary assessment of just-use obligations for intangible forms of property. Catholic social thought has been unequivocal in its affirmation that even personal skills and talents are also meant for the welfare and benefit of others. As early as *Rerum Novarum*, "just use" has been understood to encompass both material goods and personal gifts.

> The substance of all this [referring to the just use of property] is the following: whoever has received from the bounty of God a greater share of goods, whether corporeal and external, *or of the soul*, has received them for this purpose, namely, that he employ them for his own perfection and, likewise, as a servant of Divine Providence, for the benefit of others (RN #36, emphasis added).

> [T]he goods of nature and *the gifts of divine grace* belong in common and without distinction to all human kind . . . (RN #38, emphasis added).

The individual's skills and knowledge are personal in nature, but they are nevertheless still imbued with a communal dimension and subject to the expectations of stewardship.

The move toward an information-based economy has expanded the scope and sharpened further the social character of labor and its embodied human skills and knowledge. The central role of human capital in an information-based economy brings with it the obligation to contribute to society. The heavy and unavoidable use of societal inputs to develop and nurture human capital produces a debt to the community. In addition, specialization has made individuals interdependent to an even greater degree. Whichever way one looks at it, nurturing human capital is an endeavor that is intrinsically social. In the same way that material private property is viewed as a social mortgage, it would appear that personal endowments are also bound to the same social mortgage, perhaps bound to an even stricter social obligation. *Rerum Novarum*'s distinction between just ownership and just use of private property would seem to apply also to personal human skills and knowledge, and on even more compelling moral grounds, because the greater interdependence ("socialization" as *Mater et Magistra* describes it) of work organization and economic activity has intensified and expanded the social character of personal gifts. Standards for personal accountability and stewardship for the gift of labor become more exacting as work requires even more interaction with others. There are ample grounds within the tradition to argue for attendant prima facie "just-use" obligations to personal gifts and skills.[15] However, the form, the correlative rights (if any), and the strength of the claims from such obligations remain to be worked out.

Characteristic #4: Higher Entry Cost

The knowledge-based economy raises the standards, requirements, and inputs for *Populorum Progressio*'s integral human development. Human flourishing occurs within community and is heavily, although not wholly, time- and culturally-conditioned. The shift to a knowledge-driven economy necessarily changes the understanding of what it is to thrive in life arising from alterations in what the individual and the community come to expect of each other.

Community expectations

A technologically advanced society leads to higher expectations of what people are supposed to bring to the common life. The shift to a knowledge-based economic order raises the "entry cost" for meaningful participation in the life of the community. The provision of the basic essentials for physical survival and health is no longer sufficient to guarantee a significant level of meaningful interaction with others. There is a higher threshold of requisite skills expected as reflected in the more stringent demands for literacy and numeracy even for entry-level employment. Such changes in minimum skills and learning lead to a corresponding rise in both the quantity and the quality of material goods needed by individuals for their integral development. This is also caused in part by the even greater time intensity or more roundabout nature of human capital formation that has become key to productive and purposeful engagement in an information-based economic order.

Personal expectations

A higher threshold of what is acceptable as "human" living leads to a corresponding rise in what is expected of the community. Individuals demand more from the community in the same way that the community requires more of individuals. People also come to expect more from each other.

Advances in social organization, science, and "miracle" technologies have greatly expanded the array of resources and aids available not only for basic survival and health but also for growth and development. A wider variety and a more refined set of policy tools has enhanced and honed the state's ability to intervene effectively and unobtrusively in the political economy without unduly stifling private initiative. Coupled with a greater sensitivity to human rights, this breathtaking and unrelenting advance on a wide front has made the marginalization and poverty of people increasingly unacceptable. Modern technology and new forms of social organization can (and are expected to) make life more human.

Changes in what constitutes the minimum standards for "human" life and the continuing refinement in the understanding and organization of community life necessarily translate into a shift in the boundaries that social life imposes on the private realm of autonomous action. In particular, practices that may have been tolerated in the past may no longer be tenable in the present. For example, violations of human rights and the large-scale loss of lives to famine or genocide are less likely to be accepted compared to earlier epochs.

Impact on universal access principle

The "entry cost" for meaningful participation in society is much higher in the knowledge economy because of the greater expense of furnishing people with access to the requisite goods for integral development. The usual approach of providing people with purchasing power to meet their minimum needs is no longer sufficient. More is required: that of providing people with the necessary skills to sustain a substantive participation in socioeconomic life. Land reform, welfare entitlements, or workfare will not satisfy the full obligations of a transformed universal access principle in a knowledge-based economy. Having access to the gifts of the earth is only a first step; it must be accompanied by access not only to information but access also to the necessary skills to acquire, process, and use that information. This is essential both for people's economic lives and for their participation in the larger affairs of the community. Economic policy can no longer be content with the natural rate of unemployment. The three to five percent unemployed, even if provided with welfare entitlements as a safety net, will need additional assistance in the development of their human capital. The mere creation of employment opportunities is no longer sufficient but must be accompanied by the cultivation of the person's full potential.

The major changes wrought by an information-driven order are reflected in corresponding changes in the norms of justice and in the moral standards of social life. The immediate concerns of social justice are no longer limited to issues of how to divide societal output or of how to ensure humane working conditions. The urgent issues are now much broader and include the whole question of social development where people have the chance to grow intellectually, culturally, morally, and spiritually.

The shift in expectations of what the community must provide also has moral implications for international aid projects. In a society where human capital is the key factor to participation in social life, assistance to the marginalized must go beyond simple handouts. More than ever, the admonitions of *Mater et Magistra, Gaudium et Spes*, and the post–Vatican II documents on giving succor to the poor take on a new urgency. Relief and development efforts must be self-empowering, where the recipient's capacity for self-help is enhanced. Assistance in both social and economic development assumes equal importance. And even the nature of this economic help is changing with a greater emphasis on institution building directly related to human capital development. All this is reflective of what has been known in development work since the 1950s (Meier 1995).

Finally, changes in what is acceptable and expected in both personal behavior and collective action lead to corresponding alterations in the complementarity of the universal access principle to the other tenets of the tradition. As seen in the preceding survey in this chapter, the modern social documents have closely associated this principle with the primacy of labor and private property ownership. After all, in a natural resource–based economy, applying one's labor to some form of property (whether one's own or others') is the predominant manner of earning sufficient purchasing power to gain access to the necessary goods of life.

The shift in importance from tangible to intangible property highlights the centrality of human development, both in its intrinsic and instrumental roles. Integral human development is no longer merely the end result of access to and subsequent use of the fruits of the earth; it has itself become a necessary means (and an even more important means) to ensuring access in the postindustrial economy. One can, therefore, expect that *Populorum Progressio*'s integral human development would be closely associated with, indeed be inseparable from, the universal access principle in the knowledge economy in the same way that the primacy of labor has been so closely linked to this principle in dealing with the social questions of the past hundred years.

Characteristic #5: Widening Inequality

Left to itself, a knowledge-based economy may increase the likelihood of further marginalization for the trailing segments of the population. Walzer's (1983) notion of *dominant goods* provides a convenient framework with which to examine this feature of the transformed economy. Dominant goods are distinctive in that they go beyond the boundaries of their own spheres to shape and control access to goods in the other spheres of life. As a consequence, the allotment of dominant goods determines the distribution of other goods. In the postindustrial economy, knowledge and skills have become the dominant goods.

As seen in the preceding chapter, the dynamics of an information age will most likely worsen relative inequality. Slight differences in knowledge and skills (or the opportunity to acquire such) ultimately result in larger disparities in final outcomes. A knowledge-based economy can easily relegate to the fringes people who do not have the requisite skills and knowledge either to contribute to society or to avail of its benefits. As a result, people whose poverty prevents them from acquiring the means of developing their human capital will find themselves left even farther behind from the rest of society. The unskilled and the uneducated's comparative standing will be even worse in the subsequent rounds of economic activity as the minimum level of learning ratchets ever higher.

Besides the preceding ethical concern, there is a purely economic argument for a lower tolerance for relative inequality in the diffusion of skills and knowledge within society. Sustaining continued knowledge creation requires greater equity in the distribution of both tangible and intangible resources. Just as a sizable and stable middle class is indispensable for long-term economic growth, a broad-based social development is essential for an information age. The development of knowledge is not linear but exponential; knowledge expands from earlier knowledge and cannot thrive in isolation. It is auto-correlated, builds on itself, and prospers in direct proportion to the degree by which knowledge is nurtured and shared within a broad community-wide improvement in human capital. It is essential to provide depth and breadth in the social development of the population base that provides the medium for the further maturation of knowledge and skills. A wider diffusion of human capital enhances societal capacity for knowledge-induced and knowledge-sustained growth.

The preceding ethical and pragmatic perspectives imbue the universal access principle with greater urgency in its task of ensuring that the new dominant goods are within the ready reach of members of the community. Safeguarding a reasonable and fair access to such goods requires narrower margins of acceptable relative inequalities in the opportunities for human capital development. The benefits of social and economic development need to be more widely diffused.

Characteristic #6: Less Contentious Redistribution

The knowledge-based economy does not remove the problem of scarcity, but it does open up new possibilities for a less contentious sharing of society's key dominant goods. Human skills and knowledge are not subject to rival consumption in use unlike material goods.[16] An individual's use of particular data, for example, does not preclude others from availing of the same information. The accumulated stock of human knowledge is a public good from which many could simultaneously reap benefits. In contrast, tangible goods are governed by scarcity in their use and consumption and, therefore, subject to competition. Knowledge, as a dominant good, provides a wider latitude for sharing, compared to natural resources. In fact, it has the peculiar characteristic of growing even further as it is more widely shared.

This feature of the transformed economy provides the universal access principle with a new avenue for equity-oriented policies. Since human capital functions as a dominant good just like tangible property in the natural resource-based economy, inequities in traditional property and wealth holdings can now be ameliorated through policies that promote social development. Inequities in traditional property holdings could be corrected by skewing the distribution of opportunities for human capital formation in favor of the destitute and the marginalized. What we have, in effect, is a new avenue for reducing wide income disparities that is less contentious and less disruptive in rectifying inequalities compared to the redistribution of already-owned tangible properties through heavy taxation or outright expropriation. Human capital formation provides an effective and less disputed avenue for leveling the playing field. It is the key to allowing people to catch up, improve their social standing, and participate on an equal footing in socioeconomic life.[17] The nonrival feature of this pivotal dominant good opens new channels of less controversial modes of equity-oriented policies. In particular, resource reallocations for social development can mitigate the need for the redistribution of tangible properties and wealth, the erstwhile critical goods in the natural resource–based order. The upward mobility afforded by the software industry to the educated poor of India and the Philippines is an apt example.

Given the nonrival nature of knowledge in consumption, has the information age rendered the superfluous income criterion completely obsolete?[18] Since human skills and knowledge are intangible and not readily commensurable, and since they are directly constitutive of human perfection, can human capital be even said to be superfluous? Answers to these questions lie in the distinction between use or consumption, on the one hand, and formation, on the other.

Human capital cannot be superfluous in consumption or use since skills and knowledge are intangible and not subject to a zero-sum phenomenon. However, the question of whether they can be superfluous is still relevant when it comes to the issue of human capital formation. The acquisition and development of skills and knowledge require exhaustible inputs, such as time and material goods, which are subject to rival consumption and, therefore, competing uses. Human skills and knowledge can be "superfluous" in this sense. For example, a constant problem in development planning in poor countries is the tradeoff in national investment between higher education and primary schooling (Meier 1995, 313–26). Should scarce resources allotted to education be spent on training Ph.D.s in a few universities, or should such monies be spent instead on extending the reach of primary and high schools to the poor and the marginalized of society? In terms of relative privation and urgency of need, it would seem that the resources poured into securing a doctorate degree for a few are superfluous *relative* to the need for basic schooling for many in an impoverished nation.

The public good nature of knowledge does not remove the need for the superfluous income criterion since human development still requires physical inputs. Material goods still retain their importance even in an economic order whose wealth-generating capacity has shifted to human capital. Even as skills and knowledge have become the proximate causes for wealth creation, tangible goods are still requisite complementary inputs that make the development of such human gifts possible in the first place. Anything that uses scarce resources is subject to the superfluous income criterion whether directly or indirectly. After all, scarcity is the fundamental reason that makes the principle of universal access necessary in the first place.

Characteristic #7: Greater Role of Virtue

Monitoring and enforcement of just-use duties in a knowledge-based economy become more difficult because of the intangible and personal nature of its chief dominant goods. The shift to a knowledge-based economic order strengthens further the role of personal and social virtues in community life. Both the distribution and use of natural resources are observable and, therefore, easier to monitor for their adherence to the demands of justice. On the other hand, knowledge and skills are intangible and do not readily lend themselves to observation and measurement.

The moral obligation attached to human skills and knowledge is the need to share and contribute these to the community in a spirit of stewardship and solidarity. The enforcement of this obligation is very difficult, if at all possible. There is always the problem of moral hazard where individuals do not fully share their skills and talents with the community for purposes of enhancing their own personal gain at some point in the future. There is also the dilemma of free ridership where individuals benefit from others' contributions without doing their full share for the common good by not expending themselves in developing their special skills and talents. Furthermore, there is also the possibility of using human capital inappropriately to dominate or monopolize critical resources. In most of these cases, the proper application of knowledge and personal skills relies heavily on personal initiative, self-restraint, and prudence.

Because human capital is internal and unobservable, the moral obligations pertaining to the sharing of human capital can be effectively monitored and enforced only by personal integrity. Much depends on the goodwill and the virtues of the individual. The knowledge-based economy provides unique opportunities to grow deeper in solidarity and charity in view of the extended social externalities of knowledge and the enhanced potential of people in affecting the lives of their neighbors for good or for ill given their greater interdependence. Human capital as a dominant good in the transformed economy does not lend itself so readily to oversight and measurement. It is this feature that provides personal and social virtues a much larger role to play in the operation of the universal access principle in a knowledge-based socioeconomic order.

UNIVERSAL ACCESS VIA PARTICIPATIVE EGALITARIANISM

The dual phenomena of expanding markets and emerging information technologies have precipitated an accelerated dynamism, a revolution of expectations, a shift from natural to "created" comparative advantage, and an ever higher entry cost to securing choice roles in economic life. These characteristics of the postmodern economy converge in two of their normative implications: (1) a widening relative inequality with (2) universal participation as its key ameliorative principle.

Principle of Participation Revisited

The principle of participation has neither the wide usage nor the prominence of the tradition's mainstay principles such as universal access, solidarity, subsidiarity, and primacy of labor. It has been adumbrated because its key tenets can be found in varying degrees in the other principles and norms. Thus, *Rerum Novarum*'s just-use obligation is also about letting workers partake of the fruits of their employers' private ownership of the means of production. Conceptually, participation is a subset of *Quadragesimo Anno*'s principle of subsidiarity inasmuch as Pius XI's whole thrust is to nurture the exercise of private initiative. *Mater et Magistra*'s principle of socialization is about safeguarding the public space available for the individual's exercise of the private initiative promoted by subsidiarity. And, of course, *Pacem in Terris* goes right to the core of participation by setting out as inviolable those spheres that are critical for the person's self-actualization. *Laborem Exercens*'s call for alternative work arrangements is founded on the need to involve people in the affairs and decisions that affect them.

A globalized, information-driven economy provides the occasion to develop the principle of participation in its own right, if only because we are forced to do so. The U.S. bishops' pastoral letter on the economy has already begun this process by stressing the moral obligation of creating an economic life where no one is excluded (National Conference of Catholic Bishops 1986).

The principle of participation can be defined as the equitable allotment of the burdens and gains of community life—a balanced sharing that affords everyone a meaningful chance to contribute to and benefit from the common life. It flows from the fundamental understanding that the use of reason and will are constitutive of human dignity. This, in turn, gives rise to a requirement of integral human development: that people grow in the use of these signal faculties only as they are given authentic opportunities to exercise them. Meaningful participation in community life is sine qua non to nurturing and developing intelligent and responsible freedom.

The notion of participation as an essential condition of self-actualization is not original to these social documents. It is found in salvation history itself as seen in the human instrumentality that has always been present in God's saving act from the call and formation of the nation Israel, to the apostolic mandate of preaching the Gospel to the ends of the earth. God is unfailing in providing for people through each other. Christ inaugurated and continues to build the Kingdom of God through human agency. Contributing toward life in community is no less an avenue for authentic human integral development. Formalizing and accentuating participation as a principle is merely a retrieval of what has always been part of the tradition.

From *Having* to *Being*

The information economy holds much promise for a lived and better understanding of the teleology of economic life. A perennial concern in economic ethics has been the reversal in the importance attached to *having* and *being*. Where *having* is accorded primacy of place, accumulation becomes the overriding goal of economic life. Catholic social thought has repeatedly stressed that while *having* is constitutive of *being* (as seen, for example, in Leo XIII's defense of private property, RN #7–23), it should never be given a value far beyond its end of preserving and maintaining *being*. The shift to a knowledge-based economic order and the premium that it assigns to human capital refocuses attention on the preeminence and centrality of the human person.[19]

Human capital is brought to center stage given the higher threshold for minimum skills, many of which are relatively more technical, more scientific, more roundabout, and more time consuming in acquisition when compared to earlier historical periods. In sharpening human capital, even if only for its instrumental value, a beneficial side effect is that such human development is itself already a constitutive element of human flourishing. Thus, the massive campaign to promote education in poor countries has the dual effect of producing high economic returns (the instrumental role) while opening to the poor, at the same time, the rich experience and the joy of literacy and numeracy (the intrinsic dimension). Proficiency in the speculative and practical sciences, the enjoyment of the arts and literature, profiting from what the general culture has to offer, the development of personal gifts and talents to a level of excellence, human learning and contemplation–these have always been fundamental elements of human flourishing. The heightened dual role of integral human development in its intrinsic and instrumental values may succeed in overshadowing wealth accumulation as the more common, proximate end of economic activity, perhaps even to the point of reversing the materialist ethos of prizing *having* over *being*. The desire for self-improvement may yet supplant the acquisitive drive as the animating spirit of *homo oeconomicus*.

This unique opportunity, however, does not come without its risks. In particular, there is always the danger of focusing exclusively on the instrumental role of human development in producing wealth. If so, we would be back to *having* and accumulation as the ultimate measures of success, this time not only of economic activity but of human development itself. Such a utilitarian posture results in the subordination of integral human development as a means to the end of accumulation, of *being* serving the end of *having*. In this case, the analogical use of "capital" in human capital would have been completely misunderstood.

Being as a Function of Both *Having* and *Doing*

The central importance of human skills in an information-based economic order highlights *being* as a function of *doing*. *Being* necessarily entails exercising personal skills and developing the rational faculties. That agency plays a central role in human existence is reflected even in the recent literature on political economy where freedom and capabilities have become measures of economic performance.[20] *Doing* is constitutive of *being*.

A knowledge economy highlights the need to incorporate the principle of participation within the three-way nexus of human labor, the principle of universal access, and the right to life. There is a difference in the dynamics between human labor and natural resources, on the one hand, and between human labor and skills development, on the other. The interaction between human labor and natural resources is one-way in direction. Human labor makes the inert gifts of the earth fruitful, productive, and suitable for human use and enjoyment. In contrast, the interaction between human labor and skill development moves two ways. In the first place, we have the traditional direction where labor utilizes human skills and knowledge as "inputs" to make the goods of the earth fruitful. But there is a new element in this equation. Skills and knowledge are not merely inputs in work, but they are also end results since they develop further as human labor is expended.[21] Learning-by-doing is an operative phenomenon in this case. This is an interaction in the reverse direction where the stock of human capital is enhanced through its exercise in human labor, an important feedback that must now be taken into account. Unlike natural resources that are depleted from use, human skills and knowledge are further augmented and enhanced through their application in human labor.

The principle of participation will most likely prove to be *the* key postindustrial social principle because of the central importance of tacit knowledge and its auto-correlated nature in a knowledge economy. Because information technologies have become the primary engine for growth and development, the ability to manage, interpret, and use data becomes essential. Candice Stevens describes the process succinctly:

> But there are some types of knowledge that are more difficult to codify and exchange in a market. There is "tacit" knowledge—skills which often cannot be reduced to mere information. Some human capabilities, such as intuition, insight, creativity and judgement, resist codification. And it is these tacit skills which are essential to selecting, using and manipulating the knowledge which can be codified. The ability to select relevant (and disregard irrelevant) information, to recognise patterns in information and to interpret and decode information is not easily bought and sold.
>
> While codified knowledge is the material to be transformed (the "know-what"), tacit knowledge is the tool for handling it (the "know-how"). The most important tacit skill may be the ability to learn continuously and to acquire new skills [footnote: Paye (1995)]. The process of continuous learning is more than merely obtaining a formal education. In the knowledge-based economy, learning-by-doing is paramount. Individuals must upgrade their skills in both codified and tacit knowledge continuously so as to keep up with fast-moving technologies. . . . Learning, creativity and flexibility matter more in the knowledge-based economy, experience and tradition less (Stevens 1996).

These features of tacit knowledge are consistent with empirical findings on the positive effects of mother's education on child health through a better ability to process information in allocating scarce household resources (Barrera 1990, 1991). They also account for Schultz's (1975) observation that people with well-developed human capital are in a better position to deal with disequilibria.

The greater role of tacit knowledge accents the earlier observation on the higher "entry cost" to meaningful engagement in the transformed economy. In the first place, formal schooling has taken on even greater importance given the need to deal with ever greater quantities and ever more complicated codified data. On top of this is the equally significant need for nonbook learning in broadening one's background knowledge. Both of these bring participation to even greater importance. In a natural resource–based economy, access to livelihood-generating properties is a precondition for partaking in economic life. Thus, in its agrarian setting, *Rerum Novarum* encourages the landless to offer their services to the propertied. In this case, the universal access principle takes logical priority to the principle of participation.

In a knowledge-based economy, on the other hand, participation takes greater significance because subsequent access to property is contingent on the skills and tacit knowledge developed in earlier rounds of economic activity. This is a tacit knowledge shaped in large part by the quality and extent of one's role in the preceding periods. Thus, in the postmodern economy, the principle of participation will most likely be invoked simultaneously with the universal access principle; it may even take precedence over the latter.

A second insight offered by tacit knowledge is the central importance of its auto-correlated nature. As previously discussed, knowledge builds on earlier knowledge, and not necessarily on one's own either. One can build on others' knowledge, *for as long as one has access to what they have.* This requires an active engagement with others. Moreover, knowledge expansion in the transformed economy occurs largely through a greater specialization of labor, and such a division of labor means interacting with others. One can avail of and contribute to the stock of knowledge only through participation.

A third characteristic of knowledge creation is its increasing returns to scale. The synergy of the individual parts is greater than their sum especially when a completely new breakthrough is achieved. These scale effects mean that a failure to keep pace with knowledge creation spells an ever wider gap that will be even more difficult to close. This is consistent with the earlier observations in the preceding chapter on the dynamic, "created" comparative advantage and its attendant risk of marginalizing further the trailing segments of the economy. Failure to participate in knowledge processes would most likely result in greater relative inequality.

These characteristics alert us to a potential problem of increasing relative inequality in a globalized information economy. This social problem could be avoided altogether or at least minimized if everyone is assured of a meaningful participation in economic life. Affording everyone the opportunity of learning-by-doing over and above formal schooling becomes *de rigueur* to be part of mainstream economic life.[22]

The understanding of *being* as a function of *doing* adds richness to the earlier notion of work as a personal value. It makes the obligation of providing gainful employment even more urgent because such employment is an important venue for satisfying the requirements of the principle of participation. Since work is instrumental in the development of human capital, the provision of jobs becomes even more imperative in a knowledge-based economic order. Not only do work opportunities provide a livelihood, but they also enhance human capital as an important part of human perfection. The link between the universal access principle and the primacy of labor in the natural–resource based regime is thus modified to a triumvirate that now includes the principle of participation. There is a new intersection, an amplified complementarity between these three principles in the postindustrial political economy. The principle of participation may be described as the Archimedean point because it is the key to keeping relative inequality at bay and preventing the emergence of a permanent, growing underclass of people unable to traffic in the coinage of the transformed economy–knowledge.

SUMMARY AND CONCLUSIONS

The standards for human flourishing are partly time- and culturally-conditioned. The shift from a natural resource- to a knowledge-based economy transforms the context in which the person achieves integral human development. The change in the fundamentals of the economy causes corresponding adjustments in the necessary economic dimension of human flourishing and gives rise to derivative alterations in the operation of the universal access principle. In a globalized information age, the object of the principle has become both more expensive to provide (given the stiffer "entry costs" to societal participation) and more urgent to acquire (given the even more severe marginalization of the unskilled and the unlettered). Its scope is extended beyond tangible goods to encompass even intangible personal endowments.

The transformation of the economy also provides an excellent opportunity to address gray areas of the principle that have never been sufficiently addressed before: whether the principle covers only subsistence rights or includes the means necessary for human thriving, and whether just-use obligations extend beyond material to include intellectual properties. The emergence of knowledge as a dominant good, together with its nonrival feature in consumption, provides the universal access principle with new and less contentious venues for achieving equity through social development. The knowledge-based economy also presents occasion for growth in personal and social virtues given the special difficulties of monitoring and enforcing the obligations attendant to these dominant goods in the external forum.

The market-generated redistribution of burdens and benefits brings the principle of participation to center stage. As will be argued in the conceptual synthesis of part V, all the principles are important since their complementarity reveals different facets of social problems that are often multidimensional in their complexity and requirements. However, it is the principle of participation that will most likely take the lead because of its immediate relevance to the development of knowledge, the animating core of the postindustrial economy.

Notes

1. See, for example, Hollenbach (1979); Coleman (1981); Curran (1985a, 1985b, 1986).

2. In his classic work "Are There Any Natural Rights?" Hart (1955) notes that if there is such a thing as a natural right, it has to be the right to life.

3. Human labor is not the only means of gaining access to the goods of the earth. Welfare entitlements are another avenue. Human labor cannot be made the sole means of entitlement to the goods of the earth because not all are capable of toiling, such as the very young, the elderly, the infirm, and the disabled, all of whom also enjoy the right to preserve life.

4. Wage labor is defined as human work exchanged for cash through the labor market.

5. There are empirical studies of a tradeoff between wage levels and employment opportunities, between private economic initiative and equity-oriented policies. Private property ownership and market operations are necessary conditions for the provision of gainful employment sustainable into the long term. Hence, the rankings of these rights relative to each other (i.e., the right to a job, the right to a living wage, the right to private property ownership, and the right to economic initiative and action) cannot be established a priori and must be handled on a case-to-case basis, taking into account the particular circumstances of the situation and the requirements of the common good. Note how discussions in the social documents regarding the provision of a living wage and employment opportunities have always been balanced with calls for the need to weigh other considerations, like business conditions and the requirements of the common good (as in QA #70–75).

6. Pius XII (1941, 221) writes: "The native right to the use of material goods, intimately linked as it is to the dignity and other rights of the human person . . . provides man with a secure material basis of the highest import, on which to rise to the fulfillment, with reasonable liberty, of his moral duties. The safe guardianship of this right will ensure the personal dignity of man, and will facilitate for him the attention to and fulfillment of that sum of stable duties and decisions for which he is directly responsible to his Creator."

7. Paul VI (PP #23) observes: "If there should arise conflict 'between acquired private rights and primary community exigencies,' it is the responsibility of public authorities 'to look for a solution.'"

8. This, of course, is nothing new. The critical role of human capital in growth has been widely discussed and verified empirically in the economics literature since the 1950s. Note, for example, the works of R. Solow, T. W. Schultz, and E. Denison. Human knowledge accounts for the bulk of the rapid growth experienced in the post–World War II era.

9. It is important to understand the sense in which the term "human capital" is used in this book. The use of "capital" should not be taken as an endorsement of the purely economic approach of commodifying human labor and treating it as

an input no different from factors of production such as land and capital. I use human "capital" analogically in order to highlight the key productive role of personal gifts and the critical importance of such in shaping subsequent rounds of human activity and the future opportunity set available to the person.

10. This is not to deny that there are still pockets of severe destitution and economic practices that are more feudal than modern.

11. If so, then the shift from a natural resource- to a knowledge-based economy does not make that much of a difference inasmuch as the provision of basic needs for survival remains unchanged. In fact, if anything at all, these needs would be easier to fill.

12. In technical language, there is an increase in the marginal product of labor (MPL) given the continued upward shift of the production function in response to improvements in human capital.

13. Virtues are important not only because they are *instrumental* to achieving perfection, but also because they are *constitutive* elements of human perfection. In other words, virtues are part of what it means to attain human perfection. The same can be said of intellectual property (human skills and knowledge). These are not merely instrumental to the attainment of the various human goods needed for growth and development, but they are also constitutive of human perfection itself. The value of making this distinction is that "constitutive means" certainly enjoy a higher rank in the hierarchy of values and claims when compared to means that are merely functional in nature. Hence, as "inputs" in the production process, human skills and knowledge enjoy a greater excellence compared to material goods. This could also be used as an argument in supporting the teaching that labor always has priority over factors of production such as capital.

14. All this is not even to touch on the question of whether there are comparable *correlative rights* that provide the unskilled with claims on the accomplishments of the talented.

15. Finn (1995) proposes a rethinking of the doctrine of property to take better account of proprietal claims arising from human creativity.

16. Note, however, that they are subject to scarcity when it comes to the formation and acquisition of these skills and knowledge. A scholarship for individual A at a top university means one less available scholarship for others seeking admission into that same program of studies. Moreover, the market value of some skills or knowledge can be be raised by restricting their diffusion.

17. Of course, the emergence of human capital as a dominant good has a downside to it as well. Human skills and knowledge (as dominant goods) can be used to dominate others by monopolizing or limiting access to the knowledge base.

18. Recall that this criterion is important because of the moral obligations it imposes on sharing one's tangible resources with others.

19. Note, for example, the relatively greater attention accorded to social development today by development planners (United Nations Development Programme 1990).

20. See, for example, Sen (1985a, 1985b, 1988a).

21. However, human labor is not the only means by which human skills and knowledge are acquired. We also have education and training as other channels.

22. The nineteenth-century Industrial Revolution provides a very good illustration of the importance of learning-by-doing. One reason why Great Britain is

the first to enter the industrial age is its ready supply of mechanics, engineers, and other tinkerers with experience working with mechanical devices. This is a pool that is created during the proto-industrialization that precedes the eighteenth century. Not only does Great Britain have the supply of experienced personnel ready to staff the factory system when it finally replaces the cottage industries, but it also has the pool of innovators who will be responsible for the major technological breakthroughs in the first wave of industrialization. Germany takes the lead in the second wave of the Industrial Revolution (chemicals and electricity) partly because it has the better preparation in the natural sciences compared to Great Britain at the end of that century. This strategic positioning determines whether one leads, lags, or is able to keep up with the rest. See Landes (1969).

Chapter 11

SUPERFLUOUS INCOME CRITERION REFINED

INTRODUCTION

The importance of participative access in the knowledge economy underscores the need for new standards of equity. The superfluous income criterion, as part of the universal access principle, has to be refined and further developed if it is to be useful in postindustrial economic ethics.

There is a necessary economic dimension to human flourishing regardless of whether a full and perfect life is defined as one of virtue, of self-realization, or of self-determination. After all, the person is both body and soul requiring material inputs. This brings us into the realm of rival consumption where an individual's use of a scarce resource leaves that much less available for the rest of the community.[1] A consequence of scarcity is to move consumption from a purely private act into the social sphere. The limited supply of goods in the face of insatiable human needs and wants is the fundamental constraint that conditions the nature and severity of the social question in whatever form or way it is encountered. The starting point of any exercise in political economy is the acknowledgment that the social order operates in an environment of finite means.[2]

Political economy deals primarily with the allocation of scarce resources to competing claims using various criteria such as public interest, need, contribution, effort, ability, market operations, and equality (Rescher 1966, 73). There is little consensus on which of these to use, much less on how to define and measure these standards. For the most part, the market is the principal vehicle for the orderly, timely, and efficient distribution of goods and services to their manifold uses. However, this supply-demand interaction has limitations that are serious enough to warrant the use of extra-market mechanisms. There are market failures where the price system is unable to apportion scarce resources consistent with larger societal objectives. Recent examples abound as in the conflict between protecting the logging industry or preserving biodiversity, between maintaining coal-mining jobs or preventing acid rain, and between providing comprehensive health care for a few or legislating a modest package of health benefits with universal coverage. And, of course, there is the perennial problem of destitution where segments of the population are unable to participate and benefit from market operations for lack of the requisite purchasing power. Allocation in these cases can be channeled through extra-market mechanisms of regulation and entitlements should society choose to hold itself up to standards it deems desirable.

Allocation according to need is a heavily favored alternative or supplement to market operations. A. Gewirth (1985, 28) resolves clashing economic rights in favor of the party whose functional ability is at greater risk. The strength of individual claims is directly proportional to the need for such goods in order to function as a person. Sen (1984b, 1984c, 1985b) sees the development of human capabilities as a primary allocative criterion. W. J. Samuels (1994) presents the manifold dimensions of need as a mode of discourse in the distribution of the burdens and benefits of the common productive effort. He notes, however, that agreeing to need as a criterion for allocation is a completely different matter from the more demanding charge of defining the substantive content of that need.

The precise specification of human needs, in addition to prioritizing them, is not an easy task. For example, it is difficult to agree on how to appraise human well-being, an essential first step in establishing human need (e.g., Hausman and McPherson 1993, 690). Should it be based on subjective preference satisfaction or on more objective measures that avoid problems related to misinformed preferences and interpersonal comparisons of utility? Different notions on the nature of human beings lead to different formulations of need that deserve preferential treatment from society. Furthermore, some needs are time and culture bound. Consequently, Samuels (1994) cautions that such a listing of human needs cannot be prescribed but can only be the subject of a continuing social conversation.

As a necessary first step for this discussion, it is important for various ethical traditions to be clear as to how their respective understanding of human nature and well-being shapes their views on compelling human needs that have to be satisfied. The object of this chapter is to contribute to this dialogue (that accepts *need as a mode of discourse*) by providing greater specificity to a theological approach that has long sought to supplement the market with allocation according to need: Catholic social thought's *superfluous income criterion*.

Rerum Novarum, the seminal encyclical of modern Catholic social thought (CST), deals with the bitter clash of labor and capital over the proper distribution of societal output. The notion of rightful property ownership and use is examined. For early CST, the central task of its theological reflection is to "define the boundaries imposed by the requirements of social life upon the right of ownership itself or upon its use" (QA #48). In the face of scarcity, the goods[3] of the earth are governed by limits both (1) in their ownership and (2) in their use. The tradition has come to locate and anchor these limits within the principle of universal access to the goods of the earth. Hence, while staunchly defending private property ownership as an essential human right, *Rerum Novarum* maintains that there is an important distinction between the just ownership and the just use of private property; the former is a right, the latter an obligation. More importantly, the two are inseparable. As seen in the preceding chapter, the goods of the earth are meant for the common benefit of all, regardless of how the titles of ownership to them are assigned (RN #14, #35–36). This duty to use one's income and property for the welfare of others is rooted in the *Genesis* (1:26–30) mandate to exercise dominion over the earth and to make it fruitful in meeting human needs.

It turns out that this principle also effectively addresses the central concern of political economy: the equitable allocation of resources to competing uses in the social order. This is so because the issue of private property ownership and the larger question of equity both arise from the same phenomenon of scarcity. The boundaries drawn by social life around private property ownership and use are the same boundaries that fuse the legitimate demands of the individual with the requirements of the community.

The universal access principle is brought to bear on issues pertaining to competing claims through its *just-use* requirement that, in turn, is developed further in the *superfluous income criterion* where resources are allocated according to need. Recall that in defining superfluity, early modern teachings follow St. Thomas Aquinas (1947/48, II–II, q. 32, a. 6, reply) in defining excess income as the residual earnings not needed to maintain one's station in life (RN #36). John XXIII replaces this inward orientation to self with an outward focus toward the neighbor. Buried in an obscure footnote in *Gaudium et Spes* is a different approach that recaptures the scriptural and patristic understanding of the obligation as having "to reckon what is superfluous by the measure of the needs of others."[4]

Whether superfluous income is measured in terms of one's station in life or of others' needs, it is clear that the operative rule of distributive justice in this approach is the priority accorded to satisfying unmet needs (whether one's own or others'). This, in effect, gives rise to a twofold typology of goods: (1) what is needed and (2) what is not.

The formulation of this norm of distributive justice based on superfluity alone is, unfortunately, inadequate. Using "unmet needs" as the primary yardstick is problematic because the insatiability of human wants and the difficulty of separating needs from wants (not to mention the problem of moral hazard even if such distinction were readily available) result in an ever growing basket of goods that are needed for oneself.[5] We cannot base our moral distinctions on the basis of a very broad standard of unmet needs alone because people, whether rich or poor, will always have unfilled demands, especially in the light of the multidimensional nature of a flourishing life. This is particularly true in a dynamic modern economy where the rapid advance of science and technologies is most often accompanied by a corresponding creation or expansion of new and unforeseen needs. Unless a more refined classification can be found, a distributive justice that assigns a higher claim to unmet needs based solely on the concept of superfluous income can easily be obviated, if not postponed expediently or indefinitely. Conventional economics avoids this problem altogether by not distinguishing between wants and needs.

The notion of unmet needs is too amorphous and requires refinement. For example, how does one measure needs, and how does one compare them across different individuals? What decision rule is used to rank these needs? Most of all, is equity in the satisfaction of these unmet needs an equality in outcomes or an equality in opportunity-access? The absence of any finer specification of unmet needs spills over into the difficulty of talking about proportional equality with any great precision.[6] Christiansen (1984, 666), for example, could only talk of relative equality in general terms: as the attainment of that sororal-fraternal harmony that allows people to work together effectively. Unmet needs is a measure that requires much further work if it is to be of practical value.

The thesis of this chapter is that modern Catholic social thought can, at this point, offer a much richer specification of superfluity by distinguishing the varying degrees of necessity within *unmet needs*. The social documents, as a whole, already furnish fine distinctions in weighing and prioritizing needs than is explicitly advanced in the teachings pertaining to surplus income. This is accomplished by deriving the different uses of goods on the basis of the necessary economic dimension of human flourishing that gives rise to these varying degrees of need in the first place. A better understanding of the notion of unmet needs is relevant for the application of the superfluous income criterion in the postmodern economy.

THE NECESSARY ECONOMIC DIMENSION OF HUMAN FLOURISHING

Human flourishing has been described in manifold ways: as self-determination, self-realization, a life of virtue, the pursuit and lived experience of values, happiness, a fullness of life, a certain development as a person, and a meaningful existence.[7] Common to these models is the basic understanding of the human person as *embodied intelligent freedom* (Ashley and O'Rourke 1989, 168). Two features of the necessary economic dimension of human flourishing flow from this premise, namely:

1. the human person's need to consume material goods as an embodied being, and
2. the human person's need for inclusion in community life as a free and intelligent individual.

The Human Person as an Embodied Being

The human person is both body and soul. As an embodied being, the person needs material inputs both to survive and to thrive in that continued existence. The first distinction can be made at this point with respect to varying degrees of necessity by differentiating between the functional and the dysfunctional use of created goods.

All creation is good and the end of the material world is to reflect the wisdom and the beauty of God (*Genesis*). As part of this divine plan, the human person is sustained in the natural order through the use of the goods of the created world. Employed according to their proper ends, earthly goods help the human person mirror the gift of a divine image (SRS #29). The use of goods in such manner can be described as *functional*.

Beneficial gains accruing to continued consumption do not increase indefinitely. There is an ideal mean in the use of physical resources for purposes of achieving integral human development. In the same way that authentic development puts a floor to consumption below which human survival is not possible, it also defines a ceiling, an upper limit. There are two ways by which the use of goods becomes dysfunctional: through inappropriate use or through immoderate consumption. There is a threshold beyond which these goods may be detrimental (negative marginal benefits) to the person's pursuit of a full and perfect life, such as excessive eating or drinking. An inordinate accumulation of wealth that only serves to fuel an avarice injurious to the pursuit of higher human values makes the use of these goods dysfunctional. They hinder rather than promote the ability of the person to flourish (SRS #28d–i; CA #36b, #36d, #41d; OA #9). Sin has made the proper dominion over these divine gifts much more difficult. The capacity of the human person to misuse them in ways contrary to the moral order is real and potent. The goods of the earth sustain human life, but they can also be used in *dysfunctional* ways that make life less human, whether for others or for oneself.

A second distinction has to be made within the various functional uses of created goods due to their varying importance for human flourishing. As an embodied being, there is a requisite basket of goods below which physical health and survival are not possible. The consumption of any economic resource that is essential for a person's physical survival and subsistence, such as food, clothing, and shelter, is *constitutive* of human life in the most fundamental way.[8]

Integral human development calls for balance in the allocation of the gifts of the tangible world and suggests two broad categories that are helpful in sorting out degrees of unmet needs in weighing competing claims: (1) the use of goods as *constitutive* (i.e., the minimum requirements for physical survival and basic health) and (2) the use of goods as *dysfunctional*. There is an optimal band in consumption levels bounded by underdevelopment and superdevelopment, by destitution and overindulgence (GS #31b). The *constitutive* and *dysfunctional* consumption of goods define the two endpoints of the continuum that encompasses the manifold contribution of the material realm to human perfection. It also delineates for us the boundaries, indeed, the two extreme poles when it comes to weighing competing uses where the constitutive use of goods lays the first and the strongest claim versus the dysfunctional use of goods that carries neither weight nor legitimacy in its claims. The understanding of the human person as an embodied being gives rise to the first characteristic feature of the necessary economic dimension of human flourishing: there is an indispensable minimum consumption basket of material goods necessary for physical survival and basic health.

The Human Person as Intelligent Freedom

There is a second category within the functional use of goods. The human person as intelligent freedom requires community. Reason has to be nurtured and formed if it is to mature. Human will has to be exercised if individuals are to grow in the prudent use of their moral agency. Responsibility has to be given if the person is to grow in reasoned freedom. In both cases, the full attainment of human well-being can only come about in fellowship with others. The integral development of the person has an essential social dimension. Basic human goods and values can be achieved and cultivated only through interaction with other people. And even for those goods that are not inherently relational, cooperation (or lack thereof) on the part of others still plays a significant role in facilitating or hindering human perfection. After all, freedom is actualized fully only in community.

The individual's engagement in social life involves contributing to and deriving benefits from the social order. This two-way interaction between the individual and society takes place through intermediate social entities ranging from the family, to the local community, to the nation, and to the global family as a whole. Whichever level or whatever degree of involvement may be available for people's choice, one economic factor remains inescapable: They need to use some requisite complementary material goods if such engagement is to take place at all. Contributing to and deriving benefits from the common life require the use of created goods either as direct inputs or as tools that enable, facilitate, and enhance such interpersonal interactions. People are limited in what they can or cannot do by the type and quantity of physical resources available to them.

The nature and central importance of this particular class of necessary, complementary goods that shape the extent and quality of an individual's involvement in the commonweal are best illustrated by two instances of ethical reflection over scarce resources, notably, the Old Testament's *Jubilee Law* and modern Catholic social thought's (CST) *full employment at a living wage.*

Old Testament Jubilee Law

The Chosen People of God is formed into a nation different from all the other surrounding kingdoms and peoples. Among its distinctive features is a political economy rooted in a covenantal understanding of equality and basic sufficiency for all. This is reflected in the keen awareness of a collective duty to provide for those who are unable to fend for themselves. In particular, note the wisdom behind the gleaning laws in furnishing the disenfranchised with access to life-sustaining food (Leviticus 19:9–10, 23:22).

What is of even greater significance for purposes of this chapter is the way the debt- and slave-release laws[9] extend this obligation beyond merely assuring the means for physical survival. Responsibility for others is broadened to include restoring into the mainstream of socioeconomic life those who have fallen on hard times and have been marginalized to subservient roles. Even more telling, however, is the expansion of the moral obligation for each other's welfare in the Jubilee Law.[10]

The affirmation that land is an inheritance from God serves to underscore both the special divine favors accorded to the Chosen People and the nature of the goods of the earth as gifts. It is a reminder that stewardship, rather than ownership, is the proper attitude to take with respect to the material world. However, the significance of the Jubilee Law extends beyond its theological import to include practical economic considerations. The return of ancestral land is an indirect but ingenious way of guaranteeing a stable livelihood for everyone. Coinciding with the release of slaves and debt, the Jubilee Law is also a pragmatic way of ensuring that these newly emancipated members of the community have the necessary productive base to grow in that freedom and not revert back into debt slavery (Gnuse 1985, 44). In an agrarian setting, land is the economic base for sustenance and sufficiency. Access to land is an avenue for sustaining autonomous participation in the community into the long term. Beyond its theological meaning as the assurance of God's providence and the mark of the Chosen People's special calling, land also takes on a more practical value as a vital economic resource for human fellowship and well-being. Consequently, the Jubilee Law reveals comprehension and acceptance of a fundamental moral obligation of ensuring that members of the community have the necessary means to engage themselves in socioeconomic life as free and intelligent men and women.[11] Note that the spirit of this duty is once again reflected in the biblical instructions on interest-free loans where there is an injunction against taking as a pledge for a debt the person's means for a livelihood.[12]

Both the Jubilee Law and the norms governing loans ensure that members of the community are not left bereft of the means of production regardless of their particular circumstances. They accentuate a distinctive feature of the universal access principle in that if everyone is to benefit from the gifts of the earth as intended by God, then people will have to be provided with the means to gain access to and avail of these created goods.

Modern full employment at a living wage

The central role played by a special class of material goods in facilitating individual participation in the socioeconomic life can once again be seen in *Rerum Novarum*'s staunch defense of private property. Leo XIII justifies the ownership of private property as an important avenue for ensuring access to productive resources. For this reason, widespread property ownership is valued as an essential attribute of an ideal economic order just as it is in the Levitical laws. *Rerum Novarum* is realistic enough to concede that in a world of second-best solutions, most people will not have ownership of such means of production and will, therefore, have to enter the labor market (RN #14). In fact, this is the more common experience in the industrial social order.

In spite of the numerous shifts and discontinuities observed in the modern Catholic social documents, a perennial feature of this tradition has been the stress on the societal obligation to provide for gainful employment, that is, full employment at a living wage. In a modern wage-labor economy, exchanging one's services for wages has become the principal means of securing access to the necessary goods and services for daily living. Reflecting on Leo XIII's teachings on private property ownership and its practical importance, *Mater et Magistra* (MM #106–08) notes the transformation in the concept of productive private property from mere land and physical capital to include professional skills as well. The labor market has replaced land as *the* critical resource that ensures the individual's entry into the communal productive effort.

Consequently, it should not be surprising at all to see that the modern social documents have devoted a disproportionate amount of attention to the urgent need and the moral obligation to provide for humane working conditions, an adequate wage, and abundant employment opportunities for all.

Gainful employment is a cornerstone of a just economy. For example, Pius XI views the use of superfluous income in generating employment opportunities as an act of commendable liberality (QA #51). John Paul II imbues investment decisions with a moral dimension because of their consequences for job creation (CA #36d). The U.S. bishops' pastoral letter on the economy goes against accepted wisdom in economic thought and policy by advancing economic rights that include, among others, an ambitious program of full employment for all. So highly valued is human labor that *Laborem Exercens* assigns accountability for employment generation and working conditions to both direct and indirect employers (LE #77–81).

Common to both the Old Testament's Jubilee Law and modern Catholic social thought's full employment at a living wage is the implicit acknowledgment that the duty we owe to each other's welfare does not end with the mere provision of goods that are constitutive of physical survival. Such a moral obligation extends to furnishing the essential temporal resources for a sustained, meaningful, productive, and free participation in the socioeconomic life of the larger community. It is an engagement that has to be:

- productive in the way it procures for the individual the other goods and services necessary to sustain and enjoy life.
- meaningful in the way it allows the person to use the gifts of reason and will in ways that nurture further growth in a well-formed intelligence and a well-informed freedom.
- free in the way it affords the individual the necessary latitude to exercise personal initiative in availing of the fruits of the earth without undue hardship and endless toil stemming from natural or social obstacles.
- sustained in the way it generates a continuous two-way flow of contributions rendered to society by the person and of benefits drawn from the community by the individual.

In an agrarian economy, the means to such an engagement lies in the possession of, or at least access to, a parcel of land to till; in a modern wage-labor economy, it is gainful employment. In the emerging knowledge-based economy, such means may well lie in computer literacy.

Whatever form these requisite avenues to community involvement may take (whether it is land, gainful employment, or advanced skills) or however we may expand the notion of property as John XXIII does, we arrive at an economic dimension of human flourishing that is inescapable: *Bringing about these means to participation in socioeconomic life requires the use of material resources.* Even intangible professional and human skills ultimately depend on the prior consumption or use of tangible physical resources such as matriculation in schools and a wide variety of educational inputs. In the final analysis, the abundance or dearth of such requisite complementary material inputs shapes the nature, the quality, and the scope of the individual's productive fellowship in the mainstream of community life. The availability or absence of such necessary resources will either enhance or impair the person's ability and chances of participating in society in a sustained, free, meaningful, and productive manner. Michael Walzer (1983, 10) is incisive in his observation that there are some goods that serve as a "social version of the gold standard" in the way they can assign value to other spheres of distribution and exercise command over a wide range of other goods with significant ramifications for equity. Gewirth (1982) and Hollenbach (1989) argue in a similar fashion when they justify the need to make some goods the object of positive economic rights. Consequently, over and above the use of goods that secure physical survival and basic health, there is another class of needs whose satisfaction determines the opportunity set available to the individual for successful inclusion in the social order.

This class of goods can be aptly called *regulative* since they give the person access to other scarce resources and, consequently, exert great leverage on the extent of an individual's participation in society and profoundly shape the person's prospects for a flourishing life. Walzer refers to them as *dominant goods*[13] and suggests that physical strength, reputation, religious or political office, landed wealth, capital, and technical knowledge have at various points in history functioned in such capacity. They can be appropriately described as a doorway to a sustained and necessary interaction with the rest of society.

Beyond their importance in facilitating insertion into community life, this regulative use of goods deserves careful attention because of their distributional ramifications, especially for an increasingly knowledge-based economy. Living in community has a reflexive nature to it. As already noted, involvement in the commonweal occurs through a twofold exchange whereby the person contributes to the welfare of the community, while the community, in turn, redistributes to the individual the benefits and costs of social life. This interaction reflects the dynamism inherent in the common good. Individuals are engaged in social life in varying degrees. Not all contribute nor receive benefits in uniform amounts, nor are they expected to. Differences in personal gifts, skills, talents, and experience account for some of these disparities. However, part of these variations in contributions and appropriations stems from differences in the individuals' degree of engagement in the social order. People's ability to derive benefits from and contribute to the common good is dependent on their previous contributions made and gains received. In other words, the degree and extent of individuals' current and past position in the community shape their later prospects for participation in social life.[14] This cumulative, self-reinforcing effect increases the likelihood of greater inequalities within the social order. Those who are at the fringes of social life will be even more marginalized in subsequent rounds of socioeconomic activity.

This reflexive nature to living in community adds even greater weight and urgency to the norm of nonexclusion where no individual may be disenfranchised in the social order. The requirements and standards of proportional equality for goods that are regulative in their impact ought to be more stringent than those that are applicable for ordinary types of economic resources. As discussed in preceding chapters, slight variations in the distribution of these goods can easily translate into magnified differences in life outcomes. Greater equity in their allocation is necessary because of their disproportionate influence over the individual's ability to secure other resources indispensable for a flourishing life.[15] This is especially true in a knowledge-based economy where human capital has become the key to a purposeful and productive affiliation in economic life. This narrower tolerable margin for inequality in the appropriation of goods that are regulative in their use is reflected in the shifts of the various policy prescriptions and guidelines offered by CST for the political economy.[16] Ensuring an equitable distribution of these goods goes a long way toward satisfying the principles of participation and solidarity and is in line with the principle of subsidiarity's cardinal norm of nurturing private initiative through free and meaningful opportunities.

Reference to one of the most successful projects of recent development economics is an appropriate way of capping this discussion of the unique, pivotal role of these goods with a regulative impact. The Grameen Bank of South Asia and its microenterprise variants in Latin America bring to the fore the enormous difference that a selective provision of critical resources can make in poverty alleviation.[17] A new world of empowerment, self-respect, livelihood possibilities, and higher standards of living has been opened to Third World women and their families through such a simple measure as making previously inaccessible credit suddenly available. The creation of a grassroots credit market for small loans has been instrumental in successfully integrating marginalized segments of the informal economy back into the mainstream of social life; it demonstrates the strategic importance of some economic resources in shaping the opportunities available to people. Credit, in this case, is an example of a good that is regulative in its impact on these poverty-stricken communities.

Goods as Functional and Life Enhancing

I have now identified two classes of human needs that merit special attention: those whose use are constitutive or regulative. One other category remains to be acknowledged in order to complete this categorization of needs. All creation is good and the gifts of the earth have been entrusted to a human stewardship that includes both the use and care of these temporal resources. Material goods have an instrumental value in promoting human well-being and are said to be functional when they fulfill this end.

As noted earlier, goods are functional in their use when their consumption sustains the individual by "contributing to the maturing and enrichment of that subject's 'being'" (SRS #28d) and the attainment of the person's vocation. In contrast to dysfunctional goods whose consumption is neither life affirming nor life enhancing whether through inappropriate or intemperate use, functional goods live up to their instrumental value in promoting human well-being. Thus, while eating moderately replenishes one's vigor and strength, food when taken in excessive amounts becomes dysfunctional in its effect on both health and virtue. The functional use of goods advances the manifold dimensions of integral development—social, cultural, intellectual, moral, and spiritual. The enjoyment of these goods becomes a channel for the further growth of the human personality in a life consistent with the "quest for truth, beauty, goodness and communion with others" (CA #36d). From this, it is easy to see that this class of goods is necessarily broad. As already noted, the functional use of goods can be further refined according to their varying degrees of necessity. There are goods that are constitutive for survival and basic health, and then, there are those that are regulative of the individual's access to other goods. Those that are neither constitutive nor regulative may be lumped together under a catch-all category as *life-enhancing*.

Goods that are considered regulative condition the prospects for the person's engagement in socioeconomic life by supplying the necessary physical resources for the establishment of that *minimum* opportunity set that the social nature of the human person demands. In other words, they ensure the existence of this opportunity set. This third category in the functional use of goods is one step removed from such urgency but serves to expand the boundaries of this opportunity set beyond that minimum. Thus, in the case of unemployed, homeless people, access to a place to live, shower, and receive mail or phone messages is a good that is regulative of their chances of securing and keeping a job. However, procuring a cellular phone carries less urgency and can be treated as merely life-enhancing in the sense that it serves primarily to broaden the scope of one's enjoyment of the gifts of the earth. Or take the case of a Third World family for whom a simple $100 loan is regulative in the way it can open new livelihood possibilities in crafts or a household piggery. This is in contrast to a bank loan for the construction of a garage extension, the end of which is a further refinement of one's comfort in life.

In summary, the *functional use* of goods can be differentiated according to their varying degrees of necessity:

1. the use of goods as constitutive for physical survival and basic health
2. the use of goods as regulative of life prospects
3. the use of goods as life-enhancing

After all, the gifts of the earth are essential means for autonomy and for the instantiation of moral perfection in integral human development.[18]

WEIGHING CRITERION

The overarching principle of justice governing this ranking model is the universal access principle that imbues a social nature to both labor and capital, indeed, to all created goods. The operative standard is proportional equality using the following criterion:

Competing claims for scarce resources are weighed and resolved in light of unmet needs ranked in the following descending order of urgency and importance:

1. as constitutive
2. as regulative
3. as life-enhancing

The dysfunctional use of goods has no claims at all.

The graduated level of urgency and importance in the demands of justice across these categories is founded on the universal access principle's hierarchy of claims where the preservation of life takes precedence over other economic interests; human survival is the most immediate end of temporal resources. This allocative rule flows from these categories' respective importance and contribution to integral development. The demands of justice become stricter as goods become more essential to sustaining life, as in the case of goods that are constitutive for physical survival and basic health.

The standards of equity are also expected to be more stringent for goods that are determinative of the person's access to other material goods and that configure the individual's opportunity set for communion with the larger world. The strength of legitimate claims falling within the categories of goods as constitutive and regulative is compelling because of their significant foundational role in shaping the possibilities and the economic base for a meaningful life.[19] Thus, a starving person has a greater claim to a loaf of bread (goods as constitutive) than one who is well fed (goods as functional or maybe even dysfunctional in use). This is consistent with traditional teachings that in cases of extreme necessity, the poor may appropriate for their own and their family's survival what belongs to others (Aquinas 1947/48, II–II, q. 66, a. 7). In the event of extreme need, goods become common, even those that are the subject of private property rights (GS #69a, especially footnote 11). Looking at the other end of the continuum, the dysfunctional use of goods has no claim at all because it goes against an end of material goods: the promotion of human well-being.

UNRESOLVED ISSUES

Further work remains to be done on a number of issues. In the first place, there is the intertemporal question. It is not always clear whether income is superfluous or not because accumulation is most often pursued for the purpose of either building a prudent cushion for a rainy day or bequeathing something to one's heirs. The addition of a time dimension greatly complicates matters because of (1) the varying degrees of obligations owed to family, future heirs, and contemporary neighbors, and (2) the problems of commensurability in the nature of urgency between present and future contingencies. This is not even to mention the difficulties introduced by imperfect information.

A second related issue is the question of how far one's obligations extend. How wide is an individual's circle of responsibility within which competing claims may be validly presented? What are its determinants? To what extent may a poor Third World family's constitutive need for clean water and food be considered as a competing claim against a New Yorker's recreational enjoyment (life-enhancing use) of an evening out at the movies? To what extent are these needs comparable and how far may their legitimate claims reach?

A third unresolved question is the disagreement over what should be classified as constitutive or regulative in use. There are manifold visions of a flourishing life, each advancing its own basket of basic human goods. With the possible exception of food, the specific content of these two categories cannot always be defined a priori, removed from the particular context. For example, depending on their phase of development, economies may require varying minimum levels of education as a prerequisite for incorporation into the productive activities of the community. Some may require only a basic high school education as in the case of some Fourth World countries; others may call for a college or even a postgraduate degree as in the case of most developed economies. As Samuels (1994) observes, needs are time- and culture-specific. We have seen this in the differences in the emphasis of the Old Testament's Jubilee Law, modern Catholic social thought's full employment at a living wage, and the Grameen Bank's provision of small loans to the poor in the informal sector of the economy. These questions reflect the larger problem of definitively establishing, to the extent possible, the basket of goods and services that integral human development requires.

A fourth issue that requires further work is the formulation of a distributive principle for competing claims for scarce resources falling within the same class of needs. In particular, how does one weigh the merits of clashing claims in what we expect to be the largest category of goods, those that are life enhancing? Should such claims be even weighed at all according to unmet needs, or should other criteria be used such as contribution, effort, ability, market operations, and equality? After all, some of these may not even properly qualify as needs but should perhaps be viewed as wants. A different set of criteria is required for the latter.

A fifth dilemma is the need to understand the interrelationship between production and distribution. Talking of equity in distribution and defining the living wage or the minimum basket of consumption goods that must be guaranteed is pointless if the community cannot produce that which is to be apportioned equitably in the first place. What makes this concern even more significant is the empirical evidence on how equity-oriented policies alter the incentives structures within the economic order and exacerbate an inequitable situation further. Thus, the redistributive strategies of the more nationalistic or socialistic developing nations in the 1970s and 1980s distort incentives, discourage private initiative, scare capital away, and precipitate a drop in output, thereby worsening poverty (Meier 1995). While relative equality is improved, it is a sharing not of wealth and prosperity, but of even more severe destitution. This accounts for the emergence in the 1990s of more market-oriented policies in reaction to the disappointing results and the failed promises of seizing the "commanding heights" of the economy (Yergin and Stanislaw 1998).

SUMMARY AND CONCLUSIONS

While this ranking model is many steps removed from practical implementation, it provides a convenient conceptual framework for dealing with many contentious problems in political economy dealing with competing claims over scarce resources. The moral imperative of providing goods that are constitutive in use is fairly well understood and accepted as evident in the ready outpouring of aid in times of famine and other natural or civil disasters. What is yet to be developed, however, is a moral sensitivity to the second tier of needs that can substantially affect the individual's prospects for a flourishing life. This chapter's typology of goods is a step in that direction by highlighting the nature and the role of goods that are regulative in their impact. Nevertheless, just like the other approaches described in chapter 9, this ranking model requires much further work if it is to find ready application.

The two dimensions of the person as an embodied being and as intelligent freedom both converge on the unavoidable need for consuming certain requisite material resources as a necessary economic dimension of human flourishing. The person as an embodied being uses temporal goods that are constitutive for physical survival and basic health. The person as intelligent and free also requires access to material resources either as inputs or as tools for participating in the life of the community. These goods are aptly described as regulative because they are vital for establishing and, then, shaping the economic base that defines the quality and the extent of an individual's involvement in the commonweal.

The principal contribution of this framework lies in its refinement of the concept of superfluous income by distinguishing varying degrees of unmet needs through a classification that provides key distinctions with respect to function, theological warrants, and strength of claims. This is schematically summarized in table 11.1 where different categories of uses are identified. Given an understanding of the human person as an embodied intelligent freedom, one can articulate the basis for claims attendant to these various human needs. In doing so, one opens the door to a more nuanced application of distributive justice. Competing claims can be weighed according to a sliding scale where the demands of justice become stricter and the tolerance for inequality becomes much narrower as unmet needs progressively move from being life enhancing, to being regulative of life prospects, to being constitutive of survival and basic health. The strength of claims is directly proportional to the urgency of these unmet needs. Unlike the amorphous notion of superfluous income, this gradation in unmet needs allows for flexibility in varying the standards of equity depending on the type and uses of the goods that are the subject of competing claims.

Finally, in being sensitive to the ethical warrants of goods that are regulative of life prospects, we highlight a dimension of our moral obligation for each other's well-being that is usually overlooked. This is the duty not only of providing the marginalized with the means for physical survival but also of assisting them back into the mainstream of socioeconomic life. It is imperative to furnish them also with the requisite means for participating meaningfully and productively as free men and women, thereby granting them access to the other goods of creation that can further enrich their lives. Thus, the superfluous income criterion requires an intelligent use of investments in simultaneously creating both work and commodities that are truly useful (QA #51).[20] The framework in table 11.1 provides focus and facilitates the identification

Table 11.1. Defining Degrees of Unmet Needs

Categories of Uses	Sources of Claims	Strength of Claims	Standard of Equality	Tolerance for Inequality
Functional				
as constitutive of survival and basic health	Person as embodied being.	strongest/ most urgent	absolute measure	narrow margin
as regulative of life prospects for (a) access to goods (b) participation in social life	Person as intelligent being.		absolute and proportional measures	
as life-enhancing for greater enjoyment of life	Creation as gift for human flourishing.	less compelling	proportional measure	wider margin
Dysfunctional		no claim at all		

of such commodities of real value by offering a more refined classification of unmet needs together with the basis and the strength of their legitimate claims. The ideal economic order is more than merely an economics of survival. It is also an economics of sufficiency where people are provided with the necessary means for satisfying the economic dimension of human flourishing.

Notes

1. Hence, *Centesimus Annus* (#36d) could claim that investment decisions (and consequently, consumption and savings behavior) are moral decisions. For an excellent exposition on this moral dimension, see Worland (1996).

2. Note that this is not a strictly zero-sum phenomenon inasmuch as productivity gains and renewable resources allow simultaneous increases in consumption both within and across generations.

3. Readers should be alerted to the manifold uses of "goods" in this chapter. This term is used in one of two senses: (1) as a moral ideal of fullness and perfection, as in "human goods," "individual good," and "common good," or (2) as a commodity subject to depletion and competition, as in "material goods." It is the latter that is the subject of the model proposed. The context and the modifiers should make clear which usage is relevant.

4. GS, footnote #10, chapter 3, part II. The emphasis is on the obligations attendant to consumption in community life. Note that this reappropriation of the stricter patristic position is consistent with Christiansen's (1984) claim of a more stringent egalitarianism after Vatican II.

5. Keeping this distinction in mind is important for Catholic social thought because of the difference in the strength of claims between wants and needs. Furthermore, there are limits to want satisfaction in order to avoid the consumerism that reflects an overly indulgent lifestyle that has been consistently criticized by this tradition. In contrast, there are no such limits to want satisfaction in conventional economics beyond the time and budget constraints of economic agents. For a fuller discussion of the distinction between wants and needs, see O'Boyle (1994) and Danner (1994).

6. See O'Boyle (1994) for a succinct discussion of the difference between absolute and relative equality.

7. See Finnis (1980, 67–68) for a listing of works on basic human goods.

8. What is less clear is the specific composition of this *constitutive* consumption basket. What are the minimum levels of consumption deemed necessary? This is an issue beyond the scope of this study. My immediate concern is to establish the preeminence accorded to goods whose consumption falls under this category.

9. Exodus 21:2–3; Deuteronomy 15:12–18; Leviticus 25:39–43; Nehemiah 10:32.

10. The Jubilee Law calls for the return of ancestral land to the families or heirs of their original owners. This is to be done every fifty years. Consequently, any sale of land is merely the sale of the produce of that land until the next Jubilee year. See Leviticus 25:13–17, 23–28.

11. Whether the law is actually implemented or not is another issue. See Ginzberg (1932) and North (1951).

12. Exodus 22:24–25; Deuteronomy 23:20; Deuteronomy 24:6, 10–13; Leviticus 25:35–38.

13. This chapter's formulation of goods with a *regulative* impact is similar to, but not identical with, Walzer's *dominant goods*. Walzer (1983) is perceptive in advancing the second proposition of his theory of goods where people's concrete identities are shaped by the moral and material worlds that have nurtured them (p. 8). I would, however, hesitate from going too far in ascribing a role to material goods as "the crucial medium of social relations" (p. 7). People are significantly, though not exclusively, shaped by their access to and possession of these social goods that affect the opportunity set available to them. As *Centesimus Annus* (#38b) observes, moral agency imbues the human person with an innate capacity to rise above whatever social or material obstacles and difficulties they may encounter.

A second point of divergence lies in the way Walzer views distributive principles as arising from the subjective meanings assigned to goods by the particular time and place. I would take this a step further by noting that there also essential, *objective* requirements that govern distributive principles. After all, there are objective standards arising from the order of creation, such as the laws of economics (e.g., technical requirements of productive technologies) that are independent of people's subjective preferences. Finally, note that my notion of goods that are *regulative* in their impact is derived teleologically by examining the necessary economic dimension of human flourishing as the starting point.

14. For example, in the early days of the modern market economy when wealth is principally generated from natural resources, individuals who reap a disproportionate amount of the fruitfulness of these resources accumulate even more wealth and power that enable them to contribute and appropriate more from the subsequent rounds of economic activity. This leads to the economic domination and concentration that *Quadragesimo Anno* addresses as a threat to the very foundations of the economic order (Pius XI 1931). Hence, ownership of natural resources and industrial capital are examples of goods in the modern economy that are regulative in their use. They serve to constrain or to facilitate an individual's subsequent acquisition of many other human goods that are essential to a full and perfect life.

15. The unusual leverage exercised by these goods in securing other human goods makes them a valuable policy tool for correcting inequalities within the social order. They have the added advantage of being less controversial compared to other means of redistribution (such as taxation and outright expropriation) inasmuch as it is future income and wealth streams that are affected.

16. Note, for example, the increasing urgency attached to partnership contracts in labor-management relations. In *Rerum Novarum* and *Quadragesimo Anno*, partnership contracts are presented merely as ideal, nonbinding models. By the time of *Mater et Magistra* and especially *Laborem Exercens*, they have become normative with a relatively greater moral imperative attached to profit sharing, co-management, and co-ownership.

17. The Grameen Bank is an innovative grassroots livelihood program whose object is to nurture and give vent to the private initiative of the poor through the establishment of microenterprises. The poor are provided hitherto inaccessible loans that are monitored and managed through peer moral suasion. See Wahid (1993).

18. See Worland (1996, 60–63) for a succinct discussion of the instrumental nature of created goods.

19. Consequently, Catholic social thought, including the U.S. bishops' pastoral letter on the economy, has consistently championed a preferential option for the poor and the helpless.

20. See also Worland (1996, 68).

Part V

CONCEPTUAL SYNTHESIS

Social questions need to be addressed from a sociohistorical approach and, consequently, the modern Catholic social documents do not claim an immutable, universal application of their teachings on political economy.[1] Even when this body of literature is referred to as a social doctrine, it is not viewed as a closed system because people are expected to draw upon the resources offered by faith and the human sciences to assess intelligently and compassionately what a just and Christian social order requires.[2] In what has become an informal guide on the scope of binding claims that can be made regarding the social condition, Paul VI proposes:

> In the face of such widely varying situations it is difficult for us to utter a unified message and to put forward a solution which has universal validity. Such is not our ambition, nor is it our mission. It is up to the Christian communities to analyze with objectivity the situation which is proper to their own country, to shed on it the light of the Gospel's unalterable words and *to draw principles of reflection, norms of judgment and directives for action from the social teaching of the Church* (OA #4, emphasis added).

Even as it acknowledges the contextual setting of social questions, Catholic social thought constantly stresses certain root values. These axioms are by no means comparable to the permanence and the primacy of place accorded to the Sacred Scriptures, but they nevertheless provide coherence and an overarching framework for theological reflection. Thus, the *Instruction on Christian Freedom and Liberation* (#72) sees the need to balance "contingent judgments" with "principles that are always valid." *Sollicitudo Rei Socialis* (#3) is emphatic that even as attentive and "opportune adaptations" are needed to respond to the historicity and context of social problems, they must also be founded on the unchanging "fundamental inspiration" that animates Christian social action. The vitality of the tradition is dependent on striking a delicate blend of continuity and renewal.

Continuity presupposes foundational values that serve as a starting point, indeed, a prism with which to examine social issues. Unfortunately, it can be a particularly frustrating exercise in the theory and practice of Catholic social thought to search for this oft-cited set of *principles of reflection, criteria for judgment,* and *directives for action* (OA #4). Very little has been done to systematize, much less identify, these perennial tenets. For example, the U.S. Bishops' Conference condenses these into five or six themes.[3] This method of straight enumeration is a good beginning, but it is not sufficient because it implicitly assigns equal weights to these principles without examining their warrants or differentiating their importance. And even in more nuanced expositions[4] that rank these principles, much work still remains to be done in situating these principles within their historical context and in establishing their precise relationship and complementarity with each other. Moreover, their links to the common good remain largely unexplored.[5] The object of the next three chapters is to synthesize into a conceptual framework the mainstay principles that have been repeatedly employed by the social documents in proposing just solutions to the contentious public questions of their day.

The ad hoc nature of these teachings partly accounts for this lacuna in the literature; it also leads to objections that such a systematization is not viable because these social documents are not homogenous. After all, these documents are not comprehensive academic treatises but are either commemorations of earlier encyclicals or theological reflections on social disorders. Not surprisingly, commentators observe shifts and discontinuities in both methodology and content within this corpus of social teachings.[6]

The ad hoc nature of these social documents can be used to good advantage because it provides valuable multiple observations through time. Thus, we have a body of moral deliberations not only on a wide range of social issues but also on the different dimensions of longstanding problems, examined under varying conditions during a century of rapid and often disruptive economic changes. Equally important are the repeated observations afforded scholars on the use of the same principles to work through diverse social issues or new dimensions of perennial debates.

In grappling with the socioeconomic issues of their day, these documents exhibit an observable pattern of identifying the injustices to be addressed, of appropriating theological and philosophical insights from earlier works, and of proposing new approaches to dealing with the social questions at hand. There is an unmistakable regularity in their methods: (1) repeatedly appealing to a set of foundational premises on the transcendent dignity of the person and the community, these documents

(2) identify the necessary and manifold economic dimensions of human flourishing, and, then, (3) articulate the requisite principles and norms for a just socioeconomic order. It is these patterns and uniformities that provide the basis for a conceptual synthesis of the nature and structure of modern Catholic social thought on political economy.

Later documents reinterpret, spell out in greater detail, disabuse misconceptions, provide new applications, and reformulate the grounds of earlier teachings. For example, *Quadragesimo Anno* builds on *Rerum Novarum*'s defense of the rights to association and to private property ownership in order to advance the principle of subsidiarity in response to the economic crisis of the interwar years. *Mater et Magistra* adopts Leo XIII and Pius XI's acknowledgment of a rightful role for government in economic affairs and provides it with renewed importance in the post–World War II phenomenon of socialization. Moreover, John XXIII expands *Rerum Novarum*'s notion of property to encompass both tangible capital and professional skills. Part I of *Gaudium et Spes* summarizes the theological anthropology of this tradition. *Laborem Exercens* systematically lays out the philosophical arguments for the primacy and the special place of labor, a precept that has been a hallmark since Leo XIII's passionate advocacy of worker welfare. *Sollicitudo Rei Socialis* creatively sets *Populorum Progressio*'s integral human development and the principle of solidarity within the new demands of justice in the rapidly evolving geopolitics of the Cold War. *Centesimus Annus* develops further *Rerum Novarum*'s universal access principle and re-centers it in the radically changed setting of a knowledge-based economy. Indeed, the shifts, discontinuities, and development of the tradition's teachings on political economy highlight the multifaceted dimensions of the key principles that have been staple for these documents. The tradition lends itself particularly well to a coherent synthesis because there are sufficient patterns, similarities, and uniformities in the fundamental anthropological premises, principles, and norms to which these social documents have consistently appealed in reflecting on the social questions of their day. To readily dismiss the feasibility of synthesizing these social documents into a conceptual framework is to miss the opportunity of examining the rich tapestry of theological reflections on the economy that continues to evolve as the tradition grapples with some of the more exacting dilemmas of the postmodern age.

The following chapters present a synthetic conceptual structure for understanding and using the modern Catholic social principles together as a single framework. The listing is nonexhaustive and the focus is only on the key tenets that have been instrumental in unraveling the social questions of the past hundred years. Part I dealt with these principles' historical context; this section of the book is a speculative exercise in plumbing their theological warrants. The following exposition gleans through the recurring arguments that have been used by these social documents to advance these principles. One must remember that the bases for these teachings are not always explicitly nor systematically laid out as there is often a seeming presumption that they should be self-evident to readers. Hence, the following model is offered merely as an interpretive device and should neither be read as definitive nor viewed as exhaustive. Figure 12.1 is a schematic summary of this effort and shows the preeminence of human dignity and integral human development as first-order principles from which other second-order principles are logically derived. Moreover, the framework underscores the complementarity of these principles both in the way they mutually reinforce each others' norms and in the way they prevent the misuse or abuse of these tenets. The common good viewed as due order and due proportion also provides a better appreciation for the role of these principles in social ethics.

Notes

1. Note that the precision and thorough nature of teachings on sexual or personal morality cannot be replicated to the same degree when it comes to precepts for the political economy. Economic policy is fraught with both theoretical and empirical uncertainties. Thus, exceptional prudential judgment is required for socioeconomic ethics regardless of how well we are able to articulate conceptual frameworks of analysis.

2. Congregation for Catholic Education (1989); Sacred Congregation for the Doctrine of the Faith (1986).

3. The United States Catholic Conference (1990) summarizes the social teachings into six basic themes: the life and dignity of the human person; the rights and responsibilities of the human person; the call to family, community, and participation; the dignity of work and the rights of workers; the option for the poor and vulnerable; and solidarity.

4. For example, the Congregation for Catholic Education (1988) suggests the following three permanent principles of reflection: human dignity, human rights, and the sociality of the person from which are derived other principles such as the common good, solidarity, subsidiarity, participation, the organic concept of social life, and the universal destination of goods. See also Byron (1998).

5. The absence of such a systematic framework probably accounts for the difficulties observed by the United States Catholic Conference (1998) in disseminating this tradition.

6. See for example, essays by Curran, Hebblethwaite, and Hehir in Curran (1985a).

Chapter 12

FIRST-ORDER PRINCIPLES

HUMAN DIGNITY

Vital Core

Catholic social thought's ethical methodology is founded on an understanding of human nature and the needs that flow from it. A common characteristic of these writings is the inevitable reference to and reiteration of the unique value of the human person. Through all the disparate social questions of the past century, each posing its particular challenges and requiring fresh thinking, *Centesimus Annus* (#11c) notes that it is the singular worth accorded to the person that has provided the consistency, indeed, "the main thread and in a certain sense the guiding principle" of this heterogenous body of literature.

At the heart of Catholic social thought and action is the protection and the promotion of human dignity. This is the bedrock of Christian theological reflection on social issues, and four constitutive elements can be discerned in the vital core of this inalienable dignity that is consistently ascribed to the human person.

1. *Each person is created and sustained by God with a personal love*. A proper understanding of the theological notion of *creation* and of its difference from the common, anthromorphic usage of the term reveals the full depth of this tenet. The theological creation of human life entails bringing nonexistence into existence (something out of nothing) and then maintaining that created being in continued existence through divine providence. In effect, every moment of human experience and history is an ongoing act of creation; every moment is a continuing engagement of the human with the divine in a tandem of Creation-Providence.

2. *The person is made in the image and likeness of God and endowed with the signal gifts of reason and freedom that are
   unique in all of creation.* The person is endowed with intelligence and a free will and is, consequently, fully capable not only
   of knowing and loving God but of choosing whether to do so or
   not. Goodness is intelligible to the person. Such faculties mark
   the individual as clearly distinct and above all the other creatures of the earth.[1] *Centesimus Annus* (#44b) aptly refers to this
   quality as a transcendent dignity that makes the person the "visible image of the invisible God."
3. *The person has been redeemed by Christ.* Human dignity also
   arises from the person's inseparability from Christ. It is a union,
   a filial bond, effected in the economy of salvation that culmi-
   nated in the mystery of Christ's incarnation, passion, death, and
   resurrection. This redemption won for each individual the new-
   ness of liberty from sin and participation in divine life. It revealed the true condition of the person's liberty: the new
   freedom to be a child of God and to love. Each person is important and deserves to be accorded the unique dignity that has already been secured at the price of Christ's death (John Paul II
   1979).
4. *The person is the subject of a special divine friendship and is
   destined for eventual union with God–the human final end,
   perfection, and fulfillment.* The person has a transcendent destiny. Human dignity's ultimate worth is rooted in the invitation
   to a communion with God. The person's uniqueness and great-
   ness lie in that capacity to cooperate with grace in surmounting
   the fragility and transience of earthly realities for that final place
   in heaven. In addition to the gifts of intelligence and freedom,
   the individual has been singled out for a special relationship of
   intimate friendship with God both in the present time and in
   eternity, the only creature in all of creation made by God for its
   own sake. Moreover, the person is the object of the Creator's
   continued providence and reverential treatment seen in the divine respect for the human exercise of the gift of free will.[2]

Freedom as the Existential Terrain of Human Dignity

These four elements in the vital core of human dignity can be viewed together as the potency of a divine-human friendship awaiting full realization and completion. Such actualization is a function of the dual
determinants of grace and human assent. This much-awaited response,
actively and patiently elicited by God, points to the centrality of human
freedom. In this regard, four characteristics of freedom can be gleaned
from these modern social documents.

Characteristic #1: The person is the subject of freedom.

Moral agency is constitutive of personhood where rectitude takes on a meaning and significance that are accessible to human reason. In criticizing the anthropology of socialism, *Centesimus Annus* (#13a) argues that intelligence and free will turn the human creature into "an autonomous subject of moral decision" and imbue the individual with the capacity to distinguish right from wrong, to deliberate, to shape one's surrounding environment, to make choices, and to form one's character. The perfection of this moral agency lies in its openness to its most promising possibility: friendship with God. Only a personal response can accept this proffered gift of divine life and happiness. Neither the community nor anyone else can provide the assent for an invitation that is profoundly and inherently personal to begin with.[3]

Such moral agency is, by its nature, the most secure of freedoms because of its interior nature; nothing and no one can deprive the person of what lies within the self. Even as its exercise is conditioned and facilitated or impeded by countless extraneous factors, authentic human freedom can never be determined nor destroyed by these.[4] For this reason, the *Instruction on Christian Freedom and Liberation* (#73a) describes freedom as the "essential prerogative of the human person."

Characteristic #2: Freedom finds its authenticity in an objective truth.

The person's fundamental autonomy should not, however, be confused with an ethical individualism that views the person as the final and supreme arbiter of human values expressed through personal choices (Lukes 1973; Montefiore 1966). Far from being a Kantian moral autonomy, authentic human freedom can only claim, at best, to be a participation in *Subsistent Freedom*, God. Human freedom is situated within a given, well-defined divine order. Its reference point in a professed objective truth is perhaps the most striking contrast between Catholic social thought's religious individualism and secular ethical individualism. The Second Vatican Council expresses it well when it notes:

> Only in freedom can man direct himself toward goodness. Our contemporaries make much of this freedom and pursue it eagerly; and rightly to be sure. Often however they foster it perversely as a license for doing whatever pleases them, even if it is evil. For its part, authentic freedom is an exceptional sign of the divine image within man (GS #17a).

The Instruction on Christian Freedom and Liberation is even more explicit on the objective foundation of human freedom.

> [M]an is called to be like God. But he becomes like God not in the arbitrariness of his own good pleasure but to the extent that he recognizes that truth and love are at the same time the principle and the purpose of his freedom (CFL #37d).

Truth is both the fountainhead and the yardstick of authentic freedom. The person's liberty of action is indeed boundless, but only by virtue of the truth in that natural law written in the human heart, shared by all, and known to all. It is, thus, a rational freedom where reason presents to the will the good that is worthy of desire. In its objective sense, this truth consists of the historical trajectory of creation-sin-redemption and of the natural and moral structure that the person receives as part of personhood.[5]

This foundational law embraces both the wounded nature of the human person and the healing balm of grace. Sin is an exaggerated claim of autonomy from God that impedes richness and life from blooming in the individual's personality (CFL #40). In sapping the person of creativity and power to mold and form one's unique character to the fullness that one could possibly be, sin turns the moral agent away from God, the only Good that satisfies completely and profoundly. Hence, emancipation from sin is a necessary starting point of freedom if it is to be genuine.

Freed from the inevitability of sin and death, the human person nevertheless still bears their vestiges and is the subject of a constant internal struggle (SRS #30c–f). On the one hand, the person is afflicted with the effects of original sin, which readily dissipates divine gifts. On the other hand, the divine law is also deeply rooted in the individual, yearning to reach for the highest degree of love of God and neighbor. *Octogesima Adveniens* (#48b) expresses the deep conviction that "beneath an outward appearance of indifference" is a human heart longing to live in justice and peace.

The person, therefore, is torn by an unrelenting battle between the sublime and the base, between sinfulness and righteousness. One yearns for the good even as one is drawn to evil.[6] But because of a graced, transcendent dignity, the person bears both the capacity for and the obligation to rise above such self-indulgence and to live a life that is truly human.

Through all these struggles and despite the severity and the pervasiveness of social ills, there is a deep-seated optimism on the outcome of this struggle for the human heart. This hopefulness is rooted in the unwavering belief that the human person is fundamentally good, having been made in the image and likeness of God, redeemed by Christ, and sustained by supernatural grace. The individual is fully capable of surmounting the structures of sin and restoring justice. Social difficulties and conflicts, complex and intractable as they may be, can be resolved because everyone is endowed with the spiritual and moral aptitudes for interior conversion that pave the way to the heights of the new freedom inaugurated by Christ.[7] The extent to which the person lives out this human dignity determines the nature and the breadth of the freedom enjoyed. Human freedom deepens only as it situates itself within the economy of salvation.

The human person's likeness to God implants an innate quest for that which is true, good, and enduring. It is only in satisfying this manifest longing that one arrives at a self-understanding of one's inmost being. This persistent yearning provides a dynamism to authentic freedom. Truth in freedom is constitutive of the person as a moral agent because it is in its pursuit and appropriation that the person forms and takes responsibility for that personal response to divine initiative. Despite all the obstacles of sinful social structures that make righteous moral decisions even more difficult to make, the human person "remains above all a being who seeks the truth and strives to live that truth" (CA #49c).

Characteristic #3: Authentic human freedom is characterized by an intrinsic dynamism.

Liberation from sin and perfect union with God are the two endpoints that define the person's sojourn; they also define the varying degrees by which the person successfully reaches the fullness of such liberation. The inherent dynamism implicit in this lies in the second moment that follows the initial liberation from sin and death: the need to develop further and exercise this newly received freedom.[8]

Avoiding sin is the initial step of this deliverance. This interior freedom necessarily overflows and manifests itself in the person's external behavior. This initial liberation sets the stage for the subsequent easier and more spontaneous pursuit of the good. Authentic freedom is a dynamic process because it entails living up to the human person's destiny of service to God and neighbor.[9] Hence, it is better described as a *freedom for* rather than as a *freedom from* something. It is a freedom for goodness since the end of Christian liberation is holiness of life. Its authenticity is manifested in serving others in love and in the full realization and appreciation of the unique, unmerited human participation in the creative act of God.

It is Christ who animates authentic freedom, for it is He who effected liberation from sin and who sustains this new lease of life through the Holy Spirit. Thus, freedom's staying power is measured by its openness to Christ as both the paragon and the source of love.[10] Every human act can be said to perfect its own freedom in the measure that it is made in communion with the divine from whom it draws its inspiration, its potency, and its meaning.[11]

Characteristic #4: Happiness in God is the final end of human freedom.

Just as freedom, truth, and goodness are inseparable, so are happiness and freedom indivisibly linked. The yearning to be free is the obverse of the human heart's persistent longing to be happy. This is an aspiration that grows in intensity as the person matures in self-understanding in the course of responding fully, purposefully, and intelligently to God's invitation to share in divine life. It is an ever-growing discovery, awareness, and appreciation for one's unique transcendent end; this, in turn, allows the grounding of human freedom in the image and likeness of God to emerge and shine to its full brightness. It is, consequently, a participated freedom that derives its significance and life from God, a love that "comes from God and goes to God" (CFL #68b).

These four characteristics of authentic freedom locate the human person within an incessant quest to achieve fulfillment in that transcendent dignity. It begins with overcoming the domination of both personal and communal sinfulness in order to make the ensuing choices of the good both easy and spontaneous. It blooms into a charity and selflessness that take root in, permeate, and guide the person's will and actions, and makes the individual come fully alive to God. Living together as a community, therefore, must aim for the fullness of every human person's singular destiny.

Substantive Claims and Critique

In contrast to the more formalistic notions of freedom, these social documents present a substantive vision of human good and liberty. It should not come as a surprise, therefore, to read of their recurring critique of completely secularized notions of freedom. Thus, for example, the *Instruction on Christian Freedom and Liberation* (#13a, #18, #21a) laments the claims that freedom is the license to do as one pleases for as long as nobody is hurt, and that dependence on others is a diminution of one's own liberty. These views are criticized for giving rise to an excessive individualism with its concomitant selfishness and greed. Moreover, they have spawned a misleading sense of independence from God. God and the human person are seen as competitive to one another, and it is believed that only in rejecting God is the individual fully liberated, especially from the shackles of the moral teachings that flow from a divine order. Related to this rejection of dependence on God is the equation of freedom with achievements in science and technology that afford the person better control over the external world.

Centesimus Annus (#17a) disputes the common idea that the individual's liberties can be enhanced and expanded only by restricting others' enjoyment of liberties. The unrestrained pursuit of self-interest and the wanton disregard for the rights of others, far from demonstrating a liberty of action, are paradoxically a bondage in and of themselves, a reversion to the servitude of sin.

Gaudium et Spes (#4–10, #17) and *Octogesima Adveniens* (#8–21) trace what they describe as the modern paradox to these harmful misconceptions of autonomy. Despite tremendous strides achieved in modernity, its freedom often seems to be more apparent than real. For example, great poverty exists amidst the production of new and vast amounts of wealth. Advances in science and technologies mitigate the uncertainties of nature's forces but replace them with the dangers engendered by the new weapons of mass destruction. Unprecedented prosperity, while expanding the range of human choices, has only made the search for human values even more elusive than ever before. These documents observe that instead of leading to happiness, misplaced notions of liberty have only led to a characteristic dissatisfaction of emptiness and restlessness, a regression in the enjoyment of true freedom.

Catholic social thought advances a specific vision of the good, of a thinking and choosing human person brought into existence through the creative act of God, divinized and supernaturalized by God's redemptive act, and invited to a transcendence of communion with God in eternity. Its vision of freedom is, therefore, also necessarily substantive and unequivocal; authentic human freedom is, at its core, about responding to these divine initiatives. The literature refers to this in various ways, as perfectibilism (Griffin 1986, chapter 4; Passmore 1970), as human flourishing (Aquinas Summa, I–II), or as integral human development (*Populorum Progressio*).

INTEGRAL HUMAN DEVELOPMENT

Freedom in the Confluence and Continuum of the Temporal and the Transcendent

Having established the centrality of human dignity and its constitutive freedom in the first tier of our teleological framework (figure 12.1), I am now ready to move on and examine the second level of our conceptual synthesis. Integral human development is the actualization of human dignity. It can be viewed as the degree to which the person achieves authentic human freedom at the intersection of one's potency (defined by human dignity) and one's historicity. It is the full blossoming of personal gifts within the lived conditions and circumstances of temporal experience.

Centesimus Annus (John Paul II 1991, chapter 6) underscores the centrality of the person in this social tradition and goes so far as to describe the individual as "the primary and fundamental way for the Church."[12] However, it is quick to note that the subject of this tradition is not the abstract individual but the real, concrete person located within a narrative that is unique to the self. These social documents are concerned with the human in the midst of the daily events and exigencies of life with all its pain, sufferings, joys, and hopes. They are about the person who longs to be released from need, to be liberated from the earthly contingencies of hunger, destitution, ignorance, and strife. These teachings deal with the individual who yearns for autonomy and control over the insecurities of the vagaries of natural and social processes. They are

Figure 12.1. Modern Catholic Social Principles: An Interpretive Conceptual Framework

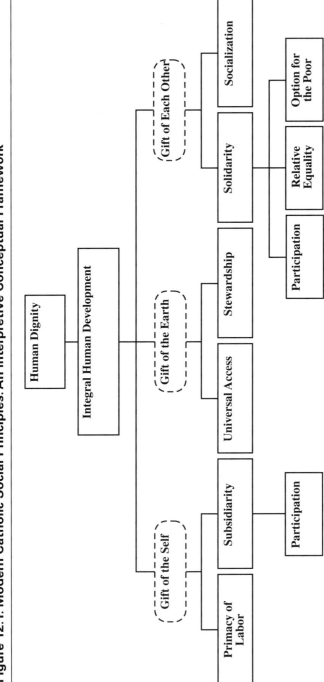

about the human longing to be emancipated from sinful social structures that impede living a full life.

This body of literature is not a speculative exercise in abstract modeling. Its concerns are of a practical nature in that it advances its teachings to alleviate suffering in the human order, to put hopes and dreams within easier reach, and to foster greater respect and appreciation for one another. It advances authentic human values of justice and charity in real life-and-death issues and situations as it aims to make life more attuned to God's vision of creation, to the extent possible. For this reason, the tradition professes to be watchful of the *signs of the times*. This attentiveness and empathy for the real, rather than the abstract, person is succinctly captured in the opening paragraph of the Conciliar document on the self-understanding of the Church in its role in the modern world, *Gaudium et Spes* (#1):

> The joys and the hopes, the griefs and the anxieties of the men of this age, especially those who are poor or in any way afflicted, these are the joys and hopes, the griefs and anxieties of the followers of Christ. Indeed, nothing genuinely human fails to raise an echo in their hearts.

The realism inherent in Catholic social thought also accounts for why these documents have been adamant in staking their claim and their right to teach on matters that are viewed to be secular. A constant criticism leveled against this tradition is that the Church has no business teaching on matters that lie outside the scope of its competence. The tradition responds to this by noting that the temporal and the transcendent, while distinct from each other, form a single continuum in the life of the human person in view of the latter's unique invitation to share in divine life for eternity. Thus, it is inappropriate to truncate the person's earthly existence from its future end, just as it is impossible to compartmentalize the person's life into fully hermetic spheres where professional, family, spiritual, and social experiences do not mutually inform, overflow, and shape each other. Consequently, the tradition considers it both as a right and an obligation to speak up on anything that puts human dignity at risk, be it in the secular realm or otherwise.

Advancing Across the Broad Spectrum of Human Giftedness

There are many competing notions of what constitutes human well-being (Griffin 1986). This interpretive synthesis offers integral human development as one such approach. Integral human development can be viewed as human freedom unleashing the vitality and creativity of the manifold giftedness of the human person—finitude and temporality blooming into transcendence through the nurturing medium of grace.

The premise that the human person has moral agency carries with it the duty to work toward one's own personal fulfillment and perfection. Temporal life provides the occasion to develop fully personal endowments so that the individual may live a full life in the present and attain the perfection of happiness in the next.[13] This is such a fundamental obligation that not even the individual has the right to do to one's own person anything that is contrary to human nature and perfection (RN #57, #60, #63).

Temporal life is a way station as the person moves toward the ultimate destiny of sharing eternity with God. Working for human well-being, therefore, cannot be limited to temporal concerns and must necessarily include those pertaining to the next life. Hence, efforts to perfect the person are envisioned to encompass body, mind, and spirit. Life, therefore, becomes more than just the satisfaction of the most basic requirements for preserving bodily integrity such as food, clothing, and shelter. It also involves nurturing the fundamental values that lend meaning to existence, qualities of life that are open to and specific to the human person: beauty, excellence, freedom, justice, solidarity, peace, and charity. These values grow and take root in proportion to the person's maturation in the cultural, social, and spiritual realms.

This understanding of human nature and its needs accounts for why the end of the economic order is nothing less than an *integral* development of the human person. Economic life is organic in the sense that it is merely one aspect of a much larger order. Consequently, in contrast to mainstream economic thought, this social tradition goes beyond the confines of *homo oeconomicus* in addressing social questions. Personhood is far more complex than a simple amalgamation of material and bodily wants and desires. Integral human development is diametrically and irreconcilably opposed to economism (SRS #28). Thus, *Populorum Progressio* and *Sollicitudo Rei Socialis* are critical of the notion of development that casts economic activity only in terms of the allocation of scarce resources to meeting these needs.[14] *Octogesima Adveniens* (#41) sets higher standards of what true progress is; it goes beyond being merely quantitative to encompass the qualitative as well. *Centesimus Annus* (#24a) argues that human welfare is genuinely advanced only when it occurs on a wide front, that is, only when it is accomplished with due consideration and respect for the human person within the context of culture, language, and history, and only when it addresses the person's fundamental existential encounters with the mysteries of life, love, suffering, death, and God.

To be personally fulfilled is to achieve the good through the proper development and use of one's manifold giftedness: the gift of the self, the gift of each other, and the gift of creation (CA #32c, #38a). If human life is primarily about responding to God's invitation of friendship and eternal life, then it is incumbent upon the person aspiring for an authentic human development to exercise stewardship not only over the earth but also over the gift of personal talents and the gift of each other. The moral imperatives flowing from these three gifts are examined in the next chapter.

Notes

1. RN #57; MM #208; GS #12c, #68a; LE #1, #13; CFL #28; CA #11c, #44b.

2. *Gaudium et Spes* part I, chapter I. See also RN #33, #38, #57; QA #118, #136; CFL #28; GS #24c; CA #13d.

3. Lukes (1973) describes this as religious individualism.

4. CA #25b observes: "[T]he manner in which the individual exercises his freedom is conditioned in innumerable ways. While these certainly have an influence on freedom, they do not determine it; they make the exercise of freedom more difficult or less difficult, they cannot destroy it." See also CFL #1a.

5. CFL #3, #4, #26. See also QA #43; GS #16a, #78a; CFL #19b, #74d; CA #38a, #44b.

6. GS #13b notes: "[M]an is split within himself. . . . [A]ll of human life, whether individual or collective, shows itself to be a dramatic struggle between good and evil, between light and darkness. . . . For sin has diminished man, blocking his path to fulfillment." See also QA #132; GS #13a, #14a, #37b–c, #78a, #83a; CFL #38d; OA #15b; CA #13d, #25c–d.

7. CFL #52, #75; SRS #47b; CA #38.

8. MM #180; CFL #23b.

9. GS #17a; CFL #26c, #27a, #71.

10. PP #15–16 remarks: "[T]his harmonious enrichment of nature by personal and responsible effort is ordered to a further perfection. By reason of his union with Christ, the source of life, man attains to new fulfillment of himself, to a transcendent humanism which gives him his greatest possible perfection: this is the highest goal of personal development."

11. CFL #24d. See also chapter 3, CFL #3, #4c.

12. See also John Paul II (1979, section 14, part III).

13. As *Populorum Progressio* (#15–16) notes: "[E]very man is called upon to develop and fulfill himself, for every life is a vocation. At birth, everyone is granted, in germ, a set of aptitudes and qualities for him to bring to fruition . . . which will . . . allow each man to direct himself toward the destiny intended for him by his Creator. . . . [T]]his self-fulfillment is not something optional." See also QA #118.

14. In the same way that the end of individual human activity is more than just the mere satisfaction of material and bodily wants, the life of the nation revolves around more than just the maximization of its gross national product (GNP). Development in its full sense involves an advance on a wide front, where economic progress is accompanied by improvements in the social and cultural life of the community. The vibrancy of a nation is measured in terms of social, political, economic, and cultural well-being.

Chapter 13

SECOND-ORDER PRINCIPLES

H ere I continue my derivation of the key social principles of this tradition and their teleological warrants. The preceding chapter dealt with the first two tiers of our framework (human dignity and integral human development) from which second-order principles can be justified (see figure 12.1). As already noted, integral human development can be measured in terms of how well the person thrives in the threefold gifts of the self, of each other, and of the earth. The conditions for flourishing in these gifts can in turn be described in terms of the social principles that have undergirded most of the teachings in the modern tradition. It is to these derived principles that I now turn my attention.

GIFT OF THE SELF: EMBODIED INTELLIGENT FREEDOM

Quadragesimo Anno's principle of subsidiarity and *Laborem Exercens*'s primacy of labor can be derived from an understanding of what it takes to blossom in the gift of the self.

Growth in Rational Freedom and the Principle of Subsidiarity

One way of appreciating the gift of the self is by looking at the person as *embodied intelligent freedom* (Ashley and O'Rourke 1989, 168). The principle of subsidiarity seeks to protect individual initiative from being unduly stifled. It is the unspoken premise undergirding *Rerum Novarum*'s staunch defense of both the capitalists' right to private property ownership and the workers' right to form their own associations for the protection of their interests. It finds its classic formulation as a fundamental principle in *Quadragesimo Anno*'s proposal to reorganize the troubled social order of the 1930s:

> [J]ust as it is wrong to withdraw from the individual and commit to the community at large what private enterprise and industry can accomplish, so, too, it is an injustice, a grave evil and a disturbance of right order for a larger and higher organization to arrogate to itself functions which can be performed efficiently by smaller and lower bodies (QA #79).[1]

The warrants for this principle are found in the moral agency that stems from human dignity. As seen in the preceding chapter, people have a transcendent end in the invitation to share in the fullness of God's divine life. The response to this can only come from individuals as subjects in their own right who are able to decide for themselves and be held responsible for the good or evil in their actions. To deprive individuals of this subjectivity in favor of a collective or a social institution (like the market) is to deprive them of the fullness of personhood. It is to diminish their innate moral agency, the ability to exercise their rightful and unique responsibility for good or evil in their lives.

Freedom is an indispensable condition both for the individual's response to God's invitation and for the stewardship of gifts received; it is both a prerequisite and a means for personal fulfillment. Accompanying this freedom is the duty for its responsible use, a charge that becomes easier and second nature to the person the more one is properly formed in the knowledge of right and wrong, together with being afforded the occasion to exercise it. Human freedom can be enjoyed in its fullness only if the individual can act as a subject in all aspects of life: personal, social, and spiritual.

From the use of subsidiarity in many of the social documents, it is evident that at the heart of this principle is the conviction that people achieve self-respect and personal growth in character when they are able to manage and contribute to the affairs that affect them. Thus, even as it is Pius XI that clearly defines the principle of subsidiarity, Leo XIII already cautions in the seminal document of this tradition that undue interference from without can easily sap the vitality of human action and initiative (RN #75, #68, #52).[2]

In expanding further on the principle, *Quadragesimo Anno* (#78, #80) observes that the wisdom of subsidiarity is not only that it strikes a balance between the legitimate demands of individual initiative and collective action, but that it also allows for a fuller and richer specification of the latter. The state is no longer the only institution that can work toward the protection and promotion of the common good; it can also rely on various social institutions and associations of individuals to discharge this duty. Nonlegal means are added to the legal avenues by which the commonweal is advanced. Hence, the principle of subsidiarity opens the door to an echelon of intermediate bodies to fill in the spectrum defined by two familiar endpoints: the individual, on the one hand, and the state, on the other. The "division of labor" that it effectively introduces is not merely an option but is in fact an obligation. It prevents the state from being hopelessly saddled with responsibilities that could not be performed by people acting singly on their own, but which could be accomplished through the cooperation of individuals acting together in groups. This enables the state to devote its resources and attention to tasks that properly belong to it. Besides, as *Mater et Magistra* (#120) argues, there are just too many unforseen needs and contingencies that the state cannot cover by virtue of its natural limitations.

Gaudium et Spes (GS #69b) counsels that in providing social services as part of the universal access principle, care should be taken that recipients do not develop a dependence but are encouraged instead to put their talents and gifts at the service of society. *Octogesima Adveniens* (#4a) leaves it to the local communities to take the lead in working out and applying the principles, norms, and directives of action that are appropriate to their particular circumstances. And, of course, whenever this tradition speaks of aid to less-developed areas, it is always within the context of private initiative taking precedence and allowing beneficiaries to accomplish as much as possible for themselves. Finally, *Centesimus Annus* emphasizes the importance of private initiative in economic life in the wake of the historical lessons left by the Soviet Union's collapse. Indeed, the principle of subsidiarity has been very much at the core of this tradition's understanding of the dynamics of integral human development.

Primacy of Labor Principle

Commemorating the ninetieth anniversary of the modern papal social tradition, *Laborem Exercens* is a systematic exposition on the significance and role of human work. John Paul II uses it as an occasion to synthesize the conceptual foundation for the Church's teachings on worker welfare. His primacy of labor principle affirms that the subjective takes preeminence over the objective dimension of work, that labor cannot be treated as if it were just a factor of production, and that the value of work output must ultimately be founded on the provision of a living wage to the laborer.

There are three dimensions to the subjective character of labor. Work is inextricably linked to human personhood because: (1) In its personal dimension it is a human good and serves as an avenue for personal growth; (2) It is necessary for the sustenance of the person; and (3) It is a means by which the individual can contribute to the common good. Personal fulfillment, sustenance for life, and the advancement of the common good are the ends of work. Consequently, work is not only a right of every human person, but it is a duty as well (LE #38–45).

1. Work as a personal value

   Work has a personal dimension for three reasons. In the first place, people are distinct from all of creation because they are created by God in His own image and likeness and endowed with reason and freedom. Thus, *Laborem Exercens* (#24) notes that humans imbue their labor with a special ethical nature. After all, only the person is capable of a rational act. Furthermore, the Second Vatican Council (GS #34, #67), Paul VI (PP #27), and John Paul II (LE #1, #13, #112–17; SRS #29c) all highlight the Genesis mandate to care for the gifts of nature and to exercise dominion over the earth. It is through labor that individuals discharge this commission, and in the process, work serves as a channel through which the creative work of God continues to unfold. Labor, therefore, moves the person ever closer to the likeness of the Creator through a sharing in the act of creation. It also allows the person to be part of the redemptive work of Christ through the toil that labor often brings in its wake.

   Second, Leo XIII (RN #15, #62) and John XXIII (MM #106–07) argue that work has personal value because it comes directly from the self and, through it, people imprint a part of themselves on the product of their sweat and toil. Labor, therefore, is the person's self-expression.

   Third, work allows people to transform the gifts of nature with their creativity. This, in turn, redounds to further their own growth and development in body, mind, and soul. Work, then, is a means by which individuals develop themselves through the acquisition of new skills and the improvement of personal qualities. It is a necessary condition for personality development and the achievement of true human fulfillment (LE #40–41; GS #35, #67). Consequently, meaningful employment is a key element in the perfection, character development, and growth of the person.

2. Work as a necessity

   Work is a personal necessity. Among the basic rights enumerated by *Pacem in Terris* are those that pertain to the preservation and development of life. The satisfaction of these basic rights is possible only through work by which people can earn a livelihood (RN #14, #62; MM #18). This includes provisions for education and a modest amount of property that provides stability and protection to the family. Work, then, is not only a necessary condition for family formation, it is also an honorable means of supporting life (RN #9, #31; LE #42).

3. Work as a social value

   Work is an avenue for exercising stewardship. In the first place, the gifts of nature can be made productive only with human care and cultivation (RN #15). Furthermore, work is the means by which the family, the most basic unit of society, is formed and maintained. It is the guarantee of the family's viability; it can either make families flourish or break up, with dire consequences for society. The social character of labor finds expression in the modern phenomena of skills specialization, division of labor, economies of scale, and organized units formed around work functions. These new and increasingly complex work arrangements require close cooperation and interdependence. Thus, human labor provides unique opportunities for community building, for strengthening human bonds of kinship and friendship, and for developing a sense of responsibility, duty, and charity toward neighbors regardless of class lines. Work is a means through which individuals contribute to the common good.[3]

GIFT OF EACH OTHER

As seen in figure 12.1, the principles of solidarity, preferential option for the poor, participation, relative equality, and socialization flow from valuing each other as a gift. Lest Catholic social thought's singular focus on the person be construed as methodological individualism, it is best to remember that the human dignity it espouses can be actualized in its fullness only within community.[4]

The role of society is pivotal. People, after all, are not born in a vacuum. They receive the gift of life and are nurtured, educated, and formed in a particular family. The values of the larger culture can encumber or foster their thriving. Their neighbors' noble virtues or malevolence can advance or obstruct their pursuit of excellence in the moral life. The community can furnish the necessary assistance, remove impediments, and maintain the best conditions for human development. This role is so vital to the point where the end of the community is deemed to be the perfection of the human person. On their own, individuals cannot achieve the fullness of their potential, much less survive; they need the help and the company of others. Social interaction is necessary both for survival and perfection. People belong to the larger family of humankind and share the same hopes, goals, and fundamental experiences. The common good is an essential condition of individual well-being (RN #70; MM #65; GS #12d, #24–26).

Both theological and pragmatic arguments undergird the longstanding claim that the human person is a social being. In the first place, the human history of creation-sin-redemption has a communal dimension to it. The Divine Providence that underwrites this human narrative unfolds through human instrumentality. God works in and through the human community. This is evident in the Sacred Scriptures. God created man and woman together that they may support one another and keep each other company; God dealt with Israel as a Chosen People. The New Testament affirms the social nature of the individual in the example of Christ's life and work, in His teachings on justice and charity toward neighbors, in His table fellowship with society's outcasts, in His unconditional welcome for all, and in His universal invitation to partake in the building of the Kingdom of God in the here and now (GS #39). Moreover, the redemptive act of Christ effected a twofold union: of God to the human person and of people to each other. Finally, the three divine Persons of the Blessed Trinity serve as the model for human fellowship, the quintessence of justice and charity in relationships.[5] The person's transcendent end itself points to this communal dimension.

Second, the glory of God is too infinite to fathom or to capture in the totality of creation. One could only catch glimpses of it both in the wonders of nature and in human interaction. Social life is built upon the uniqueness of both personal and shared human experiences. The glory of God that is unveiled in the harmonious communion of peoples is in direct proportion to the richness, truth, and vitality that permeate human relationships within the community. How the person lives in the unity of mind and heart with others serves as an avenue for God's self-revelation.[6]

A third theological argument for the person's social nature is that it is through this facet of life that the individual attains the fullness of freedom. In the preceding chapter, I focused on how authentic human freedom is a dynamic process of moving from the nascent stage of liberation from sin to the terminus of union with God, a movement characterized by an increasing self-diffusiveness that finds expression in service. Human fellowship is a necessary condition to authentic freedom. It is achieved when true interpersonal, reciprocal bonds are formed, and when responsibilities are willingly embraced, rather than avoided. Freedom necessarily overflows in a desire to self-donation. The degree to which one attains genuine freedom is a function of the quality of one's communion with God and neighbor; it is determined by the depth of one's love. The human person approaches a full realization of self when one offers the gift of self (GS #31b; OA #45a; CFL #26b; CA #39a). After all, the fullness of freedom rests in the experience of what it is to be a person—to love and be loved.

A fourth theological argument reinforces the claim that individualistic morality is not tenable. Particular human activity is necessarily situated within the larger society and takes its significance from being ordered to the common good. The obligation to contribute to the public welfare as best one can stems from justice and charity and should be considered a primary duty (GS #30; OA #24). There is a reflexive nature to the human act where the exercise of moral agency comes back to define and form the agent as subject.

The attainment of individual good is unavoidably conditioned, though not determined, by the larger world; thus, there are also numerous pragmatic reasons for the social nature of the person. The first is the phenomenon of the scarcity of material goods that are necessary for human survival and flourishing. People draw from the same pool of created gifts of the earth that are subject to rival consumption. The limited supplies of these material goods (relative to both human needs and wants) require a sharing of these means. Thus, these social documents are constantly concerned with relative inequality inasmuch as resource allocation has a material impact on the ease or the difficulty with which people are able to work for their self-perfection. The post–Vatican II social documents, in particular, have been resounding in their dismay over grinding poverty, especially since destitution can severely frustrate development in the noneconomic dimensions of life: physical, cultural, intellectual, and emotional. Extravagant luxury and conspicuous consumption are condemned because such behavior can inflict poverty on others, and they are the antithesis of integral human development and stewardship. Both extremes of destitution and of superabundance impede human flourishing.

A second practical argument is the importance of people's roles in society. Human flourishing is often a function of how well the person contributes to and draws from common life. The satisfaction of one's rights and the performance of one's obligations are determined by the degree to which the person interacts within the larger community. This is often dependent on the place one occupies in community, where roles and positions are scarce, subject to rival consumption, and, therefore, the object of competing claims (Hirsch 1976). How these positions are apportioned can significantly affect the ease or the difficulty with which individuals set and attain worthwhile goals for themselves.

Externalities provide a third pragmatic consideration. Given the unavoidable interdependence in social life that is exacerbated by the scarcity of both material goods and social roles, individual action can have unintended effects on others (Hausman 1992). This is especially true for acts that are of a moral nature in economic life. Advances in science and technologies have been moving socioeconomic life toward an ever greater and more intense reliance on each other. How well one is able to act effectively is increasingly dependent on how well others have lived up to what is expected of them.

In light of these theological and practical reasons, the particular circumstances of social living do affect, although not determine, people's journey to their transcendent end. Growth in perfection that is genuinely human can only occur in community. It is in interaction with other human beings that love and the responsible use of freedom find their medium for development. It is in fellowship with others that one discovers, feels, and is sustained by the personal love of God. There is a necessary social dimension to human flourishing. This is the intersection that provides social ethics its subject matter. Indeed, the quality of the interfacing between the natural and the supernatural (i.e., the attainment of the person's ultimate good) is a function of the quality and dynamics of another interface, this one between the person and the community. The interaction between the person and the community is reflected in and feeds back to the interaction between the temporal and the transcendent.

Not only is there a social dimension to human flourishing, but there is also an intrinsic link between the good of the individual and the good of the community. Much has been written on the subject matter, especially on the question of primacy between the good of the person and the good of the community. Implicit in this issue of preeminence is the assumption that authentic individual good and the common good can be at odds with each other. Jacques Maritain's (1947) *Person and the Common Good* dispels this idea and argues that one cannot properly weigh them against each other as both form a single continuum. The good of the person and the community are distinct but inseparable. They are necessary conditions to each other. It is a case where the finite blossoms into a transcendence in the most personal manner but within a most public medium of individuals growing in holiness in the midst of their neighbors. This point is also emphasized by *Gaudium et Spes* in reflecting on the human person in community and in fellowship with others. From this intrinsic sociality, one can derive the principles of solidarity and socialization. Solidarity, in its own turn, gives rise to what could be called the tradition's principles of nonexclusion: participation, relative equality, and preferential option for the poor. Figure 12.1 provides a schematic illustration of these interrelationships.

Principle of Solidarity

John Paul II (1987) presents the essence of the principle of solidarity in *Sollicitudo Rei Socialis* (#38f):

> [S]olidarity. . . is not a feeling of vague compassion or shallow distress at the misfortunes of so many people, both near and far. On the contrary, it is *a firm and persevering determination* to commit oneself to the *common good*; that is to say to the good of all and of each individual, because we are *all* really responsible *for all* . . . a commitment to the good of one's neighbor with the readiness, in the gospel sense, to "lose oneself" for the sake of the other instead of exploiting him, and to "serve him" for one's own advantage (emphases in the original).

At the heart of this solidarity and animating it is the belief that every person is a child of God and a fellow sojourner.

The principle of solidarity calls for individuals to put the interests of the larger community ahead of their own. It is a summons to a readiness for selfless sacrifice and for service to others. It is founded on justice and charity that create a nurturing environment of freedom and humaneness, where the promotion of the social good is made both feasible and easy.

This principle has been called by various names, as *friendship* by Leo XIII, as *social charity* by Pius XI, and as the *civilization of love* by Paul VI (CA #10c). It is a fundamental tenet of the Christian vision of the social and economic order. As in the preceding sections, I can show the close link between this principle and the tradition's anthropological axioms of human dignity and integral human development.

The transcendence of the human person gives the principle of solidarity its distinctive Christian cast compared to other philosophies of human solidarity and collective action where others are viewed merely as partners in contractual agreements. Christian solidarity goes beyond this. It sees deep, natural, and human bonds that arise from a fundamental equality and from a shared created contingency. As individuals with a common transcendent end, people share the same invitation to partake of divine life and the same friendship and filiation with God. It is a unity in Christ as a result of His salvific act. And because each individual is made in the image of God, this divine likeness is perfected to the extent that people emulate the paradigmatic unity, that intimate communion of love that characterizes the Oneness of the three divine Persons in the Blessed Trinity. Consequently, under the principle of solidarity, people can never be treated in a utilitarian manner and valued only for their productive contribution to society. Rather, the principle calls for each person to be viewed as the living image of God. Community is not contractual but familial in nature with ties that go deeper than mere mutual compacts.

As moral agents, people are invited to embrace interdependence and accept responsibility for each others' well-being. One grows in freedom as these mutual bonds and commitments are forged. The freedom of self-lessness in the service of God and neighbor is the attendant obligation of the liberation from sin effected by Christ's redemptive act. The human act takes its significance only when ordered toward others. For this reason, solidarity is said to be a virtue, a Christian virtue that stresses the unity of mind and heart.[7] Note that the principle of solidarity provides justification for other derived principles: participation, preferential option for the poor, and relative equality (see figure 12.1).

Principle of participation

Both the principles of solidarity and subsidiarity provide the warrants for the principle of participation. The principle of participation is concerned with ensuring that no one is excluded from active engagement in the common social, political, and economic life. It is through these interactions that individuals are able to draw from and contribute to the common good. The principle calls for the promotion of the welfare of all regardless of race, creed, nationality, and gender. It sees the common good as the good of all and of each individual. Thus, nonexclusion is a central norm of this principle.

Solidarity furnishes the moral imperatives for guarding against the marginalization of members of the community. Each individual has been treated in the trajectory of creation-sin-redemption with reverence and respect; the invitation to a privileged divine friendship is extended in a universal call to holiness. Moreover, every person is the object of Christ's redemptive act (CA #53a). Nothing less than this reverential treatment of the person is expected from the socioeconomic order that must, in its own turn, respect the value and the primacy of each life that is imbued with transcendent dignity.

The principle of subsidiarity provides the grounds for the right to be actively involved in the social affairs and decisions that affect one's personal development. As a social being, the human person can flourish and attain perfection only within community. Social interaction is essential for such growth and development, possible only if one partakes in a meaningful manner in social life. Among the person's innate rights is being able to engage others as an equal and contributing to the common good. Both solidarity and subsidiarity make the principle of participation a requirement of distributive justice.

The principle of subsidiarity can also argue for the principle of participation on the basis of moral agency. The human person needs to learn and grow in the responsible exercise of the unique capacity for choosing between right and wrong. This, in turn, is a function of personal moral formation and exposure to the values of fellowship, justice, and charity. However, these can only be experienced primarily through a well-rounded growth that takes place within community.

Moral agency also brings with it corresponding responsibilities. The faculties of intelligence and free will carry the correlative obligation of nurturing and using these gifts. Individuals mold and form their own character in the way they exercise freedom in choosing between right and wrong. They are capable of intelligent, disciplined, and creative work but only when they are given the opportunity to do so and only when they are given the chance to develop the requisite strengths. Their life in community is an important avenue for them to exercise their moral agency and to own up to the consequences of their actions. Participation is a means of moral formation by which individuals are given occasion to make decisions and, in the process, develop the virtues conducive to responsible judgments. Human beings as subjects must be accorded the right and the chance to have a hand in the formulation and execution of decisions that bear directly on their life. Besides, such participation is a critical component of individuals' sense of self-worth.

The principle of participation also issues forth from the demands of legal justice stemming from the needs of the community. The contribution of all is a necessary condition to a stable, peaceful, and prosperous order and the establishment of a genuine community. Particular human decisions and actions are the building blocks from which the social order and culture are formed. This is also acknowledged in the affirmation that the first step toward transforming societal structures of sin is personal conversion. Society takes its character and life from the quality of the human interactions upon which it is founded. Furthermore, in the same manner that no one may be left out of the processes and benefits of the social order, no one, rich or poor, is exempt from the demands of the principle of solidarity to provide for the common good out of one's own means. Besides, "only the vast numbers and rich diversity of people can express something of the infinite richness of God" (CFL #33a).[8] The demands of justice and love within the task of creating a vibrant and stable social order can only be satisfied if individuals contribute to the common good in the full measure they can.

Preferential option for the poor and the principle of relative equality

To treat people as subjects is to nurture the exercise of their God-given creativity and talents in an environment that encourages and protects individual initiative and freedom. It is to ensure that they have the space and the means to gain a sense of self-worth. Providing the person with the opportunity to participate is not enough. *The nature and the quality of one's participation in society are also important and are demarcated by the principles of a preferential option for the poor and of relative equality.*

Preferential option for the poor The principle of solidarity calls for a total and radical identification of the self with one's neighbor through a deep and abiding sense of empathy. Such a commitment deepens in the measure of others' need and destitution. *A preferential option for the poor* necessarily flows from the principle of solidarity.

Society, including economic life, exists only that it may serve and help individuals achieve perfection in a manner consistent with their human dignity and freedom.[9] The end of any social institution is the protection and promotion of this dignity; the justification for its continued existence is contingent on its observance and pursuit of this end. Furthermore, the breadth and depth of an individual's contribution to the formation of culture are dependent on the degree to which the "whole" individual is engaged. Marginalization through deprivation in some sphere of life can seriously hinder such requisite engagement.

Ignoring those who are left at the fringes of economic life is not even tenable in the long run as the very fabric of society is gravely undermined. Disorders in the social order arise whenever people are deprived of venues to grow in the freedom of personal development. Peace and prosperity arise only to the extent that the rights of all are respected, especially those pertaining to self-formation.

Relative equality A genuine and active concern for others is necessarily manifested in an attentiveness to equity in the distribution of resources. Thus, the principle of solidarity necessarily gives rise to the principle of relative equality. Characterizing post–Vatican II egalitarianism, Christiansen (1984, 666) notes:

> [T]he basic thrust of the norm [relative equality] is that the distance between any set of groups ought to be curbed so that their ability to act in a fraternal/sororal way toward one another is not subverted.

An equitable distribution of burdens and benefits is essential to living together as a community. Solidarity recognizes the inextricable link between the individual and the social good where each is a necessary condition for the attainment of the other.[10]

The principle of participation can be derived from the principle of subsidiarity because of the claim that the full development of the gift of the self requires the ability to relate and interact well with other fellow humans. However, the quality of such interpersonal relationships is dependent on being able to interact with others *as an equal*. Severe relative inequality makes it difficult for the community to nurture its individual members in the human values of friendship, justice, and charity.

In living together as a tangible community of care and concern for each other, especially for the marginalized, God is made present in human affairs. The socioeconomic order derives its vibrancy from the dynamism of its constituent individuals as they both contribute to and derive benefits from each other. This vital synergy is impeded by severe inequalities within the community.

As seen in the chapters on the postindustrial economy, the case for universal participation and limits on relative inequalities in economic life is further strengthened by the transformation of the modern economy where the principal source of wealth creation has shifted from natural resources to human skills. More than ever, participation in economic life has become an essential condition for the person's growth and perfection in the information economy. To exclude individuals from the channels through which they can develop their skills and productivity is, in effect, to shut them out from meaningful participation both in the short term and, even more seriously, into the future. Thus, the principles of relative equality and participation are even more closely linked to each other in a knowledge-based economy.

Principle of Socialization

People are a gift to each other. Stewardship of this gift requires living up to the obligations of the principle of solidarity, such as universal participation, a preferential option for the poor, and the rectification of severe relative inequalities. All of these suggest that higher bodies have the obligation to step in and assist lower bodies when the latter are unable to discharge functions that are essential both for themselves and the common good. J. Bryan Hehir (1998) refers to this as the principle of socialization.

There is question on whether this duty should be treated as a separate principle (i.e., as the principle of socialization), or whether it is already implicit in the principle of subsidiarity. In the first place, *Quadragesimo Anno*, in the paragraph following its definition of the principle of subsidiarity, immediately qualifies its position on private initiative by stressing the greater efficacy with which the state should be able to discharge its duties once it is relieved of having to accomplish what individuals and lower bodies are able to do for themselves:

> The state . . . will thus carry out with greater freedom, power and success the tasks belonging to it, because it alone can effectively accomplish these, *directing, watching, stimulating and restraining*, as circumstances suggest or necessity demands. Let those in power, therefore, be convinced that the more faithfully this principle be [*sic*] followed, and a graded hierarchical order exist between the various subsidiary organizations, the more excellent will be both the authority and the efficiency of the social organization as a whole and the happier and more prosperous the condition of the state (QA #80, emphasis added).

Observe the seamless nature with which Pius XI moves from a delineation of private initiative's protected spheres to a statement of the state's obligation to assist individuals and lower bodies.

Second, John XXIII never refers to it as a separate principle even as he describes the phenomenon of socialization. In fact, the greater leeway and role he accords government in economic life is always within the context of the principle of subsidiarity.

> At the outset it should be affirmed that in economic affairs first place is to be given to the private initiative of individual men who, either working by themselves, or with others in one fashion or another, pursue their common interests.
>
> But in this matter, for reasons pointed out by our predecessors, it is necessary that public authorities take active interest, the better to increase output of goods and to further social progress for the benefit of all citizens.
>
> This intervention of public authorities that encourages, stimulates, regulates, supplements, and complements, is based on the *principle of subsidiarity* as set forth by Pius XI in his Encyclical *Quadragesimo Anno* . . . (MM#51–53, emphasis in the original).

Even the choice of terms to describe the action of the state–encouraging, stimulating, regulating, supplementing, and complementing–are reminiscent of Pius XI's own discussion of the state's roles. *Populorum Progressio* provides substantiation that this passage should be properly interpreted both as an account of the principle of socialization and as an affirmation of its intrinsic and inseparable link to the principle of subsidiarity. In referring to the need for programs and planning in poverty alleviation, Paul VI carefully notes:

> Individual initiative alone and the mere free play of competition could never assure successful development. . . . Hence programmes are necessary in order to *"encourage, stimulate, coordinate, supplement and integrate"* [footnote reference to *Mater et Magistra*, AAS (1961, 414)] the activity of individuals and of intermediary bodies. It pertains to the public authorities to choose, even to lay down the objectives to be pursued, the ends to be achieved, and the means for attaining these, and it is for them to stimulate all the forces engaged in this common activity. But let them take care to associate private initiative and intermediary bodies with this work. They will thus avoid the danger of complete collectivisation or of arbitrary planning, which, by denying liberty, would prevent the exercise of the fundamental rights of the human person (PP #33, emphasis added).

The exact quote that is taken from *Mater et Magistra* (#53) is an obvious emphasis on the rightful role and obligation of government to assist in economic affairs. Furthermore, the context also provides evidence of the inescapable connection between the principles of socialization and subsidiarity. Paul VI circumscribes his endorsement of government's role by simultaneously cautioning against stifling individual action, thereby making immediately clear that there are limits to such state actions. This suggests that in determining the proper order of operation (i.e., in designating the appropriate entity responsible for undertaking a particular action), the principle of subsidiarity is applied first, to be followed by the principle of socialization should the private initiative of individuals and intermediate bodies be inadequate to satisfy the requirements of the commonweal.

All principles must be viewed within the larger backdrop of these documents' understanding of society as being comprised of multiple tiers of human associations. Participation in the social order occurs primarily through the individual's membership and involvement in various associations and groups. It is an order comprised of layers upon layers of intermediate societal institutions starting from the family as the most basic unit, to the local communities and professional groupings, all the way up to regional, national, and international bodies.[11] These provide the individual with the nurturing environment within which to flourish as a person. Equally important is the function these societal institutions play in providing people with venues to help each other in their common effort of seeking their transcendent end and in contributing to the public good. The economic order is, thus, viewed as organic in the sense that it is a complex entity whose totality is greater than the mere summation of its members. Consequently, in discussing the common good, John XXIII is quick to reiterate the importance of situating the public authorities' obligations within the exercise of private initiative.

> That these desired objectives be more readily obtained, it is necessary that public authorities have a correct understanding of the common good. . . . Hence, we regard it as necessary that the various intermediary bodies and the numerous social undertakings wherein an expanded social structure primarily finds expression, be ruled by their own laws . . . (MM #65, emphasis added).

Implicit in both Pius XI's (QA #79) and John XXIII's (MM #51–53) formulations is a mirror image between the right to exercise private initiative and the obligation of higher bodies to step in once lower bodies are unable to discharge those functions that are essential for the common good. Hence, Hehir's principle of socialization could also be properly called part II of the principle of subsidiarity.

Instead of describing these as the two parts of subsidiarity, J. Verstraeten (1998, 135–36) takes a slightly different approach and describes the nexus instead as the twofold meaning of the principle–a positive and a negative formulation. That part of the principle that calls for the nonintervention of higher bodies in functions that lower bodies are fully capable of discharging is viewed as the negative sense of subsidiarity. The positive formulation pertains to the obligation of higher bodies to actively participate in the affairs of lower bodies for the sake of the common good. Note the similarity of this categorization and the language used with Berlin's (1969) exposition on positive and negative rights.

There are advantages to keeping these two parts together as a single principle. First, it prevents the abuse of the norm. Hehir (1998) himself cites the example of misusing the principle of subsidiarity as a justification for the privatization of federal welfare assistance. He laments this as a lack of appreciation for the larger tradition in which the principle is to be found and interpreted. Such inappropriate use of the principle of subsidiarity is not only a lack of appreciation for the context provided by the larger tradition but is perhaps an even more fundamental failure to grasp *the fullness of the principle of subsidiarity itself*. By casting the obligation of higher bodies as the mirror image of the right to private initiative (i.e., calling it part II of the principle of subsidiarity), we are able to counterbalance the principle from within itself, rather than having to rely on a completely separate principle of socialization to complement subsidiarity. Arguments extolling the eminent position of private initiative are, consequently, restrained within the boundaries imposed by the internal structure of the principle that carries within itself the important qualifier that the right to private initiative takes place within the higher body's obligation to be the guardian of the common good. It is not an absolute right to private initiative.

A second reason to conflate socialization as the second part of the principle of subsidiarity is the advantage of presenting both principles (halves) as a single continuum. Regardless of which definition of subsidiarity one embraces (Peterson 1994), it can be likened to a ladder with the lower rungs as the proper realm of action for the individual or lower bodies; higher rungs correspond to the appropriate range of action for ever higher bodies. Subsidiarity can be viewed as a continuous spectrum of spheres whereby larger aggregations of collective action leave to their lower counterparts (or individuals) functions that these smaller groups can effectively perform for themselves, while taking on those tasks that lower bodies are unable to accomplish for the community. To move up *the ladder of subsidiarity* is to rely on ever higher bodies to perform critical complex functions. This imagery of a continuum is lost in presenting John XXIII's further elaboration of the principle of subsidiarity as a separate principle of socialization instead of being viewed as the oft-forgotten mirror image of Pius XI's formulation in 1931.

A third benefit to formulating subsidiarity as a two-part principle is that it highlights the common good's role in defining the dividing line between the two halves (or how high up to climb the ladder of subsidiarity). The commonality of both principles (halves) is accented in the common good as a necessary end of private initiative, and the common good as a source of higher bodies' obligation to promote and protect individual welfare. Not only is the commonweal an excellent divide between the principles (halves), but it also serves as a pivotal foundation for both.

Despite these intrinsic links between the principles of socialization and subsidiarity, it is probably best to keep them separate because of the different warrants for their justification. The principle of subsidiarity is founded on the need to exercise private initiative in order to flourish in the gift of freedom, while the principle of socialization flows from the social nature of the person. However, whichever approach one chooses— whether to use them as a single principle of subsidiarity with two parts or as two separate principles of subsidiarity and socialization—it is important not to lose sight of the inseparability of the positive and negative formulations of the principle from each other.

In summary, the understanding that people are a gift to each other gives rise to manifold obligations that are succinctly defined by the principles of solidarity, socialization, participation, relative equality, and a preferential option for the poor. It is only in living up to the duties that flow from these principles that one blossoms in the gift of each other as part of genuine, integral human development. *Gaudium et Spes* (#31b) describes this phenomenon well:

But human freedom is often crippled when a man encounters extreme poverty, just as it withers when he indulges in too many of life's comforts and imprisons himself in a kind of splendid isolation. Freedom acquires new strength, by contrast, when a man consents to the unavoidable requirements of social life, takes on the manifold demands of human partnership, and commits himself to the service of the human community.

GIFT OF THE EARTH

As seen in figure 12.1, the principles of stewardship and universal access can be derived from an understanding of the earth as a trust and as a gift.

Principle of Stewardship

Stewardship is the least developed and discussed of the key principles of the modern tradition. This is in part a reflection of the relatively late sensitivity to ecological concerns in ethical discourse. Aside from *Ecological Crisis: A Common Responsibility*, there are relatively few and minor references to the person's responsibilities and rights regarding the environment in these social documents.[12]

The principle of stewardship is the obligation of caring properly for the goods of the earth and of using them for the ends for which they were created: to meet human needs and to reveal the glory of God. This principle follows from the view that the goods of the earth have been entrusted to human beings for their care. It is a correlative obligation of the universal access principle's right to work, to manage, and to own the gifts of nature as means toward achieving both individual and societal good.

The human person is the steward of the earth, and *Genesis* provides the scriptural foundation for this understanding. God gave people the use of the earth together with the gifts of reason and free will. They were given the duty of tending the earth to make it yield its riches for their own needs and to make the wisdom of God manifest in creation.

All earthly creatures have their reference point in the human person as the "center and crown" through whom they are able to reveal their perfection (GS #12a, #14a). After all, it is only the human person, of all earthly creatures, who shares in divine life. As part of this moral agency, the human person is accountable for the stewardship of created goods. The fruits of nature are meant to facilitate the human response to God's invitation to divine friendship; they become means with which the individual can work toward perfection and the good of the community. It is in this sense that one can say that creation finds its perfection and crown in the human person. Finally, in working the earth to make it yield its abundance and riches, the person participates in God's act of creation as a "co-creator" through fidelity to the divine mandate of caring for the earth.

The principle of integral development brings into sharp focus the proper disposition in using the fruits of nature. Since the end of the human person is nothing less than union with God and sharing in divine life for eternity, the proper attitude toward wealth and material goods is one that differentiates *having* from *being*.

Material goods are acquired not for the sake of sheer accumulation but to facilitate the individual's quest for a full life. Individual self-identity and self-worth are not measured by pecuniary possessions but by growth in the virtues and in the fundamental human values of truth, excellence, justice, and charity. Human well-being is not appraised in terms of *having* but in terms of maturation in strength and integrity of character, in *being* more of a person–a subject with a moral agency fully capable of deliberation, choice, action, and, most of all, love. As repeatedly emphasized in the preceding discussions of integral human development, how people use what they have is more important than how much they have.[13] Such a stance requires a change in economic behavior from profit-maximization to satisficing and from consumerism to prudent consumption as argued in part III of the book.

While the conceptual ramifications of the principle of stewardship are fairly straightforward and easy to articulate, the principle itself is not always simple to apply in practice. Note, for example, the perennial conflicts between the pressure to develop natural resources for employment creation versus the advocacy for strict environmental laws that curtail economic growth. This is a hard tradeoff between the legitimate claims of providing a livelihood for people (principles of universal access and primacy of labor) as against the values of safeguarding the delicate ecology (principle of stewardship).

Principle of Universal Access

People have the obligation to respect each other's role as costewards of the earth. Consequently, no one may be excluded from enjoying the fruits of nature.[14] This is a necessary condition for any social order to thrive in lasting peace, prosperity, and stability. The principle of universal access to the goods of the earth affirms that people are entitled to the use the gifts of nature for their own sustenance and development. This claim comes from that initial act of gift-giving when God created the earth and gave it to all for the satisfaction of human needs. Its bountifulness is meant for the enjoyment of everyone. In view of its importance in ensuring the physical survival of the individual, this principle gives rise to rights that are innate to the dignity of the human person. Furthermore, the satisfaction of this right is not contingent on the outcomes of institutional or social arrangements such as the market. The person's physical well-being takes precedence. Note, however, that this should not be cause for a free-rider problem. Individuals have the corresponding obligation of contributing to the public good to the fullest extent possible. This is discussed at greater length in the following section.

Both the principles of stewardship and universal access are made even more relevant in the knowledge economy where interdependence between people and nations has become the era's distinctive feature that has brought both fresh dangers and opportunities in its wake. There is an increasing appreciation for the finitude of goods of the earth and for the delicate balance of its ecology that is easily upset by indiscriminate consumption and production patterns that are indifferent to their disexternalities. How well and how judiciously people use and manage the goods of the earth within the scope of their responsibilities will determine how much will be available for others both in the contemporaneous and subsequent generations.[15] Furthermore, the distinction between *having* and *being* accords value to how well the goods of the earth are used for worthwhile ends, rather than on how much of them is consumed or accumulated.

The universal access principle can also be argued from the social character of the principle of stewardship. The earth is vast in terms of the breadth and variety of its creatures. The extent to which the glory of God can be witnessed in creation is dependent on how well and how much individuals work together to unveil the earth's bountifulness and beauty. It is evident, then, that the more people can work together with each other in properly managing and using the gifts of nature, the more profoundly will the earth yield its hidden richness and beauty that are reflective of God's wisdom.

SYNERGY: NECESSARY COMPLEMENTARITY

The conceptual synthesis schematically summarized in figure 12.1 not merely highlights the teleological derivation of the tradition's norms, but it also accentuates the complementarity of the principles of the modern Catholic social documents and the advantages of using them together as a unit. Principles and norms can be misused to justify extreme positions either through misinterpreting or stretching the principles beyond their original spirit and intended application. The use of these principles together within a single framework of analysis minimizes such improper uses since they complement each other; one cannot be selective in using only some of the principles for one's ends without heeding the requirements of the rest of the model.

The universal access principle, for example, can be inappropriately employed in many ways. It can be used as a license for the wanton exploitation of the earth under the pretext that the primary finality of the goods of the earth is to satisfy the human person's needs anyway. This, of course, goes beyond the intent of the principle since there is a difference between needs (the proper object) and wants. Moreover, access is meant for all, including future generations. There is an intertemporal dimension to this principle. The principles of stewardship, solidarity, and relative equality define the limits to which the universal access principle can be used in this regard. At the same time, however, the universal access principle, in its own turn, balances out the principle of stewardship and prevents the misuse of the latter in justifying extreme environmentalism where preservation and conservation become ends in themselves to the detriment of legitimate human needs and livelihoods. The universal access principle in this case affirms the sustenance of the human person as an important end of the gifts of the earth.

Another instance is the unintended consequence of abetting dependency. One can, for example, take no responsibility for earning an honest livelihood or for saving since one can simply rely on the universal access principle's moral suasion on the community to safeguard everyone's basic needs for survival and development. The principles of subsidiarity and the primacy of labor preclude this problem of opportunism with the obligations to exercise private initiative and to work assiduously and sincerely for one's own integral development. Moreover, the principle of solidarity addresses the problem of free ridership through its concomitant duty of contributing to the common good. The principle of participation echoes this because the right to meaningful opportunities of engagement in social life brings with it the corresponding responsibility of sharing proportionately both in the benefits and the burdens of community living.

The outward orientation toward others in the principle of solidarity can be carried to extremes where the individual is absorbed by the collective or the larger body. Subsidiarity is the balancing principle in this regard as it affirms the importance of preserving and nurturing private initiative.

In its own turn, the principle of subsidiarity can be abused where individual interests are inordinately pursued to the total disregard of the common good, all in the name of private initiative. Arguing against welfare assistance on the grounds of subsidiarity is one such example as Hehir (1998) notes. This extreme can be avoided by an appeal to the principle of solidarity where private action must always be imbued with a genuine concern for the common good. Besides, there is also the principle of socialization (part II of subsidiarity), which serves as a counterpoise to the unfettered pursuit of exclusive interests. The reverse is, of course, also true. Subsidiarity balances socialization and prevents the latter from being used as a rationalization for unduly curtailing private initiative. This, in fact, is the delicate balance that *Rerum Novarum* and

Centesimus Annus take in condemning the stifling collectivism of socialism while at the same time criticizing the systemic failures of classical liberal markets. Hehir (1998) and *Christian Freedom and Liberation* (#73) recognize the mutually balancing relationship between the principles of solidarity and subsidiarity by juxtaposing them.

The principle of participation (that calls for nonexclusion from meaningful and productive engagement in community life) can be used as a basis for a radical egalitarianism where everyone has an equal share in the exercise of rule (the collective leadership of the group). This, of course, is an abuse of the spirit of the principle of participation, which calls for equity, and not absolute mathematical equality in the distribution of burdens and benefits within the community. This improper application is negated by the principle of socialization, which makes it an obligation of a higher body to take responsibility for the commonweal.

The primacy of labor principle may precipitate the moral hazard of shirking. Since workers are paid a living wage that is ultimately based on need rather than performance, incentives for greater effort and productivity may suffer as a consequence. Such an adverse consequence is avoided if one remembers that the principles of solidarity, stewardship, and participation all impose obligations on everyone to contribute to the good of society in the measure of one's gifts and position within the community.

Knowing precisely how and why these principles flow from human dignity and integral human development prevents the employment of these principles beyond their intended ends. For example, the value accorded to the protection of private initiative in the principle of subsidiarity may lead to an exaggeration of the claims made in the name of the right to exercise freedom. Often, the right to the liberty of expression is taken to be so absolute as part of subsidiarity so as to preclude any legitimate room for government or community oversight. The roots of this principle in human dignity and integral human development prevent such an abuse of subsidiarity. A closer examination of the foundational premises of the tradition would show that the exercise of freedom is not an end in itself but is merely the means to the much greater end of authentic human flourishing. Besides, it is rooted in the objective demands of truth as seen in the preceding chapter. In anchoring these principles to their origins in human dignity and integral human development and in using these principles together as a single analytic framework, one can avoid the inadvertent or deliberate application of these principles to justify extreme positions.

Finally, human beings, as trustees of both the goods of the earth and their personal skills, stand a better chance of discharging their stewardship well if they understand the essence of the threefold gifts entrusted to them and if they appreciate their own end and that of their fellow stewards. The joint use of these principles makes intelligible the distinct but inseparable facets of the gift of each other, the gift of the earth, and the gift of the self as an embodied intelligent freedom.

CONCLUSION

Most scholars will readily agree that human dignity is *the* foundational principle of the Catholic social tradition. However, approaches vary when it comes to the second-order principles and the various ways by which this human dignity is actualized. This should not come as a surprise since human experience is multifaceted. Therefore, any attempt at synthesizing and putting a theoretical structure to the modern Catholic social principles cannot claim to be exhaustive nor definitive, and this caveat is also true for this proposed interpretive model.

It is best to end with a brief reprise of the analytical terrain covered in the last two chapters. The value of the framework proposed in figure 12.1 lies in its demonstration of the teleological method to deriving and justifying the mainstay principles that have been repeatedly used in clarifying the social issues of the last century. Using a theological conception of human dignity as a starting point, we come to appreciate the wide spectrum of human needs that must be satisfied if the person is to thrive. This integral human development is attained to the degree that the individual is able to respond to the threefold giftedness of the human experience: the gift of the self, the gift of each other, and the gift of the earth. The various social principles flow from a reasoned derivation of what it takes to truly flourish in each of these gifts. Thus, figure 12.1 schematically shows the relationship of these principles to each other and the hierarchical ranking of principles, with human dignity and integral human development forming the bedrock from which all other social principles proceed. Since the various spheres of human giftedness cannot be hermetically compartmentalized but instead overflow into and shape one another, social principles cannot be used singly or in isolation of each other. The elements of the model have to be employed together as a single framework, with different facets of social problems examined with the use of different principles. This point cannot be overemphasized given the selective or inappropriate use of some of these principles.

There are other functional benefits offered by such a conceptual synthesis besides underscoring the complementarity of principles and preventing their misuse. This constructive proposal breaks down the complexity of social questions by putting in the foreground a listing of various dimensions to examine such as the different relationships highlighted by due order. It enables one to distinguish what is permanent from what is contingent in the formulation and use of norms by paying attention to their core elements. The warrants of these principles become readily comprehensible when viewed as flowing from human nature; the likelihood of their abuse is minimized through a cogent familiarity with the principles' original spirit and intent, their *epikeia*. Moreover, in understanding the historical context, the teleological reasoning, and the structure undergirding the social teachings of the past hundred years, one is better prepared to draw fresh principles of reflection, norms of judgment, and directives for action that embody both continuity and renewal in tackling unfamiliar problems that are expected to arise in the rapidly emerging and evolving postindustrial economy.

We can gain an even better appreciation for the need to use these principles together by understanding *how* and *where* they fit in within the larger end of the common good. It is to this that I now turn my attention in the concluding chapter of the book.

Notes

1. See also QA #80; CFL #73d.

2. Moreover, he argues that enormous benefits flow from the self-help initiatives among employers and employees through the formation of foundations and groups that provide mutual help and insurance in hard times and which also care for the old and the disabled. Besides, the principle delineates boundaries in family life that the state should not cross.

3. See also RN #14; MM #92; GS #67; PP #27–28; LE #1.

4. Thus, Hollenbach (1994) argues that Catholic social thought straddles key elements from both liberalism and communitarianism.

5. GS #12d, #24c, #32; JW #31; SRS #29d; CA #53a.

6. CFL #33b observes: "[S]ocial life, in the variety of its forms and to the extent that it is in conformity with the divine law, constitutes a reflection of the glory of God in the world."

7. SRS #38–40; OA #24a; CFL #26, #73; CA #51a.

8. QA #75 remarks: "For then only will the economic and social organism be soundly established and attain its *end* when it secures *for all and each* those goods which the wealth and resources of nature, technical achievement, and the social organization of economic affairs can give" (emphasis added); SRS #26e notes: " . . . [T]he good to which we are all called and the happiness to which we aspire cannot be obtained without an effort and commitment on the part of all, nobody excluded, and the consequent renouncing of personal selfishness." See also MM #65, #74; GS #64; PP #47; JW #18; CA #34a, #53.

9. MM #219 argues: "The cardinal point of this teaching [on the social life of the person] is that individual men are necessarily the foundation, cause and end of all social institutions. We are referring to human beings . . . raised to an order of existence that transcends and subdues nature." GS #63a notes: "In the economic and social realms, too, the dignity and complete vocation of the human person and the welfare of society as a whole are to be respected and promoted. For man is the source, the center, and the purpose of all economic and social life."

10. GS #25a remarks: *"Man's social nature makes it evident that the progress of the human person and the advance of society itself hinge on one an-*

other. For the beginning, the subject and the goal of all social institutions is and must be the human person, which for its part and by its very nature stands completely in need of social life" (emphasis added). See also OA #24.

11. CA #13b; CFL #32a; Congregation for Catholic Education (1989), #38.

12. QA #53; SRS #29a; LE #13; CFL #34; GS #12c; RN #57.

13. RN #33; PP #19; GS #35a; SRS #28.

14. GS #69a observes: "God intended the earth with everything contained in it for the use of all human beings and peoples. Thus, . . . created goods should be in abundance for all in like manner." See also PP #22; CA #31b; SRS #42e; CFL #90.

15. The social dimension of the obligation of stewardship can be seen in SRS #30g–h. It is interesting to note how John Paul II turns the parable of the talents (Matthew 25:26–28) into the *"duty* . . . to work together for the full development of others" (SRS #30h, emphasis in the original).

Chapter 14

THE COMMON GOOD AS DUE ORDER AND DUE PROPORTION

INTRODUCTION

There is much truth and appeal to Hollenbach's (1996) observation that theology's distinctive contribution, especially in postmodernity, is the continued articulation of its perspectives on the "ultimate questions about the human good." Much of this engagement will be in social ethics where differences in notions of the common good will stand center stage. This is where theological traditions will face the question of just how "thick" or "thin" a conception of the common good they should advance in a pluralistic epoch. Before they can get to this, however, there is an even more fundamental task that remains to be done: providing a more lucid self-understanding and statement of the constitutive elements of the common good. What is its structure and what are its foundational principles? Without the benefit of such a clearly formulated framework, one cannot begin to see where accommodations for a common ground can be made. Catholic social thought is not exempt from this deficiency. As William Byron (1998) laments:

> [O]ne (admittedly only one) reason why the body of Catholic social teaching is underappreciated, undercommunicated and not sufficiently understood is that the principles on which the doctrine is based are not clearly articulated and conveniently condensed. *They are not "packaged" for catechetical purposes* like the Ten Commandments and the seven sacraments (emphasis added).

In order to ensure the clarity of the Christian contribution in the public square, it is imperative to have a well-formulated vision of the common good.

The common good has been the cornerstone of Catholic social ethics. However, two gaps are worth noting. First, the concept itself has to be made more accessible for practical use by describing its content with greater specificity. What, for example, are the minimum conditions that must be satisfied in protecting and promoting the common good? What are its defining characteristics? Discourse on this subject matter has generally been so abstract as to make its application to particular issues frequently ad hoc, with diametrically opposed positions justifying themselves by claiming the same high ground of the common good. There is need for a more precise enumeration, to the extent possible, of the requirements imposed by legal, distributive, and commutative justice operating within the confines of the common good. The Catholic Bishops' Conference of England and Wales's (1996) *The Common Good and the Catholic Church's Social Teaching* is a good first step. Unfortunately, it does not provide a much-needed condensation that outlines its salient features.

A second gap is the pressing need to systematize the various warrants used extensively in the social documents that follow in the wake of *Rerum Novarum*. The common good has been generally accepted to be the operative core of this tradition. In spite of this, very little has been done to show how its principles and norms flow from the common good. Overviews of this field[1] merely enumerate these principles and norms without showing how they are related to each other or how they are derived from the common good. Moreover, unless the content of the common good is specified in a systematic and coherent way, it would be difficult to use the concept in a practical way or even sustain arguments made on its behalf.

This chapter addresses these two gaps by providing an overarching framework for the common good and the principles that flow from it. This interpretive synthesis is presented in table 14.1. It is a condensed diagnostic framework for examining issues through the spectacles of the common good. Readers would find it easier to understand the arguments of the next sections by supplementing them with reference to the diagram. Two essential characteristics of the common good are first identified together with their anthropological premises (first column). Principles and norms are then derived from these axioms (second column) followed by a nonexhaustive checklist of questions (third column) that highlight some of the critical aspects of the common good that may be at risk or neglected as competing claims and solutions to social issues are weighed for their relative merits.

REVIEW OF THE LITERATURE

The notion of the common good has received considerable attention in the literature. Germain Grisez (1983, 271) views it as the set of basic human goods sought and enjoyed collectively by members of a community. It is

Table 14.1. Framework for Applying the Common Good in Particular Cases

Anthropological Premises	Derivative Principles and Norms	Specific Effects Requiring Examination
Common Good as Due Order		
The human is oriented toward the transcendent.	integral development subsidiarity	How does it affect a person's relationship to God?
The human is oriented toward each other.	solidarity	How does it affect an individual's relationship to others?
All persons enjoy a fundamental equality.	preferential option for the poor, participation	How does it effect a community's relationship to the marginalized?
The end of community is the individual.	primacy of labor, socialization, participation	How does it effect a community's relationship to the individual?
The person is a steward of the goods of the earth.	stewardship	Does it care for the earth?
Common Good as Due Proportion		
The goods of the earth are meant for all.	universal access stewardship	Do the goods of the earth benefit all?
There are legitimate inequalities in society.	universal access relative equality	Is there an equitable distribution of burdens and benefits the within community?
There are limits to these legitimate inequalities.	universal access, participation relative equality, option for poor	
There is a balance between goods of the body and soul.	integral development	Does community serve the *whole* person and *every* person?

nothing more than the just pursuit of social goods by persons living together (Grisez 1983, 273–74). Maritain (1947, 39–40) and Yves Simon (in Cochran 1978, 232) argue that it is not merely a summation nor a multiplication of individual goods. Rather, it is a distinct kind of good attained and enjoyed by individuals in communion with each other.

Clarke Cochran, Mortimer Adler, and Walter Farrell see the common good as a set of normative standards and an imminent reality unattainable in this life but, nevertheless, worth striving for.[2] It is the life of the community, the bond of solidarity, and the loyalty that holds the community together (Cochran 1978, 237–38). Bruce Douglass (1980) accepts the common good as a perfection requiring universal participation as it pertains to all, with benefits accruing to all. These gains must be good in a moral sense. Sylvanus Udoidem (1985, 220) describes it as the horizon, the nurturing medium for the pursuit of individual good.

Eberhard Welty (1960, 158, #48) calls it the end peculiar to the community, a relative end that deals with the sphere of secular life. It is an "ensemble of goods" achievable in history (Finnis 1980, 154–55; MM #65). Hollenbach (1989, 85) views it as a set of conditions that enables the members of a community to achieve their ends; common values and objectives need not necessarily be shared by all members of the community. *Mystici Corporis* (#61) describes it as a moral association that is oriented toward the ordination of "all in general and of each single member in particular."

Much thought has been given to the attributes that can be reasonably expected of the common good. "[R]elationality is a key descriptive and normative term" so much so that it must be steeped in the language of impartiality and distribution (Brady 1988, 201). This means that it must encompass conditions that nurture a dialogue between equals (Brady 1988, 274; Dorr 1983, 184). It must be characterized by desirability, availability, accessibility, shareability, durability, and communality (Udoidem 1985, 215). It presupposes authority (Maritain 1945, 7–11; Simon 1962).

The notion of the common good can often be shaped and tailored to fit the user's own ends. Part of the difficulty lies in the absence of a consensus on the "good" that is supposed to be pursued in common. However, a shared and a more defined vision of the good is no guarantee of agreement either, especially when it comes to its application. Thomas Rourke's (1996) comparison of Michael Novak and Simon's approaches to the common good and capitalism illustrates the disparities that still arise even within the confines of the same tradition. Indeed, clarifying the nature of the common good[3] in its manifold uses is not an enviable task. No authoritative treatise within the tradition has examined the common good systematically or in any great depth. St. Thomas talks about it but does not provide a comprehensive treatment of the subject matter. He only refers to *bonum commune* in his works, and he does so in an equivocal way (Froelich 1989). Furthermore, many treat the common good as if it were a self-evident concept. In addition, political philosophers[4] use it interchangeably with general welfare and public interest (Held 1970, 2–3).

John XXIII defines the common good in *Mater et Magistra* as "the sum total of those conditions of social living, whereby men are enabled more fully and more readily to achieve their own perfection" (MM #65). But what specifically are these "conditions of social living" that constitute the common good?

St. Thomas notes that every principle is reflective of some order from whence it is derived.[5] Given an understanding of the basic features of this order, it is possible to list specific characteristics expected of the common good. Order has been defined as the "estimation of the relative worth of the various sorts of goods" (Adler 1941, 212). This implies a need for (1) a vision of equity for right distribution, (2) harmonizing principles to maintain that order, and (3) a concept of *the good* that defines a requisite proportion. At the very least, therefore, the essential conditions for the common good should include due order and due proportion (Adler and Farrell 1941, 628–29). I develop this in greater detail in the following sections.

DUE ORDER

Order is the confluence of numerically distinct units into a whole that is regulated by an all-encompassing principle. Brian Coffey (1949, 7) summarizes St. Thomas's notion of *ordo* as "the arrangement of a plurality of things or objects according to anteriority and posteriority in virtue of a principle." The existence of an order necessarily implies the ability to define the following: the end(s) of these distinct elements, their relation to each other, and their place within the whole. In fact, it is through these characteristics that the order lends itself to description.

The primary order flows from and is sustained by Divine Wisdom. The all-encompassing principle that governs and provides the numerically distinct units not only their definition but their being itself is God, the *First Principle*. Consequently, due order in social life mirrors a much larger moral order. The natural and social structures governing the human community operate within the broader sphere of the eternal law of Divine Wisdom. The attainment of both the individual[6] and the common good necessarily entails an acknowledgment of and conformity to this larger moral order, an objective external harmony within which the individual and the community thrive (PT #85; see also #1, #5, #38). In fact, juridical life is meant to be "an outward refraction of the social order willed by God, a luminous product of the human spirit which is in turn the image of the Spirit of God" (Pius XII 1942, 50c).

Order in social life is not merely an externally imposed harmony. Rather, it is also an intrinsic unity of a plurality held together in a cohesion whereby members are inseparably bound (QA #84). After all, the perfection and completion that come with goodness necessarily includes an immanent coherence. The centripetal ties of this intrinsic unity flow from at least five fundamental axioms that define the constitutive elements of a *due order* that can be reasonably expected to be a hallmark of the common good.

1. The human person is oriented toward God, the Common Good.
    The primary principle of internal order is the orientation of the human person and the community to the transcendent. The human person is made in the image and likeness of God, enjoys reason and freedom, and is endowed with a natural and moral structure (SRS #38a). Two principles necessarily flow from this orientation to the divine: integral human development and subsidiarity.
    Integral human development pertains to the individual's right and obligation to work, in cooperation with grace, for union with God as the crown of human experience. It involves not only preserving one's life but flourishing in all its dimensions: physical, intellectual, moral, emotional, and spiritual. Consequently, authentic human growth can make the following claims:
    a.   Since the human person is both body and soul, personal survival and maturation require that the individual be able to procure the necessary goods and time for nourishing both body and soul.
    b.   Consumption of these requisite goods, however, must conform to the true hierarchy of values that subordinates *having* to *being*, the material to the spiritual. The former is merely instrumental to the latter. Physical welfare is necessary, but it is not sufficient; it must set the stage for and move further into spiritual well-being.
    Only within this integral development can the human person enjoy genuine freedom in all spheres of life (MM #246; PP #42; SRS #28g, #46d, #39d–e). Given the fundamental orientation of the person to God and the principle of integral human development that flows from it, due order in the common good requires the provision of conditions that pave the way for the fullness of human experience through both physical and spiritual growth.
    Integral human development can only be attained in the responsible and rational exercise of human freedom, as it is only the individual who can provide the requisite personal response

to God's grace. Thus, it is important to afford the person with the opportunity to grow in the use of the signal faculties of reason and will. This requirement gives rise to the principle of subsidiarity.

The principle of subsidiarity follows from the creation of the human person in the image and likeness of God. Moral agency is the distinctive feature of human experience. Human intelligence and free will endow the individual with ultimate responsibility and accountability for personal growth and development.

While the community and numerous extraneous factors heavily influence the individual's attainment of a full life, the human person is not determined by these. Grace and the human orientation to the divine empower the individual to transcend social institutions in reaching out to truth and goodness (CA #38b). There is a right and an obligation to self-help.[7] However, the community has a key role in shaping the environment and in providing vital assistance for this self-development. The individual has to be afforded not only the necessary formation for discharging this responsibility in a fitting manner, but the opportunity to exercise this agency must also be furnished.[8] This is the underlying spirit behind the principle of subsidiarity that seeks so zealously to protect and to nurture the exercise of private initiative (QA #79).

2.   The human person is oriented toward others.

A second constitutive element of due order is the orientation of the human person toward others. Catholic social thought's understanding of the common good flows from its theology of the human community whose exemplar is the Blessed Trinity; three Persons in one God, distinct but inseparably bound and animated by a unity of love (Pius XII 1942, 47d). While it bears a distant and poor resemblance to this divine communion, the human community nevertheless shares an essential characteristic with its primary analog in one important respect: love as the fundamental bond of human community. The ties that hold men and women together in community are anchored in the same love that has brought about the human drama of creation, covenant, and salvation. Because of this inescapable outward orientation to God and to others, due order imbues the individual with a duty and a right to work toward both one's own fulfillment and the welfare of others (PP #16; SRS #26e). Consequently, the good of the individual and the good of the community are intrinsic to each other; they are necessary conditions to one another (GS #25a; see also MM #194).

While the human person is the "only creature God willed for itself" (GS #24c), God desired to create, to sustain, and, then, to save and re-create this person not merely as an individual but as a member of a community. Since the paradigm for the human community is the union between the three divine Persons of the Blessed Trinity, human relationships can be properly forged and reach their full flowering only in charity. Moreover, the common good is not merely the sum of private individual interests as there is an essential communitarian character to human existence, salvation, and perfection (GS #32; PP #17; see also GS #25). Consequently, there is a dual dimension to human interaction. The individual's relationship with God is inextricably linked with the person's association with others. Divine-human and human-human interaction feed into each other. St. Thomas says it well when he notes that the orientation of the whole to God defines the relationship of the parts (in this whole) to each other. The vertical and horizontal dimensions of any human relationship are distinct, yet indivisible and reflective of each other (RN #38; GS #24; JW #31, #34). This second premise gives rise to the principle of solidarity, also known as the principle of social charity.

Solidarity refers to a firm commitment and an active genuine concern for the well-being of others.[9] Justice is an essential element, if not *the* starting point, of any human relationship. However, justice finds its completion only in charity. The perfection of the individual and the community comes about only through a love that reaches out to others. The individual achieves happiness, self-knowledge, and integral development only through a sincere gift of self, that is, only through a self-donation to others (GS #24c).

In the static orientation of St. Thomas's notion of order, sharing the goodness of God does not adequately capture the fullness of the purpose of creation. Each must take a step further in communicating that goodness and perfection to others according to one's nature and capabilities. In its dynamic orientation, this order calls for the parts to contribute toward moving the whole to its end, with intelligent creatures achieving their fullness in union with God (Coffey 1949).

The human person holds a special and unique place in this twofold order. Freedom and intelligence make the human person distinct from all other creatures. It is in exercising these faculties that the human person makes a unique contribution toward communicating the goodness and perfection of God. However, freedom and intelligence have a peculiar property as gifts. They have to be nurtured if they are to grow further.[10] Note, however, that freedom and reason can only be nurtured and developed within community. It is the community, after all, that provides the human interaction and exchange so essential to growth and development in intelligence and free will. Due order in the common good, therefore, requires living out the principle of solidarity with its selfless orientation toward others that is manifested in mutual support and genuine compassion for each other.

3. All human persons enjoy a fundamental equality.

A third feature of due order in the common good is the fundamental equality of all. This equality is rooted in the conviction that humans belong to the same special place reserved for humanity in the divine plan of creation. All have been equally created by God, redeemed by Christ, called to partake of divine life, and sustained by divine Providence (GS #29a). Everyone shares a common contingency of creatureliness. Men and women find a bond in the realization and appreciation that theirs is a derivative existence where all are created out of nothing. However, people's ties go beyond mere shared creatureliness to a common filial relationship with God. This fundamental equality adds further arguments for the necessity of the principle of solidarity discussed in the preceding section.

Given the fundamental equality of all, the community has to ensure the meaningful participation of all. Extra attention and assistance are warranted for members of the community who face even greater hurdles to living out the fullness of human dignity. Thus, a preferential option for the poor follows in the wake of acknowledging such a fundamental equality for all.

4. The end of the community is the perfection of the individual.

A fourth premise of due order asserts that the object of human community is to nurture and assist individuals flourish and be true to their creation in the image of God (Pius XII 1942, 48b, 49d–50a). The person is the foundation, the end, and the cause of social institutions (MM #219; PP #34). In fact, the human community attains its perfection only when it is faithful to this end. This is true for all human associations (RN #41). Nothing less than the promotion of integral human development is expected. This means that as part of its obligations from the principle of socialization, the community has to provide the necessary conditions for the advancement of the individual on a broad front that encompasses all aspects of personality: the economic, social, intellectual, and spiritual dimensions of human existence. It is in life with others, after all, that the individual's personal gifts can evolve and flourish.[11]

The enjoyment of human freedom is necessarily conditioned by social life. External circumstances provide the conditions that can either enhance or impede the exercise of moral agency. Social life can either make it easier for the person to flourish or make it that much more difficult by throwing up obstacles. Social structures can provide either a nurturing or a hostile environment for developing the fundamental human values of truth, freedom, justice, and charity. Both destitution and overindulgence affect the quality of one's *being*. For this reason, due order requires a social life that is supportive of a human and social "ecology" conducive to a full and perfect life for the individual.[12]

The end of the common good is the welfare and perfection of the person. A common good cannot be considered as a good on its own without reference to the person's welfare. Two observations follow from this:

a. The *political* common good is not an end itself but is merely an intermediate end for an even greater end. This is true even in the natural order (even before talking of the transcendent end in God) because it does not enjoy the formal property of a last end, that is, it does not encompass all the other goods, nor does it satisfy all the natural desires of the human person. Only natural temporal happiness can satisfy this requirement as it embraces the totality of all the goods that a person can properly and naturally desire. For this reason, the political common good is a transitional end ordained toward a greater end in the temporal order, that is, the natural happiness of the individual. It has a nonultimate character and is only one among many other goods desired, achieved, used, or enjoyed in common for purposes of achieving the last end (Farrell 1945, 42–43).

b. The common good may be detached as it is desired, but it is always immanent in the person when enjoyed. It is both intrinsic and extrinsic to the person. It is a separate good because it is an object desired, pursued, and loved. On the other hand, it is also an immanent good because the perfection of the community is likewise a perfection of its individual members. The common good is a social good immanent in the individual (Adler and Farrell 1941, 603).

"The common good is common *because it is received in persons*, each of whom is a mirror of the whole" (Maritain 1947, 39, emphasis added). The common good subsists only when it is embodied in persons. It achieves reality in the temporal order only as it is enjoyed by its members. The notion that the common good is a perfection immanent in its members (Adler and Farrell 1941, 603) has important implications for the principles of distribution and participation in the social order. This sharing in the perfection and well-being of the community implies access to social goods for all.

The fundamental equality enjoyed by all, the end of the community as founded on the perfection of the individual, and the orientation of individuals to each other all give rise to the principles of nonexclusion (solidarity, participation, relative equality, and preferential option for the poor). No one may be excluded either from contributing to the common effort (primacy of labor) or from partaking of communal goods. Harmony within the social order—indeed, its very integrity—cannot be preserved if segments of the population are marginalized and excluded from leading a meaningful life.[13] Due order requires a distributive dimension to the common good. Individual members must be able to partake of the common life.

5. The human person is a steward of the goods of the earth.

Goods of the earth fulfill their function of communicating and revealing God's goodness by their very being. Furthermore, they provide the human person with the necessary means for survival, sustenance, and growth.

Apart from the mandate given in *Genesis* to care for the goods of the earth, human beings are charged with the stewardship and use of the earth by virtue of their freedom and intelligence. As already noted, creatures are meant not only to share in the goodness of God, but they are also meant to communicate this divine goodness according to their nature and capacities. Human intelligence allows the individual to grasp the intelligible laws governing the natural world as part of the whole of creation. Human freedom allows the individual to render fitting regard for the gifts of the earth in the manner revealed by these comprehensible laws.

The gifts of human intelligence and freedom are instrumental in allowing the person and the goods of the earth to communicate the goodness and perfection of God in each other: the person through the care of the goods of the earth and the goods of the earth through providing for human needs.

DUE PROPORTION

Due proportion is a logical consequence of due order. While due order deals with intrinsic unity and structure, due proportion pertains to balance within the social order. Harmony among the distinct elements of the social order can only be achieved when there is appropriate symmetry in relationships especially among members in the community. The balance and harmony embodied by due proportion are necessary if the unity of the whole is to be preserved. Four premises undergird due proportion in the common good.

1. The goods of the earth are meant to benefit all.

   As noted earlier, goods of the earth communicate the goodness and perfection of God by their existence and by providing for the needs of the human person. In this latter function, material creation assists the person's quest to preserve life and to live it to the fullest. After all, the human person is both body and soul and needs material inputs. This gives rise to the universal access principle.

   The universal access principle maintains that the goods of the earth are meant for the benefit of everyone regardless of how titles of ownership are assigned. This was discussed at length in chapter 10. Stewardship, rather than proprietorship is the proper attitude toward the earth. Neither the private ownership nor the use of property is absolute. The just-use obligation attendant to ownership makes it a duty of the propertied to employ their goods both for their own benefit and for their needy neighbors' welfare.

2. There are legitimate inequalities in the order of the universe.

   Order presupposes a plurality. The beauty of this order lies in the way it encompasses a full array of creatures sharing the perfection of God in varying ways and degrees. This variety manifests the inexhaustible and manifold dimensions of God in the created order. Such diversity necessarily brings about differing ways by which creatures embody a created likeness to God.

   While due order assigns a fundamental equality rooted in creation, redemption, and a transcendent human orientation, due proportion finds its starting point in the acknowledgment of legitimate human differences within the social order.[14] People are endowed with a wide variety of talents, skills, and personal gifts. It is these variations in natural qualities that provide richness and vitality to social life. Disparities in natural endowments lead to inequalities in individual performance and outcomes in community life. There is a rightful place for these differences.[15]

3. There are limits to these legitimate inequalities.

   Despite the acknowledgment of legitimate inequalities as part of the very notion of order, there are limits to these disparities. The same beauty that is afforded by variety can be marred by the lack of harmony in such a plurality.

   These limits to inequalities stem from the nature of the common good. As an object of love, it "elicits a concordance of wills." As an object of desire, it "requires concerted" action.[16] St. Augustine adopts Cicero's definition of justice and notes that a people ceases to be a community when there is neither a shared vision of justice nor mutual cooperation for a collective goal.[17] Extremes in the distribution of the benefits and burdens of community life are injurious to the foundations of commonality in purpose, will, and action. Reciprocity and the willing participation of individuals are impeded when members perceive themselves as aggrieved victims of injustice.

While accepting the legitimacy of inequalities in the social order, due proportion imposes limits beyond which disparities in outcomes and positions become unsettling and untenable. There comes a point when inequalities disrupt, rather than assist, parts of the whole in communicating the goodness and perfection of God according to their nature and capabilities. Beyond a certain threshold, an overly skewed distribution of the gains and costs of social living threatens the harmony of the community itself. The difficulty, of course, is in identifying this threshold. This is where the social principles provide some helpful preliminary criteria.

Limits to legitimate inequalities give rise to the principles of relative equality, participation, and a preferential option for the poor. Obligations and rights are not parceled out on the basis of an absolute, mathematical equivalence. Individuals participate in social life and contribute to the social order in varying degrees according to their capacities, circumstances, and roles within the community (RN #50, #71). Stewardship demands that personal responsibilities owed to the community become heavier and more extensive the greater the individual's powers and endowments (GS #34c, #30–31; PT #87–88; LE #116; SRS #23c–d).

Natural human differences also lead to disparities in needs. Due proportion in the social order necessarily entails variations in the manner by which the benefits of social life are dispensed. People draw benefits from the common good according to their needs and their degree of participation in society.[18] Individuals receive special assistance and protection from the community to the extent that they cannot fend for themselves. The powerless, the infirm, the very young, and the very old deserve more attention and support compared to those who are able to provide for themselves (RN #54, #32; PT #56).

4. There is a requisite balance to satisfying the needs of the body and the soul.

A fourth foundational premise is that authentic human development requires balance in meeting the needs of both body and soul. Even as the spiritual enjoys a higher rank than the material in the hierarchy of values, both the physical and the spiritual well-being of the person require solicitous care. Both are needed for a full and perfect life (PT #57–59). Material and spiritual goods have to be provided in their proper proportion in sustaining the individual. Extremes of underdevelopment and superdevelopment can be deleterious. Whether it is in a dearth or excess of material goods, the individual's advance toward genuine human development can be rendered more difficult either by imposing obstacles (such as destitution in underdevelopment) or by impeding progress (through overindulgence in superdevelopment) (PP #18–21; SRS #28; CA #41d).

Even as the material is subordinate to the spiritual, this hierarchy in the order of goodness does not mean expendability. Goods of a higher order of goodness are not any more indispensable than all or any of the other goods of lower rank. After all, physical well-being, much less survival, requires material inputs.

SYNTHESIS: A DIAGNOSTIC FRAMEWORK

It is difficult to define the material content of the common good a priori, given the fluidity and uncertainties of many social questions. Besides, taking context into account is a prerequisite. However, this should not discourage efforts to come up with useful guidelines that define the minimum conditions that must be satisfied if the common good is to be achieved. The understanding of the common good as due order and due proportion lends itself particularly well as a way of assessing competing solutions to social problems.

Figure 14.1 is a schematic summary of the terrain covered thus far. Its last column turns this framework into a workable tool for examining various aspects of social dilemmas and their proposed solutions as they promote or impinge upon the minimum requirements that can be reasonably expected of the common good.

Order is constituted by relationships.[19] Consequently, relationships take a defining role in personhood. Given competing claims in social problems, one must evaluate their impact on at least four relationships that form the due order of the common good:

1.   Relationship of the person to God
       How do the competing claims affect individual growth in the highest of human values (of truth, love, friendship, and justice) that are characteristic of integral human development? What do they do to people's relationship with God? [principle of subsidiarity; integral human development]
2.   Relationship of the individual to others in the community
       How do opposing claims affect the individual's contribution to the community? Are they animated by genuine, mutual caring and self-giving? [principle of solidarity]
3.   Relationship of the community to the marginalized

What do the contending solutions accomplish with respect to the community's commitment to the marginalized? [principles of participation, relative equality, and preferential option for the poor]

4. Relationship of the community to the individual

Do the various proposed solutions promote the community's end of assisting individuals in their quest for a flourishing life? [principles of socialization, participation, and primacy of labor]

5. The individual and community as regards the goods of the earth

Do the rival claims help the person discharge the obligation of caring for the gifts of the earth in a manner that reflects the goodness and perfection of God? [principle of stewardship]

The following checklist evaluates for due proportion.

1. How do these vying claims affect the distribution of benefits flowing from the use of the goods of the earth? [universal access principle]
2. Is there an equitable distribution of gains and burdens across the community? [principles of relative equality, preferential option for the poor, and participation]
3. How well do these contending solutions promote service to the whole person and every person? In other words, is every person able to access ample resources for the satisfaction of the needs of both body and soul?[20] [integral human development]

These questions must be answered satisfactorily if the ideal common good is to be served. It is important to remember, however, that the ideal cannot be achieved in its fullness in the temporal order and can only be approximated.

There are problems yet to be worked out with this proposed model. In particular, how does one resolve cases where there are apparent conflicts among these requirements? For example, in the debate over preserving biodiversity or jobs in the Pacific Northwest, there seems to be a conflict between the common good's requirement of providing for its members' needs versus the charge of stewardship for the gifts of the earth for both current and future generations. Much prudential judgment is needed in applying this model of the common good as due order and due proportion.

SUMMARY AND CONCLUSIONS

Due order and due proportion can be used effectively as an overarching structure from which to identify the minimum requirements of the common good. These constitutive characteristics, in turn, facilitate an articulation of the tradition's social principles using the language of the common good. Furthermore, due order and due proportion provide a diagnostic framework for weighing competing claims. By identifying and then defining its constitutive elements with a little more precision than heretofore available, the notion of the common good stands a better chance of going beyond abstract generalities and lending itself as a practical tool for examining competing claims.

This interpretive synthesis of the common good as due order and due proportion does not, by any measure, avoid the problematic "thick" conception that may make its use difficult in postmodern pluralism. However, by articulating a more detailed notion of the common good, we can begin to identify at which points premises can be "thinned" out without unduly compromising the fundamentals of the tradition in an intelligible conversation in the public square.

The modern Roman Catholic social documents aim for a more daunting notion of the common good and pursue a more difficult path of twofold objectives because of the tradition's longstanding convictions on the nature of the person. Its views on human dignity necessarily lead to higher expectations and stricter measures of performance for an economy that has to conform to a larger divine order. However, the same anthropological axioms that compel Catholic social thought to be stringent in its standards also provide it with an optimism that these lofty goals can be reached. In particular, this theological tradition believes that because of the transcendent dignity of people, they can rise above the difficulties and conflicts that come with living together as a community. The human person is fully capable of selfless behavior and cooperation with others in a spirit of justice and charity manifested in a mutual solicitude for each other's well-being. Within economic life and its seemingly intractable competing claims lies a deep-seated, grace-transformed human capacity to use freedom intelligently, responsibly, and wisely to reach out for the Good that truly fulfills and endures.

Notes

1. See, for example, Congregation for Catholic Education (1988).

2. Cochran (1978, 236). See also Adler and Farrell (1941, 619) for their differentiation of the ideal-potential versus the existential common good.

3. It is important to distinguish the proper from the customary usages of the common good. The common good must be an *end simpliciter*, that is, it must be the final end—the culmination of the person's development and the satisfaction of all the desires of the human person. Consequently, only God can be called the *Common Good* in its proper usage, as God is the Final End. The customary usages of common good pertain to the well-being of the entire community or to the material or human goods managed and enjoyed in common. Unless otherwise indicated, "common good" for the rest of the chapter refers to its customary usage.

4. Gustafson (1984, 18) notes that a consensus is hard to come by in defining the common good. There is little agreement regarding its scope and content. Diggs (1973, 283) notes that political philosophers differ on the particulars of the

common good but generally agree that it is, at the very least, the end of government and pertains to the good of all citizens. Locke views it as the supreme law of the people. Hume equates it with the "public" or the "common" interest. Madison considers it as the "public," "common," or "general" good that is closely associated with the justice that government and civil society seek to promote. Rousseau proposes it as the object of the general will and as the end of the state.

5. St. Thomas notes: "As Aristotle says in the *Metaphysics* the terms *before* and *after* are used with reference to some principle. Now order always implies a *before* and *after*. Hence, wherever there is a principle there must always be some kind of order" (Aquinas 1947/48, II–II, q. 26, a.1).

6. I will use "individual" and "person" interchangeably in this chapter fully aware of the distinctions of Maritain (1947, chapter III).

7. Paul VI (PP #34) notes that the person is only truly human "in as far as, master of his own acts and judge of their worth, he is author of his own advancement, in keeping with the nature which was given to him by his Creator and whose possibilities and exigencies he himself freely assumes." See also PP #15–16; JW #17, #71.

8. For this reason, Catholic social thought has always stressed self-determination and self-help as critical values to uphold across a wide array of social remedies from workers' associations to agricultural development to international aid for less-developed countries. See, for example, MM #150–52; PT #123; PP #54–55, #65, #77; SRS #32c, #44–45; CA #28a.

9. See SRS #38–40, especially #38f. See also CA #10c; QA #137; PP #66–70.

10. Hence, the need for the principle of subsidiarity that seeks to foster private initiative as discussed in the preceding section.

11. QA #118; Pius XII 1941, 222, 1st par.; PT #139, #55; GS #26b–c; PP #34, #14, #20–21; SRS #28i, #33.

12. GS #25c; CA #25b, #46b, #37–38; SRS #15; MM #63–67.

13. QA # 75. See also JW #18; CA #27c. For this reason, Pius XI observes that it is a grave error to think that either capital or labor can appropriate for themselves the fruit of societal output to the total exclusion of the other party (QA #57–58).

14. Pius XII (1942, 48c) describes this well: "If social life implies intrinsic unity, it does not, at the same time exclude differences which are founded in fact and nature. When we hold fast to God, the Supreme Controller of all that relates to man, then the similarities no less than the differences of men find their allotted place in the fixed order of being, of values, and hence also of morality."

15. RN #26. In fact, Leo XIII calls the socialists' version of egalitarianism an "absurd equality" (RN #55). See also SRS #15b.

16. Adler and Farrell (1941, 604). See also Simon (1960).

17. Augustine (1958, book 2, chapter 21).

18. See chapter 11 for a threefold categorization of unmet needs.

19. In fact, *ordo* can be treated as synonymous to relations. See Coffey (1949).

20. This last question may be the most problematic. In a complex world of scarcity amidst insatiable wants and needs, providing every member of the community with full opportunities for integral human development will be an extremely difficult obligation to fulfill.

APPENDIX. THE ECONOMICS OF
QUADRAGESIMO ANNO'S
VOCATIONAL GROUPINGS

INTRODUCTION

R eligious economic thought's dual objective of a family wage and
full employment is schematically presented in a standard supply
and demand framework in figure A.1.[1] The demand curve in the
labor market represents the value of the marginal product of labor and
can be succinctly represented by the following equation:

$$\text{wage} = \text{price of output x marginal product of labor}$$
$$= \text{value of marginal product}$$

The family wage level can fall anywhere between points E and A.[2]

An immediate effect of this dual-objective strategy is an expected increase in unemployment. *Quadragesimo Anno* is aware of a possible in-
verse relationship between wage levels and employment in the labor
market. This tradeoff is explicitly acknowledged:

> Another point, however, of no less importance must not be overlooked,
> in these our days especially, namely, that opportunities for work be pro-
> vided for those who are willing and able to work. *This depends in large
> measure upon the scale of wages, which multiplies opportunities for
> work as long as it remains within proper limits, and reduces them if al-
> lowed to pass these limits.* All are aware that a scale of wages too low,
> no less than a scale excessively high causes unemployment (*Quadrage-
> simo Anno* #74, emphasis added)

Von Nell-Breuning's (1937, 185–89) exposition on the different wage
theories undergirding the relationship between employment and wage

Figure A.1. Labor Market

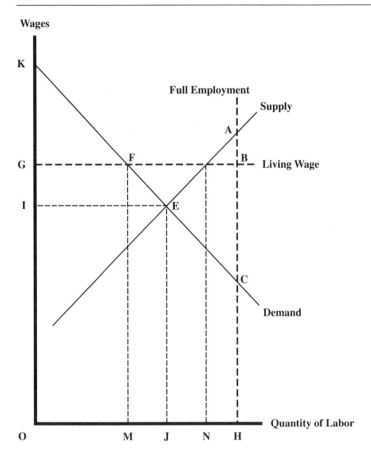

levels shows a keen appreciation for the difficulties involved in striking a balance between the two objectives of a family wage and full employment.

An increase in the wage rate from that set by point E to the new family wage will expand the labor force to include (1) new workers who have heretofore stayed out of the market because their opportunity cost of time is much higher than the former wage level at E; (2) discouraged workers who had stopped looking for employment but who have now been enticed back by higher wage rates; and (3) part-time workers who now want to put in more hours of work at the new higher rate. Instead of OJ laborers in the market, there will now be a total of ON workers looking for employment. However, employers are willing to hire only OM workers at the new higher wage rates. There will, therefore, be a total unemployment of HM workers in contrast to an earlier unemployment of HJ workers at the theoretical competitive equilibrium (point E).[3]

A total wage bill represented by the rectangle OGBH is required. Left on its own, the market would merely come up with a total wage bill of OIEJ, which is substantially smaller because of a lower employment level (OJ) and a lower wage rate (OI). Assuming perfect competition in the product market and letting the price of output be equal to one (P = 1), the total value of output produced by labor OJ is defined by the trapezoid OJEK. This is divided between the wage bill for labor (OJEI) and the employers' profits (IEK). The problem, then, is to shift the final market outcome from the free market operation's equilibrium at point E to the more desirable "full employment at a living wage" equilibrium at point B. This could be accomplished in any of the following ways:

1. By funding the shortfall represented by FBC from part of the employers' profits or through subsidies from the government (which, in turn, raises issues of tax incidence and welfare losses).
2. By increasing the selling price of the industry's goods and services thereby shifting the demand curve for labor to the right.
3. By increasing the marginal productivity of workers thereby shifting the demand curve for labor to the right.

These are not mutually exclusive means; they could be combined in a policy package to reach the ideal equilibrium at point B.

FUNCTION OF INDUSTRY-LEVEL VOCATIONAL GROUPINGS

Opportunities

One way of providing full employment at a living wage is for employers to accept a smaller share of the output, that is, if employers pay a wage that exceeds the value of the workers' marginal product. This leads to lower profits and is, de facto, a form of profit sharing where part of the normal profits is foregone and is plowed back as worker compensation. A number of difficulties must be surmounted with this approach.

In the first place, even without such transfers, employers already experience a decline in their profits (IEK > GFK) under the new regime (from point E to point B). This is directly attributable to the two new constraints of a family wage and full employment. At the family wage rate (OG), employers are willing to hire only up to OM. This is the employment level at which the value of marginal product is equal to the family wage. Anyone hired beyond this (i.e., MH workers) will not be contributing enough to the work effort to warrant the payment of a family wage in a profit-maximizing world. This means that the payment of a family wage to workers beyond OM would have to be subsidized by a third party if employers are to keep their profits intact. However, a second constraint is imposed on the market: There has to be full employment, that is, OH workers will have to be hired. If the full brunt of this second constraint were to be placed entirely on the employers, this means that they have to hire an additional MH workers whose productivity and contribution to the work effort do not produce a value equal to the family wage. This shortfall is graphically represented by the triangle FBC. If the employers are not subsidized for these workers, the shortfall of FBC would have to be taken out entirely from the employers' share of the output (GFK) which, as we have seen, is already much smaller to begin with compared to the previous regime of perfect competition (equilibrium at point E). Note, however, that there is a limit to how much employers can bear the brunt of this dual objective. The shortfall of FBC cannot exceed the employers' share of the output GFK. Moreover, this will lead to sluggish job creation in subsequent rounds of economic activity because of an expected decline in profits available for reinvestment. And on top of all this, we have no reason to presume that shareholders are willing to sacrifice their profits voluntarily in favor of workers. Given ever more efficient financial markets, owners of capital can readily find alternative investment vehicles that provide for better returns.

A second difficulty pertains to the futility of a single firm acting on its own to pay a living wage above the market rate. The willingness to take a cut in profit levels may not be good enough because individual firms acting alone will find it difficult to sustain the payment of a living wage into the long term without running the risk of substantially eroding a critical internal source of capital financing (profits for reinvestment) or of altogether pricing itself out of the market, or both. A concerted action on the part of other employers is necessary. And even with this cooperation from others, interindustry competition may still prevent the payment of above-market wages. Products and services can substitute for each other, and entire industries can price themselves out of the market. The steep oil price drop of the last two decades of the twentieth century in the aftermath of the OPEC embargoes of the 1970s is a good example of the risks of disregarding market signals. Even if industry owners were willing to reduce their profits to avoid raising prices and incurring interindustry product substitution, they would still face the problem of being uncompetitive in attracting capital relative to other industries that are able to provide better corporate earnings and returns.

Note that *Quadragesimo Anno*'s proposal of vocational groupings has the added attractive feature of achieving what individual firms acting alone could not accomplish—moving the labor market from point E to point B. What the market could not reach (i.e., covering a shortfall of FBC if full employment at a living wage is to be achieved) is now made feasible through industry-level negotiations, namely, income transfers from the employers' profits to the workers' wages. Just like the medieval guilds, these vocational groupings would have the power and the means both to protect the welfare of their members and to take an active role in formulating decisions that shape their work environment. *With vocational groupings, point B (full employment at a living wage) can be secured while allowing the principle of subsidiarity to operate (through worker-management negotiations) without having recourse to government intervention.* All this presupposes that both parties will cooperate with each other. However, there are no a priori's that should lead us to believe that they will in fact have harmonious relations. Furthermore, as noted earlier, the substitutability of goods and services across industries may lead the virtuous industry to price itself out of the market relative to other parts of the economy, including capital financing. And even if all domestic industries were to follow suit, there is still the import competition that must be considered. Indeed, there are formidable dynamics working against reaching an equilibrium of full employment at a living wage (point B) through nonmarket means.

Risks

There are significant economic ramifications in allowing such vocational groupings of employers and workers to set wage and employment levels outside of a freely operating market. Four outcomes are possible as a result of this arrangement. The most optimistic scenario is that both employers and workers cooperate with each other and arrive at an amicable resolution of their many competing claims. This in itself should lead to an increase in the marginal product of labor by attenuating intra-industry and firm-level labor strife (O'Boyle 1998). A second possible case is where the shortfall of FBC is simply too large to be covered by transfers from industry profits.

The third possible outcome is the risk of an indeterminate solution. Even after industry-wide associations of employers and workers have been formed and face each other across the bargaining table, there is no guarantee that they will in fact cooperate and not treat each other as adversaries. The erstwhile atomistic economic actors of the preassociation regime who were simple price takers, now suddenly find themselves with real control over market outcomes, thanks to a new industrial organization where collective action is the norm. With their newly acquired effective influence over market outcomes, these vocational groupings can appropriate ever more benefits for their respective constituencies. Gaining leverage and bargaining power can become their overriding concern as these take on greater importance in the distribution of societal resources. Consequently, there is a greater likelihood of dissipating resources and entrepreneurial energies in directly unproductive activities.

The fourth possible outcome is the worst-case scenario. In grouping the industry employers together, one effectively creates a monopsony. Prior to such industry-wide associations of employers, it is very likely that the entire industry's employment and wage levels were determined by the supply and demand for labor. The individual firm faced a strictly horizontal supply curve, that is, its level of hiring did not affect the going wage rate in the market. With the advent of an industry-wide wage-setting mechanism, and assuming that employers maximize their profits as a group, the labor market turns into a monopsony. Because employers can act in concert as a group, they now face an upward sloping supply curve, that is, their hiring levels influence the wage rate in the market.[4] To maximize profits, employers will hire labor only to the point where the value of the marginal product from the last worker hired is equal to the marginal factor cost, that is, the increment in the total wage bill as a result of bringing in that last worker at a higher wage rate. This means that the equilibrium point will be defined by the intersection of the marginal factor cost curve and the demand curve. This results in lower wages and employment levels, higher profits for the employers, and a welfare loss for the rest of society.

An additional risk is that of setting a precedent and providing a ready-made avenue for cooperation not only in the labor market but in the product market as well. Coordination in hiring practices in the labor market could very well spill over to collusion in the product market. Prior to this industry-wide mechanism of cooperation, the industry product market could have either been a perfectly competitive one, or an oligopoly, or a monopolistic competition, but not a monopoly. However, this proposed industry-wide association of employers opens up an opportunity for the industry to act as a monopolist. If so, the industry product market equilibrium will no longer be determined by the intersection of the supply and demand curves but by the marginal revenue curve and the industry marginal cost curve. Again, this leads to lower output, higher prices, and a sizable welfare loss for society.

There is another dimension to this risk of collusion. The establishment of this grouping of employers may easily translate into barriers to entry in the industry, thereby encasing the market further in a monopolistic structure. This would move the industry farther away from a perfectly competitive ideal, create inefficiencies, introduce rigidities in the movement of resources across industries, and hinder the development of private initiative, enterprise, and innovation.

Industry-level vocational groupings may have the unintended consequence of creating a monopsony-monopolist industry if there is little oversight or if there is no credible and viable countervailing force from a corresponding industry-wide association of workers. This arrangement produces the largest welfare losses for society as a whole. This situation is illustrated in figure A.2. For purposes of simplicity, let us assume that

Figure A.2. Monopsonist–Monopolist Industry

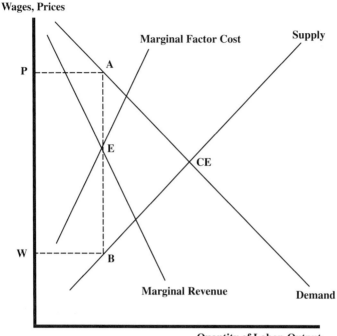

the particular industry has only one product that uses a single input, labor. Let us further assume that each unit of product uses exactly one unit of labor. There are no substitutes for the product and there are no other buyers for this particular type of labor. Under these conditions, the industry, which in effect is a monopolist in the product market and a monopsonist in the labor market, will arrive at its profit-maximizing level of output by equating the marginal factor cost and the marginal revenue curve (point E). This market outcome produces maximum profits for the employers as a group. Given perfect competition in both the labor and product markets, the equilibrium would have been at point CE with no economic profits for the employers. This monopolist-monopsonist structure is the farthest from a perfectly competitive market equilibrium (point CE) and leads to the most severe welfare losses (defined by the triangle A-B-CE) for society, larger than any of the other three possible scenarios.[5] It produces the lowest level of output (and consequently employment), the lowest wage rates, the highest price levels for output, and the biggest economic profits.

These difficulties highlight the importance of government as the third institution in this proposed tripartite arrangement. The use of

industry-wide associations of employers and employees, either to supplement or to override market operations, requires vigilant oversight by a
disinterested third party if the rest of the economy is to be protected from
possible welfare losses from rent-maximizing behavior that vocational
groupings may find too tempting to forego. In addition, there may also be
need to correct for distortions as a result of deviating from a market-
determined allocation of scarce resources.

The proposal for vocational groupings is never advanced again by
any of the subsequent social documents of the tradition. Some attribute
this silence to its unwelcome association with the corporatism of fascism. Whether this claim has any merit or not, one can say that the microeconomics of *Quadragesimo Anno*'s vocational groupings presents
welcome possibilities of full employment at a living wage within a spirit
of subsidiarity. However, it also brings in its wake potential hazards that
include economic indeterminancy and large welfare losses arising from a
monopoly-monopsonist industrial structure. It is not clear from the literature whether von Nell-Breuning (1937, 1986) takes these risks into consideration in the drafting of *Quadragesimo Anno*.

Notes

1. There are two possible combinations of the family wage and the full employment levels in relation to the supply and demand curves. We can either have
the family wage and the full employment levels intersect above the supply curve
or below it. The first case goes against common sense because the intersection of
the full employment line with the supply curve (i.e., the point at which people are
willing to engage themselves fully in the market) is still below the family wage.
This is irrational as it would mean that people are willing to supply their maximum work effort in exchange for wages that are not even sufficient to meet their
needs and to bring them into the folds of the middle class. The second case is the
more sensible scenario and will be the one used for the rest of this exposition.

2. Only cases above point E would make for an interesting study. If the family wage were below the competitive equilibrium, point E, one could simply let
the market set wage levels. The problem of unemployment could then be dealt
with using standard Keynesian fiscal policies. Note that the family wage level
cannot exceed point A as this would be the irrational case explained in the preceding note.

3. This tradition has a more stringent notion of "full employment" in going
beyond what is commonly described in economics as the natural rate of unemployment to include the entire labor force, to the extent possible. Moreover, even
as the labor market clears at point E, it would still view the gap represented by HJ
as unacceptable unemployment that needs to be addressed.

4. Employers, as a group, would now no longer be content with simply having the equilibrium at the intersection of the supply and demand curves. Hiring
an additional laborer can only be achieved by offering a higher wage rate. However, in offering this higher wage to the last worker, they must also offer the same

higher rate to everyone else hired earlier. Consequently, the entire wage bill goes up. This marginal increase in the total wage bill brought about by hiring the last worker is reflected in the upward sloping marginal factor cost curve.

5. There are four possible scenarios: (a) The industry is perfectly competitive in both markets; (b) The industry is perfectly competitive in the product market but a monopsonist in the labor market; (c) The industry is a monopolist in the product market but a perfect competitor in the labor market; and (d) The industry is a monopolist in the product market and a monopsonist in the labor market.

REFERENCES

Adler, Mortimer. 1941. A Dialectic of Morals. Parts 1–3. *Review of Politics* 3, no. 1: 3–31; 3, no. 2: 188–224; no. 3: 350–94.

Adler, Mortimer, and Walter Farrell. 1941. The Theory of Democracy, Part II. The End of Political Activity: The Common Good. *Thomist* 3 (4): 588–652.

Anderson, Elizabeth. 1993. *Value in Ethics and Economics*. Cambridge, Mass.: Harvard University Press.

Aquinas, Thomas. 1947/48. *Summa Theologica*. Translated by the Fathers of the English Dominican Province. 3 vols. New York: Benzinger Brothers.

Archibald, Katherine. 1988. The Concept of Social Hierarchy in the Writings of St. Thomas Aquinas. *The Historian* 11 (1949–50). Reprint, in *St. Thomas Aquinas on Politics and Ethics*, translated and edited by Paul E. Sigmund. New York: Norton.

Arrow, Kenneth J. 1979. The Division of Labour in the Economy, the Polity and the Society. In *Adam Smith and Modern Political Economy*, edited by G. P. O'Driscoll. Ames: Iowa State University Press.

Ashley, Benedict, and Kevin O'Rourke. 1989. *Healthcare Ethics: A Theological Analysis*. St. Louis, Mo.: Catholic Health Association of the United States.

Ashley, William. 1925. *An Introduction to English Economic History and Theory*. 2 vols. New York: Longmans.

Augustine. 1958. *City of God*. New York: Doubleday.

Austin, Vincent. 1981. *Rural Industrial Development: A Practical Handbook for Planners, Project Managers, and Field Staff*. London: Cassell, Ltd.

Avila, Charles. 1983. *Ownership: Early Christian Teaching*. London: Sheed and Ward.

Ayres, C. E. 1936. Fifty Years' Developments in Ideas of Human Nature and Motivation. *American Economic Review* (Supplement: Papers and Proceedings) 26 (1): 224–36.

Baddeley, Michelle, Ron Martin, and Peter Tyler. 2000. Regional Wage Rigidity: The European Union and United States Compared. *Journal of Regional Science* 40 (1): 115–42.

Bairoch, Paul. 1975. *The Economic Development of the Third World Since 1900*. Berkeley: University of California Press.

Baldwin, John W. 1959. *The Medieval Theories of the Just Price: Romanists, Canonists, and Theologians in the Twelfth and Thirteenth Centuries*.

Transactions of the American Philosophical Society, Vol. 49, Part 4 (series paper). Philadelphia: American Philosophical Society.

Barnet, Richard, and Ronald Mueller. 1975. *Global Reach.* New York: Simon and Schuster.

Barone, Enrico. 1935. The Ministry of Production in the Collectivist State. In *Collectivist Economic Planning,* edited by Friedrich August von Hayek. London: Routledge.

Barrera, Albino. 1990. The Role of Maternal Schooling and Its Interaction with Public Health Programs in Child Health Production. *Journal of Development Economics* (1990) 32: 69–91. Reprint, *Economic Growth Center Paper,* No. 438, New Haven, Conn.: Yale University Press.

———. 1991. The Interactive Effects of Mother's Schooling and Unsupplemented Breastfeeding on Child Health. *Journal of Development Economics* 34: 81–98.

Bartell, Ernest. 1962. Value, Price, and St. Thomas. *Thomist* 25 (3): 325–81.

Barth, Desire. 1960. The Just Price and the Costs of Production According to St. Thomas Aquinas. *New Scholasticism* 34: 413–30.

Bauer, P. T. 1984. Ecclesiastical Economics: Envy Legitimized. In *Reality and Rhetoric.* Cambridge, Mass.: Harvard University Press.

Becker, Gary. 1974. A Theory of Social Interactions. *Journal of Political Economy* 82 (6): 1063–93.

Bentham, Jeremy. 1907. *An Introduction to the Principles of Morals and Legislation.* Oxford: Clarendon Press.

———. 1954. The Psychology of Economic Man. In *Jeremy Bentham's Economic Writings,* edited by W. Stark. Vol. 3. London: George Allen and Unwin Ltd.

Berlin, Isaiah. 1969. *Four Essays on Liberty.* London: Oxford University Press.

Bettio, Francesca, and Samuel Rosenberg. 1999. Labour Markets and Flexibility in the 1990s: The Europe-U.S.A. Opposition Revisited. *International Review of Applied Economics* 13 (3): 269–79.

Bhaskar, V., and Ted To. 1999. Minimum Wages for Ronald McDonald Monopsonies: A Theory of Monopsonistic Competition. *Economic Journal* 109 (455): 190–203.

Bokenkotter, Thomas. 1990. *A Concise History of the Catholic Church.* Rev. and exp. ed. New York: Doubleday.

Boland, Vivian. 1994. Mater et Magistra. In *The New Dictionary of Catholic Social Thought,* edited by Judith Dwyer. Collegeville, Minn.: Liturgical Press.

Bonar, James. 1893. *Philosophy and Political Economy.* London: Swan Sonnenschein.

Brady, Bernard Vincent. 1988. Rights, the Common Good and Roman Catholic Social Thought. Ph.D. diss., University of Chicago.

Braudel, Fernand. 1967. *Capitalism and Material Life: 1400–1800.* New York: Harper Colophan.

Bruton, Henry. 1970. The Import Substitution Strategy of Economic Development. *Pakistan Development Review* 10 (2): 123–46.

———. 1989. Import Substitution. In *Handbook in Development Economics,* edited by Hollies Chenery and T. N. Srinivasan. Vol. 2. Amsterdam: North-Holland.

Buchanan, Allen. 1985. *Ethics, Efficiency, and the Market.* Totowa, N.J.: Rowman and Allanheld.

Byers, David. 1985. *Justice in the Marketplace*. Washington, D.C.: United States Catholic Conference.

Byron, William. 1998. Ten Building Blocks of Catholic Social Teaching. *America* 179 (13): 9–12.

Calvez, Jean-Yves. 1964. *The Social Thought of John XXIII: Mater et Magistra*. Chicago: Henry Regnery.

Camp, Richard. 1969. *The Papal Ideology of Social Reform: A Study in Historical Development 1878–1967*. Leiden: E. J. Brill.

Card, David, Francis Kramarz, and Thomas Lemieux. 1999. Changes in the Relative Structure of Wages and Unemployment: A Comparison of the United States, Canada, and France. *Canadian Journal of Economics* 32 (4): 843–77.

Carlen, Claudia, comp. 1981. *Papal Encyclicals, 1790–1981*. Wilmington, N.C.: McGrath Publishing Co.

Carter, John R., and Michael Irons. 1991. Are Economists Different, and If So, Why? *Journal of Economic Perspectives* 5 (2): 171–77.

Catholic Bishops' Conference of England and Wales. 1996. *The Common Good and the Catholic Church's Social Teaching*. London: Catholic Bishops' Conference of England and Wales.

Cawson, A. 1986. *Corporatism and Political Theory*. New York: Blackwell.

Charles, Rodger. 1998. *Christian Social Witness and Teaching: The Catholic Tradition from Genesis to Centesimus Annus*. Leominster, Herefordshire (England): Gracewing.

Chenery, H. B. 1960. Patterns of Industrial Growth. *American Economic Review* 50 (4): 624–54.

Christiansen, Drew. 1984. On Relative Equality: Catholic Egalitarianism after Vatican II. *Theological Studies* 45: 651–75.

Cipolla, C. 1976. *Before the Industrial Revolution: European Society and Economy 1000–1700*. New York: Norton.

Clark, J. B. [1899] 1956. *The Distribution of Wealth*. New York: Kelley and Millman.

Coase, R. H. 1976. Adam Smith's View of Man. *The Journal of Law and Economics* 19 (3): 529–46.

Cochran, Clarke E. 1978. Yves R. Simon and "The Common Good": A Note on the Concept. *Ethics* 88 (3): 229–39.

Coffey, Brian. 1949. The Notion of Order According to St. Thomas Aquinas. *The Modern Schoolman* 27 (November): 1–18.

Coleman, John. 1981. What Is An Encyclical? Development of Church Social Teaching. In *Origins* 11 (3): 33–41.

Congregation for Catholic Education. 1989. *Guidelines for the Study and Teaching of the Church's Social Doctrine in the Formation of Priests*. Washington D.C.: United States Catholic Conference, 1989. Reprint, *Origins* 19 (11): 169–92.

Cornia, G. R. Jolly, and F. Stewart. 1987. *Adjustment with a Human Face*. Vol I. *Protecting the Vulnerable and Promoting Growth*. Oxford: Clarendon Press.

Cramer, Dale L., and Charles Leathers. 1981. Schumpeter's Corporatist Views: Links Among His Social Theory, *Quadragesimo Anno*, and Moral Reform. *History of Political Economy* 13 (4): 745–71.

Curran, Charles, ed. 1985a. *Directions in Catholic Social Ethics*. Notre Dame, Ind.: University of Notre Dame Press.

——. 1985b. A Significant Methodological Change in Catholic Social Ethics. In *Directions in Catholic Social Ethics*, edited by Curran. Notre Dame, Ind.: University of Notre Dame Press.

——. 1986. The Changing Anthropological Bases of Catholic Social Ethics. In *Readings in Moral Theology: No. 5, Official Catholic Social Teaching*, edited by C. Curran and R. McCormick. New York: Paulist Press.

Danner, P. L. 1994. The Person and the Social Economy: Needs, Values, and Principles. In *The Social Economics of Human Material Need*, edited by J. B. Davis and E. J. O'Boyle. Carbondale and Edwardsville: Southern Illinois University Press.

Dasgupta, A. K. 1985. *Epochs of Economic Theory*. Oxford: Basil Blackwell.

Davis, J. B., and E. J. O'Boyle, eds. 1994. *The Social Economics of Human Material Need*. Carbondale and Edwardsville: Southern Illinois University Press.

Dempsey, Bernard. 1943. *Interest and Usury*. Washington D.C.: American Council on Public Affairs.

——. 1958. *The Functional Economy: The Bases of Economic Organization*. Englewood Cliffs, N.J.: Prentice-Hall.

Denison, E. 1962. *The Sources of Economic Growth in the United States and the Alternatives Before Us*. New York: Committee for Economic Development.

Desai, S. S. M. 1967. *History of Economic Thought*. Poona, India: Continental.

Diggs, B. J. 1973. The Common Good as Reason for Political Action. *Ethics* 83: 283–93.

Dorr, Donal. 1983. *Option for the Poor: A Hundred Years of Vatican Social Teaching*. New York: Orbis.

Douglass, Bruce. 1980. The Common Good and the Public Interest. *Political Theory* 8 (1): 103–17.

Douglass, M. 1994. The "Developmental State" and the Newly Industrialised Economies of Asia. *Environment and Planning* 26 (4): 543–66.

Dworkin, Ronald. 1981a. What is Equality? Part I: Equality of Welfare. *Philosophy and Public Affairs* 10 (3): 185–246.

——. 1981b. What is Equality? Part I: Equality of Resources. *Philosophy and Public Affairs* 10 (4): 283–345.

The Economist. 1952. The Uneasy Triangle. Parts 1–3. *The Economist*, 9 August: 322–23; 16 August: 376–78; 23 August: 434–359.

——. 1991. Freedom and Prosperity. *The Economist*, 29 June: 15–18.

Edgeworth, F.Y. 1881. *Mathematical Psychics: An Essay on the Application of Mathematics to the Moral Sciences*. London: C. K. Paul.

——. 1925. *Papers Relating to Political Economy*. New York: Burt Franklin.

Elster, Jon. 1982. Sour Grapes–Utilitarianism and the Genesis of Wants. In *Utilitarianism and Beyond*, edited by A. K. Sen and B. Williams. Cambridge: Cambridge University Press.

Epstein, Gerald, James Crotty, and Patricia Kelly. 1996. Winners and Losers in the Global Economics Game. *Current History* 95 (604): 377–81.

Farrell, Walter. 1945. Person and the Common Good in a Democracy. *Proceedings and Addresses of the American Philosophical Association* 20: 38–47.

Fei, John, and Gustav Ranis. 1964. *Development of the Labor Surplus Economy: Theory and Policy*. Homewood, Ill.: R. D. Irwin.

Ferguson, C. E., and J. P. Gould. 1975. *Microeconomic Theory*. 4th ed. Homewood, Ill.: R. D. Irwin.

Finkelstein, Joseph, and Alfred Thimm. 1973. *Economists and Society: The Development of Economic Thought from Aquinas to Keynes.* New York: Harper.

Finn, Daniel Rush. 1995. Catholic Social Thought on Property: An Urgent Need for Extension and Renewal. Paper presented at conference, The Legacy of Msgr. Ryan. St. Paul, Minn.: University of St. Thomas.

———. 1998. John Paul II and the Moral Ecology of Markets. *Theological Studies* 59 (4): 662–79.

Finnis, John. 1980. *Natural Law and Natural Rights*, Oxford: Clarendon Press.

Fitzgibbons, Athol. 1995. *Adam Smith's System of Liberty, Wealth, and Virtue: The Moral and Political Foundations of the Wealth of Nations.* New York: Clarendon Press.

Flubacher, Joseph F. 1950. *The Concept of Ethics in the History of Economics.* New York: Vantage.

da Fonseca, Eduardo Giannetti. 1991. *Beliefs in Action: Economic Philosophy and Social Change.* New York: Cambridge University Press.

Fortin, Ernest. 1992. "Sacred and Inviolable": *Rerum Novarum* and Natural Rights. *Theological Studies* 53 (2): 203–33.

Frank, Robert, Thomas Gilovich, and Dennis Regan. 1993. Does Studying Economics Inhibit Cooperation? *Journal of Economic Perspectives* 7 (2): 159–71.

Frankena, William K. 1973. *Ethics.* 2nd ed. Englewood Cliffs, N.J.: Prentice-Hall.

Freemantle, Anne, ed. 1956. *The Papal Encyclicals in Their Historical Context.* New York: New American Library, Mentor Books.

Friedman, David D. 1980. In Defense of Thomas Aquinas and the Just Price. *History of Political Economy* 12 (2): 234–42.

Friedman, Milton. 1987. Good Ends, Bad Means. In *The Catholic Challenge to the American Economy: Reflections on the US Bishops' Pastoral Letter on Catholic Social Teaching and the US Economy*, edited by Thomas Gannon. New York: Macmillan.

Froble, Folker, J. Heinrichs, and O. Kreye. 1980. *The New International Division of Labor.* Cambridge: Cambridge University Press.

Froelich, Gregory. 1989. The Equivocal Status of Bonum Commune. *New Scholasticism* 63 (1): 38–57.

Georgescu-Rogen, Nicholas. Utility. *International Encyclopedia of Social Sciences.* New York: Macmillan and Free Press.

Gewirth, A. 1982. *Human Rights: Essays on Justification and Applications*, Chicago: University of Chicago Press.

———. 1985. Economic Justice: Concepts and Criteria. In *Economic Justice: Private Rights and Public Responsibilities*, edited by K. Kipnis and D. Meyers. Totowa, N.J.: Rowman and Allanhead.

Giersch, Herbert. 1991. *The World Economy in Perspective.* Northampton, Mass.: Edward Elgar.

Ginzberg, E. 1932. Studies in the Economics of the Bible. *Jewish Quarterly Review* 22: 343–408.

Glendon, Mary Ann. 1991. *Rights Talk. The Impoverishment of Political Discourse.* New York: Free Press, Macmillan.

Gnuse, R. 1985. Jubilee Legislation in Leviticus: Israel's Vision of Social Reform. *Biblical Theology Bulletin* 15: 43–48.

Gordon, Barry. 1975. *Economic Analysis Before Adam Smith: Hesiod to Lessius.* New York: Barnes and Noble.

Gossen, Hermann H. [1854] 1938. *The Laws of Human Relations*. Cambridge, Mass.: MIT Press.

Grabowski, Richard. 1994a. The Failure of Import Substitution: Reality and Myth. *Journal of Contemporary Asia* 24 (3): 297–310.

———. 1994b. Import Substitution, Export Promotion, and the State in Economic Development. *Journal of Developing Areas* 28 (4): 535–54.

Griffin, James. 1986. *Well-Being: Its Meaning, Measurement, and Moral Importance*. Oxford: Clarendon Press.

Grisez, Germain. 1983. *The Way of Our Lord Jesus Christ*. Vol. I, *Christian Moral Principles*. Chicago: Franciscan Herald Press.

Groenewegen, Peter. 1987. Political Economy and Economics. In *The New Palgrave Dictionary of Economics*, edited by John Eatwell, Murray Milgate, and Peter Newman. London: Macmillan.

Gustafson, James. 1984. *Ethics from a Theocentric Perspective*. Vol. 2. Chicago: University of Chicago Press.

Halevi, Joseph. 1987. Corporatism. In *The New Palgrave Dictionary of Economics*, edited by John Eatwell, Murray Milgate, and Peter Newman. London: Macmillan Press.

ul Haq, Mahbub. 1980. Beyond the Slogan of South-South Cooperation. In *Dialogue for a New Order*, edited by Khadija Haq. New York: Pergamon Press.

Hardin, G. 1968. The Tragedy of the Commons. *Science* 162: 1243–48.

Hargreaves Heap, Shaun. 1989. *Rationality in Economics*. New York: Basil Blackwell.

Harper, Malcolm. 1984. *Small Business in the Third World: Guidelines for Practical Assistance*. New York: John Wiley and Sons.

Harsanyi, J. 1955. Cardinal Welfare, Individualistic Ethics, and Interpersonal Comparisons of Utility. *Journal of Political Economy* 63 (August): 309–21.

———. 1982. Morality and the Theory of Rational Behaviour. *Social Research* (1977), 44 (4): 623–56. Reprint, in *Utilitarianism and Beyond*, edited by A. K. Sen and B. Williams. Cambridge: Cambridge University Press.

Hart, H. L. A. 1955. Are There Any Natural Rights? *Philosophical Review* 64 (April): 175–91.

———. 1982. *Essays on Bentham: Studies in Jurisprudence and Political Theory*. Oxford: Clarendon Press.

Hausman, Daniel. 1992. When Jack and Jill Make a Deal. In *Economic Rights*, edited by Ellen Frankel Paul, Fred Miller, and Jeffrey Paul. Social Philosophy and Policy Foundation, Bowling Green, Ohio. New York: Cambridge University Press.

———. 1994. When Jack and Jill Make a Deal. In *Economic Rights*, edited by Ellen Frankel Paul, Fred Miller, and Jeffrey Paul. New York: Cambridge University Press.

Hausman, Daniel, and McPherson, Michael. 1993. Taking Ethics Seriously: Economics and Contemporary Moral Philosophy. *Journal of Economic Literature* 31 (June): 671–731.

———. 1996. *Economic Analysis and Moral Philosophy*. Cambridge: Cambridge University Press.

Hebblethwaite, Peter. 1985. The Popes and Politics: Shifting Patterns in Catholic Social Doctrine. In *Directions in Catholic Social Ethics*, edited by C. Curran. Notre Dame, Ind.: University of Notre Dame Press.

Hebert, R. F., and Ekelund, R. B. 1984. Welfare Economics. In *Economic Analysis in Historical Perspective*, edited by J. Creedy and D. P. O'Brien. London: Butterworths.

Hehir, J. Bryan. 1998. Catholic Social Teaching and the Challenge of the Future. In *Woodstock Report*, No. 54 (June). Washington, D.C.: Woodstock Theological Center.

Heilbroner, Robert. 1975. *The Making of Economic Society*. Englewood Cliffs, N.J.: Prentice-Hall.

Held, Virginia. 1970. *The Public Interest and Individual Interests*. New York: Basic Books.

Helleiner, Gerald K. 1982. *For Good or Evil: Economic Theory and North-South Negotiations*. Toronto: University of Toronto Press.

Hirsch, Fred. 1976. *Social Limits to Growth*. Cambridge, Mass.: Harvard University Press.

Hirschman, Albert. 1958. *The Strategy of Economic Development*. New Haven: Yale University Press.

———. 1968. The Political Economy of Import-Substituting Industrialization in Latin America. *Quarterly Journal of Economics* 82 (1): 1–32.

Hollander, Samuel. 1965. On the Interpretation of the Just Price. *Kyklos* 18: 615–34.

Hollenbach, David. 1979. *Claims in Conflict: Retrieving and Renewing the Catholic Human Rights Tradition*. New York: Paulist Press.

———. 1989. The Common Good Revisited. *Theological Studies* 50 (1): 70–94.

———. 1994. A Communitarian Reconstruction of Human Rights: Contributions from Catholic Tradition. In *Catholicism and Liberalism*, edited by R. Bruce Douglass and David Hollenbach. Cambridge: Cambridge University Press.

———. 1996. The Common Good in the Postmodern Epoch: What Role for Theology? In *Religion, Ethics, and the Common Good*, edited by James Donahue and M. Theresa Moser. The Annual Publication of the College Theology Society, Vol. 41. Mystic, Conn.: Twenty-Third Publications.

Hollis, Martin. 1981. Economic Man and Original Sin. *Political Studies* 29 (2): 167–80.

Iglesias, Enrique. 1992. *Reflections on Economic Development: Toward a New Latin American Consensus*. Washington, D.C.: Inter-American Development Bank.

Jessop, B. 1979. Corporatism, Parliamentarianism and Social Democracy. In *Trends Toward Corporatist Intermediation*, edited by P. C. Schmitter and G. Lehmbruch. London: Sage.

Jevons, William Stanley. [1871] 1965. *The Theory of Political Economy*. New York: Augustus M. Kelley. Reprint, London: MacMillan and Co., 1888.

John XXIII. 1961. *Mater et Magistra*. Boston: Daughters of St. Paul.

———. 1963. *Pacem in Terris*. Boston: Daughters of St. Paul.

John Paul II. 1979. *Redemptor Hominis*. Boston: Daughters of St. Paul.

———. 1981. *Laborem Exercens*. Boston: Daughters of St. Paul.

———. 1987. *Sollicitudo Rei Socialis*. Boston: Daughters of St. Paul.

———. 1990. *The Ecological Crisis: A Common Responsibility* (Message for the Celebration of the World Day of Peace, January 1, 1990). Rome: The Vatican.

———. 1991. *Centesimus Annus*. Boston: Daughters of St. Paul.

Johnson, Luke. 1981. *Sharing Possessions: Mandate and Symbol of Faith*. Philadelphia: Fortress Press.

Kahneman, Daniel, Jack L. Knetsch, and Richard Thaler. 1986. Fairness as a Constraint on Profit Seeking: Entitlements in the Market. *American Economic Review* 76 (4): 728–41.

Keynes, John Maynard. 1936. *The General Theory of Employment, Interest, and Money.* New York: Harcourt Brace.

Keynes, John N. 1891. *The Scope and Method of Political Economy.* London: Macmillan and Co., Ltd.

Kinsley, Michael. 1995. The Case Against the States. *Time,* 16 January, 78.

Kirshner, Julius. 1974a. Raymond de Roover on Scholastic Economic Thought. In *Business, Banking, and Economic Thought in Late Medieval and Early Modern Europe: Selected Studies of Raymond de Roover,* edited by Kirshner. Chicago: University of Chicago Press.

———. ed. 1974b. *Business, Banking, and Economic Thought in Late Medieval and Early Modern Europe: Selected Studies of Raymond de Roover.* Chicago: University of Chicago Press.

Krueger, Anne. 1997. Trade Policy and Economic Development: How We Learn. *American Economic Review* 87 (1): 1–22.

Kuznets, Simon. 1966. *Modern Economic Growth: Rate, Structure and Spread.* New Haven: Yale University Press.

Landes, David. 1969. *Unbound Prometheus: Technical Change and Industrial Development in Western Europe from 1750 to the Present.* London: Cambridge University Press.

Landreth, Harry. 1976. *History of Economic Theory: Scope, Method, and Content.* Boston: Houghton Mifflin Company.

Lange, Oskar. 1936/37. Mr. Lerner's Note on Socialist Economics. *Review of Economic Studies* 4: 143–44.

Langholm, Odd. 1982. Economic Freedom in Scholastic Thought. *History of Political Economy* 14 (2): 260–83.

———. 1987. Scholastic Economics. In *Pre-Classical Economic Thought: From the Greeks to the Scottish Enlightenment,* edited by S. Todd Lowry. Boston: Kluwer.

———. 1992. *Economics in the Medieval Schools: Wealth, Exchange, Value, Money and Usury according to the Paris Theological Tradition 1200–1350.* Leiden, New York, and Köln: E. J. Brill.

Laslier, Jean-Francois, Marc Fleurbaey, Nicolas Gravel, and Alain Trannoy, eds. 1998. *Freedom in Economics: New Perspectives in Normative Analysis.* Routledge Studies in Social and Political Thought. London and New York: Routledge.

Lay Commission on Catholic Social Teaching and the U.S. Economy. 1984. *Toward the Future: Catholic Social Thought and the U.S. Economy: A Lay Letter.* New York: Lay Commission.

Leo XIII. 1891. *Rerum Novarum.* Boston: Daughters of St. Paul.

Lewis, W. Arthur. 1952. World Production, Prices and Trade, 1870–1960. *Manchester School of Economic and Social Studies,* 20 (May).

———. 1954. Economic Development with Unlimited Supplies of Labor. *Manchester School of Economic and Social Studies,* 22 (May): 139–91.

———. 1955. *Theory of Economic Growth.* Homewood, Ill.: R. D. Irwin.

Lichtenstein, Peter M. 1983. *An Introduction to Post-Keynesian and Marxian Theories of Value and Price.* Armonk, N.Y.: M. E. Sharpe, Inc.

Love, Joseph. 1980. Raul Prebisch and the Origins of the Doctrine of Unequal Exchange. *Latin American Research Review* 15 (3): 45–72.

Lukes, Steven. 1973. *Individualism*. Oxford: Basil Blackwell.

Lutz, Mark, and Kenneth Lux. 1988. *Humanistic Economics: The New Challenge*. New York: Bootstrap Press.

MacIntyre, Alasdair. 1966. *A Short History of Ethics*. New York: Macmillan.

Macpherson, C. B. 1962. *The Political Theory of Possessive Individualism: Hobbes to Locke*. Oxford: Clarendon Press.

Malthus, Thomas. [1798] 1958. *An Essay on the Principle of Population, As It Affects the Future Improvement of Society with Remarks on the Speculations of Mr. Godwin, M. Condorcet and Other Writers*. 2 vols. New York: Dutton.

Maritain, Jacques. 1945. *Rights of Man and Natural Law*. Translated by Doris Anson. New York: Charles Scribner's Sons.

——. 1947. *Person and the Common Good*. Translated by John J. Fitzgerald. New York: Charles Scribner's Sons.

Marshall, Alfred. [1890] 1961. *Principles of Economics*. 9th (variorum) ed., with annotations by C. W. Gulillebaud. London: Royal Economic Society, Macmillan and Co.

Marx, Karl. [1867] 1906. *Capital: A Critique of Political Economy*. New York: Modern Library.

——. 1904. *A Contribution to the Critique of Political Economy*. Chicago: Kerr.

Massaro, Thomas. 1998. *Catholic Social Teaching and United States Welfare Reform*. Collegeville, Minn: Liturgical Press.

McConnell, John. 1943. *The Basic Teachings of the Great Economists*. New York: New Home Library.

McCormack, Arthur. 1963. *World Poverty and the Christian*. New York: Hawthorn.

McGoldrick, Terence. 1998. Episcopal Conferences Worldwide on Catholic Social Teaching. *Theological Studies* 59 (1): 22–50.

McKinley, Erskine. 1965. Mankind in the History of Economic Thought. *Economics and the Idea of Mankind*, edited by Bert Hoselitz. New York: Columbia University Press.

McKinnon, Ronald. 1966. Foreign Exchange Constraints in Economic Development and Efficient Aid Allocation. *Economic Journal* 76 (301): 170–71.

McLaughlin, Martin 1994. Agriculture. In *The New Dictionary of Catholic Social Thought*, edited by Judith Dwyer. Collegeville, Minn: Liturgical Press.

McPherson, Natalie. 1994. *Machines and Economic Growth: The Implications for Growth Theory of the History of the Industrial Revolution*. Contributions in Economics and Economic History, No. 156. Westport, Conn.: Greenwood Press.

Meier, Gerald M. 1984. *Leading Issues in Economic Development*. 4th ed. New York: Oxford University Press.

——. 1995. *Leading Issues in Economic Development*. 6th ed. New York: Oxford University Press.

Mill, John Stuart. [1836] 1948. On the Definition of Political Economy; and on the Method of Investigation Proper to It. *Series of Reprints of Scarce Works on Political Economy*, No. 7. London: London School of Economics and Political Science. Reprint, in *Essays on Some Unsettled Questions*. London: John Parker, West Strand, 1844.

———. [1838] 1974. Bentham. In *London and Westminster Review* (August 1838). Reprint, in *Utilitarianism, On Liberty, Essay on Bentham*, edited by Mary Warnock. New York: New American Library.

———. [1863] 1962. *Utilitarianism*, Edited by Mary Warnock. New York: Meridian.

———. [1885] 1929. *Principles of Political Economy*. London and New York: Longmans, Green and Co.

———. 1965. *On the Logic of the Moral Sciences*. Edited by H. M. Magid. New York: Bobbs-Merrill.

von Mises, Ludwig. 1935. Economic Calculation in the Socialist Commonwealth. In *Collectivist Economic Planning*, edited by Friedrich August von Hayek. London: Routledge.

Mokyr, Joel. 1990. *The Lever of Riches: Technological Creativity and Economic Progress*. New York: Oxford University Press.

Montefiore, Alan. 1966. Fact, Value and Ideology. In *British Analytical Philosophy*, edited by Bernard Williams and Alan Montefiore. London: Routledge and Kegan Paul.

Morris, M. D. 1979. *Measuring the Conditions of the World's Poor: The Physical Quality of Life Index*. Oxford: Pergamon.

Morton, Kathryn, and Peter Tulloch. 1977. *Trade and Developing Countries*. New York: John Wiley and Sons.

Muench, Aloisius. 1948. Social Charity. In *Summa Theologica* by Thomas Aquinas. Translated by the Fathers of the English Dominican Province. Vol. 3. New York: Benzinger Brothers.

National Conference of Catholic Bishops. 1986. *Economic Justice for All: Pastoral Letter on Catholic Social Teaching and the U.S. Economy*. Washington, D.C.: NCCB.

von Nell-Breuning, Oswald. 1937. *Reorganization of Social Economy: The Social Encyclical Developed and Explained*. English edition prepared by Bernard W. Dempsey. New York: Bruce Publishing Company.

———. 1986. The Drafting of *Quadragesimo Anno*. In *Readings in Moral Theology, No 5: Official Catholic Social Teaching*, edited by C. Curran and R. McCormick. New York: Paulist Press.

Nitsch, Thomas O. 1981. On Human Nature Presuppositions in Economics: The "Men" of Adam Smith, Karl Marx, et al.–Part I. *Midsouth Journal of Economics* 5 (2): 21–30.

———. 1983. On Human Nature Presuppositions in Economics–Part II: Homo Oeconomicus and Homo Socioeconomicus. *Midsouth Journal of Economics* 7 (1): 13–35.

Noonan, John. 1957. *The Scholastic Analysis of Usury*. Cambridge: Harvard University Press.

Nordhaus, W., and J. Tobin. 1972. Is Growth Obsolete? *Economic Growth: Fiftieth Anniversary Colloquium*. New York: National Bureau of Economic Research.

North, Douglass. 1981. *Structure and Change in Economic History*. New York: Norton.

North, R. 1951. The Biblical Jubilee and Social Reform. *Scripture, The Quarterly of the Catholic Biblical Association* 4 (2): 323–34.

Novak, Michael. 1984. *Freedom with Justice: Catholic Social Thought and Liberal Institutions*. San Francisco: Harper and Row.

Nurkse, Ragnar. 1953. *Problems of Capital Formation in Underdeveloped Countries*. Oxford: Basil Blackwell.

O'Boyle, Edward J. 1994. Human Physical Need: A Concept That is Both Absolute and Relative. In *The Social Economics of Human Material Need*, edited by J. B. Davis and E. J. O'Boyle. Carbondale and Edwardsville: Southern Illinois University Press.

———. 1998. *Personalist Economics: Moral Convictions, Economic Realities and Social Action*. Dordrecht and London: Kluwer.

O'Brien, D. P. 1975. *The Classical Economists*. Oxford: Clarendon Press.

O'Brien, David, and Thomas Shannon, eds. 1977. *Renewing the Earth: Catholic Documents on Peace, Justice and Liberation*. New York: Image Books.

O'Rourke, Edward. 1963. The Encyclical and Agriculture. In *The Challenge of Mater et Magistra*, edited by Joseph Moody and Justus Lawler. New York: Herder and Herder.

Oser, Jacobs. 1963. *The Evolution of Economic Thought*. New York: Harcourt, Brace and World.

Oxford English Dictionary. 1933. Vol. 6. Oxford: Clarendon Press.

———. 1982. *Supplement*. Vol. 1. Oxford: Clarendon Press.

———. 1986. *Supplement*. Vol. 4. Edited by R. W. Burchfield. Oxford: Clarendon Press.

Paauw, Douglas, and John Fei. 1973. *Transition in Open Dualistic Economies*. New Haven: Yale University Press.

Pagano, Ugo. 1985. *Work and Welfare in Economic Theory*. Oxford: Basil Blackwell.

Pareto, Vilfredo. 1927. *Manuel d'Economie politique*. Translated by Alfred Bonnet. 2d ed. Paris: Marcel Giard.

Parsons, Talcott. 1968. Utilitarianism: Sociological Thought. *International Encyclopedia of the Social Sciences*. Vol. 16. New York: Macmillan and Free Press.

Passmore, John. 1970. *The Perfectibility of Man*. New York: Scribner Sons.

Paul VI. 1967. *Populorum Progressio*. Boston: Daughters of St. Paul.

———. 1971. *Octogesima Adveniens*. Boston: Daughters of St. Paul.

Paye, Jean-Claude. 1995. Making Life-Long Learning a Reality for All. *OECD Observer*, #193 (April/May).

Peterson, John. 1994. Subsidiarity: A Definition to Suit Any Vision? *Parliamentary Affairs* 47 (1): 116–33.

Petrella, Frank. 1972. The Liberalization of the Scholastic Theory of Socio-Economic Policy. *Review of Social Economy* 30 (3): 352–65.

Phan, Peter. 1984. *Social Thought. Message of the Fathers of the Church*. Wilmington, Del.: Michael Glazier.

Pius XI. 1931. *Quadragesimo Anno*. Boston: Daughters of St. Paul.

Pius XII. 1941. The Social Question in the New Order [Pentecost Address]. *The Catholic Mind* 39 (923): 1–16.

———. 1943. The Holy Season of Christmas and Sorrowing Humanity (1942 Christmas Message). *The Catholic Mind*, 41 (961): 45–60.

Polanyi, Karl. 1944. *The Great Transformation*. New York: Farrar and Rhinehart.

Popper, Karl. 1952. *The Open Society and Its Enemies*. 2d ed. London: Routledge and Keagan Paul.

Postan, M. M., E. E. Rich, and Edward Miller, eds. 1963. The Gilds. In *The Cambridge Economic History of Europe*. Vol. 3. Cambridge: Cambridge University Press.

Prebisch, Raul. 1979. Neoclassical Theories of Economic Liberalism. *CEPAL Review* 7 (April): 167–74.

Quandt, R., and J. Henderson. 1980. *Microeconomic Theory: A Mathematical Approach.* 3d ed. New York: MacGraw Hill.

Radin, Margaret Jane. 1996. *Contested Commodities.* Cambridge, Mass.: Harvard University Press.

Rawls, John. 1971. *A Theory of Justice.* Cambridge, Mass.: Harvard University Press.

Renard, Georges. 1918. *Guilds in the Middle Ages.* Translated by Dorothy Terry. London: G. Bell and Sons.

Rescher, N. 1966. *Distributive Justice: A Constructive Critique of the Utilitarian Theory of Distribution.* Indianapolis: Bobbs-Merrill.

Ricardo, David. 1971. *On the Principles of Political Economy and Taxation.* Harmondsworth (England): Penguin.

Riga, Peter. 1966. *John XXIII and the City of Man.* Westminster, Md.: Newman Press.

Rima, Ingrid Hahne. 1996. *Development of Economic Analysis.* 5th ed. London and New York: Routledge.

Robbins, Lionel. [1932] 1949. *An Essay on the Nature and Significance of Economic Science.* 2d ed. London: Macmillan.

de Roover, Raymond. 1958. The Concept of the Just Price: Theory and Economic Policy. *Journal of Economic History* 18 (4): 418–34.

——. 1974a. Monopoly Theory Prior to Adam Smith: A Revision. *Quarterly Journal of Economics* (1951) 65: 492–524. Reprint, in *Business, Banking, and Economic Thought in Late Medieval and Early Modern Europe: Selected Studies of Raymond de Roover,* edited by Julius Kirshner. Chicago: University of Chicago Press.

——. 1974b. The Scholastic Attitude toward Trade and Entrepreneurship, *Explorations in Entrepreneurial History,* 2d ser., (1963) 1: 76–87. Reprint, in *Business, Banking, and Economic Thought,* edited by Julius Kirshner.

——. 1974c. Scholastic Economics: Survival and Lasting Influence from the Sixteenth Century to Adam Smith. *Quarterly Journal of Economics* (1955) 64 (2): 161–90. Reprint, in *Business, Banking, and Economic Thought,* edited by Julius Kirshner.

Rosenberg, Nathan, and L. E. Birdzell, Jr. 1986. *How the West Grew Rich: The Economic Transformation of the Industrial World.* New York: Basic Books.

Rosenstein-Rodan, P. 1943. Problems of Industrialization of Eastern and South-Eastern Europe. *Economic Journal* 53 (June–September): 204–07.

Rourke, Thomas R. 1996. Michael Novak and Yves Simon on the Common Good and Capitalism. *Review of Politics* 58 (Spring): 229–68.

Routh, Guy. 1975. *The Origin of Economic Ideas.* White Plains, N.Y.: International Arts and Sciences Press.

Sacred Congregation for the Doctrine of the Faith. 1986. *Instruction on Christian Freedom and Liberation.* Boston: Daughters of St. Paul.

Samuels, W. J. 1994. Need as a Mode of Discourse. In *The Social Economics of Human Material Need,* edited by J. B. Davis and E. J. O'Boyle. Carbondale and Edwardsville: Southern Illinois University Press.

Schuck, Michael. 1991. *That They Be One: The Social Teaching of the Papal Encyclicals, 1740–1989.* Washington, D.C.: Georgetown University Press.

Schultz, T. Paul. 1988. Economic Demography and Development: New Directions in an Old field. *The State of Development Economics: Progress and Perspectives*, edited by Gustav Ranis and T. Paul Schultz. Oxford: Basil Blackwell.

Schultz, T. W. 1975. The Value of the Ability to Deal with Disequilibria. *Journal of Economic Literature* 13 (3): 827–46.

———. 1980. Nobel Lecture: The Economics of Being Poor. *Journal of Political Economy* 88 (4): 639–51.

Schumpeter, Joseph A. 1954. *History of Economic Analysis*. Edited by Elizabeth Booth Schumpeter. New York: Oxford University Press.

Scitovsky, T. 1959. Growth–Balanced or Unbalanced. In *The Allocations of Economic Resources*. Edited by M. Abramovitz. Stanford, Calif.: Stanford University Press.

Seers, Dudley. 1969. The Meaning of Development. *International Development Review* 11 (4): 2–6.

———. 1972. What Are We Trying to Measure? *Journal of Development Studies* 8 (3): 21–36.

Sen, Amartya Kumar. 1979. Rational Fools: A Critique of the Behavioural Foundations of Economic Theory. *Philosophy and Public Affairs* (1977) 6: 317–44. Reprint, in *Philosophy and Economic Theory*, edited by F. Hahn and M. Hollis. Oxford: Oxford University Press.

———. 1980. Levels of Poverty Policy and Change. *World Bank Staff Working Paper*, No. 401 (July). Washington, D.C.: World Bank.

———. 1984a. Ethical Issues in Income Distribution: National and International. In *The World Economic Order: Past and Prospects*, edited by S. Grassman and E. Lundberg. London: Macmillan, 1981. Reprint, in *Resources, Values, and Development*, by Sen. Cambridge, Mass.: Harvard University Press.

———. 1984b. Goods and People. In *Resources, Values, and Development*.

———. 1984c. Rights and Capabilities. In *Resources, Values, and Development*.

———. 1985a. *Commodities and Capabilities*. Amsterdam: North-Holland.

———. 1985b. Well-being, Agency and Freedom: The Dewey Lectures 1984. *Journal of Philosophy* 82 (4): 169–203.

———. 1988a. Freedom of Choice: Concept and Content. *European Economic Review* 32 (2/3): 269–94.

———. 1988b. The Concept of Development. *Handbook of Development Economics*, Vol. I. Edited by Hollis Chenery and T. N. Srinivasan. Amsterdam: North Holland.

Sibley, Mulford. 1970. *Political Ideas and Ideologies: A History of Political Thought*. New York: Harper and Row.

Sidgwick, Henry. [1886] 1968. *Outlines of the History of Ethics*. Enl. ed. Boston: Beacon Press.

Simon, Herbert. 1959. Theories of Decision Making on Economics. *American Economic Review* 49 (4): 253–83.

Simon, Yves. 1960. Common Good and Common Action. *Review of Politics* 22 (2): 202–44.

———. 1962. *A General Theory of Authority*. Notre Dame, Ind.: University of Notre Dame Press.

Simonazzi, Annamaria, and Paola Villa. 1999. Flexibility and Growth. *International Review of Applied Economics* 13 (3): 281–311.

Smith, Adam. [1776] 1937. *The Wealth of Nations*. Edited by Edwin Canaan. New York: Modern Library.

Sowell, Thomas. 1974. *Classical Economics Reconsidered*. Princeton, N.J.: Princeton University Press.

Spengler, Josef J. 1968. Hierarchy vs. Equality: Persisting Conflict. *Kyklos* 21: 217–38.

Stevens, Candice. 1996. The Knowledge-Driven Economy. *OECD Observer*, June–July, 6–11.

Stewart, Frances. 1976. The Direction of International Trade Gains and Losses for the Third World. In *A World Divided*, edited by G. K. Helleiner. Cambridge: Cambridge University Press.

Streeten, Paul. 1954. Keynes and the Classical Tradition. In *Post Keynesian Economics*, edited by Kenneth K. Kurihara. New Brunswick, N.J.: Rutgers University Press.

———. 1981. *Development Perspectives*. London: Macmillan.

Synod of Bishops. 1971. *Justice in the World*. Boston: Daughters of St. Paul.

Taussig, F. W. 1924. *Principles of Economics*. 3d ed. New York: Macmillan.

Tawney, R. H. 1926. *Religion and the Rise of Capitalism*. New York: New American Library of World Literature.

Thanawala, Kishor. 1998. Justice and International Development from *Mater et Magistra* to *Centesimus Annus*. *International Journal of Social Economics* 25 (11–12): 1739–54.

Udoidem, Sylvanus Iniobong. 1985. Authority and the Common Good in the Social and Political Philosophy of Yves R. Simon. Ph.D. diss., Catholic University (Washington, D.C.).

UNCTAD. 1977. *New Directions and New Structures for Trade and Development*. Report by the Secretary-General of the United Nations Conference on Trade and Development to UNCTAD IV. New York: United Nations.

United Nations Development Programme. 1990. *Human Development Report 1990*. New York: Oxford University Press.

———. 1998. *Human Development Report of 1998*. New York: Oxford University Press.

United Nations General Assembly. 1974. *Declaration on the Establishment of a New International Economic Order*. Resolution No. 3201 (S-VI), General Assembly, Sixth Special Session.

United States Catholic Conference. 1990. *A Century of Social Teaching: A Common Heritage, A Continuing Challenge* (A Pastoral Message of the Catholic Bishops of the United States on the 100th Anniversary of *Rerum Novarum*). Washington D.C.: USCC (November).

Vatican Council II. 1965. *Gaudium et Spes*. Boston: Daughters of St. Paul.

Verstraeten, J. 1998. Solidarity and Subsidiarity. In *Principles of Catholic Social Teaching*, edited by David Boileau. Milwaukee, Wis.: Marquette University Press.

Viner, Jacob. 1958a. Adam Smith and Laissez Faire. *Journal of Political Economy* (1927) 35 (April): 198–232. Reprint, in *The Long View and the Short: Studies in Economic Theory and Policy* by Viner. Glencoe, Ill.: Free Press (1958).

———. 1958b. Bentham and J. S. Mill: The Utilitarian Background. *American Economic Review* (1949) 39 (2): 360–82. Reprint, in *The Long View and the Short*.

———. 1958c. Full Employment at Whatever Cost. *Quarterly Journal of Economics* (1950) 64 (3): 385–407. Reprint in *The Long View and the Short.*

———. 1978. *Religious Thought and Economic Society.* Edited by Jacques Melitz and Donald Winch. Durham, N.C.: Duke University Press.

Vinogradoff, Paul. 1957. Feudalism. In *The Cambridge Medieval History,* Vol. 3, edited by H. M. Gwatkin, J. P. Whitney, J. R. Tanner, and C. W. Previte-Orton. Cambridge: Cambridge University Press.

Wahid, A. N., ed. 1993. *Grameen Bank: Poverty Relief in Bangladesh.* Boulder, Colo.: Westview Press.

Walzer, Michael. 1983. *Spheres of Justice: A Defense of Pluralism and Equality.* New York: Basic Books.

Waterman, A. M. C. 1991. The Intellectual Context of *Rerum Novarum. Review of Social Economy* 49 (4): 465–85.

———. 1999. Market Social Order and Christian Organicism in *Centesimus Annus. Journal of Markets and Morality* 2 (2): 220–33.

van der Wee, Herman. 1987. *Prosperity and Upheaval: The World Economy 1945–1980.* Translated by Robin Hogg and Max R. Hall. Berkeley: University of California Press.

Weisskopf, Walter A. 1973. The Image of Man in Economics. *Social Research* 40 (3): 547–63.

Welch, C. 1987. Utilitarianism. In *The New Palgrave: A Dictionary of Economics,* edited by J. Eatwell, M. Milgate, and P. Newman. London: Macmillan Press.

Welty, Eberhard. 1960. *A Handbook of Christian Social Ethics.* Vol. 1. *Man in Society.* New York: Herder and Herder.

Weston, Samuel C. 1994. Toward a Better Understanding of the Positive/Normative Distinction in Economics. *Economics and Philosophy* 10: 11–17.

Wheeler, Sondra Ely. 1995. *Wealth as Peril and Obligation: The New Testament on Possessions.* Grand Rapids, Mich.: Eerdmans.

Wicksteed, P. H. 1910. *The Common Sense of Political Economy.* London: Macmillan.

Williamson, Jeffrey. 1996. Globalization, Convergence, and History. *Journal of Economic History* 56 (2): 277–306.

Wilson, George W. 1975. The Economics of the Just Price. *History of Political Economy* 7 (1): 56–74.

Winkler, J. T. 1976. Corporatism. *European Journal of Sociology* 17: 100–36.

Worland, Stephen. 1967. *Scholasticism and Welfare Economics.* Notre Dame, Ind.: University of Notre Dame Press.

———. 1977. Justum Pretium: One More Round in an "Endless Series." *History of Political Economy* 9 (4): 504–21.

———. 1996. The Investment Decision as Moral Choice. In *Social Economics: Premises, Findings, and Policies,* edited by E. J. O'Boyle. London and New York: Routledge.

World Bank. 1991. *World Development Report, 1991: The Challenge of Development.* New York: Oxford University Press.

Yergin, Daniel, and Joseph Stanislaw, 1998. *The Commanding Heights: The Battle Between Government and the Marketplace That is Remaking the Modern World.* New York: Simon and Schuster.

INDEX

Numbers in *italics* refer to paragraph numbers in the Catholic social documents.